THE LONDON & NORTH WESTERN RAILWAY

Articles from the Railway Magazine Archives

The Victorian Era and the early 20th Century

THE LONDON & NORTH WESTERN RAILWAY

Articles from the Railway Magazine Archives
The Victorian Era and the early 20th Century

Neil Smith

With many additional photos from
The London & North Western Railway Society

PEN & SWORD
TRANSPORT
AN IMPRINT OF PEN & SWORD BOOKS LTD.
YORKSHIRE - PHILADELPHIA

Special Note from the author:

Proceeds from the sales of this book will be donated to St. Luke's (Cheshire) Hospice

First published in Great Britain in 2021 by
Pen & Sword Transport
An imprint of
Pen & Sword Books Ltd
Yorkshire – Philadelphia

Copyright © Neil Smith, 2021

ISBN 978 1 52678 137 6

The right of Neil Smith to be identified as Author of this work has been asserted by him in accordance with the Copyright, Designs and Patents Act 1988.

A CIP catalogue record for this book is available from the British Library.

All rights reserved. No part of this book may be reproduced or transmitted in any form or by any means, electronic or mechanical including photocopying, recording or by any information storage and retrieval system, without permission from the Publisher in writing.

Typeset in 12/15 pt Times New Roman
by SJmagic DESIGN SERVICES, India.
Printed and bound by Printworks Global Ltd, London/Hong Kong

Pen & Sword Books Ltd incorporates the Imprints of Pen & Sword Books Archaeology, Atlas, Aviation, Battleground, Discovery, Family History, History, Maritime, Military, Naval, Politics, Railways, Select, Transport, True Crime, Fiction, Frontline Books, Leo Cooper, Praetorian Press, Seaforth Publishing, Wharncliffe and White Owl.

For a complete list of Pen & Sword titles please contact

PEN & SWORD BOOKS LIMITED
47 Church Street, Barnsley, South Yorkshire, S70 2AS, England
E-mail: enquiries@pen-and-sword.co.uk
Website: www.pen-and-sword.co.uk

Or
PEN AND SWORD BOOKS
1950 Lawrence Rd, Havertown, PA 19083, USA
E-mail: Uspen-and-sword@casematepublishers.com
Website: www.penandswordbooks.com

Contents

	Introduction	7
	Acknowledgements	8
	The London and North Western Railway Society	9
	Index	11
Chapter 1	Engine Drivers and their Duties	12
Chapter 2	Frederick Harrison	23
Chapter 3	Willesden	33
Chapter 4	Wolverton Carriage Works	45
Chapter 5	A Trip on the LNWR "American Special"	60
Chapter 6	The London and Birmingham Railway	71
Chapter 7	The Irish Mail and The Emerald Isle via Holyhead	87
Chapter 8	"Precedents"	102
Chapter 9	The Grand Junction Railway	118
Chapter 10	Crewe – The Result of Railway Enterprise	131
Chapter 11	To Manchester via Ashbourne	146
Chapter 12	Euston Station in 1899	155
Chapter 13	Francis William Webb M.I.M.E.	171
Chapter 14	Birmingham New Street	182
Chapter 15	LNWR Liverpool Express	194
Chapter 16	Carlisle Citadel	203
Chapter 17	Webb Compounds	212
Chapter 18	Cross Country Train Services of the LNWR in 1901	231

Chapter 19	Manchester London Road	237
Chapter 20	Earlestown Wagon Works of the LNWR	248
Chapter 21	The London and Birmingham Express Train Services – 1838–1901	257
Chapter 22	The Opening of the Liverpool and Manchester Railway	262
Chapter 23	LNWR Locomotive and Rolling Stock in the United States	275
Chapter 24	Preston	280
Chapter 25	New LNWR Royal Saloons	287
Chapter 26	New Goods Warehouse at Sheffield	294
Chapter 27	A Depopulated Railway Town (Crewe During the Holiday Week)	297

Introduction

This book is a wonderful miscellany of the London & North Western Railway. Here is a delightful new illustrated history of the "Premier Line" drawn from the Railway Magazine Archives which covers the close of the Victorian Era and the start of the 20th Century. Topics of the 27 chapters include:

- Personal Interviews with F. Harrison (General Manager), F.W. Webb (CM&EE)
- Notable Stations – Birmingham New Street, Carlisle Citadel, Crewe, Euston, Manchester London Road, Preston and Willesden
- Wolverton Carriage Works and Earlestown Wagon Works
- Engine Drivers and their Duties by C.J. Bowen Cooke
- The Irish Mail and the 'American Special' trains
- Webb Precedent and Compound Locomotives
- Royal Saloons
- The opening and early years of three LNWR constituent companies – The Liverpool & Manchester, The Grand Junction and the London & Birmingham Railways

The present author/compiler has excluded most of the original photos and diagrams due to their poor quality, however –

The large number of new illustrations and photos, mostly from the London and North Western Railway Society's archive, make this a great historical record and a very special book.

Acknowledgements

Special thanks to the Railway Magazine (Mortons Media Group) for permission to use their wonderful archive material and the London & North Western Railway Society for extensive use of their photographic collection. Thanks also to Edward Talbot, Norman Lee, Sue Brown and Michael Wilcock for their help in the preparation of the book and to Tony Hisgett for the Curzon Street photo.

Thanks also to Gerald Broom GRA for two of his wonderful colour paintings in chapters 9 & 17.

Dedication

To my wife Ann and my children Fiona and Stuart with thanks for their support and encouragement over many years.

The London and North Western Railway Society

The Society was founded by the late Eric Rayner in 1973 to bring together all who are interested in the LNWR, its constituent companies and associated lines.

Members receive four Journals and four Newsletters a year, as well as other occasional publications, plus greatly reduced prices on publications that we are associated with. Society events include the Annual Crewe Luncheon at The Crewe Arms Hotel which has a long association with the LNWR, the 'Steam Up' where we visit a Model Engineers' track and members run their live steam LNWR locomotives, and an Open Day at Kidderminster Railway Museum featuring illustrated talks on LNWR subjects, displays and sales stands, relics and archives and an enormous Gauge 1 running track in the station concourse.

The Society has its own Study Centre at Kenilworth housing an extensive library and collection of archive material, photographs, plans, drawings and relics. Meetings and Research Days are frequently held there for members. The Centre houses sophisticated equipment for scanning books, drawings and large plans.

Applications for membership may be made on-line at lnwrs.org.uk or to:
The Membership Secretary
19 Totternhoe Road, Dunstable
Bedfordshire LU6 2AF
membership@lnwrs.org.uk

Other publications by The London & North Western Railway Society:

LNWR 42Ft Carriages of Richard Bore.	Richard Ball, Peter Chatham	£15.00
L&NWR wagons (suppl. No1)	Peter Ellis	£7.50
F.W. Webb, a Bibliography	J.E.Spink, notes by Edward Talbot	£15.00
Garston & Stalbridge Docks	Mike G. Fell	£15.00
Wolverton Carriage Works	Reprint of 1906 LNWR publication	£4.95
L&NWR Non-Corridor Carriages	Philip Millard, Ian Tattersall	£29.95
Railway Photos of P.W. Pilcher	David Patrick	£9.95
The War Record of the L&NWR	Edwin A. Pratt (reprint)	£8.95
The Diary of Thomas Baron, Engineman	Edward Talbot	£20.00

Prices include post and packing. More information on publications is available on the Society's Website and by email to: sales@lnwrs.org.uk

Copies are available from The LNWRS Sales Officer
58 Shire Road,
Corby, Northants NN17 2HN

Journals and Portfolios that have long been out of print are available in PDF format for £7.50. Price includes sending via email or CD. Please add £5.00 for a USB memory stick.

1. Premier Portfolio No1: A Miscellany of Subjects
2. Premier Portfolio No2: A Miscellany of Subjects
3. The Locomotive Nameplates of the London & North Western Railway
4. The Webb Experiment Compounds
5. Crewe Works Narrow-Gauge System
6. The L.N.W.R. Bloomers. Wolverton's 7ft. Singles
7. Selected L.N.W.R. Carriages. A detailed commentary
8. The Holyhead Steamers of the L.N.W.R.
9. L.N.W.R. One Man's Passion. A tribute to G. D. Whitworth
10. Gateway to the West. A History of Riverside Station, Liverpool
11. LNWR Great War Ambulance Trains
12. Recollections of Oxenholme
14. Bill Finch, Building a Jumbo £7.90
15. Six-wheeled Carriages £7.95
16. LNWR Company Houses. Last few remaining £3.50

Index

SHOWING ORIGINAL PUBLISHING DATES IN THE RAILWAY MAGAZINE

1. Engine Drivers and their duties (Aug 1897)
2. Frederick Harrison, General Manager (Sep 1897)
3. Willesden – 24 hours at a railway junction (Sep 1897)
4. Wolverton Carriage Works (Nov 1897)
5. A trip on the LNWR "American Special" (Jan 1898)
6. The London & Birmingham Railway (Feb 1898)
7. The Irish Mail (Dec 1898)
8. Precedents – some wonderful little engines (Mar 1899)
9. The Grand Junction Railway (May 1899)
10. Crewe – the result of railway enterprise (Sep 1899)
11. To Manchester via Ashbourne (Oct 1899)
12. Euston – notable railway stations (Jan 1900)
13. F.W. Webb – a personal interview (Feb 1900)
14. Birmingham New Street – notable railway stations (Apr 1900)
15. LNWR Liverpool Express (June 1900)
16. Carlisle Citadel – notable railway stations (Nov 1900)
17. Webb Compounds (May 1901)
18. Cross Country Train Services of the LNWR in 1901 (June 1901)
19. Manchester London Road – notable railway stations (Oct 1901)
20. Earlestown Wagon Works (Dec 1901)
21. London and Birmingham Express Train Services 1838 to 1901 (Dec 1901)
22. The Opening of the Liverpool & Manchester Railway (Mar 1902)
23. LNWR Locomotive and Rolling Stock in the United States (Apr 1902)
24. Preston – notable railway stations (Feb 1903)
25. New Royal Saloons (Mar 1903)
26. New Goods Warehouse at Sheffield (Mar 1903)
27. A Depopulated Railway Town – Crewe Holiday Week (Apr 1904)

Chapter 1
Engine Drivers and their Duties
by C.J. Bowen Cooke
District Locomotive Superintendent LNWR

"Oh! The Engineer's joys, to go with a locomotive," sings Walt Whitman, the American poet, and although the self-same poet yearned after a great variety of emotional experiences, there is no doubt that the first experience of a ride upon the footplate of an engine working an express train is a pleasurable excitement equal to the mental exhilaration to be got from any form of recreation.

Charles John Bowen Cooke, Chief Mechanical Engineer 1913.

I am speaking, however, now of the probable sensation which you, my reader, might experience were you fortunate enough to obtain a "permit" to ride upon an engine; but the purpose of this article is to give a little insight into the duties of the men who spend their lives upon the footplate, and from whom the romance of the situation is taken away by long usage, by the knowledge of the responsibilities devolving upon them, and from the fact that upon the manner in which those duties are performed depends not only the means of existence for them and their families, but also the lives of the passengers whose safety depends on their vigilance.

To become a first class engineman requires a vast amount of experience and training. The period of training is longer than the ordinary term of apprenticeship considered necessary to render a man an expert craftsman in any other particular trade which he may take up as a means of earning his livelihood, and to follow the career of an engine driver from the time he enters the railway service until he is promoted to the position of express passenger train driver would take more space than can be allotted to this article. In most trades the skill of the workman is equally valuable wherever he may be employed; but unfortunately this is not altogether the case with the engine driver, whose knowledge is essentially limited to his particular line. A very important part of his training is to "learn the road" – that is to gain a knowledge of the gradients and signals on every part of the line over which he has to run. He must be able to read off at sight the meaning of every signal, and to pick out those he must obey from the gigantic array when he approaches a complicated junction or busy station.

It takes a driver years to thoroughly learn all the signals over a large railway system, and the knowledge, when acquired, is only of use upon the line on which he is trained.

In the early days of railways, engine drivers were usually men who had previously been employed as mechanics, in many instances assisting in building the machines of which they afterwards took charge. However, it soon became evident that these were two entirely different branches of locomotive work, and that a good mechanic did not necessarily make a good engineman.

A separate department, therefore, sprang into existence, which was called the "Running Department", and it is through the various grades in this department that men rise step by step until the highest rank – viz. that of an express passenger train driver – is attained.

The larger railways are divided into districts with a staff of drivers attached to each. Thus on the London and North Western Railway the men working local trains about Birmingham, Wolverhampton, and Walsall are thoroughly acquainted with the complicated junctions and signals in that part of the country, but do not know the main line. In the same way Crewe drivers, who know the road over 300 miles from London to Carlisle, could not work trains on the branch lines. On the London and North Western Railway alone there are 17,000 signals lighted every night, and the driver working from Crewe to London and back for his day's work is controlled by no less than 570 signals, to say nothing of those coming under his observation which do not affect the working of his train.

The youth who enters the railway service with the aspiration of ultimately becoming an engine driver first commences work as a cleaner, and has to pass the various stages before he reaches the top rung of the ladder. Promotion goes by seniority combined with merit. A cleaner who takes a pride in the thoroughness of his work and the appearance of the engine with the cleaning of which he is entrusted should be singled out for promotion before one whose only idea is to do the minimum amount of work that will enable his engine to be passed by the foreman.

The cleaner who eventually succeeds as an engine driver is always trying to learn something; while he is employed in the running sheds he has constant opportunities of seeing the fitters at work on different parts of the mechanism of the engines, and, if he is bright and intelligent, that will be useful to him hereafter.

The man who keeps his eyes open and intelligently observes what is going on around him, whether he be cleaner, fireman, or driver, is the one who will surely work his way to the front, while his fellow-servant who has not made the most of his opportunities is still compelled to remain in the lower grades of the service.

To the uninitiated the life of an engine driver appears to be a pleasant and perhaps an easy one. It cannot be denied that, even to the many who gain their living by the occupation, it has a fascination that never wanes, and when once a man has attained the position of an express passenger train driver his lot is one that well may be envied by the majority of the artisan class. His rate of pay is high; his hours are short, and his work neither monotonous nor arduous.

But on the other hand, it has cost him many years of real hard work to gain this position; and, although the life may have its picturesque side, it must be remembered that the responsibilities are great, and that the driver is called upon to take his turn on night duty and to be out in all weathers at all seasons of the year. It is no light matter to be responsible for the safe conduct of an express passenger train through the country in the dead of night at the rate of fifty or sixty miles an hour, past busy stations and mazy junctions.

We will not attempt to follow the different gradations of service in the Running Department, but will try to gain some idea of the duties of the engine-driver during his day's work.

Rugby Signal Gantry with 44 signals (22 above, repeated below) due to Great Central bridge crossing behind. The signalbox is Rugby No.1 which was built in 1885 and was then the largest on the LNWR – 96 ft. long with 159 levers.

Every engineman is supplied weekly with printed notices giving particulars of extra trains arranged, signal alterations, repairs to the permanent way, and all special arrangements of every kind and description affecting the part of the line over which he has to work.

A careful driver will take these notices home with him and look them over, so that when he goes on duty, he has all the instructions fixed in his mind, and can give his whole attention to his engine. When there are important alterations to the signals or roads at any station, it is the practice on the London and North Western Railway to supply every driver with a diagram giving full details of all such alterations. This is an excellent system, and keeps the men well advised of everything of the kind that is going on. The driver, however, must not be satisfied with the information to be gleaned from these printed notices, but whenever he books on duty, his first care must be to study the special notice-board hung up in the shed, upon which he will find posted all special instructions which are issued from time to time.

Many of these instructions refer to the Locomotive Department only, and are not included in the traffic superintendent's weekly notices. A water pipe has burst somewhere, and there is no water to be obtained at that station; the driver must therefore make a special stop to fill his tank elsewhere. Complaints have been made that trains are running through some particular junction too fast, and drivers are cautioned to moderate the speed. Some irate householder has written to the General Manager, complaining of the noise or smoke made by engines standing at some signal in the vicinity of his residence, and the locomotive superintendent threatens dire penalties to the offender who again transgresses in this respect. These are the kind of notices the driver finds displayed upon the special notice-board.

But we are going to follow him through his day's work, and we have somewhat anticipated. His first duty is to "book-on" – that is, to give his name in at the "check-office" at the gate, where the time of his coming to work is recorded, together with his train and number of his engine. The keys of his tool boxes are kept at this office, and must be obtained by the driver or fireman.

Having booked on duty and examined the notice-board, the driver proceeds to his engine, which he finds ready placed in a convenient position for moving off the shed. His next business is to examine his engine. To make a really satisfactory and efficient examination, a man must not be content with spending a certain amount of time in making a general survey of the different parts of the machinery, but he must so train himself in habits of minute and careful observation as to be able to make his examination without overlooking the smallest and apparently least important detail. There are men who have been driving for years, and have daily inspected their engines, as they thought, thoroughly, and who may, however, have habitually overlooked some one small part, which has eventually led to a bad failure on the road from want of proper supervision. Everything that could possibly go wrong should be examined, no matter how improbable any mishap may be.

Having completed all this work, the engine is, if necessary, taken to the turntable to be turned and to the water column to have its tank filled. The driver then "whistles up," and the engine is run off the shed road to stand in some convenient place till the arrival of its train, or, if starting from a terminal station, to back on to the train, and start "right away" when time is up.

After the engine is backed on to a train there are certain duties to be performed by the driver before starting. With a train fitted with the automatic brake the following work has to be done between the time of backing up and starting away.

The fireman's duties are:
1. To hook the engine shackle on to the carriage draw-bar hook and screw it up tightly.
2. To couple up the vacuum pipes.
3. To attach the communication cord.
4. To take the tail lamp from the rear of the tender and place it on the front buffer-plank.

The driver's duties are:
1. To deliver up his "ticket" to the guard, who will, during the journey, record upon it particulars of the running of the train.
2. To ascertain from the guard the number of vehicles upon the train and the brake power under his control.
3. To raise the vacuum by opening the ejector and keeping it open until the vacuum gauge shows the required amount to be maintained while running.
4. To re-create the vacuum after it has been destroyed by opening the emergency valve in the rear van to test the continuity of the vacuum pipes.
5. To pull back the communication cord and close the whistle after the cord has been pulled from the rear of the train to test its continuity.

If the driver does not raise sufficient vacuum in the train pipe, a white flag is held out of the rear van, and he must again open the ejector and continue to "blow up" until the flag is waved – an indication that the proper figure is registered by the rear van vacuum gauge.

When the time is up and this station business is completed, the guard gives a "right away" signal by exhibiting a green flag (by day) or a green lamp (by night). This signal is only an indication to the engine driver that so far as the station business is concerned he has permission to start the train. Before he does so he must, however, be careful to look at the starting signal, and see that it is "off," and the line ahead is clear for him to proceed.

When he has satisfied himself on these points, he must carefully open the regulator. If it is suddenly thrown wide open there is a severe strain on the pistons and valve gear, and the result frequently is that the wheels spin round on the rails without moving the engine.

The ease or otherwise with which the driver starts his train depends greatly on the state of the rails. The adhesion per ton of load on the driving-wheels varies from 200lb, when the rails are slippery, to 600lb when they are dry. In starting, the driver has to take into consideration the state of the rails, the load of the train, and the gradient upon which the engine and train are standing.

As already explained, every engine carries a supply of dry sand, stored in boxes fitted with outlet valves worked from the footplate. When rails are slippery the sand is allowed to stream upon them, and thus promote adhesion. It is the fireman's duty to manipulate the sanding gear, and he must exercise care in the discharge of this duty, which is a very important one; for, in frosty weather, for instance, when the rails are covered with rime, it is almost as useless to attempt to start a train with a single engine without opening the sand valves as without opening the regulator.

If the engine is slipping badly, and the sand valves are opened while steam is on, the wheels pass directly from a slippery rail upon which they are spinning round on to a well sanded rail, and they thus receive a sudden check which causes a great strain upon the machinery – in fact, axles have been known to break from this cause.

When once the train is well on the move, and the engine begins to feel the load, the regulator may be more fully opened and the engine allowed to run for a short distance with the reversing lever or wheel over in full gear. A few beats of the engine in "full throw" help clear the tubes of any small cinder or ashes that may be left in them, and the strong blast gives a good start to the fire. After running a short distance with the lever in this position the driver should "pull the engine back" a little at a time as the speed increases.

The terms "pull-back" or notch-up mean to place the reversing wheel, or lever, or whatever kind of apparatus is used for this purpose, in the position for working steam expansively. When the engine is in "full-throw" the lever is right over, and the steam is admitted to the cylinder during the greater part of the stroke of the piston. As the engine is "pulled-back" the period of "cut-off" is shortened, until eventually "mid-gear" is reached.

The way in which the reversing gear is manipulated must depend on the gradient of the road and the load of the train; but it may be laid down as a general rule that the notching up should be done gradually as the speed increases, without shutting the regulator.

The driver must stand on his engine in such a position that he can best see straight ahead. His side of the footplate is that always upon which the reversing-gear is placed; but this varies from right to left on the different lines. The reversing screw on the London and North Western Railway engines is always on the left side. The driver's position is therefore on the left of the footplate, and in this position he is, with few exceptions, on the same side as the platform and the starting signal, which is a great advantage. The regulator is in a convenient position for his right hand, the reversing wheel for his left, and the window in the cab is just in front of him. He can therefore manipulate the regulator and reversing gear without taking his attention off the signals.

Having followed so far the starting away of an engine with a passenger train, let it be supposed that the engine is working an express from Rugby to London and back. The train has travelled some 200 yards, and a speed of from fifteen to twenty miles an hour attained. The engine has been partly notched-up, but is still emitting sonorous puffs, the steam as yet only being cut off at about half, because the engine must continue to work hard until a higher speed is attained. As long as it is running in full gear, or only partly notched-up, a great quantity of steam is being used for working the engine; also the fire has not yet developed the fierce heat which the blast will shortly produce, and consequently the pressure drops back a little, because the steam used exceeds that which the fire at this stage is capable of producing. Having started away with a full boiler, the driver can, however, afford to lose a little steam at first, because he need not put on the ejector until the water level is considerably reduced.

By the time the train has travelled about half a mile or so, if everything is right, the blast has so acted upon the fire that the whole mass has burst into flame, and in a short time the fire develops sufficient heat to generate steam faster than the engine is using it, and the needle of the steam pressure gauge, which has perhaps gone back 5lb or 10lb, gradually begins to rise, until it again reaches "blowing-off point." By this time the water-line will show about half way up the gauge glass, whereas before starting it was out of sight in the top stand.

As soon as the engine shows signs of blowing-off, then is the time for the fireman to commence firing. The fact that the pressure gauge needle has crept round to this point indicates to him that his fire is in good order, and has properly burned through before starting. He may therefore put on his first instalment of fuel without fear of throwing it upon other coal not yet burned through. To heap coals upon a fire in this latter condition is a most fatal thing to do. If the engine does not begin to make steam at once it will not mend matters to commence putting coal on, In such a case the fireman should wait until he sees the pressure-gauge needle moving in the right direction, and in the meantime keep the feed off as long as is consistent with safety.

While running, the fire must be kept of the same structure and thickness as when made up in the shed before starting – viz. right up to the door at the back, and thin in the front. An unskillful fireman, instead of properly directing it into the front corners, will sometimes shoot the coal against the brick arch; the coal then falls into the centre of the fire-box, and impedes the circulation of air through the fire. In such a case the front of the fire next to the tube-plate burns away, and the bars become uncovered, and draw cold air directly on to the tube-plate.

The fireman, by putting on the first lot of coal, has in doing so caused the steam pressure to drop a few pounds, partly through the admission of cold air into the fire-box, and partly through the heat of the fire being checked by the fresh coal thrown upon it.

In a few seconds, as the fire gets hold of the fresh coal, the needle again reaches blowing-off point, and it is now time to put the feed on. The injector is therefore set to work by the fireman, and commences to supply the boiler with water. When the ejector is once put in, if the train be a heavy one, it should not be necessary to again shut it off until the next stop. The water regulating wheel must be screwed down and adjusted until the supply to the boiler is just equal to the water evaporated by the working of the engine.

A skillful fireman will manage this, and if everything goes right he will not have to shut the injector all the way from Rugby to Willesden; and during the whole run the water in the boiler will not vary half an inch, nor the steam pressure more than a pound or two to the square inch. The steam should always be just at blowing-off point, without the pressure being sufficiently high to cause the safety valve to lift, and allow a quantity of steam to pass from the boiler to the atmosphere without any work being got out of it.

Upon the skill and care of the fireman to a great extent depends the amount of coal consumed by the engine. If a driver finds his mate is not possessed of the necessary skill, it should be his duty to train and instruct him until he is satisfied with the manner in which the work is performed.

The train has now got well under way, and has travelled some five or six miles, during which distance the driver has notched the engine up. The speed has considerably increased, but the line is on a gentle rising gradient for the seven miles from Rugby to Welton, and a great speed is not attained between these points, and the engine must not be pulled back too far.

Having passed Welton the gradient is descending, the engine is notched-up to its maximum, and the speed increases to fifty or sixty miles per hour.

The engine has now settled down to its work. The glass gauge shows the water in the boiler at its full working height, the steam gauge records the maximum pressure without blowing-off, the vacuum gauge twenty inches of vacuum, and the sight feed lubricator is working and passing about four or five drops of oil per minute into the steam chest to lubricate the valves and pistons.

The fireman fires up at regular intervals, his attention being called to the necessity of doing so by the fact that the safety valve shows signs of blowing off. When the door is opened and coal put on the pressure is slightly reduced, and the steam does not begin to blow off again until it is time to put on some more coal.

The damper must be so adjusted as to bring about the regular routine of firing every time the engine begins to blow off; if opened too wide the engine steams too freely, and begins to blow off before it is time to fire; if not open wide enough, the time to fire arrives before the blowing-off point is reached, and the engine will gradually go back in steam.

When the engine is steaming properly, it should never be necessary to touch the fire-irons; and good firemen, with a good driver, and a good engine, will never need to use them at all when running.

Sometimes, when the fire begins to go wrong, a gentle stirring up with the pricker may put things right again; and there are circumstances when it is necessary, but they should be exceptional, for the more the fire is knocked about by the fire-iron the greater the consumption of coal.

There are no heavy gradients between Rugby and Bletchley, and having once got up express speed, and put the reversing wheel and regulator in the proper position, it should not be necessary to alter them between these two points.

The driver's attention should be concentrated ahead upon keeping a strict look out ahead, occasionally glancing at the gauges to see that everything is right, and swinging the door for the fireman when coal is put on.

Between Castlethorpe and Wolverton are the first water troughs and the moment the engine gets on to them the scoop must be let down by the fireman, and as soon as the tank is full the driver must assist in shooting back the scoop-handle. During the night great watchfulness must be observed not to miss the water troughs; but the sound made in travelling over them is sufficient to call the driver's attention to his whereabouts.

The fireman must, when not engaged in firing or breaking coal in the tender, assist the driver to keep watch ahead, and should always make a point of being on the look-out when passing through stations or junctions, where extra care is required in sighting the signals.

After passing Bletchley the line is more or less on a rising gradient as far as Tring, the last four miles from Cheddington being on a pretty stiff gradient. Here it is necessary to give the engine a little more lever – that is to say, to work in fuller gear. Having passed Tring, the ruling gradient is downwards all the way to Willesden, except between Bushey and Pinner, where there is a piece of level road and another water-trough, from which the water tank must again be replenished as before.

During the last fifteen or twenty miles the fire is gradually worked down, little or no coal being put on after passing Watford, 17½ miles from

London. To work the fire down a rake is used to gradually push forwards the thick part of the fire in the back of the firebox a little bit at a time as the thin part of the fire in front burns away. By the time the train arrives at Euston there should be a level thin fire covering the fire-bars.

Before the stop at Willesden is made, special preparations are made by the driver. The speed from Watford is very high – greater as a rule than any other part of the up journey. After passing this station there is an excellent piece of road, slightly down hill, and, if there is a minute or two to be made up, the driver need not be afraid of spoiling his fire and knocking his engine "out of time" by "punishing" it – that is running at a high speed with the engine nearly in full gear. He is close to a stop, and can get up steam again while standing, besides which he has only another five miles from Willesden to complete the journey. This hard running makes an extra powerful blast, and the consequence is that the fire, which is being run down, develops a very fierce heat, which is not checked by the addition of fresh coal.

If the driver were to shut off steam while working in these conditions, the steam would continue to be generated very rapidly, and, finding no outlet through the cylinders, would blow off furiously at the safety valve, causing a great nuisance whilst standing at the station, besides wasting fuel by the generation of steam to no purpose.

To avoid this, before the time arrives for shutting off steam, the damper is lowered, the fire-hole door opened, and the injector shut off. The two former operations reduce the heat in the fire-box, and the latter lowers the water in the boiler. By thus lowering the pressure there is, when the regulator is shut, a margin for the accumulation of steam before it reaches blowing off point, and its further generation can be checked by putting on the injector and filling up the boiler.

The last station to pass before reaching Willesden is Sudbury, soon after passing which the regulator should be shut and the steam jet put slightly on to clear away the smoke and sulphur from the fire.

After closing the regulator the vacuum brake should be partially applied, in order that the driver may satisfy himself that it is in good working order and properly checks the speed of the train. Finding this to be the case, he should again release the brake and allow the train to run forward. This partial application of the brake will check the speed, and, the regulator being shut, the train will gradually slow down as it approaches the station. The second application must be made on nearing the platform, and the brake must be so regulated to bring the train to a stand exactly at the proper

Crewe North Shed 1911. Mechanical coaling plant showing wagon being tippled and coal moving up conveyor to the bunker.

place. Of course the manipulation of the brake, and the decision as to how far from the station it ought to be applied, must depend upon the speed and weight of the train and the state of the rails; but in any case the speed should be so far reduced on the first application as to render it unnecessary to apply the brake to its fullest extent in making the final stop. The driver thus has a reserve of power to make use of if necessary when entering the station. As the train comes to a stand the brake should be in the act of being released. This causes the train to stop without any unpleasant jar to the passengers; whereas when a driver runs sharply up to a station and then turns the brakes fully on, keeping them so till the train comes to a stand, he brings up with a sudden jerk. This is especially the case with a heavy main line train with long buffers between the carriages.

After leaving Willesden the train passes through a thickly signalled piece of line to Euston. For the last mile and a quarter the line is on a steep, falling gradient, and special care must be observed in approaching the station. A terminal platform cannot be overshot with the same immunity from an accident as a roadside station, and disastrous consequences must ensue unless the train is brought to a stand at a proper place, and accordingly a terminal station at the foot of a descending gradient must be approached with extra precaution. In order to ensure this is being done, engine drivers are instructed to use their handbrakes only when approaching Euston station, so that the speed must be checked a considerable distance outside, and, if by any chance the speed is a little too fast, there is always the continuous brake to use in case of emergency. Its use in this case proves that a man has not had his train under sufficient control, and the fact of its being necessary to apply it gets the driver into trouble.

Stockport Edgeley Loco Shed 1890 showing DX Locos and LNWR bracket signal sideways on.

Improved Precedent No.867 "Disraeli" on Shrewsbury shed.

For ordinary stops where the vacuum brake is used the guards do not apply their handbrakes, but they should render assistance in descending the Euston incline.

After arrival at Euston the driver obtains his ticket from the guard, and the fireman detaches the engine, which is then taken on the turn-table and turned with the head towards Rugby. Adjoining the table are the different engine-pit roads, on to one of which the engine is to run.

When the time for leaving approaches, the same preparations are made as before starting from Rugby, and the engine is backed up on to the train, which stands ready at the platform.

Immediately after leaving Euston the heavy gradient to Camden Town has to be faced. This gradient is in some places as steep as 1 in 70. An ordinary coupled engine is capable of working twelve or thirteen vehicles up the incline, and the driver knows he must have his engine in the best possible trim to take the train up the bank.

There have been a considerable number of cases of trains "sticking" on the incline through starting away with a fire not in good condition. The driver should therefore be thoroughly satisfied that everything is right in this respect before attempting to take a heavy load out of Euston without a pilot engine.

The run down from London is always a little more troublesome than the up journey, because there is a continuous rising gradient nearly all the way to Tring, a distance of thirty miles; on the other hand, the stop at Willesden gives the driver a chance to make a good start again in case he has run short of steam through "punishing" his engine when working up the incline.

The usual time taken in running from Euston to Tring, a distance of thirty miles, with an express train is about forty-eight minutes, and, as many of the trains are timed at an average speed of fifty miles an hour from London to Rugby, some good running has to be made after passing Tring.

If the engine is going to finish its trip at Rugby, care must be taken to run the fire down as low as possible before arriving at the end of the journey. When an engine is run with a big fire of blind coal, firing must be discontinued some twenty or thirty miles before the point at which the trip ends. The thick part of the fire at the back of the box must be gradually pushed forward by the fire-irons until there is a thin fire of equal depth all over the bars. If properly managed, the lower the fire gets the fiercer the heat developed, and may be run down until not more than five or six inches deep on the bars.

If the fire gets down as low as this a few miles before the end of the trip, and steam cannot be kept up without putting on more coal, a few shovelfuls of small coals should be put on as required, being lightly scattered over the whole surface of the bars, so that when the engine arrives at its destination the grate is just covered by the fire. When the fire gets very low, and is composed only of incandescent cinders, the pressure will drop; but so long as the gauge shows 60lb at the time of closing the regulator the heat in the fire-box will go on generating steam after the regulator is shut, so that probably on arrival at the station there is sufficient pressure to make a shunt or two if necessary, and then take the engine on to the shed.

A great deal of experience and skill is required in judging exactly how to run the fire down so as to maintain sufficient steam to the last, and yet avoid waste by taking the engine on the shed with an unnecessary amount of fire in the fire-box.

Upon detaching from the train the driver obtains his ticket from the guard and takes his engine into the locomotive yard, where he places it over a pit near the coaling stage, gives it over to the care of the turner, and gives instructions as to the amount of coal to be put on the tender for the next trip.

Both men should then proceed to the engine shed; the driver makes out his tickets, which record particulars of the run he has made and the stores obtained. He must also insert in the "repairs book" particulars of any repairs required to his engine, and make out reports of special circumstances that have arisen in connection with working his train.

Chapter 2

Frederick Harrison

General Manager, London and North Western Railway
A Personal Interview
by G.A. Sekon

I am expecting this interview with you, Mr Harrison, to be of an interesting character, as the London and North Western Railway occupies a leading position among the great railways. It is I believe the leading line in several respects?"

"Well of course, one must not boast but there is no harm in saying that from most points of view the 'North Western,' as we generally call it for shortness, is the biggest undertaking in this country – if not in the whole world. Indeed, it is commonly believed to be the biggest joint-stock corporation in the world. There are other railways with a larger mileage it is true and, for the purposes of the mileage tables, a mile of single unproductive railway counts just the same as a mile of quadruple railway in the busiest part of the country. But, if you take either the invested capital, the earnings, the number of people employed, or any of the usual statistics the North Western is easily first. Our authorised capital stands at close on £120,000,000 and our gross revenue for the past year has been twelve million and a half. We carried during the year over a hundred million passengers, including season ticket holders, and more than forty million tons of goods and we employ about seventy thousand people. It must be admitted that these figures represent considerable quantities and value."

"A further interesting feature is the historical importance of the railway, as it includes amongst its many other important amalgamations the first public passenger railway (the Liverpool and Manchester), and also the original great railway – the famous London and Birmingham?"

"Yes, there is no disputing our claim to be 'the oldest established firm in the business.' The Liverpool and Manchester Railway, now part of our system, was opened in 1830, which represents the dawn of the railway era; and the London and Birmingham, which may be taken to be the parent tree on which all the other branches have been grafted, was authorised by Parliament in 1833, although not opened to the public until 1838. The London and North Western Railway first came be known as such in 1846, when the London and Birmingham, the Liverpool and Manchester,

Lieutenant Colonel Sir Frederick Harrison LNWR General Manager 1893-1908.

London & North Western Railway Crest.

the Grand Junction and the Manchester and Birmingham were amalgamated under that title. Since that time the Company has been something like 'Aaron's rod,' for it has swallowed up about forty-five other railways and welded them into one homogeneous undertaking."

"Another circumstance that lends additional consequence to your railway from an historical point, is the fact that you still preserve the original minute books and other documentary details of these old lines. Since the history of railways is yearly becoming of more interest to the nation, the arguments that frequently arise as to various facts can easily be authoritatively determined by reference to these old books and documents?"

"Yes, I believe our records are pretty complete and they go a long way back; but railway men live very much in the present and are too busy making fresh history to give much time to mediating upon what is past. No doubt though, as you say, the history of the development of railway enterprise is a very interesting one and there is nothing more astonishing than its tremendous rapidity. Looking at the railway system as we know it today, it must be a matter of astonishment to those, doubtless still living, who travelled in stage coaches in their youth and thought the perfection of speed in travelling had been reached, to see the rate at which the modern expresses now travel."

"The working of railways is very much changed since the days when Edward Berry supplied the London and Birmingham Railway with locomotive power at so much per train mile and

Pickford and Company managed the whole goods traffic, excepting the locomotive power?"

"Well, you are going a long way back now; but of course, it is a fact that in the early days the railway companies had no idea of becoming common carriers. All they contemplated at first was making a railway and taking power to charge certain tolls for the use of it, just as if it were a highway, leaving other people to conduct the traffic. As time went on and they saw private firms, like Pickford and Co., making large fortunes out of the business of carrying, they began to see that these profits might as well go into their own pockets; but old institutions die very hard and it is only comparatively within recent years that the companies are beginning to cart their own goods in the large towns and dispense with carting agents. We still employ Pickford and Co. as carmen in certain towns and it is a curious thing that there are many old-fashioned firms who to this day refuse to recognise any particular railway company, and look upon Pickford and Co. as their carriers. They have given their goods to Pickford and Co. during the last fifty or sixty years, dating back perhaps to the time when they were carried by road wagons and to Pickford and Co., they will give them still, not caring what railways they are sent by. The old firm is as enterprising in this generation as ever and do us loyal service still as agents in many parts of the country."

"I believe, Mr Harrison, that nearly fifty years ago, when the broad-gauge route to Birmingham was first projected, the London and North Western Railway proposed to perform the journey between London and Birmingham by express trains in two hours. Perhaps you can inform me whether this design was ever carried into effect; but at any rate, I presume it will be within the next few years, as the opening of the Great Western Railway's shorter route is likely to cause the trains between London and Birmingham to be accelerated?"

"I cannot say I ever heard of that intention but I think you may take it from me that if the Great Western Company or any other company ran from London to Birmingham in two hours, we should do it in the same or less. We are pretty hard to beat in that way, as our East Coast friends have discovered on one or two memorable occasions in recent years, and our route from London to Birmingham is as nearly direct as it is possible to be, with better gradients than exist by any other direct route, which means easy and expeditious travelling combined with economy. In fact, the worst gradient on the route is that which Stephenson discovered to be 'the angle of repose,' or in other words, a practical level. At the same time, it is not our policy to go in for excessive speed; we prefer to establish a reputation for punctuality and comfortable travelling with our express trains and I hope we have done so. Still, we always shall maintain a reasonable rate of speed.

"At the same time, you know there is nothing very Utopian about a run of two hours to Birmingham, for you will find we have already one train which performs the journey in two hours and twenty minutes."

"The competition for the American traffic, caused by the recent remarkable development of the Southampton Docks, has, I understand, caused the Liverpool Dock authorities to be at great pains to improve their port. Of course, I am fully aware that the London and North Western Railway has most ably seconded the endeavours of the Merseyside people. I believe your 'American Boat Specials' are amongst the fastest and best equipped trains in the world. Particulars from an official log would be interesting."

"Yes, we have undoubtedly laid ourselves out for the American traffic, and it is an open secret that we have been successful in securing the cream of it. Every time one of the Cunard or White Star steamers sails from Liverpool, we run a special timed to connect with it at the Riverside Station at Liverpool, performing the journey from London to Liverpool in four hours and sometimes even less, practically without a stoppage. The trains are thoroughly up to date, with corridors throughout and containing dining saloons, in which luncheon or dinner is served, as the case may be, *en route.* We carry a large number of passengers by these trains, and sometimes have to run two specials for one steamer instead of one.

"I think a journey at the present time from London to New York exemplifies in a very high degree the extent to which luxury and convenience have been carried in modern travel. A family staying in London and wishing to go to America have really nothing to do but pack their trunks and send for one of the Company's omnibuses, and from the moment they step into it they are relieved of all trouble and anxiety either as to themselves or their luggage; in fact, they can have their heavy baggage registered through if they wish it. Arrived at Euston, they find the special waiting and by the time they have lunched or dined, they find themselves at the Riverside Station, where they simply have to alight and walk a few yards across the landing stage to the steamer. There is not so much worry and fatigue now in going from London to New York as there used to be going from London to Manchester."

"You are just now very busy in transporting to Scotland the yearly increasing multitudes of tourists who consider it fashionable to 'go North' in August. Some details of this traffic would be of great interest to the readers of the RAILWAY MAGAZINE."

"Yes, this is the busiest time of the year with us as regards passenger traffic and I can assure you that Euston Station on one of our heavy nights early in August is a sight worth seeing. But you wanted some figures. Well, during one week in July this year upwards of 33,000 people left Euston, and on one day alone we took over £7,600 over the counter at Euston. I believe that was a record for one day's bookings. The quantity of luggage people take with them is enormous, and this greatly adds to our difficulties. Last week, for instance, we had one party of fifteen people, who took four and a half tons of luggage between them, and this is not a solitary case by any means. Then the bicycles are a new trouble which we have to contend with at busy times, and it may interest your readers to hear that in three days during July we carried from Euston no less than 2,400 of these. Then great numbers of people take their horses and carriages with them; and during one week in July we had to load up nearly 600 horse-boxes and carriage trucks at Euston. Our busiest time at night in the tourist season is between eight and nine, and during that one hour we had last night to despatch from Euston no less than nine heavy express trains for the North, and in these trains, it is no uncommon thing for us to have to make up three hundred beds in the sleeping saloons. This, you will see, is equivalent to putting a good-sized hotel on wheels and transporting it through the country at the rate of about fifty miles an hour. Indeed, the analogy to a travelling hotel may be carried further, for there are separate sleeping compartments, with lavatories, attendants, hot and cold water and tea and coffee in the morning. From a return I have in my hand I see that during eight days, from July 30th to the 7th August, between six am and midnight, we had no less than 2,557 trains in and out of Euston, which you will find is at the rate of one nearly every four minutes."

"I understand too, there has been of late a great development in your tourist traffic with North Wales?"

"Yes, we have been making an experiment, and it has turned out very well. During the months of July, August and September we run every Saturday morning from London to all the popular places in North Wales at fares ranging from 18s. to 22s. for the journey both ways and the tickets are available for a fortnight. These trains have proved to be immensely popular and they are crammed with people every Saturday. Of course, the fare is cut down very low, but the numbers being so large it pays; for instance, last Saturday we had two splendid trains, conveying just upon 1,200 people."

LNWR Timetable Cover 1898.

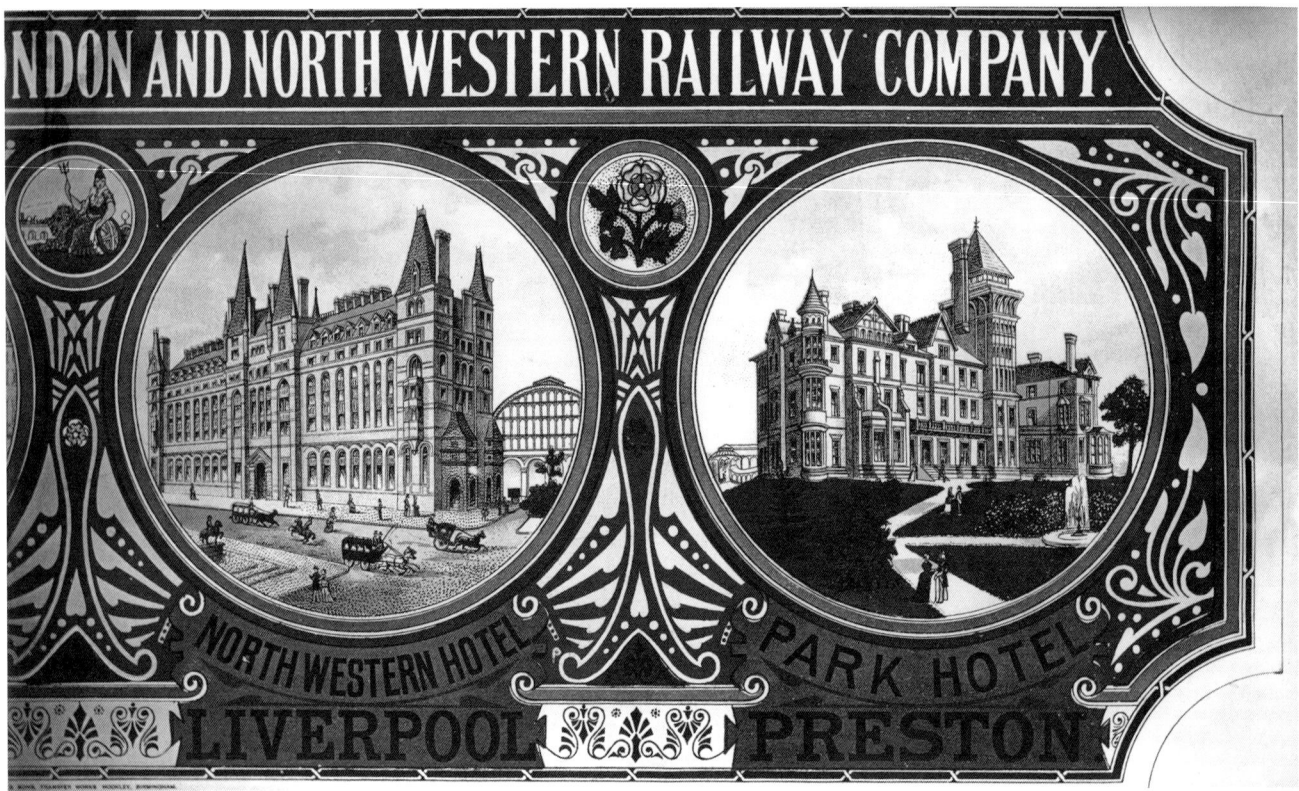

LNWR Hotels. Liverpool North Western opened in 1871. It was designed by Alfred Waterhouse in French Chateau style and had 330 rooms. Preston Park hotel was a red brick building opened in 1883 and had a connecting bridge to platform 4.

"The past few years have seen the introduction of widely divergent methods of dealing with the question of first, second and third-class traffic by the various railway managers. I am anxious to know your views on the matter, Mr Harrison."

"Ah! Now you are opening up a very large and vexed question, and one which has caused railway managers many searchings of heart. In a word, my view is that there are at least three classes of railway travellers, and that they ought to be provided for. There are first, the wealthy, who can afford to pay; secondly, the working classes, who must, and will, travel as cheaply as they possibly can; and, thirdly, the middle class, who cannot afford to travel first-class, but who like a little extra comfort and are willing to pay something for it. Our policy has always been based upon this view, and indeed, seeing that last year we carried nearly eleven millions of second-class passengers (that is, including season-ticket holders), we think that, while there are these millions of passengers who desire the accommodation and are willing to pay us something more than the third-class fare, we should be very short-sighted to throw the money away. I know the companies who have abolished second-class did so with the expectation of saving working expenses, but no statistics that I have ever seen go to show that this hope has been realised. It is true that we have dropped second-class in our Scotch trains, because the number of second-class passengers in those trains was exceptionally small in proportion to the amount of accommodation we had to provide for the different destinations. It is indeed, in many ways, an exceptional traffic altogether.

"What we are doing is to revise our second-class fares in certain districts so as to make them something like 10 per cent over the third. This has been done for the present as an experiment, and so far, as we have gone, it has proved very satisfactory, and has pleased the public, so that we shall probably go on in the same direction and make the revision a general one. We think it is a far better policy than abandoning the second-class fares altogether."

"I observe you have recently been at great expense in improving your Irish boat and train services. It would be entertaining to know details, both of the reasons prompting the special facilities now enjoyed by travellers to and from the Emerald Isle, and also as to the results of the augmented and accelerated services so liberally provided by the London and North Western Railway."

"Yes, we have been doing a good deal lately in the way of improving the service with Ireland, although it was a good service before, and had resulted in inducing a good deal of travel. As to results, it is a little too soon to say much; but as to the reasons that prompted us, well, we have always attached great importance to our Irish traffic, and we are always trying to improve it. Then, again, our Irish friends were getting a little jealous of the fine Scotch service by the rival routes, and the Post Office were getting pressure put upon them in Parliament and elsewhere to accelerate the mail service between England and Ireland. I am afraid it would take too long to tell you all we have done in this direction, but briefly, we have quickened the running of the up and down night Irish mail trains to the extent of half an hour and the City of Dublin Company, who, as you know, carry the mails across the Channel, have put on new boats and cross in about half an hour less, so that there is a saving of about an hour on the journey. Then we have done practically the same thing with the service which is conducted by means of our own boats to and from North Wall; the journey has been made about an hour less in both directions. Then, you know, we run our own boats between Holyhead and Greenore, and have a service by that route to the North of Ireland, and we have improved that service very much both by acceleration of the trains and the building of new steamers. From London to Greenore the service has been quickened by an hour and twenty minutes and from Greenore to London nearly two hours. We have two fine new steamers now performing the Greenore service – the 'Rostrevor' and the 'Connemara' – and only last week we launched a new Dublin boat, the 'Cambria', which is 337 feet in length, and has a guaranteed speed of 21 knots, and will be one of the finest vessels in the Channel service.

"You were talking just now of results and, so far as Greenore is concerned, we have every reason to be satisfied, for our carryings by that route are going up by leaps and bounds. For years past we have been unable to understand why the public did not make greater use of that route, but with better boats and a better train service it is beginning at last to get popular. The scenery round about Greenore, Carlingford Bay, Rostrevor, Warrenpoint and the neighbourhood is extremely beautiful, and there is every reason to believe that Greenore, with its comfortable North Western Hotel, will become a favourite holiday resort."

"Nearly fifty years ago, Mr Harrison, the author of 'Stokers and Pokers' used his utmost powers for the purpose of showing, by means of statistics, the enormous amount of business transacted by the London and North Western Railway. It would be very entertaining if you would give me the figures, say, for the past year, to compare them with those mentioned in the book."

"Well of course, if you contrast the figures, the growth is very striking. In 1846 our capital, instead of £120,000,000, was less than £18,000,000; our gross revenue, now twelve and a half millions, was only a little over one million. In that year we carried about six million of passengers, where we now carry about one hundred million, but I find I have not got the tonnage of merchandise in 1846."

"Now, perhaps, you will be good enough to let the readers of the RAILWAY MAGAZINE have some particulars of how the London and North Western Railway is constantly endeavouring to provide for the public convenience in the way of new lines and other improvements."

"The biggest thing we have in hand at present is the new line between Huddersfield and Leeds, which is practically the alternative to widening our existing Yorkshire Line, but we pass through new country, and open up new sources of traffic. Then we are making a new line to connect our High Peak Line near Buxton with the North Staffordshire Railway at Ashbourne, which will open up to tourists a very beautiful track of country; and we are engaged in widening portions of our Chester and Holyhead Railway, to enable greater facilities to be given to the tourist traffic."

"Will any great engineering works require to be constructed to carry out these projects?"

"There is nothing startling like the Severn Tunnel or the Runcorn Viaduct, but on the new Yorkshire Line we have got one tunnel to make nearly a mile and half long, at Gildersome, and there is another at Gomersal nearly half a mile in length. Then on the Ashbourne Line there is a tunnel nearly a quarter of a mile in length, but things of this sort modern engineers take as a matter of course and they present few difficulties."

"The London and North Western locomotives are world famed; they are unfortunately handicapped by the severe ascent from Euston to Camden. It would afford a lesson in railway development to compare the dimensions of the first engines used to draw the trains up the bank, after the abandonment of the fixed engines at Camden, with one of Mr Webb's latest creations with four cylinders and a leading bogie."

"We have no record of the first locomotive used for that purpose, but I should hardly say we are handicapped exactly by the gradient between Euston and Camden. It is 1 in 60, but we have worse gradients than that to negotiate elsewhere; for instance, in South Wales we have gradients of 1 in 40. What we do with the heaviest trains is to attach a second engine at Euston and detach it at Willesden and there is no real difficulty."

"And now, Mr Harrison, what about the Workmen's Compensation Act? Your Company is supposed to be particularly interested in that because of its effect on your own friendly societies. May one ask what you are going to do about it?"

"Well, it is rather too soon to ask me that question, because we really have not made up our minds. I believe our men were perfectly satisfied with our societies and asked nothing better than to be left alone, but there are busy people outside who are trying to persuade them that they have got a great boon in this new Act. For my part I am not so sure of that, but time will show. Of course, there is more than one course we might adopt, but at present, as I have said, we have not come to any decision. Our great desire is to preserve the good feeling and kindly relations with our men which have always existed and the point we have to decide is how we can best do that. In my opinion, it is not by legislative interference that this good feeling can be preserved, but by kindly

Richard Grosvenor, Lord Stalbridge. Chairman of the LNWR 1891-1911. Formerly an MP and Colonel of the Dorsetshire Yeomanry.

LNWR Westminster Office on the corner of Parliament Street decorated lavishly for the Queen Victoria's Jubilee in 1887.

and anxious study on the part of the directors and chief officers to promote the wellbeing of the staff in all grades, and secure their contentment, with the resulting advantage of loyalty and good service to the Company. We have done a good deal for our men, but it would take too long to describe all the organisations that we have established for them, and to which we liberally subscribe. Suffice it to say that we have superannuation and pension funds for old age, a provident fund for sickness and natural death, and the insurance societies against accident, all of which will be affected by the recent legislation. Then we have a savings bank and give our people better interest for their money than they can get outside. Indeed, the public has very little idea of the constant thought and labour devoted by the directors and officers to the examination and consideration of the circumstances affecting every grade of the staff in relation to the duties they perform. We are constantly making changes, altering rates of pay or hours of duty as the circumstances vary from time to time, and it is not putting it too high to say that this is the constant work of a considerable staff of officials."

"Having heard so much that is of general interest, RAILWAY MAGAZINE readers will naturally like some particulars of your own career, Mr Harrison."

"Oh, I don't know that there is any need to say much about that. The careers of all General Managers run very much in the same groove, because in the nature of things the General Manager of a big railway must be a practical man, who has been 'through the mill,' to use a familiar phrase, and you will find we have all begun at the bottom of the ladder. In the early days of railways there was a great idea of appointing retired army officers as General Managers, but that was soon found to be a mistake. I entered the service of the North Western in 1864, when I was twenty years of age, as a clerk at Shrewsbury, under the late Sir George Findlay, but when he came to Euston to be General Goods Manager, at the end of that year, he brought me with him and I served under him here for seven years. Then I had about three years at Liverpool as Assistant District Superintendent, about a year at Chester in the same capacity and then I came back to Euston as Assistant Superintendent of the Line. Ten years later I was appointed Chief Goods Manager and when Sir George Findlay died in March 1893, I succeeded him as General Manager."

Chapter 3
Willesden
Twenty-four Hours at a Railway Junction
by V.L. Whitechurch

A great French writer has observed that "the river is the soul of the country," but, indeed, the epithet might well be applied to the railway also, for therein lies living energy that pulsates throughout the length of the land even more than that belonging to the "silver stream." As the rivers pour themselves into the oceans so do the railways of our countries empty their streams of traffic and humanity into our big cities.

Nowhere, perhaps, can the life and energy of a railway be studied better than at one of the larger junctions, and it is my intention in this article to submit a few jottings on the working and management of such a junction – one of the most important in the country – that of Willesden, on the London and North Western Railway, about five miles out of Euston, a station known, I suppose, to thousands, and yet unknown to most of those thousands. Why is the station called Willesden? The parish and surrounding district is known as Harlesden. The postal address of the junction is "Station Road, Harlesden." The suburb of Willesden proper is some distance away. The real railway station for Willesden is not the famous Willesden Junction, but Willesden Green, on the Metropolitan Extension Line. The passenger to the North via the "West Coast Route" perhaps makes his connection there; the season-ticket holder on the North London passes through daily; the "Manchester man" gives up his Euston ticket as the train stops for a couple of minutes at "No. 3 platform"; the excursionist to the Continent has time to look about him from the window of the through coach, as he is shunted onto the Herne Hill train on the new route to Dover – these all see the surface, and not much more, for few imagine as they pass through Willesden Junction that, roughly speaking, a detachment of 1,100 men of our great "Railway Army" is constantly at work within its precincts.

Besides the London and North Western main line, Victoria, Croydon, Herne Hill and the Mansion House to Broad Street system, all worked by the same company; no less than three other companies, by virtue of running powers or working arrangements, also run their own trains to and from Willesden. The Great Western has a regular service of passenger trains from the High Level Station to Southall, thus providing an easy means of communication with the Great Western main line. The North London runs its Broad Street to Richmond or Kew trains through the same station, and its service to Broad Street via Chalk Farm from the "Bay" platform on the Low Level Station, while the London and South Western Railway, although running no passenger trains, has a very important share in the transfer of mineral and goods traffic at the "Exchange Sidings." The London and South Western trains travel from Kew over the North and South West Junction Railway, a railway probably unknown to many readers of the Railway Magazine. It was incorporated forty-six years ago, and its lucky shareholders have a minimum dividend of seven per cent in perpetuity, with an additional bonus occasionally. A couple of South Western locomotives may constantly be seen at work in these "Exchange Sidings," varying with their bright green tint the monotony of the black painted engines of the London and North Western and North London Railways.

Formerly there were two High Level Stations over the main line – the one for the reception of the North London, and the other for the Broad Street, Kensington, and Mansion House, "Outer Circle" or London and North Western trains running between – and very puzzling the unwary passenger from the country found it when he had to "change." These two stations were afterwards thrown into one, but the small accommodation on its platforms, together with the eight narrow and awkward staircases leading down to the four platforms of the Low Level station, rendered the puzzle of finding "the way out" almost as bad as getting to the centre of Hampton Court Maze – in fact, there is a facetious tradition that the Junction is haunted by ghosts of the unlucky passengers who never found their way out, and whose presence in the spiritual world is a kind of "Ixion trying to find the exit." But the opening in the autumn of 1894 of the new High Level "island platform," reached by broad and commodious stairs, and central landing, from the lower station, and having a separate exit to the exterior, turned the High Level Station into one of the finest and most convenient of its kind to be found, although for the first few weeks foolish passengers would insist upon getting out the wrong side, so that for a short time the doors on all trains had to be locked at the previous stations.

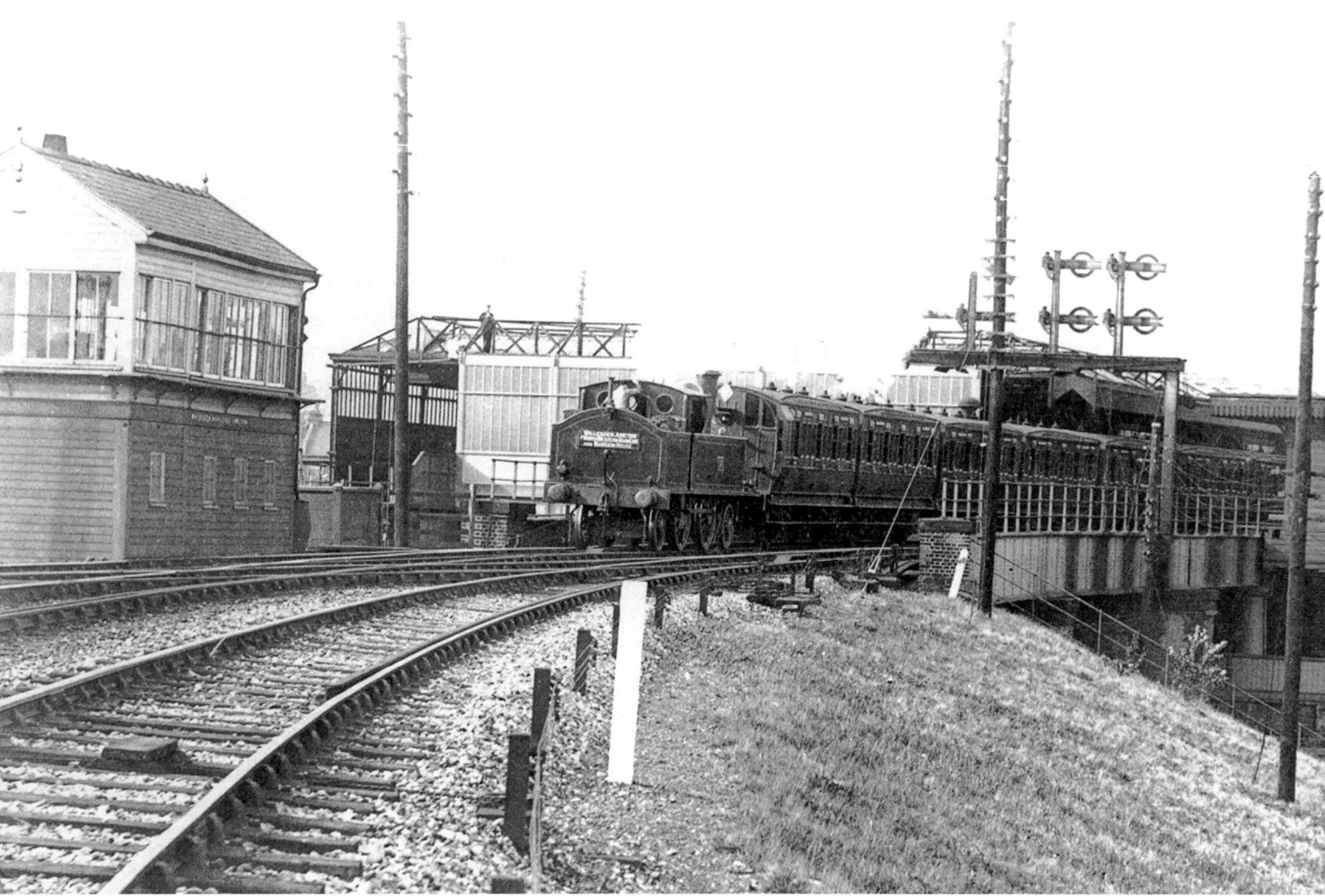

Willesden High Level: 2-4-2 tank departs bunker first with westbound train of lake "Mansion House" 4-wheeled carriages.

Willesden High Level station platform.

The following outline of the passenger trains which run through the Junction will show how varied and large the traffic is:-

1. The High Level Station
   On the down side:
   (a) L. and N.W. trains, Broad Street to Mansion House
   (b) L. and N.W. trains, Broad Street to Kensington (expresses)
   (c) N.L. to Kew and Richmond
   (d) G.W. to Southall, via Acton (G.W.)
   On the upside the corresponding services in the other direction are dealt with.

2. The Low Level (main line) Station

   No.1 Platform – for trains to and from Kensington, Victoria (L.B. and S.C.), Croydon (via Clapham Junction), and Herne Hill (L.C. and D.)

   No.2 Platform – Down main line trains (expresses)

   No. 3 Platform (Island) – On one side for up main line expresses, and the other for down local trains (Harrow and Watford)

   No. 4 Platform – Up local trains (Broad Street and Euston).

Besides these platforms there are two "bay" lines for the reception and despatch of N.L. trains to and from the city via Chalk Farm. But when we come to the number of trains themselves, our study becomes still more intricate. Sometimes the hasty traveller grumbles over the problems of "Bradshaw," but he would grumble still more had he to carry in his head the "Working Timetable" that controls the running of trains through such a junction as that of Willesden. I suppose it is part of the inherent selfishness of our nature that generally leads us to imagine that the train by which we are about to travel is the important one of the day; and now and then we are apt to complain because the porter, who often has to reckon and remember his trains by the hundred instead of by the unit, makes some slight mistake in directing us – especially at holiday seasons, when many "specials" are on and "ordinaries" are off. As a porter said to me once: "We ought to eat a 'Bradshaw' for breakfast to be able to remember all the information we are asked to give!"

To return, however, to the list of daily ordinary trains running into or through Willesden. I give it below, in brief tabulated form, including both passenger and goods:-

Willesden Junction Station entrance.

(a) **PASSENGER TRAINS**

	Low Level	High Level	Total
L. and N.W. Main Line	97	92	189
L. and N.W. Suburban	93		93
N. L.	77	77	154
G.W.		30	30
Grand Total	**267**	**199**	**466**

(b) **GOODS, MINERAL AND EMPTY WAGON TRAINS**

	Low Level	High Level	Total
L.and N.W. Main Line	76	31	107
L.and N.W. Suburban	44	16	60
N. L.	47		47
G.W.	26		26
Grand Total	**193**	**47**	**240**

The above list is exclusive of "specials," fish, meat, horse and carriage traffic, and empty coaches to and from Euston, averaging thirty per day. The following are the only main-line passenger trains which do not stop at the Junction:-

UP TRAINS
The "Scotch Mail" arriving at Euston at 5.30am.
The Liverpool "Sleeping Saloon Express" arriving at Euston 4.16am.

DOWN TRAINS
5.15am from Euston	"Newspaper Express"
7.15am	"	"Irish and North Mail"
12 noon	"	"American Special" running four or five times a month only
12.30pm	"	"American Special" running four or five times a month only
5.30pm	"	"Liverpool and Manchester Dining Saloon Express"
6pm	"	Watford and Bletchley
8pm	"	"Scotch Express"
8.45pm	"	"Irish Mail"
10.15pm	"	"Irish Night Express"
11.50pm	"	"Edinburgh and Glasgow Sleeping Saloon Express"

It will be seen that there is a daily average of 706 trains during the 24 hours through the Junction, or about one every two minutes, although it is obvious that the actual "working average" is much higher, as most of the passenger trains are running in the daytime. A very large amount of ticket collecting has to be performed every day at Willesden, not only from passengers actually journeying to that station, but also the tickets of all those travelling by the fast up trains from No.3 platform, including the immense number of passengers from the North. The number of ticket collectors on duty, therefore, is large; while the Railway Clearing House, no doubt, has a fair number of "through booked" tickets sent to them in the course of a year from Willesden Junction.

The above number of trains, of course, necessitates a very large staff on the traffic department at the Junction, and it will be interesting to note how this staff is divided. It consists of the following:-

Stationmaster	1
Assistant Stationmaster	1
Night Stationmaster	1
Porters, foremen, and ticket collectors	79
Signalmen	58
Guards	31
Brakesmen	21
Shunters and Yard Foremen	58
Telegraph, booking, and parcels clerks	18
Messengers	3
	271

So much for the traffic department staff. As now for a note about the "weapons" with which this little army combats the running, shunting, and marshalling of the 706 trains. These "weapons" may, I suppose, be characterised under two heads – the "telegraph" and the "lever." It would be rather outside the scope of this article to enter into the former; but with regard to the latter the working of traffic through the station, along the main lines, and in and out of the sidings, is controlled from no less than fourteen signal cabins, the levers of which regulate 225 signal arms and 440 points, besides many subsidiary "ground disc" signals for sidings and crossings. No wonder that 58 men are required to work them! And here let me say that the public can never understand and appreciate the smartness and wonderful accuracy of a signalman's work without paying a visit to a large signal cabin. No words, for instance, can describe the marvellous celerity of the three men on duty at Euston; and it is with a genuine feeling of awe that one remembers they carry in their heads the interlocking movements and

Willesden Junction Station. Train of horse boxes with No.165 "Star" ('Lady of the Lake' or 'Problem' class 2-2-2 with 7ft 9in driving wheels) in final form with circular smokebox door and vacuum pump. Built by John Ramsbottom in 1860 and rebuilt by Webb in 1897.

combinations of 288 levers. "But," said one of them to me, "when you are used to it it's just like the keyboard of a piano, and a musician playing a well-known tune. He can't very well make a mistake, for he's not only in perfect practice, but a `discord` jars on his ears at once." Thanks to the perfection of interlocking, the attempted "discord" jars the operator's muscles also, and he is prevented from making a mistake. This is scarcely the case with a musical instrument, so the two actions are not of so parallel a nature as suggested by the signalman.

The following is a list of signal cabins at the Junction and the number of arms actuated by each:-

Signal box	Signal arms	Distant signals outside boundary
Willesden No.1	39	5
" No.2	9	
" No.3	11	
" No.4	17	
" No.5	18	
" No.6	3	
" No.7	26	
" No.9	7	
Brent Junction	15	3
Kensal Green Junction	18	8
Old Oak Jn. (North London)	18	1
Willesden High Level Jn.	17	
Mitre Bridge Jn.	8	2
	206	19
Total		225

Working in close connection with the signalmen, of course, are the "shunters," and a very important part do they play in the work of the Junction. As one of them pithily remarked to me: "Ours is the letter-sorting department of the railway." So it is. Just as the sorter in the post-office quickly separates a huge mass of letters, and despatches them in different bags to their various centres of destination, so does the shunter deal with the heavy goods train. A score or so of loaded wagons arrive from the North or Midlands at Willesden – some to remain there, some for the London, Brighton and South Coast, others for the London, Chatham and Dover, and a few for the London and South Western. With speed the observant shunter takes in the situation, and gets to work, chalking the wagons, shouting or signalling directions to drivers and signalmen, putting a few wagons into this, and a few into that siding; until out of the apparent confusion, order is at length evolved, and the London, Brighton and South Coast, and London, Chatham and Dover wagons are "marshalled" with others into a train proceeding to Lillie Bridge and Stewarts Lane via Kensington, while the South Western wagons are conveyed to the "Old Oak Siding" alongside the Richmond High Level line, to be presently pulled off by one of their own engines via Acton.

On the down side of the line, north of the passenger station, are large sidings for goods and coal, known as "A" and "B" sidings; at these coal for the various London depots is dealt with. The "C" sidings on the opposite side of the line are also used for the reception of traffic from the North for distribution in diverse parts of the metropolis; while further down the line are sidings for sorting empty wagons returning to the North. Some idea of the tremendous extent of the work done in the shunting department can be realised when I mention the number of goods, coal, and other mineral wagons passing through Willesden amounts to a daily average of 1,500, while a similar number of "empties" is also dealt with daily.

While I am dealing with the traffic department I must not fail to mention a little about the work of the booking-clerks, porters, and ticket-collectors, who "label" and "shunt" passengers rather than wagons, and "marshal" the travelling public. The undermentioned figures, kindly supplied to me by official sources, will prove interesting, especially when it is borne in mind that they only relate to ordinary passenger traffic booked from Willesden, and do not include those coming to the Junction. I give a ten year's interval comparison:-

NUMBER OF PASSENGERS BOOKED FROM WILLESDEN JUNCTION
In 1886   530,300
In 1896   1,006,886

It may be assumed that a similar number of incoming passengers are also dealt with, and that, of course, these figures are still increasing. There are also an immense number of passengers who use the station as a point of change *en route*, and of which no record is available; besides the large number of season-ticket holders, the striking increase in which will be noticed in the following comparison of ten year's interval. Of course, these passengers are in addition to the above quoted figures. Also, it does not include those who have taken out tickets at Broad Street (NL) or Kensington, or other stations belonging to "foreign" companies working in connection with the London and North Western:-

Year	1st class	2nd class	3rd class	Total
1885	97	362	19	478
1895	144	948	152	1,244
1896	–	–	–	1,600

During this period of ten years, therefore, the number of season ticket-holders increased at the average annual rate of nearly 30 per cent, or almost 300 per cent on the whole ten years – in 1896 it has still further increased.

And here is a comparison of the number of parcels dealt with in and out of the station during the period of ten years:-

In 1886   260,220
In 1896   623,200

But we must leave these traffic statistics and go on to another department that claims our consideration. Probably the average passenger little realises the amount of work that has to be done in repairing and cleaning carriages – or "coaches" as they ought properly to be termed, out of deference to the old road vehicles they superseded. One inherently expects to find a carriage clean when one travels; but as the paterfamilias rarely understands the mystery of "spring cleaning," so the average passenger rarely thinks of how, or when, or where the railway coach is overhauled or cleaned. South of the passenger station, on the up side of the line, are the stabling and repairing sheds for main line carriage stock, which may be termed "relief" works to those at Wolverton, and under the superintendence of Mr. Park, the head of the Carriage Department. In some of these you may find a bogie coach raised by powerful machinery while a new wheel is being put on – the old one, not yet quite discarded, meanwhile being re-turned by a huge lathe in the shed hard by. In another shed a detachment of men and boys are busily cleaning out the magnificent "corridor train" which runs every afternoon out of Euston, and which is brought to Willesden every morning to be thoroughly overhauled and garnished, so that it may start in its usual trim array.

Talk about "spring cleaning!" A good housewife would think twice before she undertook the cleaning of a corridor train! Hard by stands a train of a very different calibre – the night mail, with its long post-office coaches, and its nets for picking up wayside letter bags. This, also, is being cleaned out preparatory to its evening journey to the North. In the next shed are a number of sleeping cars, which will receive clean pillows, etc, before they bear their freight of living sleepers over the railway sleepers in their Northern flight. Situated close to the station is the Company's laundry, at which all the towels for the carriage lavatories, sleeping saloon sheets, etc, are washed. In the summer as many as fifteen to twenty of the main line passenger trains are made up at Willesden before being sent to their starting point at Euston.

In addition to the above, there are other sheds close by, and also on the down side north of the station, for the stabling of suburban passenger trains. The result of these covered habitations is the preservation of carriage stock, and, besides this, the comfort of the passenger is greatly increased by reason of the carriages being protected from extreme heat or frost. This appreciably affects the temperature of the compartments during the journeys of the trains. It also prevents the doors from warping or shrinking, as they would do were the carriages allowed to stand in the open, thus causing unpleasant draughts. The number of cleaners and repairers employed in this carriage department amounts to about 100.

Leaving the passenger coaches, and turning to less showy, but by no means less important, portion of the rolling stock, we may find in another part of the station premises the "hospital for damaged wagons." Every goods train that passes through Willesden has to undergo a strict examination; and when the examiner affixes a certain red card to a vehicle it signifies that this particular wagon must not go a step – no, a wheel – further, but must enter the repairing department. Perhaps one of its wheels is a bit worn, or its couplings have become a little loose in the racket of its life's journey, or the examiner may have said in kindly tones, "This old buffer ain't no good," but when once it gets the red card on it, it is distinctly a "case" for, as every railwayman knows, it is criminal to remove it. These cards bear on them in writing, the nature of the disease – such as "blocks worn out," "spring broken," etc. This department, again, requires a body of fifty men to keep it going; repairers, rather than cleaners – for the poor coal wagon does not stand a chance of a "wash and brush up" as does its gaudy rival of the road the corridor train.

But a still more interesting department awaits our inspection as we wend our way through the huge stacks of coal, from which 80 to 100 tons are drawn daily for the consumption of the engines. I mean the "loco sheds." If the coaches require careful cleaning, so do the engines; and although the cleaning sheds at Chalk Farm contain more accommodation, and are more busy owing to their nearness to Euston, still a goodly number of iron steeds may generally be seen standing over the pits at Willesden, while men and lads are busily engaged in cleaning and inspecting them. Before each run, the locomotive has to be carefully overhauled, and on its return takes a rest while it is soothed down with oiling and rubbing like a tired athlete. It may be that the careful examiner detects some defect of more or less serious import. This must be seen to immediately; and close at hand we find large store rooms where a supply of necessaries is always kept, arranged in the most careful order, all ready for immediate use. Or, in more serious cases, the well-cared for locomotive is taken bodily into hospital and rests there while her wheels are re-turned, or her internal arrangements are taken out and cleaned.

It is astonishing what careful grooming the iron horse requires, and how particular she is in her consumption and digestion of coal, oil, and water. At Willesden Junction the latter has to be prepared for her as carefully as for the most fastidious invalid; and close at hand is the "filtering department," a place that well deserves an article in itself. By means of the most ingenious pumping machinery, worked by the water supply itself, a mixture of lime-water is passed into the hard, fresh water, resulting in a strong deposit of chalk. This chalk is removed by the water which contains it passing through huge filters under great pressure, when it is ready for the engines' consumption. By this means the boilers, being nearly free from the deposit, require cleaning only at rare intervals.

Perhaps it is "pay day" as we are making our round of inspection, and we pause for a moment to watch the stream of 400 firemen, cleaners, fitters, etc, going up to the "pay window" to receive their hard-earned weekly wages. Each man carries a metal check bearing his own particular number; while behind the window are rows of small cylindrical tins, correspondingly numbered, and bearing the exact amount of wages due on the pay sheet, the cash having been brought down by a clerk from Euston. On the personal presentation of his check each man receives the contents of the tin box – his weekly pay, lessened perchance by a fine, or perhaps increased by overtime work.

Retracing our steps to the station, we notice the grim-looking breakdown train, with its tool trucks, large crane, and carriage for the gang, standing ready to start at a moment's notice for the scene of any accident or emergency between Euston and Bletchley. Happily we congratulate ourselves that its journeys are of infrequent occurrence, thanks to the absolute block system and the careful and constant examination of locomotives, vehicles and permanent way. The latter department alone employs 135 men in the precincts of Willesden Junction, and many of these men occupy the dreary post of fog-men when the dread enemy to railway and ocean traffic alike swoops down over the semaphore arms.

Just a word or two about the housing of the company's servants at Willesden. Close to the station, situated partly in Acton and partly in Hammersmith parishes, is quite a little town, consisting of several streets of small houses owned entirely by the London and North Western Company, and inhabited by railwaymen and their families. There is a capital Institute, with reading room and a large hall for meetings and entertainments, on the platform of which the writer of this article has many times had the pleasure of appearing before his friends the railwaymen. There is also in this district a literal "barracks," a large building devoted to the accommodation of goods drivers, firemen and brakesmen coming up from the North, and enjoying a well-earned rest between the hours of duty. Day and night this building is constantly open, and the men are entering for a few hours' sleep, or starting forth on a duty. The religious needs of this district are provided for by a little iron church, worked by the clergy of All Souls', Harlesden; while for many years the Presbyterians have held services in the large room belonging to the Institute, kindly lent by the Company for that purpose.

By standing on the High Level platform of Willesden Junction and gazing around one cannot but be impressed by the enormous power of the railway over civilisation, for it is no exaggeration to say that this important station has practically "made" the huge district of bricks and mortar which lies around it. One can hardly realise that

Willesden Junction Main Line c1900. From the left are two local trains with 'Willesden' and 'Watford' headboards. In the right down fast platform there is an express double-headed by a 'Problem' and a 'Greater Britain'.

Willesden Junction station with Cauliflower Goods 0-6-0 No.447.

hard by – where the Irish Mail goes rushing and snorting, or the city train discharges its load of tired workers – in medieval England pilgrims were wending their way from distant London to visit the shrine of "Our Ladye of Wilsdon" in the forest; or that, to come down to a later period, the traveller heard the voice of the dreaded highwayman (the district was famous for these "gentry of the road") bidding him alight and hand over his cash, where now he catches the cry, "Change here for Broad Street and Kensington! All tickets ready, please!" Old inhabitants of Harlesden, where, as already stated, the station really stands, will tell you how a score of years ago they could see across the fields to the Junction, and watch a handful of passengers coming up the "lane" to the little village! Now all this has changed, for thousands of people are alive to the importance of living in a neighbourhood which offers such exceptional railway facilities.

From Willesden Junction one can practically go anywhere. The "City man" finds a splendid service of trains to and from Broad Street, from High or Low Level, by London and North Western or North London. Twelve minutes will take one to Euston; while for the West End and south London there is ample convenience via Addison Road. Perhaps one of the greatest improvements that could be made in connection with routes from Willesden Junction would be a direct communication with Paddington, and already there has been a rumour afloat of an electric railway to serve between these two points. As it is, however, Willesden Junction has developed into a unique station, one of the most important in the country; and perhaps the above notes may serve to show something of its position as a great railway centre.

The present Stationmaster, Mr Wood, has been in charge since 1885, and his post is by no means an easy one, although the manner in which the work under his direction is dealt with testifies well to his energy and ability.

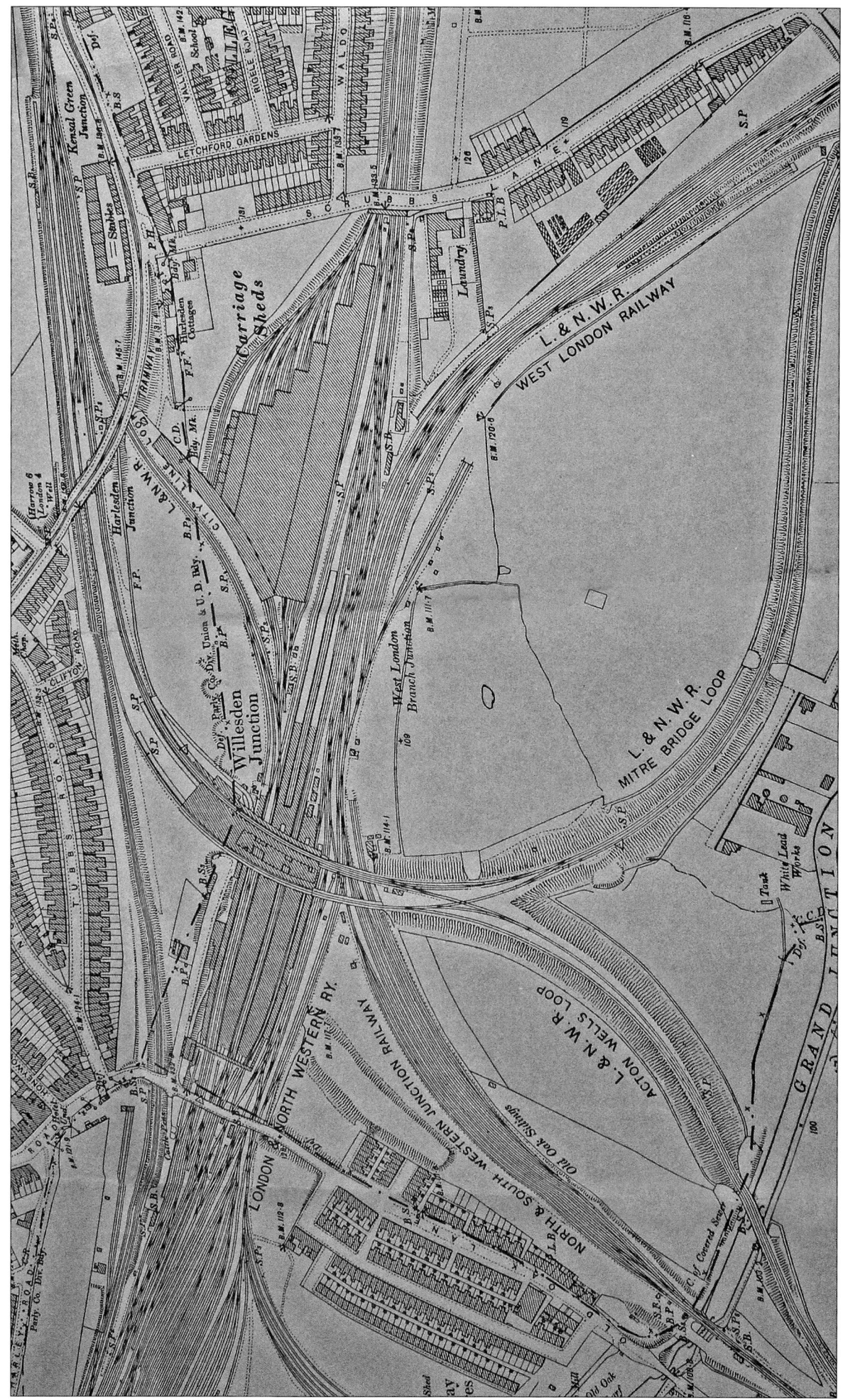

Willesden Junction Map 1894.

Chapter 4
Wolverton Carriage Works
by V.L. Whitechurch

"This is the noisiest tunnel in London," I remarked, as our train dashed into Kensal Green tunnel, just before Willesden Junction. "Yes: and do you know why?" asked my companion. I began some elaborate explanation of the reverberating echo, when he stopped me. "It's because our trains shake up the bones in Kensal Green Cemetery, and make them rattle!" "Well, some of the trains are heavy enough," I replied. "I should think so" he cried, enthusiastically, and began giving me some details about "American Specials" and "West Coast corridors." "But there," he added, "you'll see for yourself presently, when we get to the Works."

For I was *en route* for Wolverton, there, under the kindly guidance of the official detailed to conduct me thither, to gather some notes for the basis of an article in the Railway Magazine on the Carriage works of the London and North Western Railway. The time passed quickly enough, as it always does when a railway enthusiast gets face to face with a railwayman who loves and thoroughly understands his work, until the train drew up at Wolverton, and the magic word "Pass" let us through the barrier to the road. The office entrance to the works is close by the station, and I very soon found myself introduced to Mr C.A. Park, M.I.C.E., the

Wolverton Erecting Shop showing roofs of various 6-wheel carriages.

Carriage Superintendent of the Company, and seated myself opposite to him ready to draw a little information.

"I am afraid it's rather a bad day for you, in some respects. You see, we don't happen to have very much stock in just now – just after the Bank Holiday. Questions? Not too many, please, for I've a very busy day on hand."

"How long have you been superintendent of the Wolverton Works?"

"Just about ten years. I superseded the late Mr Bore."

"Have you always been in the service of the L. and N.W.?"

"Oh no! I came here from the N.E."

"East Coast to West Coast, eh?"

"Quite so. I came over from our rivals. I was formerly stationed at York, and was Locomotive Superintendent to the southern division of the North Eastern Railway. You see, I am by profession a locomotive man; but, of course, I now have nothing to do with that department."

"Does your authority extend beyond Wolverton?"

"Oh yes. I am over the carriage department at Crewe also; and then we have repairing sheds at Carlisle and Willesden. These fall under my jurisdiction. Our department is a very large one, for besides building and repairing, we are responsible for all the cleaning and examination of the whole coaching department. The average number of vehicles passed through the shop for repairs annually is 8,100."

Wolverton underframe for 57 ft. carriage.

"And how many hands have you, all told?"

"Well roughly speaking, in round numbers there are 3,200 employed at Wolverton, while outside we have 2,000 at Crewe, Carlisle, Willesden, and scattered over the line."

"Quite a little army! And are you responsible for building and repairing passenger coaches only?"

"Oh, dear no! We include, of course, brake-vans for passenger trains, horse boxes, fruit, milk and luggage vans, and also all the omnibuses, parcel carts and vans, broughams, gigs, and so on are made and repaired by us …… But here comes Mr Coker, who will prove an able guide in showing you round, and will supply you with any information about the works which you may require."

So off I started with Mr C. Coker, the chief draughtsman at Wolverton, who has been in that position for fifteen or sixteen years, but whose time in the works dated back over thirty years, before the then locomotive establishment of Wolverton was removed to Crewe. I might mention here that the present Works Manager is Mr Purslow, who entered upon that position about the time that Mr Park came to Wolverton, and who superseded Mr Panter, the present Manager of the London and South Western Railway works at Eastleigh – a very popular railwayman, who was one of those to see the development of the carriage works out of the old locomotive erecting shops at Wolverton, which, by the way, were finally removed in 1877.

"There are two chief ways of seeing the works," said Mr Coker, as we descended from the office; "either we begin at the finished coach and work backwards to the details, or to go to the beginning first and work upwards; but, at all events, you shall see as much as we can show you in a day."

When one considers that the works take up an area of between fifty and sixty acres, it can be easily realised that even this "much" was, after all, very little; but I will endeavour to give some description both of the various departments and manner of work, and also of the beautiful final results in the way of the LNW passenger rolling

Wolverton Works 1893. Pioneer WCJS corridor train in yard (with end of workshops in left background) hauled by Teutonic No.1304 "Jeanie Deans" made up of 5 42ft bogies, 3 12-wheel diners and 2 more 42ft bogies.

Wolverton 1894. Inside carriage erecting works showing 4 and 6 wheeled carriages in various stages of repair and construction.

stock that I inspected during the course of the day, and of which the Company is justly proud.

The immense timber yard is enough to make one imagine that material had been laid in for building a fleet of a hundred arks after the pattern of Noah's. There are huge logs of mahogany too from the panels in the future; long strips of oak – wood everywhere of all shapes and varieties; while under cover are stored up thousands of boards for panel, etc.

"We try and keep the panelling for three years, to get it thoroughly seasoned," explained my guide; "while other wood is dried artificially if required before it has time to get seasoned. What wood do we use chiefly? Mahogany, oak, and walnut, a vast amount of teak – one of the most useful woods in railway construction, sycamore, yellow deal for partitions, roofs and floors; elm we find of very little use, but we are now very partial to Padouk wood, though the workmen don't like it on account of its toughness." I saw a great deal of this Padouk wood when going through the finishing and varnishing shops. It hails from South Australia, and is of a beautiful deep red

Wolverton Paint Shop in 1894 with view along track of central traverser showing carriages set out in rows on either side. The traverser is positioned at the far end with a 32ft 6-wheeled brake.

colour, very tough, polishes magnificently, and is admirably adapted for chair-backs and arms in dining saloons, skirtings, mouldings, etc.

Adjoining the timber stores are the saw-mills, which occupy two large shops. The work here is very interesting. I saw a huge mahogany log, over two feet in width and thickness and very long, weighing five tons and worth twenty-five pounds, being sawn into panels by a set of vertical saws. Five boards were sawn off either side at once from end to end, and when these ten, destined for side panelling, were cut, the log was turned, and thirty boards of narrower width sawn for end panels, thus utilising all the wood possible.

Close by was a steam planing machine, while the next big thing which caught my eye was the process of making teak tabs for wheels. These are cut into their wedge shape by one machine, and then placed into a horizontal revolving frame, where endless saws cut their outer and inner circumference correct as to shape, and groove them properly. There was no time to linger in this preparatory shop, except, perhaps, to notice the clever little machine for boring square holes. A hollow, square tube of steel, very sharp at the ends, contains a revolving circular drill, cutting pretty well all the space of the square except the corners. This is brought to bear against the timber under hydraulic pressure, and in no time a cleanly bored square hole, several inches deep, is the result. Of course, there is a set of these drills, varying in size.

Closely adjacent to the saw mills is the smith's shop. "Looks more like Crewe, doesn't it?" remarked my guide, as we entered a large building resounding with the clang of the hammer, and bright with forge-fires and hot iron. In this shop are no less than one hundred forges, while fourteen steam hammers (of which two weigh three tons), three gas furnaces, and four gas-producers go to swell the machinery. One of the most important of the many articles manufactured in this shop are the steel carriage springs, each of which is submitted to a test quite as severe as that applied to guns in Woolwich Arsenal before it is sent out to administer to the comfort of the traveling public, the test chiefly consisting in the dropping of heavy weights upon the springs.

An intensely interesting portion of the 25 shops that make up the Wolverton works is before me as I enter the wheel department, for here I have the opportunity of studying in detail the basis of the running of the modern railway coach. And here I might remark that the chief point that strikes the observer as he goes through this department is the predominance of the bogie – in fact there is very little else. Ever and anon six-wheeled passenger coaches, that have been running on the main line, come into the works for repair, and are converted chiefly into composite brake-vans, and, in nearly every case, sent to work on the local lines in the future; but the actual building of the six-wheeled coach is now conspicuous by its absence, and I shall be able to give some details of its successor before the close of this article.

Queen Victoria's Day Saloon.

Queen Victoria's Day Saloon interior (postcard).

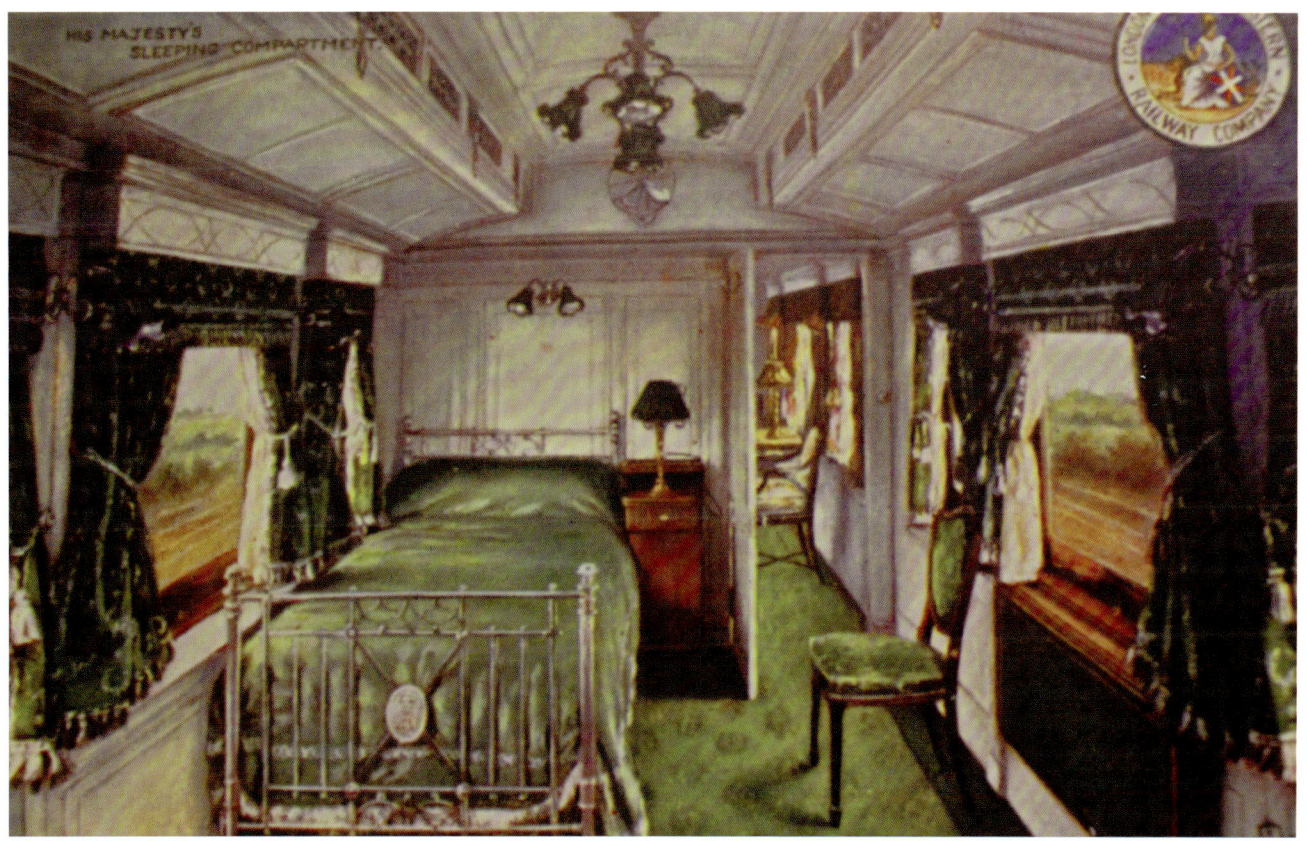
Queen Victoria's Sleeping Compartment.

The steel tyres of the wheels are brought from Crewe – every other portion except the axles being manufactured at Wolverton. These tyres are first carefully turned to the required angle of 1 in 20, and are then ready for the "tabs" to be inserted, for all the wheels manufactured here are those of the Mansel system, in which tabs take the place of spokes. These tabs, made of the best teak, are each stamped with their exact weight, so that it is easy to pick out two wheels of equal weight to run as a pair on the same axle. The tyre is placed over the tabs (fitted in a circle), the whole clamped in a horizontal case, and the tabs rammed up into the tyres by a ten inch hydraulic ram exercising a force of three tons per square inch. Inside and outside "retaining rings" are then put on, and bolted through the tabs; these retaining rings fit, at their outer edges, into grooves in the steel tyres, so that, in the event of a tyre working loose from its tabs, it is impossible to fall off, but it would revolve loosely on the retaining rings. The wheel, with its centre disc, is now ready to be fitted to the axle. A pair of wheels are pushed on their axle, one wheel at a time, by hydraulic press which exercises a force of ten tons per inch diameter, or a total pressure of 52½ tons. No wonder that the wheel can be fixed on a cold axle firm and immovable. A centre guide tells the operator the exact moment to turn off the pressure, and the two wheels are pushed on thus in a few seconds.

Each pair of wheels is then run in a balancing machine, and the unequal weight, which is generally detected, balanced by an expert by the means of nailing strips of iron on the inner side of the tabs of the lighter wheel. They are then stored away, ready to be fitted to their "axle boxes." The axle boxes themselves deserve a word of description for the sake of the uninitiated; they are cast at Wolverton, and literally "planed" down to smoothness. The upper part contains the brass bearing, a simple curved piece that fits over the journal of the axle, and is fixed on a "slipper" of iron that slips into a groove in the axle box in such a manner that it has to be removed before the brass bearings can be taken out. The lower portion of the box is filled with oil, which is carried to the journals by spongy pads, so that the journal as it revolves continually takes up a thin layer of oil as a lubrication between itself and the bearings.

"Rather better than the old system of yellow grease" said my guide.

"Yes" I answered; "and how many miles will one of these axles run without requiring new brass bearings?"

"Well, we generally calculate about a hundred thousand, but they frequently last for a much longer distance."

"And do you think that you have reached the same perfection in these axle boxes, which I understand, have been in use for about six years?"

"It is impossible to say. There may be such a thing as ball bearings applied to coaches in the future. We're already fitting them on some of the light buses and parcel vans; but at present our carriage bearings seem to leave little to be desired. They are simple, and allow of the wheels being removed in a few seconds if anything goes wrong. And now, if you please, we'll have a look at the bogie frames to which they are fixed."

Pausing for a moment to watch the working of the Bradford portable air-drill, we were soon among the bogie frames.

"You see," explained my guide, as we stood opposite an hydraulic punching machine, "these men are punching out portions of the steel frame for the reception of the upper part of the axle boxes. Of course, it tends to weaken the frame slightly; but then, as you will notice, we clamp a plate on afterwards. In modern coach-building we are obliged to do this, otherwise vehicles would become much too high, and every platform along the line would have to be raised. There you see an old discarded wooden bolster" (a "bolster," by the way is the cross piece on which the body of the coach eventually rests). "We make them all of steel now, and here you will see the difference between the four-wheeled and six-wheeled bogie.

The four-wheeler has one transverse piece, with a centre piece, hollowed, on which the greater part of the coach's weight rests, while there are end rubbing and bearing plates on either side; the six-wheeled bolster fits between the centre pair of wheels, with the centre plate over their axle, and is square, with rubbing plates at the corners, so that there are four points of bearing besides the centre. The bolsters, as you see, are resting on very strong spiral springs, the weight over which is conveyed from them to the frame, and thence to the springs over the axle boxes. Notice the easy side play of the bolsters, which allows the body of the coach to gravitate whilst rounding curves."

"And might I ask the thickness of the frames?"

"On a four wheel bogie they are twelve by four inch angle iron, three quarters of an inch thick. The frames come from Crewe – but we are quite able to make them here. And now we will begin looking at the coaches themselves in the initiatory stages, first going through the finishing shop."

This could be more properly called the joiner's shop, for it contains scores of carpenter's benches, upon which every species of detail work can be seen. One man was making door panels, another grooving door pillars; on other benches were window frames and skirtings, while a huge pendant, swinging circular saw, reminding one of Edgar Allan Poe's grim pendulum in his awful story of the Inquisition, was sawing up panels. Ventilators, sashes, rests for water-bottles – everything that one can imagine in the woodwork of a railway coach was being manufactured in this immense shop.

"We do a great deal of veneering," said Mr Coker, as he led the way through a smaller shop. "Now isn't this a pretty bit of work?" and he showed me some beautiful sycamore, as thin as pasteboard, veneered to a board of mahogany. "Yes we may have to use mahogany, for no wood that shrinks at all will do for this process. Here is a piece of sycamore before being veneered. Looks rough and crinkled, doesn't it? But we press down to the mahogany with steel plates heated in the steam oven yonder, and that soon makes it smooth enough. And now here we are at the body shops. We take the coaches away or bring old ones in by this steam traverser, which moves up and down with a coach on it, and discharges its load along the roads on either side. Now that bogies are in so much fashion we can't stow nearly the number of coaches in a road, and are very often much pressed for room. Notice, before we go inside, this pile of gas reservoirs. Those we are using beneath our new coaches are 11 feet 9 inches long, 21 inches in diameter, and contain 895 cubic feet (ordinary atmospheric pressure) of condensed gas for lighting purposes."

Entering the body shop, I speedily saw the beginning of the erection of the coach itself. The steel frames are sent down from Crewe. Those for the new carriages, which I shall describe presently, are fifty feet in length. It is obvious that as these are only supported from underneath by a bogie at either end, there is a strong tendency to bend down the frame in the middle. This is overcome by means of "truss-rods" below the frame, which act in exactly the opposite manner to a suspension bridge, and make the frame at least four times as strong in the centre, where the pressure is most acutely felt, being screwed immediately below, and thus tending to force the frame upwards. Under the frames are fixed the "spectacle eyes" for carrying gas reservoirs, while the "pull" at either end is eliminated along the whole length of the coach from coupling to coupling by a stout centre rod fitted with rubber buffers.

We entered the "body" of a corridor coach that was in a state of semi-completion, and looked, on the outside, with its rough coatings of red and white paint, something like a mammoth bathing machine. Mr. Coker pointed out to us the different woods used in various parts of the construction, The framing was of teak, and though the coach was fifty feet in length, I could detect no join in the end to end timbers, though I am told that this is now sometimes necessary, owing to the difficulty

Saloon compartment for Manchester to Llandudno trains.

of getting sufficient length in one beam. The cantrails were of oak, and the partitions, roof, and floor of yellow deal. The panels were mahogany, strengthened on the outside with stout canvas glued to the back, and supported to the angles of the framing by glued blocks. Deal was the wood used for seats, with oak for the seat rails. The roof was spanned by curved ribs of channel steel, with internal lining of the wood, for screwing the roof outside and the panels within. Such was the body of the coach in its initial stage, and, though I would have gladly lingered over details, I was taken to sundry smaller departments, where material was being arranged for interior completion.

In one shop were a group of female polishers and varnishers rubbing seat-arms and panels, posting the well-known "notices" on to slabs of tin, etc. Another step or two and we were in the upholstery department, amid piles of "rep," "leather," and rugs, while a hug "cutter," with an endless knife, was busy cutting up, ten thicknesses at a time, material to be taken to a room above, where there was a

WCJS fish Van for Scottish Services.

row of sewing machines, worked by steam, and an army of fifty women and girls stitching busily at cushions, and cordings, and hand rests, and the like, while in another room were more of the gentle sex preparing strips of leather for window straps. Next came the "stuffing" department, where seats and backs were being filled with horsehair - "real horsehair and nothing else" – stitched down with the familiar red buttons.

To get into the sheds where stood several finished trains that I wished to inspect, we had to pass through the paint shops – one of them containing thirtysix "roads" for storing coaches. Presumably the public has a very slight idea of the lengthy process which the LNWR carriages undergo before they emerge from Wolverton in the full glory of the well-known chocolate and white. I was astonished when I was informed that each coach received no less than sixteen coats of paint, distributed as follows:-

Three coats of "white priming" (white lead, linseed oil, and turpentine)

Four coats of "filling up"

One coat of red staining. This shows any surface inequalities, and the whole has to be rubbed down with pumice stone and water until not a particle of red remains.

The other coats are distributed as follows:-

PANELS – WHITE
Three coats of lead
One coat of Kremnitz white
One coat of enamel
Three coats of varnish

BODY – CHOCOLATE
One coat of brown
One coat of lake (carmine, a very expensive colour)
Three coats of varnish

The "lining" (gilding, etc) is done after the first coat of varnish. The paint is all ground and mixed on the premises.

The modern Mansion House to Broad Street trains of the LNWR are not painted at all. They are built of the best teak, polished and varnished, and are well adapted to the Underground, whereas if ordinary coloured coaches were run they would soon show dirt – as do the G.W.

The cleaners and repairers at Wolverton hate these Mansion House coaches, as both within and without they arrive in a dirtier condition than the others. Mr J.B. Williams' system of cleaning the carriages with oil is used in the works. It removes all dirt, and renders the paint supple, preserving it from cracking.

"And now," said Mr Coker, "you shall see some of the crack rolling stock – the finest trains in the kingdom."

I mildly brought in a mention of East Coast corridors, but it doesn't do to say too much to a LNW man on the subject of GN rolling stock – or anything else connected with that particular "tramway to the North, that only gets as far as Doncaster," as I once heard a high LNW official describe the rival route.

The first train that I went over was the very latest type of West Coast Joint Stock corridor, designed to run from Euston at 11.30am to Edinburgh and Glasgow, returning from Edinburgh at 11.35. This was a reserve duplicate of those now running. It is fitted with the Automatic Vacuum for the LNWR and the Westinghouse brake for the Caledonian, the pipes running along the sides, under the frames; and Peter and Co.'s American system of steam heating –

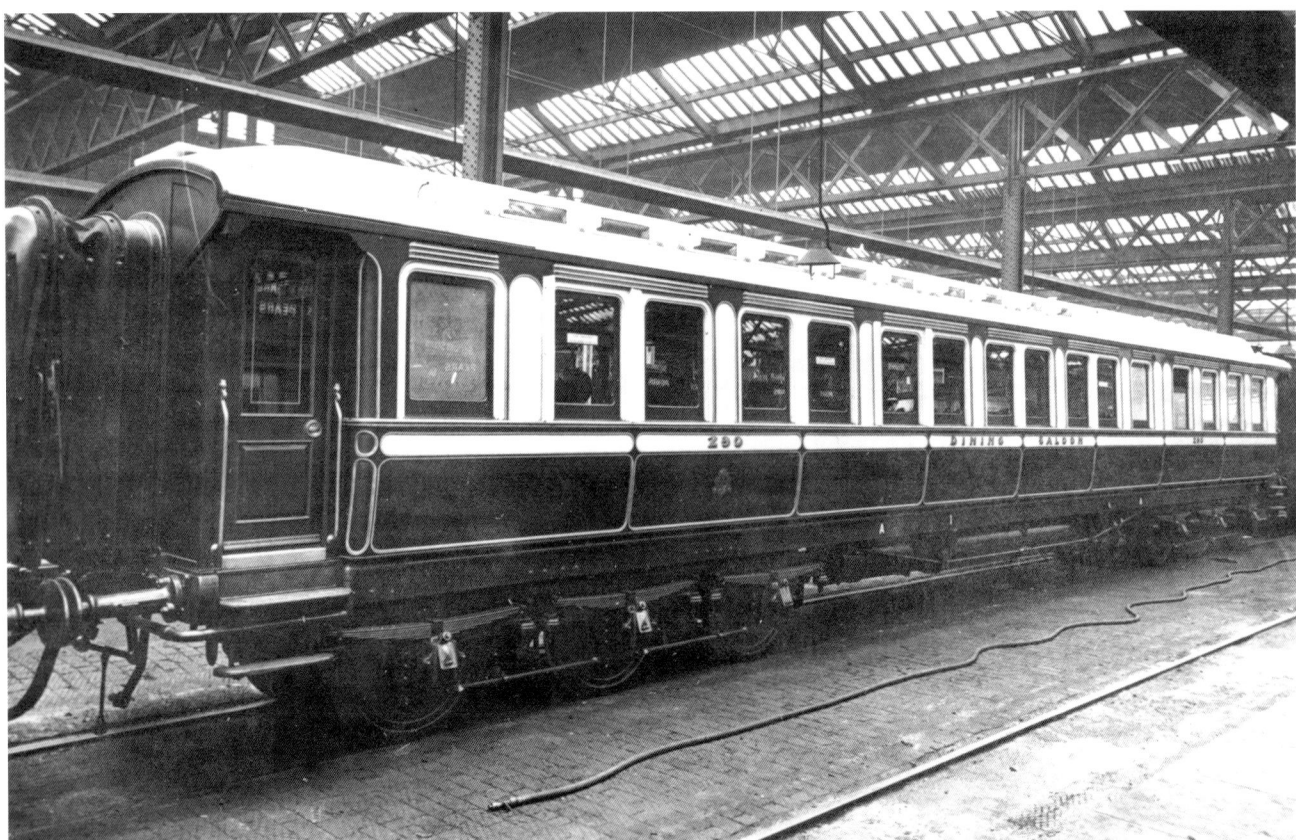

65ft.6in 12-Wheel Dining Saloon No.290 2nd & 3rd composite with clerestory roof at Euston 1905.

an inner tube filled with acetate of soda, and heated by steam from the engine sent through an outer one, the amount of heat being under control of the guard.

The coaches are fifty-four feet in length from buffer to buffer; the corridors are two feet six inches in width; the doors one and three-eighth's inches in thickness. In a third class carriage there are seven compartments, seating is three a side, each fitted with electric bell push for attendant, and a lavatory at either end. The upholstery is brown and black rep with black and red seaming cord and laces, and leather corner arm rests; the partitions are pine, and the roof covered with white lincrusta. The corridors are fitted with teak pillars and framing, and are roofed with sycamore (veneered). The floor is covered throughout with Kork linoleum. There are two fold up seats in the corridor, a water filter at one end, and twenty-four gas-burners in all.

The first class coach contains five full and one coupé compartment. The lavatories, one at either end, are fitted with silver-topped basins, and the interior finished with V-jointed American oak, with walnut mouldings and skirtings. The corridors are fitted with walnut framing, sycamore panels relieved with gold, dado of Italian walnut, sycamore roof V-jointed and banded with walnut. For the compartments black American walnut, highly polished, is used for framing, while photo prints and mirrors in walnut frames are under net racks. The panelling is of sycamore, relieved with gold beading, and the roof of Walton lincrusta, in cream relieved with gold. The upholstery is figured moquette of a crushed strawberry-coloured ground, and the floors are covered with figured Kork linoleum and matting. The dining cars on this train are of the newest West Coast pattern, first and third composite on six-wheeled bogies. The whole train is made up as follows:

EDINBURGH PORTION
1. Composite brake and first class
2. Composite dining car
3. Third class coach

Clerestory diner built for Euston to Manchester services shows sumptuous decoration and upholstery with wide single seats each side of the gangway 1890.

GLASGOW PORTION
4. First class coach
5. Composite dining car
6. Third class coach
7. Composite third class brake

Glancing at some of the "sleepers" which the Company claim as being unique, having separate compartments shut off into two-bedded rooms with their own lavatory, and possessing small rooms with one bed – which carriages, by the way, are supplied with the heating apparatus of Messrs. Dargue, Griffiths and Co., of Liverpool – and having walked through the Prince of Wales's saloon, Mr Coker next drew my attention to a class of coach that will prove of interest alike to the railway specialist and the travelling public.

"And now," he said, "let me show you the third-class coach of the future. This is a sample of four hundred which we are busily engaged in turning out, and a type of railway carriage that in time will succeed nearly all the present main line thirds on our system."

As I looked at the magnificent vehicle, I could not help thinking of the historical "Experiment" of the Stockton and Darlington Railway, or of the Exhibition excursions of 1851, when the G.W. nailed rough boards across their permanent way trucks at Didcot to accommodate their third class passengers! These new examples of modern luxury railway travelling are fifty feet in length, and mounted on two four –wheel bogies. They are corridor carriages, but differ from those of the "West Coast Joint Stock" above described in that they are slightly narrower, in order to be of uniform width with the present ordinary rolling stock, their actual body width being eight feet. But the seating accommodation is not diminished, the corridors being narrower – to wit. two feet instead of two feet six inches. "But they beat the G.W." said my companion, "For they only provide a twenty inch corridor." There are seven compartments in each coach, and a lavatory at each end. The panelling is similar to the West Coast corridors, but the roofing is white lincrusta throughout, and I was bound to say that I preferred the sycamore as being more artistic. It would also seem that more utility might be provided by arranging one luggage compartment in each coach; otherwise these new vehicles appear to leave nothing to be desired (except electric communication), and the LNW company may well be proud of them – and they are, too! As an instance of the exceeding care which is given to the finish of details, I might mention here that I went into one little department where the window-glasses for the lavatories were prepared. The panes of glass are partly ground, then laid over a pattern – containing the Company's arms, floral designs, etc – which is *outlined* by hand in Brunswick black, and the portion not intended for relief filled up with the same material .They are then exposed to an acid bath, the non-blacked portion eaten away, and the whole finished and ground afterwards.

"And how many panes can you outline and fill up in a week?" I asked.

"Three at the outside," was the reply. And yet half the travelling public know almost nothing of the care that is taken to ensure their comfort.

"Now," said my guide "you've seen about the finest thing in corridors and new main line coaches, so come and have a look at our new Watford locals – the best locals, bar none, in the kingdom."

The LNWR may be justly proud of these exquisitely finished trains. They are not corridors, as, of course, the exigencies of the local traffic scarcely render that sort of coach desirable, but are built specially for the service between Watford and Euston, and Watford and Broad Street. They are fifty foot frames on four-wheeled bogies. Three are already running, and three more will shortly be turned out of Wolverton. Two of those that are now running are fitted up with the electric light, more as an experiment than anything else.

"Just look inside this third-class compartment," I was asked. "I could mention several local lines that haven't a first to equal it. And you must notice in this new first smoker the seats and backs are fitted with embossed crimson leather. Isn't that good enough for anyone?"

These new "Watford locals" are marshalled as follows:-

1st vehicle	2nd class brake-van composite
2nd "	2nd and 1st class composite
3rd "	1st class coach
4th "	1st and 3rd class composite
5th "	3rd class coach
6th "	3rd class brake-van composite

I was drawing to the end of my time, and so I made a hasty inspection of the Queen's Saloon, which happened to be close at hand. The LNW Company are exceedingly jealous over this same saloon, claiming it is, *par excellence*, the special carriage of the Queen; and that all other so-called "Royal Trains" must take a back seat – or siding. The saloon in question consists really of two vehicles joined together, forming a carriage sixty-three feet in length, mounted upon six-wheeled bogies. The width is eight feet, and the interior accommodation is luxury itself. It consists of the following compartments:-

1. Lavatory.
2. Saloon for the Queen's dressers, upholstered with brown tabarette.
3. The Royal Sleeping Apartment, with bedstead for the Queen and a smaller one for Princess Beatrice – or the Royal Princess who may be accompanying her. This apartment is fitted with a kind of pink chintz, and green watered curtains, with white watered silk roof.
4. The lavatory – silver basins – blue silk upholstery.
5. The State drawing-room apartment beautifully fitted with blue watered silk and gilt cornices, with sofa, royal chair, table, etc.
6. The Gillies' compartment.
7. Lavatory.

The saloon is lighted throughout by electricity, accumulators being carried beneath; but rumour reports that the Queen is partial to oil lamps, and carries her own.

Other departments, which want of time and space, forbid me to notice at any length, are the huge storage rooms, where every detail of the railway coach down to the little stands for water bottles is kept, and the omnibus and parcels cart erecting and repairing shed. Another point of interest is the "brake shop," into which coaches are continually coming for repair. I was asked particularly to notice the very simple but effective apparatus for raising the coaches. It consists of an upright cylinder containing a twelve inch piston with rod two and a half inches in diameter. This is wheeled by hand and placed under the end of the coach. Compressed air, stored by a beautiful little machine on the premises, is admitted into this cylinder, the connection being made by an ordinary "Westinghouse" joint from one of the many rubber pipes leading from the air cistern (which is eighteen feet long by four feet diameter). A tap is turned, a pressure of 120 pounds per square inch applied to the piston, and up goes the end of the coach as easily as though it were a doll's house.

"And how long did this operation take under the old screw jack system?" I asked.

"About an hour and a quarter." And they do it in five seconds now! A prop is put under the coach, the air let out of the cylinder with a turncock, and off they go to raise another.

Very regretfully did I turn my back on the works, although the inner man reminded me that I was ready for the excellent repast that awaited me, served by the genial host of the Victoria Hotel, after the fatigues of sight-seeing.

Chapter 5
A Trip on the LNWR "American Special"
by V.L. Whitechurch

It was through the kindness of Mr Turnbull, Superintendent of the Line, that I found myself on one of the Euston departure platforms, armed with a pass for a trip on one of the very "crackest" of crack trains in the country, the "American Special" of the London and North Western Railway, a train that is known but little to the ordinary travelling public, but which, for many reasons, holds a unique place on the London and North Western system – perhaps a unique place even among all English trains. That regularly twice a week there is a train running from Euston to Liverpool without a stop, and accomplishing the distance to Edge Hill Station in three hours and three quarters, is a fact not known even to enthusiastic record compilers.

Euston view along departure platform showing station staff and well-dressed passengers. On the right is a short cove roofed carriage labelled 'Riverside' with a clerestory diner beyond.

"American Special", as its name denotes, has something to do with John Bull's go-ahead brother Jonathan. It is a train running in connection with the White Star and Cunard Company's boats to New York and owes its origins, in common with many other excellent arrangements on the L. and N.W. Railway, to Mr Fred Harrison, the present General Manager. The opening of the "Riverside Station" at Liverpool on June 12th, 1895 rendered it possible to transfer New York passengers direct from train to boat without the inconvenience of the transit in cabs and omnibuses from Lime Street Station across the city; and the L. and N.W. were not slow in taking advantage of this convenience, though not till Saturday February 29th, 1896, did the train run through from Euston to Edge Hill without a stop.

But I must get on with the actual journey. At 11.30 am – an hour before starting time – the train was backed into Euston, and, in company with Inspector Pollard, the "Sub-London and American Agent," I went on board for a preliminary tour of inspection. Pollard was busily pinning "reserved" labels to the various seats, but presently had time for a word or two.

"Not a very large train today, Sir; the season's getting a bit over, and besides this is an 'intermediate' boat, the White Star's 'Germanic'. But it's all the better for you that the train won't be crowded, for you'll be able to get about more easily."

American Special 1st Class Carriage compartment in 12-wheeled carriage built in 1906 with couch and arm chair.

"You know, as a rule, about the number of passengers likely to be on board, then?"

"Oh yes! That's one of the special features of the train, and it falls to my lot, as a general rule, to see to it."

"And how do you find out?"

"We canvass the different hotels at which passengers generally put up, and our various booking offices in London. In this way we get a pretty fair idea of the number likely to travel, and the train is made up accordingly." I may here remark, by the way, that as a general rule it is easy to ascertain beforehand the number of passengers within twenty, and, as far as possible the train is made up with about one-third more seats than passengers, in order to avoid overcrowding. The number of passengers carried by an "American Special" average from sixty to one hundred first class, twenty second class, and twenty third; and I shall give an outline of the number and description of the vehicles for that amount.

"I suppose you get through large numbers in the season?" I went on to ask.

"Yes. Sometimes over two hundred first-class passengers, and often we have to run the train in two parts."

"And do you always reserve compartments?"

"Not for all passengers; but many of them make up little family groups and like to be by themselves. For instance, these two seats are for a New York Judge and his wife, while I am just going to the next carriage to arrange one of the saloons for a party of five gentlemen. Of course, there's a right-of-way through, otherwise they're quite private."

And now a word or two about the composition of the train on which I was a passenger, and a comparison between it and an "American Special" destined to carry more. As I have said a very large number of persons were not expected on this occasion, so the train was accordingly arranged as follows:

First vehicle – A van for luggage only.

Second vehicle – A second class brake, with guard's compartment and three second class compartments. As the L. and N.W. have no second class corridor coaches, these were the only compartments on the train on the older system.

Third vehicle – Third and first composite corridor coach, containing two third and three first compartments, with lavatory accommodation, the thirdclass being nearest the engine and the door of the corridor closed between first and third, so as not to allow of the latter passengers entering the vestibuled portion of the train.

Fourth vehicle – A first class 50 feet corridor coach, compartments holding four passengers.

Fifth vehicle – A 42 feet vestibuled "drawing room saloon," divided as follows:

(a) "Smoking room," containing four lounge seats, one in each corner.
(b) Vestibule, with lavatory on either side.
(c) "Smoking room" with four seats, one in each corner and tables between.
(d) Vestibule (doors on either side for exit and entrance).
(e) Large Saloon, containing eight seats, tables between.
(f) Vestibule, with lavatory and stove chamber.

Sixth vehicle – A saloon exactly the same size, but divided as follows:

(a) Vestibule, with stove chamber.
(b) Corridor on left side, compartment with four lounge seats and table on right.
(c) "Ladies' saloon," with seating accommodation for eight, and right-of-way through.
(d) Vestibule, with two revolving cane-seated chairs.
(e) Saloon compartment, lounge seat in each corner, two tables.
(f) Vestibule and lavatories.

182

AMERICA
VIA LIVERPOOL.

The Special Express Vestibuled Trains run between LIVERPOOL and LONDON by the London and North Western Railway Company for American travellers arrive at, and depart from, the

RIVERSIDE STATION at LIVERPOOL,

adjoining the Landing Stage, at which the Atlantic Steamers are berthed.

Baggage of Passengers arriving from America, directly it passes through the Custom House, is placed in the Train, which is standing alongside the Custom House; and both for incoming and outgoing travellers the expense and inconvenience of crossing the City of Liverpool are entirely avoided.

During the month of August, 1898, AMERICAN VESTIBULED SPECIALS with Luncheon Cars attached leave EUSTON STATION, LONDON, for the RIVERSIDE STATION, in LIVERPOOL, as follows:—

	noon	Steamer.		noon	Steamer.
Wednesday, August 3rd—	12 30	Majestic.	Wednesday, August 17th—	12 30	Teutonic.
Thursday, ,, 4th *12	0	Yorkshire.	Thursday, ,, 18th *12	0	{Labrador. Numidian.
Saturday, ,, 6th—	12 0	Campania.	Saturday, ,, 20th—	12 0	Lucania.
Wednesday, ,, 10th—	12 30	Germanic.	Wednesday, ,, 24th—	12 30	Britannic.
Thursday, ,, 11th *12	0	{Dominion. Canada. Californian.	Thursday, ,, 25th *12	0	{Scotsman. Parisian. New England.
Friday, ,, 12th—	12 30	Cymric.	Saturday, ,, 27th—	12 0	Etruria.
Saturday, ,, 13th—	12 0	Umbria.	Wednesday, ,, 31st—	12 30	Majestic.

*—Luncheon Cars will not be attached to these Specials.

IMPORTANT NOTICE.

The London and North Western Railway Company run direct from the RIVERSIDE STATION, which adjoins the Landing Stage at Liverpool, Special Express Vestibuled Trains through to London (Euston) in connection with the Steamers from America, the journey being performed in Four Hours. Luncheon or Dining Cars are attached to these Trains.

The Ocean Steamers berth alongside the Landing Stage, and Passengers pass from the Ships to the Special Trains which leave immediately after the transfer of Passengers and Baggage has been accomplished. Application for accommodation on the Express Vestibuled Trains should be made to the Company's Officials in attendance at the Landing Stage.

NORTH WESTERN HOTEL, LIVERPOOL.—This Hotel situated at Lime Street Station, Liverpool, is lighted throughout by Electricity, and contains upwards of 250 Bedrooms, with spacious Coffee Room available for Ladies and Gentlemen, Ladies' Drawing Room, Reading, Writing, Billiard, and Smoking Rooms. The Hotel is especially appointed for the convenience of American Travellers, as it adjoins the most important Railway Station in Liverpool, from which there are Trains to London (Euston) performing the journey in Four hours and Twenty minutes. Forty minutes Hourly Service of Trains to Manchester, and Through Trains to Leeds, York, Hull, Newcastle, the Lakes, Scotland, Chester, the North Wales Coast, Bristol, Birmingham, Stratford-on-Avon, Oxford, Cambridge, and all parts of England.

MAIL SERVICES (via Dublin & Queenstown) with AMERICA.

Passengers joining or leaving the Atlantic Steamers at Queenstown can avail themselves of the following Services via Holyhead and Dublin:—

TO AMERICA.		Wednesdays.	Saturdays.
London (Euston)	depart	8 45 p.m.	4 10 p.m.
Birmingham (New St.)	,,	10 15 ,,	5 50 ,,
Bristol (via Severn T'nel)	,,	7 40 ,,	2 20 ,,
,, (via Birmingham)	,,	7 0 ,,	3 15 ,,
Chester (General)	,,	12 41 night	8 25 ,,
Edinburgh (Princes St.)	,,	6 0 p.m.	2 0 ,,
Glasgow (Central)	,,	5 55 ,,	2 0 ,,
Liverpool (Lime Street)	,,	11 10 ,,	7 15 ,,
Manchester (London Rd.)	,,	10 50 ,,	6 25 ,,
Holyhead Harbour Station	arr.	2 17 ,,	10 10 ,,
Holyhead (Pier)	,,	2 25 ,,	...
		Thursdays.	Sundays.
North Wall (Dublin)	{arrive depart	A	2 0 a.m. 2 5 ,,
Kingstown (Pier)	{arrive depart	5 30 (about) 5 45 a.m.	...
Queenstown	arrive	10 15 a.m.	6 15 a.m.

FROM AMERICA.		Week-days.
Queenstown	depart	3 0 p.m.
Kingstown (Pier)	{arrive depart	8 15 ,, 8 15 (about)
Holyhead (Pier)	,,	12 12 night
Manchester (Exchange)	arrive	3 55 a.m.
Liverpool (Lime Street)	,,	3 35 ,,
Glasgow (Central)	,,	7 50 ,,
Edinburgh (Princes St.)	,,	7 50 ,,
Chester (General)	,,	2 12 ,,
Bristol (via Birm'gham)	,,	11 37 ,,
Birmingham (New St.)	,,	4 35 ,,
London (Euston)	,,	6 10 ,,

A—Dublin passengers for the American Steamers must join the train at Amiens Street, from which place it is due to leave at 6.0 a.m.

Through Carriages are run between Kingstown Pier and Queenstown in connection with this Service. On Sunday Mornings the Through Carriages are run from North Wall Station (Dublin) to Queenstown.

American Special Time Table 1898.

Seventh vehicle – Dining car, divided into two portions, with lavatory between; the first portion seating fourteen, the second ten.

Eighth vehicle – Dining and Kitchen car; first part containing accommodation for eight diners, and the second containing the kitchen and pantry. (The right-of-way for passengers through the train ends at this car.)

Ninth vehicle – A third class brake, three third compartments, and luggage and guard, etc.

The larger dining car was mounted on six, and other vehicles on four-wheeled bogies. The train is always vestibuled throughout (with the exception of the second class compartments above mentioned), but first class passengers only are permitted to use the dining saloons, the other passengers being supplied with dinner baskets as required. As a matter of fact the bulk of the passengers are always first class, and the following are the numbers who travelled by the particular train on which I made the run:

First class   38
Second class   7
Third class   14

This hardly represents a fair average, as the season was rather late, and the boat not one of the largest. This accounts for the number of passengers being much below the average upon the occasion on which I travelled. Readers will therefore readily understand that, when the average number of passengers are travelling by these bi-weekly American boat specials, a larger train is, of course, required, in which case it is usually the custom to run another pair of drawing room saloons and two large dining cars, or, on occasions, a small one in addition. As a matter of fact, dining accommodation for half the number of first class passengers is provided, so that, in the case of eighty, forty can dine at a sitting – there being ample time to serve two dinners during the journey, allowing one and a half hours for each. These "American Specials" require a larger staff of attendants than is usually provided for ordinary passenger trains.

American Special near Crewe Coal Yard c1898. Improved Precedent No.2186 "Lowther" with a train of 6-wheeled brakes, 8-wheeled arc roof bogie carriages and 12-wheeled clerestory carriages.

Such a train as I have just described would be staffed as follows; Two guards; two train attendants, who look after every part except the dining saloons, and answer the electric bells provided throughout the train; two cooks and two waiters for each kitchen; and a page boy at times.

The passengers of the "American Special" are always worth studying, and it was with some interest that I watched them arrive and take their seats. There were the usual old stagers, who knew all about it; a group of nasal-twanged men, who settled down to play poker in one of the saloons long before the train started; some ladies crying after reserved compartments; and one wily couple who had brought a large doll with them, as big as a "life-sized" baby, and had placed it on the seat of one of the corridor first-class compartments. It was quite funny to see folks look in at the window and instantly depart, and is a dodge apparently much to be recommended to the individual who loves to be alone when he travels. Baggage was coming down marked with the "White Star" label and destined for the cabins. The North Western Company label the luggage also, but no invoices are made out for it.

The hands of the platform clock approached the half hour, the engine was on – a 6ft. 6in. coupled, with simple cylinders, the class of engine most usually employed on these trains – the guard tested the vacuum brake, farewells were said, and just at the last minute Mr C. Lowndes, who was to take the trip with me, appeared on the platform; we jumped on board the train, and the "American Special" glided out of Euston Station.

Mr Lowndes is one of Mr Turnbull's assistants, and part of his work lies on the American "Specials" by which he frequently travels for the purpose of drawing up reports, etc. As he is also greatly responsible for the running of these trains, many particulars of which are placed in his especial charge, I could not have had a better companion for the journey, and must express my thanks to him for much of the information contained in this article.

We soon settled down to our long journey – a journey that was to be performed without a single stop between Euston and Edge Hill Station, Liverpool, and which was timed to be completed in three and three-quarter hours, which, with another quarter of an hour allowed for collecting tickets and running to the Riverside Station, brings the total journey up to exactly four hours.

The Wednesday trains running in connection with the White Star boats during the season, from March to September inclusive, leave Euston at 12.30, and arrive at 4.30. The Saturday trains in connection with the Cunard line leave at 12, arriving at 4 in the afternoon.

"Are we likely to be punctual?" I asked.

"Yes, if we run as we usually do, for it is our boast that the "American Special" is scarcely over a minute early or late, and every effort is made to work these trains exactly to time. I see you are going to compare the actual running with schedule time, but you must remember that very often a driver knows the latest peculiarities of the road even better than those who draw up the working time tables, and it very often happens that he is purposely behindhand at certain stations, because he knows there is the chance of a clear run beyond."

"Is there any difference between the running of this Wednesday special and that on Saturday?"

"Yes. The Saturday train has a clearer course, for as far as Rugby we've got the 12.10 out of Euston ahead of us, and the driver knows that there may be signals against him. Now he'll slow down in plenty of time rather than have to stop altogether, for, as of course you know, it's the actual stop that most delays a train, even if it's but for an instant."

"You've got plenty of accommodation in the train." I remarked, after a stroll through.

"Yes. Did you notice the little post boxes for letters? By the way, you may note that this has been a record summer in passenger traffic, but we haven't had a single failure in providing ample accommodation, without crowding."

"You convey American passengers to, as well as from, London, do you not?"

"Yes, and perhaps you would like a few details about the up 'specials'? The train is always drawn up at the platform of the Riverside Station at least two hours before the earliest possible arrival of the boat."

"But as you cannot possibly tell the number of passengers likely to run direct to town directly the boat arrives, how do you manage if there are but a few?"

"Even if there were only two passengers wishing to proceed direct to London from the New York boat of the White Star and Cunard lines, we should give them dining car accommodation; and if there were no ordinary express leaving Edge Hill at that time we should run them special as far as Crewe, and then attach them to an up express there."

"Lunch is ready," announced the train attendant at this moment, and we proceeded to the dining car to partake of a very fair meal. I might mention that of the thirty-eight first class passengers thirty partook of this *table-d'hôte* lunch, one had some food *à la carte* while five third class passengers were served with luncheon baskets.

And now for a word or two about the actual running of the train. It must be borne in mind that the run is practically at an end at Edge Hill, and that the quarter of an hour from that station to Riverside must not be taken into account in reckoning the speed especially as a man walks in front of the train with a red flag part of the way. The worst part of the journey is between Euston and Rugby, both on account of the rising gradient to Tring and a possible block from the 12.10. A good steady bit of running brought us to Tring, three minutes and a few seconds late however by schedule time; but I was congratulating myself that this would soon be made up as we dashed away on the down grade through Cheddington and Leighton, when an ominous whistle and slight reduction in speed announced the fact that a "bit of stick" was against us at Bletchley, though as we ran through that station we were only a minute and a half after time, having done the distance from Tring in ten seconds over fifteen minutes.

Again, when nearing Rugby, the signals were against us for a moment or two, and we ran through eight minutes late, but once clear of Nuneaton the driver managed to put on some very good work; and, though we were over five minutes late, in passing through Stafford we were only three, and at Crewe two minutes behind time. Undoubtedly some of the best running was done between Stafford and Crewe, and a careful timing observation of three separate (non-consecutive) miles on this bit of the trip gave fifty-two, fifty-six and fifty-nine seconds for the mile respectively. At Crewe a permanent way operation caused us to slow down, but at Weaver Junction we were closer to the scheduled time than at any other point, being only one minute five seconds late, but instead of running to Edge Hill to time, as I had hoped, we again lost ground, and finally arrived at 4 hours 17 min 10 sec. instead of 4.15 precisely. At Edge Hill tickets were collected, and a couple of small tank engines put on to draw the train to Riverside station, the Dock Company not allowing large locomotives to run down to that point.

The following is a "log" of this particular "American Special" taken on the journey, and compared with scheduled time; but it is only fair to say that I noted the time when running between the platforms of the stations, whereas the working time table may have been arranged for passing signal cabins. The table may be of some interest to those who care for collecting speed records of long runs, though, as will be noted by those who are familiar with the track, it shows more uniformity of steady running than "record breaking" in particular places. I might state that it is a most unusual occurrence for this train to be late in the slightest degree; it generally arrives punctually to time, every care being taken that it should do so:

Station	Scheduled time in Co's Working Time Table	Actual time
	hrs. min	hrs. min. sec
Euston (dep)	12.30	12.30.0
Willesden Junction	12.38	12.40.20
Sudbury		12.43.25
Harrow		12.47.20
Pinner		12.49.30
Bushey		12.52.50
Watford	12.55	12.56.50
King's Langley		12.59.25
Boxmoor		1.2.15
Berkhampstead		1.6.40
Tring	1.8	1.11.10
Cheddington		1.15.47
Leighton		1.19.45
*Bletchley	1.25	1.26.30
Wolverton		1.33.13
Roade	1.40	1.41.56
Blisworth		1.45.24
Weedon		1.53.0
*Rugby	2.7	2.14.55
Shilton		2.21.50
Nuneaton	2.23	2.28.10
Atherstone	2.30	2.33.40
Polesworth		2.38.25
Tamworth	2.38	2.41.10
Lichfield	2.46	2.49.10
Armitage		2.56.4
Rugeley	2.54	2.57.55
Colwich	2.58	3.1.13
Stafford	3.5	3.8.0
Whitmore		3.25.13
Betley Road		3.31.20
Crewe	3.35	3.37.0
Weaver Junction	3.53	3.54.5
Halton Junction		4.2.27
Ditton	4.4	4.5.10
Liverpool (Edge Hill) arr	4.15	4.17.10
" " dep	4.18	4.21.10
The Riverside Station	4.30	4.32.40

* Signals against train

Just a word or two about the running of this bi-weekly train. At first I was under the impression that it had the proud distinction of performing the longest run without a stop of any train in England, but I fear that I was mistaken, and must yield the point to the Great Western. The latter line during the last two summers ran expresses from Paddington to Exeter, a distance of 194 miles, without a stop. Now the distance from Euston to Edge Hill Station, Liverpool, is 199 miles 36 chains, but unfortunately for the "American Special" Mr Lowndes tells me that is the distance via the old route, and that there is an allowance to be made out of this for Runcorn Bridge, which brings the distance down to 193½ miles.

However, one point *can* be claimed and proved for the train under discussion, and that is the "American Special" does the longest regular run all year round without a stop.

The Great Western run is timed to be performed in 223 minutes with an average speed of 52.1 miles an hour. The "American Special" pulls up at Edge Hill 225 minutes after leaving Euston having done the trip at the exact average of 51.6 miles per hour. I consider this a point of interest to those whose opinions are divided on the respective merits of single and coupled engines, for here, at all events, we have a very steady and, at the same time, a fast bit of running with a heavy train performed by the coupled class of locomotive, and it is a fact that should well be borne in mind when dealing with this much-divided subject. At all events the length of the run from Euston to Liverpool without a stop places the "American Special" at the head of

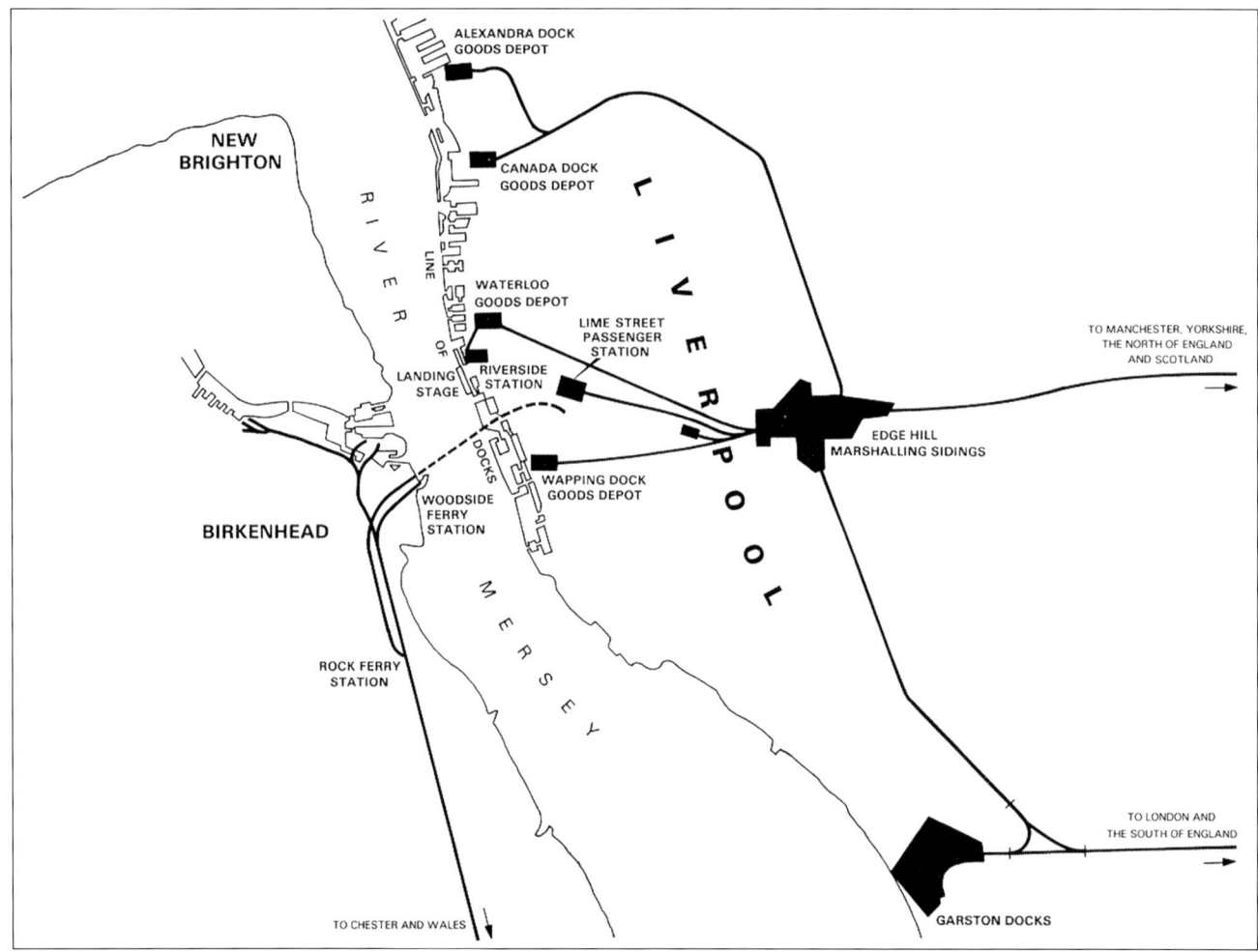

Liverpool Map showing route from Edge Hill to Riverside Station.

regularly running long distance trains on English railways, and certainly gives a chance of showing our American cousins who travel by it what the old country can do when it tries.

Mr Price, the Assistant Superintendent, came on board the train at Edge Hill, and accompanied me to the Riverside Station and embarking stage. This station is the property of the steamship companies, and the London and North Western trains are the only ones running into it.

The luggage was handed out of the vans by L. and N.W. men, and taken off in trollies by the steamship companies' porters, of whom sometimes one hundred are employed for this purpose on heavy days. Alongside the landing stage lay the fine steamer "Germanic" belonging

Liverpool Riverside Station. The station was opened in 1895 by the Mersey Docks & Harbour Board when they built a short connection from the LNWR Waterloo Goods Station to the Princes Pier Landing Stage. There is a glazed roof and passengers can move easily between train and ship without having to be exposed to the elements at all and luggage can be quickly moved with the help of hundreds of porters. Indeed a whole train load can embark on to the ship in about twenty minutes. The cream of Edwardian society has passed through together with many thousands of emigrants. The station was always kept in immaculate condition by the MD&HB. Because of weight restrictions and sharp curvature of the track in the dock area boat trains were hauled by two LNWR 0-6-0 tank engines between Edge Hill and Riverside – No.3021 "Liverpool" and 3186 "Euston". Between Waterloo Goods and Riverside trains moved extremely slowly through the dockside streets and wharves with a MD&HB man walking in front with a red flag.

Liverpool Riverside Landing Stage in 1904 with RMS "Oceanic" preparing to embark for America. The horizontal gangway on the left links to Riverside Station. This White Star Line ship was 704 feet long, weighed 17,272 tons and had a capacity for 1710 passengers and 349 crew. It had twin propellers with a maximum speed of 21 knots.

to the White Star Line, with her head pointed down the river, and a crowd of steerage passengers on her decks watching the arrival of the "saloons". Everything was done so swiftly, methodically, and quietly, that it might have been an ordinary cross-Channel boat going out instead of an Atlantic "greyhound". Half an hour is allowed for the transference, and long before this time had elapsed the very last passenger and his portmanteau were on board, and the landing platform cast off, the "look-out" posted in the crow's nest on the foremast, the captain and Queenstown pilot on the bridge, and exactly on the stroke of five the good ship "Germanic" was gliding from the landing stage and heading for the sea.

Chapter 6
The London and Birmingham Railway
by Gilbert J. Stoker

When the myriad-fingered genie, steam, was set to work in earnest in the early part of the present century, it soon became apparent that the existing means of transport were quite inadequate for the task of distributing the ever-increasing products of the loom, the forge, and the workshop, and it was but natural that the thoughts of men of business should turn for relief from the difficulty to the same power that had created it; and that they should gradually come to look with favour on the suggestions of those who were pressing the claims of railroads worked by steam engines.

The position of Birmingham and district, inhabited by a busy community continually employed in producing articles for the markets of the world, and requiring the cheapest and most expeditious transit in the directions which afforded the easiest outlets for its rapidly growing trade, very early caused attention to be directed to the advantages likely to arise from its being connected by the new system with the ports of London and Liverpool, and the populous districts surrounding them. Accordingly, we find lines between these places amongst the earliest projected. We are not at present concerned with the railway connecting Liverpool and Manchester with Birmingham, the Bill for which was passed in the same year as that for the line between London and Birmingham, but propose to give a few particulars representing the latter.

Some progress was made towards forming a company, and obtaining an Act for this line, in 1824-5, but no practical result followed until the year 1830, when the two companies were formed and routes proposed, one via Oxford, the other via Coventry. The promoters of these schemes, finding they were wasting money and energy opposing each other, judiciously united their forces, and on the recommendation of George Stephenson adopted the Coventry route, which presented the fewer engineering difficulties. Four or five miles might have been saved by keeping nearer Warwick, but this route was objected to because in that direction the line rising from the low-lying basin of the Avon would have had to ascend a higher range of the Meriden ridge at a steeper gradient that that of 16 ft. to the mile, or 1 in 330, which was fixed by Stephenson as the maximum rate of inclination, and nowhere exceeded except on the extension between Camden Town and Euston.

Parliamentary Committees in those days scrutinised very closely, and not always in the spirit of "friendly neutrality" they display at the present time, any statements made by the promoters of Railway Bills. In order, therefore, to be prepared to show that the estimates to the probable traffic were founded on something more substantial than mere opinion, men were appointed to take particulars for a fortnight of the traffic on the roads and canals between Birmingham and London. The results are highly interesting, as showing the amount of travelling at that period. We are accustomed to think of our ancestors as very sleepy, stay-at-home folks, but the information obtained does not quite bear out this idea.

It was calculated that during the year the coaches and commercial gigs on the main road,

Camden – constructing the line with cut and cover.

Primrose Hill Tunnel (near Camden in North London) was built in 1837 on land owned by Eton College who insisted on the elaborate architectural feature at the portals. It is 1100 yards long and was the first railway tunnel in London. A number of navvies were killed during construction.

with those running in connection with them, made equal to 75,909 journeys of 110 miles each, and carried 488,342 passengers, at a cost of £889,945. The private and stage vans, errand carts, etc, on the direct road made equal to 16,808 journeys and the boats on the canal equal to 11,131. There were 75 four-horse coaches, long and short distance, on the main road. If we contrast these with the one coach per week which crawled from London to Birmingham and Lichfield in three days, and back again in the next three, in 1742, we shall see that even before the advent of the railway system the world was moving at no mean rate.

In endeavouring to obtain exact data on which to base their calculations, the promoters of the Bill were more honourable than some of the later speculators; for instance, the estimates of 23½ per cent, probable dividends for the Eastern Counties Railway, and of 18½ per cent for the Sheffield and Manchester did more credit to the imagination than to the candour of the gentlemen who made them.

Such estimates were about as valuable as much of the evidence given in committee by witnesses in favour of certain lines. Here is a sample:

Counsel for the Opposition: do you mean to tell me that you ever saw an inhabited house in that valley?

Witness: Yes I do.

Counsel: Did you ever see a vehicle there in your life?

Other questions were put, and the witness was leaving the chair, when the counsel, impelled by a happy inspiration, said: May I ask you whether the vehicle you saw was the hearse of the last inhabitant?

Witness: It was.

A writer in the Cornhill Magazine relates an instance in which counsel was pulled up pretty sharply. One St. Patrick's Day, O'Connell, his hat decorated with a huge bunch of shamrock, was sitting on a Committee on an East Grinstead Bill, and was apparently asleep, when he suddenly opened his eyes and remarked to one of the counsel, who was speaking somewhat at random. "Mr. ----, I always sleep with my eyes open!"

Before a Bill could be applied for, it was of course necessary, in order to comply with Parliamentary rules, to make a survey of the country, but whilst Parliament required that certain particulars should be furnished, it gave no authority under which the engineers could go on the ground to obtain them; consequently, they were at the mercy of the owners and occupiers, who, in numerous instances, threw every possible obstacle in their way. The fixed idea of many people in the country parts being, apparently, that a body of crafty townspeople wanted to take possession of their property and use it for purposes destructive of all farming, and calculated to bring ruin and misery on every person connected with agriculture. Some of the adventures of the engineers are very entertaining. The following was furnished by Le Count to Thomas Roscoe for his book on the London and Birmingham Railway.

While Mr Gooch, the chief engineer for one of the divisions of the line, was taking levels near London, two brothers, who occupied the land, ordered him off. He walked into the next field, leaving his assistant at the last level station, nearly two hundred yards distant, but still on the brothers' land. The one nearest Mr Gooch spread out his coat tails and tried to intercept the view through the telescope, at the same time calling to the other to knock down the staff. The brother, not understanding what he said, asked the man with the staff. "Oh" replied he, "he is calling on you to stop that horse there, which is galloping out of the fold yard!" Away he ran to stop the horse, and before he got back the level was taken.

It is possible that many of the excessive claims made by owners of property were *bona fide* – the claimants being honestly afraid of the results that might follow the intrusion on their Arcadian tranquillity of the smoky monster of which they heard such strange accounts; the amounts of the claims being in proportion to the extent of their apprehensions. Such an excuse could not, of course, be admitted at the present time, when there is a fund of experience on which to draw in estimating the extent to which a neighbourhood would suffer, or be improved with a new railway. Neither could it, on the most charitable construction, be held good in numerous instances at the period of which we are writing. The reverend proprietor knew pretty well what he was about who required that six bridges should be erected to connect portions of his land severed by the railway, and then when the contract was signed and he had the company in his power found that he should for a consideration, do without one then without another, until they all disappeared. Also that other reverend gentleman, "who complained that his privacy was ruined; that his daughters' bedrooms were exposed to the unhallowed gaze of the men working on the railway; that he must remove his family to a watering place, to enable him to do which he must engage a curate. All this was considered in the compensation demanded and paid; yet no curate has been engaged; no lodgings at a watering place taken. The unhappy family have still dwelt in desecrated abode, and borne with Christian-like resignation all the miseries heaped upon them. The gilding of the pill, it seems, has rendered it palatable, and we have no doubt that if his daughters' rooms have a back window as well as a front one he would be exceedingly glad if a railroad was carried across that at the same price.

On the whole, the people whose land was taken had not much to complain of, seeing the Company paid about £320 per acre for it, which seems a fair price for what must have chiefly consisted of agricultural holdings. This does not include the £74,505 paid for the "Euston extension" from Camden Town to Euston, a price which would now be scarcely thought excessive for the same land.

We cannot be much surprised at the amount of prejudice to be overcome amongst ordinary people when we find it shared by a man like Sir Astley Cooper, the famous physician. When Robert Stephenson endeavoured to obtain his consent to the line running through his property, he raised objections to the whole scheme, clinching his argument by the sapient remark that "if this sort of thing be permitted to go on you will in a very few years *destroy the nobility*."

In spite of strong opposition, the Act for the construction of the railway was read for the first time in the House of Commons on February 20th, 1832, passed, and in due course sent to the House of Lords, where it was rejected at the instance of Lord Brownlow, who seems to have been of Sir Astley Cooper's opinion as to the deleterious effects of railways on the nobility. Some trifling alterations were made, and the Bill again brought in on 31st November in the same year, and passed both Houses, receiving the Royal Assent on 6th May, 1833.

The cost of obtaining the Act – £72,869 – was considered a very large sum at the time. Compared with some later lines, when the lawyers and others had fairly *struck the vein,* it may be considered moderate. For instance, the "Trent Valley", the Parliamentary expenses of which, George Stephenson said, were more than the cost of construction.

There was a clause in the bill which enacted that out of the twenty-four directors to be appointed at least ten must be resident within twenty miles of London, and ten within twenty miles of Birmingham. The advantage of such a provision is not very obvious, but the reason for it may possibly be found in the action of the Grand Junction Railway, the control of which was kept in the hands of the Liverpool men, none of the directors being selected from amongst the Birmingham shareholders. It was a matter of public comment at the time that no official notice was taken in Birmingham of the opening of the Grand Junction line, the first to enter the town, and that very few persons of position even went to the station to witness an event of so much importance; and this was attributed to a feeling of resentment at what appeared to be a slight on the local proprietors. Whether intentionally or not, the provision referred to effectively "dished" the Lancashire element. This particular clause was repealed in the next Act, obtained in 1835, and the Board, as constituted when the line opened, contained a fair proportion of Liverpool gentlemen.

The construction of the line was divided amongst thirty contractors, of whom ten failed, leaving the Company to finish the work, from which it would appear that the contractors at that time were very much in the dark as to the expense involved in works of this description. An enormous rise in prices took place after the contracts were given out, and no doubt was also an important factor in the unfortunate result. The well-known case of Kilsby Tunnel furnishes an illustration of the liability of a mistake being made, notwithstanding the precautions taken. The original contract was £99,000, the total cost £320,000. No wonder the contractor gave up in despair after about ten months, and the work had to be taken in hand by the Company's engineers. The difficulty arose from a kind of basin that lay in the hill, containing water, loose sand, and gravel, which was missed when the trial shafts were sunk, but made itself very unpleasantly apparent when the tunnelling commenced. It took nine months' continual pumping, at the rate of 2,000 gallons per minute, before the quicksand was sufficiently dry to admit of its being worked through.

With regard to the cutting at Roade, near Blisworth, we are enabled to give a few figures, which will assist in making a slight comparison

Gates from the Doric Arch at Euston now on display at the National Railway Museum in York.

A close-up of the London & Birmingham Railway Crest on the Euston Gates.

between work at the present time and in 1835. From the original cutting one million cubic yards were excavated, which required the use of 300,000 lb of powder. In 1881 when the cutting was widened in order to double the line, about half a million cubic feet were removed, in the course of which 34,360 lb of ordinary, 1,480 lb of extra strong blasting powder, and 2,325 lb of dynamite were used, equal in all, calculated at proportional prices, to 52,830 lb of powder, being proportionately about one third the quantity of explosive used in the original cutting. The total cost of the work also was considerably under 3s 4d per cubic yard, which is given as the figure at which the first work was done. Here, again, the contractor for the first excavation was unable to complete the work, the expense of which was £130,000 more than the contract price.

What was, perhaps, one of the most singular incidents that ever happened in connection with the construction of a railway occurred in making the Wolverton embankment. After a description of the difficulties encountered, which reminds us of the trouble with Chat Moss, Le Count goes on: "There seemed to be no end to the vagaries of this unhappy embankment. There was a portion of alum shale in it, which contained sulpharet of iron; this becoming decomposed, spontaneous combustion ensued, and one fine morning we had a novel sight of a fifty feet embankment on fire, sleepers and all, to the great surprise of a host of beholders. The inhabitants of all the neighbouring villages turned out, of course, in no small amaze, on the occasion; and various were the contending opinions as to the why and the wherefore. Some said 'the Company were hard up for cash and were going to melt some of the rails'; others 'that it was a visitation of Providence, like the Tower of Babel.' At last a village Solon settled the point. 'Dang it' said he, 'they can't make this here railway after all; and they have set it afire to cheat their creditors!'"

The cuttings and tunnels near London were very troublesome and expensive. Engineers at that time had not grasped the possibilities of the slipping and other eccentricities of London clay, and were not prepared to find the mortar being squeezed out of the joints of the brickwork, and the bricks themselves being gradually ground to dust, as happened in Primrose Hill tunnel. They did not, however, give up the task as the people did who were concerned in the construction of the tunnel through similar material at Highgate twenty-three years before. By strengthening the brickwork, and using cement instead of ordinary mortar in the tunnels, and taking these and other precautions in the cuttings, they circumvented their "slippery customer."

Whilst the road was being prepared, the question as to the best description of rails to be used was receiving very serious consideration. Experience had shown that the fish-bellied rails, weighing 35 lb to the yard, as laid down on the Liverpool to Manchester line, were too light, and doubts were expressed whether even those of 50 lb to the yard, by which they had been superseded, would be of sufficient strength. The best known expert on these matters at the time, Mr P. Barlow, FRS, was consulted, and, at the request of the directors, made a series of experiments on the Liverpool and Manchester Railway, with the result that he recommended double parallel "T" rails weighing 75 lb. to the yard, which were adopted. No doubt this was a matter of great importance, and one not to be hastily decided, but one unfortunate result of the delay in settling it was that in consequence of a rise of £4 per ton in the price of iron, which took place in the meantime, the cost of the rails was greatly increased. It was calculated that the total additional expense from the extra weight of the rails, and the rise in price, amounted to £258,000.

Amongst other absurd notions that got abroad, some wiseacre started a theory that the atmosphere of tunnels must be very injurious to health, and this opinion became so general amongst simple folks that the Company, who could not afford to lose the support of a class which forms so large a section of the community, treated it quite seriously and requested some eminent scientific men to investigate the matter. They entered into the spirit of the thing, made careful experiments, and drew up a report calculated to have a reassuring effect on the most timid. It concluded: "We are decidedly of the opinion that dangers incurred in passing through well-constructed tunnels are no greater than those incurred in ordinary travelling upon an open railway, or upon a turnpike road, and that the apprehensions which have been expressed that such tunnels are likely to prove detrimental to health or inconvenient to the feelings of those who may go through them are perfectly futile and groundless."

The engineers having got over all the unforeseen terrors that best them, of quaking bogs, running quicksands, slippery clay, etc, which their modern successors, profiting by their experience, have learned to treat so lightly, the work had so far advanced as to admit of the first length of line from London to Tring, being opened on the 1st January, 1838. On the 9th day of April in the same year it was extended to Denbigh Hall, and on the same day the section from Birmingham to Rugby was brought into use, the distance between Rugby and Denbigh Hall, 35 miles, being performed by coach. So long as the break continued, the greatest difficulty was experienced in finding a sufficient number of coaches to convey passengers arriving by rail at either end. There was almost a riot on the occasion of the coronation of Her Majesty, on the 28th June, 1838. For some days before this every place was taken – in some instances £10 was offered and refused for a seat. People went in hundreds to Rugby on the chance of getting forward, and paid as much as £4 inside and £2.10s outside, on the coach from there to Denbigh Hall. All sorts of vehicles were brought into requisition, and happy was the man who secured a donkey-cart to convey his wife and family. The link was completed and the line opened throughout, on the 17th September, 1838.

The signalling arrangements were at first rather primitive. Men with flags were stationed at intervals of from one to three miles to signal to the drivers as they passed. The uniform was similar to that worn by the London Police of the period. There were no semaphore signals as at present. It was suggested that these should be erected, and, in addition to protecting the trains, be utilised for sending messages for the public in the same manner that semaphore telegraphs were used for the government service. The writer who made the suggestion failed, in common with more distinguished railway men, to apprehend the possibilities of the electric telegraph, the first successful experiment with which had been made, by Wheatstone and Cooke, between Euston and Camden Station on 25th June, 1837. Robert Stephenson had some perception of the utility of the electric telegraph, and endeavoured to have the wires fixed between London and Birmingham. The Directors agreed only on condition that the Grand Junction Railway would consent to their being extended to Liverpool and Manchester. This they refused to do, and the honour of taking up the new invention, which has since proved of such incalculable benefit in the working of traffic, passed to Brunel and the Great Western Company.

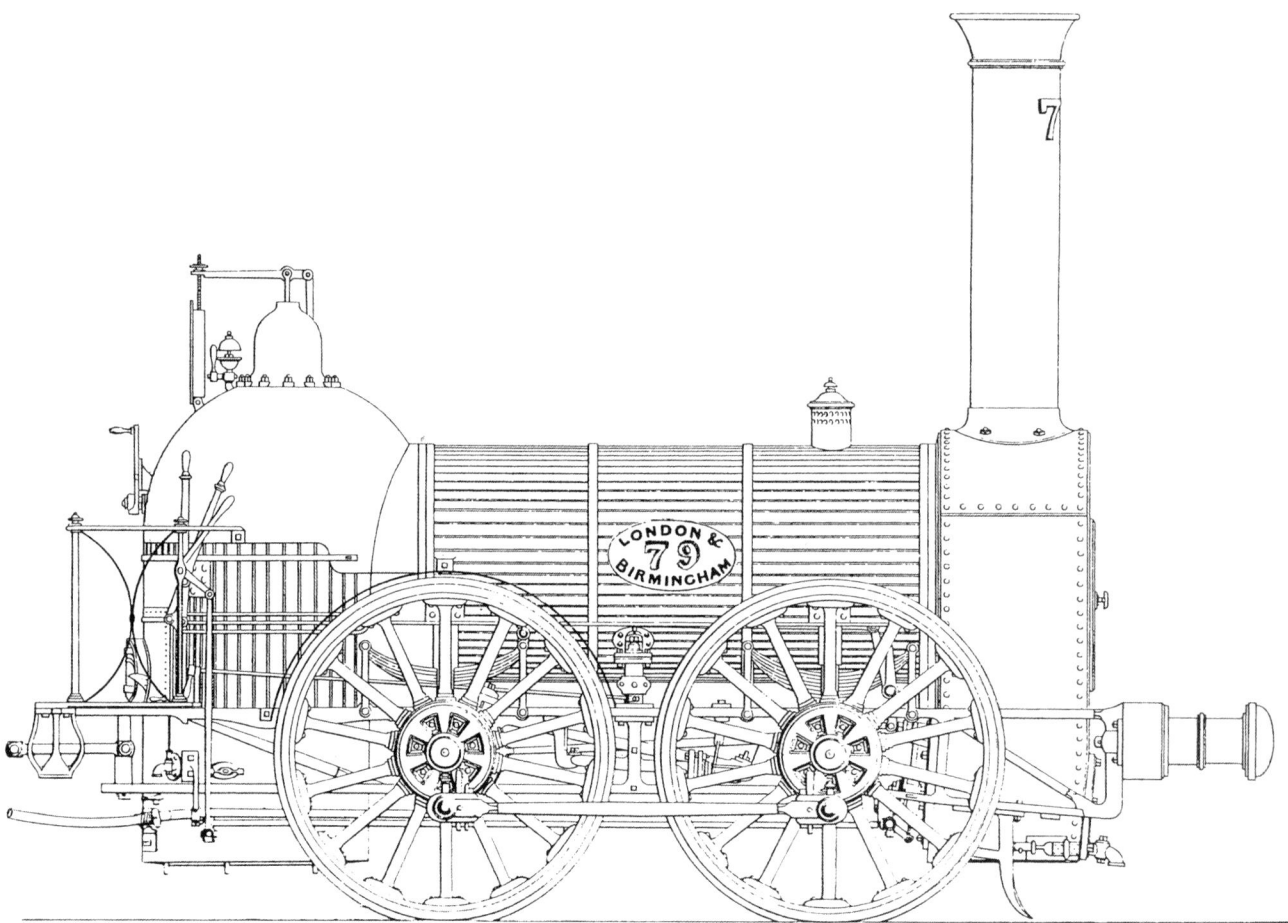

Drawing of Bury's original London & Birmingham 0-4-0 goods engine of 1838.

There is a tradition amongst North Western men, to what extent founded on fact we are not prepared to say, that the idea of distant signals originated from a labour saving apparatus constructed by an Irishman named Donegan, who was employed as a signalman at Tring. His signal was at the top of a bank, up which he had to walk every time it was necessary to work the signal – there were steps up the bank, and alongside them a handrail. To save going up and down these steps, Mr Donegan rigged up a clothes line along the rail, by means of which he moved the signal. The Superintendent, Mr H.P. Bruyeres, took note of the arrangement and made some experiments in Camden Yard, and before long "distant" signals were erected along the line.

Trevithick 6ft. 2-2-2 'Crewe' type No. 192 "Hero" built in 1848 with bright green livery (This and the following 3 pictures are examples of early LNWR Locos).

Trevithick 2-4-0 Goods engine No. 1897.

McConnell Large 'Bloomer' 2-2-2 in original condition with 7ft 6in driving wheels. Built in 1861, later named "Caithness".

'Problem' or 'Lady of the Lake' class No.1434 "Eunomia" with drop down smokebox door and no coal rails on tender. Built in 1865.

Some of the regulations issued at that period appear rather quaint and old-world to us of the present generation. Smokers will be pleased to know what was thought of their favourite habit sixty years ago, amongst the regulations was one "for preventing the smoking of tobacco, and the commission of other nuisances."

The station clocks were set to local time; to prevent mistakes a table was issued giving the time for each station as compared with London. A passenger leaving London with his watch correct would find on arrival at Birmingham that it was 7 min.15 sec. fast. For some inscrutable reason the clocks in London and Birmingham were set three minutes later than the correct time – which did not tend to simplify matters. Eventually it was decided to adopt Greenwich time all over the country. There were no platforms at roadside stations; passengers entered the carriages or alighted at either side as suited their convenience – not considering the danger of being run over by a passing train whilst wandering over the metals. The fact is, at first, people regarded railway carriages as they would road vehicles; they tried to get on and off whilst they were in motion in the same manner. Many persons were injured through jumping off open carriages to pick up their hats when blown away.

On reference to the timetable we find that there were, between London and Birmingham, nine trains each way daily. The "first class" took 5 hours 15 minutes, the "mixed" (first and second class) 5 hours 30 minutes, and the "third class" 8 hours 45 minutes – not much difference between this last and the fast coaches, which performed their journey in ten hours.

The fares were somewhat higher by the night than the day trains, the Company apparently not being disposed to provide a night's lodging free. It is well known that card tickets and the dating press, described by Albert Smith as "that wonderful machine which appears to be a cross between a nut cracker and a coffee-canister," were not invented until some years later. When tourist tickets were first issued the intending passengers had to give their names – to be written on the tickets. The public rather resented this, and the number of people whose patronymic became "Smith" for the occasion was very surprising to the clerks.

The Directors, with that caution which characterised all their proceedings, instead of committing themselves to any great expenditure with respect to locomotives, entered into a contract with Mr Edward Bury, of Liverpool, for the supply of power, the Company providing the engines, and Mr Bury keeping them in repair for three years. They commenced with quite a reasonable stud of 35 engines, made by six different makers, but all constructed exactly alike in all their parts.

In a note at the foot of the fare table issued in 1838 there is a description of the passenger coaches, and the manner in which the trains were made up: "The first-class trains consist only of mail carriages, carrying four inside (one compartment of which is convertible into a bed carriage if required), and of carriages carrying six inside. The mixed trains consist of first-class carriages carrying six inside and of second-class carriages carrying six inside, and of second-class carriages open at the side, without linings, cushions, or divisions in the compartments. The night mail train consists of first-class carriages carrying six inside, and of second-class carriages closed and entirely protected from the weather. Each carriage has a small roof lamp inside, by day and night."

The mention of the bed carriages reminds us that the sleeping carriage, as it is now called, is not a recent innovation. The bed was made by sliding a cushion, fixed to a board, into the space between the seats, filling up the place where the passengers' legs were when seated. A board, forming a door into the boot, fixed at the end of the carriage, was then lifted up, and into this receptacle the would-be sleeper pushed his feet. A stuffed pillow was also provided. In the drawing of a first-class or "mail" coach of the period the "boot" is seen at the rear. It will be observed that the lines of the stage coaches

A replica of the first Mail Sorting Coach (a converted horse box) in 1838 now in the York Railway Museum. Initially thought to have been built by the GJR recent research shows that it was initiated by the London and Birmingham Railway. The experiment was successful and became the Travelling Post Office (TPO) which was later extended throughout the country. It even had apparatus for picking up and dropping off post at speed with an extending net and a chute. The Royal VR monogram is painted on the side.

4-wheel carriage in stagecoach styling at Stratford-on-Avon thought to be ex London & Birmingham original.

A model of a London & Birmingham Break (Brake) Van. This was probably the first brake van used on a main line railway and is attributed to J. Wright & Co. of London. It is thought to date from the opening of the railway in 1838. Brake application was by means of a large lever which must have required considerable force to operate.

were preserved as far as possible, carriage builders being apparently unable to emancipate themselves from the force of old association, or, it may be, they thought the public would take more kindly to the new vehicles if presented in a form with which they were familiar. The long period during which these lines continued to be followed after their original significance was lost affords a curious indication of the influence of custom, and it may be that if all other records should be lost some future "Darwin" of the rail, treating of the development of the railway carriage, may by their means be enabled to trace it back to the original type.

On the whole, except those who could afford to pay for first-class, the new mode of travelling did not at first present itself in a very attractive guise. The expense of providing new types of carriages imposed a heavy tax on railway companies, a fact which many people overlook, but is a sufficient reason for the seemingly slow substitution of new designs for old.

In an article originally published in the Birmingham Daily Mail, Mr E. Edwards describes a journey he made from London to Coventry, in July, 1839, which gives a lively picture of railway travelling in those days, and may fitly close this sketch: - "On Sunday, the 14th of July, in the year 1839, I left Euston Square by the night mail train. I had taken a ticket for Coventry. It was a hot and sultry night, and I was very glad when we arrived at Wolverton, where we had to wait ten minutes while the engine was changed. An enterprising person who owned a small plot of land adjoining the station had erected therein a small wooden hut, where in winter time he dispensed to shivering passengers hot elderberry wine and slips of toast, and in summer tea, coffee, and genuine old-fashioned fermented ginger beer. It was the only 'refreshment room' upon the line, and people

Birmingham Curzon Street entrance 1838. (LNWR postcard).

Birmingham Curzon Street interior 1838 - the terminus of the London & Birmingham Railway. The Grand Junction Railway opened their station alongside the following year after building an extension from Vauxhall over a viaduct. There was no running line connection so passengers had to change trains. (LNWR postcard).

Birmingham Curzon Street. The original entrance as preserved. It was designed by Philip Hardwick and is similar to his famous Euston Arch (Roman inspired). It cost £28,000 to build and is one of the oldest surviving pieces of railway architecture in the world.

used to crowd his little shanty, clamouring loudly for supplies. He soon became the most popular man between London and Birmingham.

"Railway travelling was then in a very primitive condition. Except at the termini, there were no platforms. Passengers had to clamber from the level of the rails by means of iron steps to their seats. First-class carriages were built upon the model of the inside of old stage coaches. A short man could not stand upright, the height from floor to roof being 4 ft. 6½ in. The seats were divided by arms as now, and the floor was covered afresh for each journey with clean straw. The second-class coaches were simply execrable. They were roofed over certainly; but, except a half door and a low fencing to prevent passengers from falling out, the sides were utterly unprotected from the weather. As the trains swept rapidly through the country, particularly in cuttings, or high embankments, the wind, even in the finest weather, drove through 'enough to cut your ear off.' When the weather was wet, or it was snowing, it was truly horrible, and, according to the testimony of a medical man, was the primary cause of many deaths. There were no buffers to break the force of concussion of two carriages in contact. When the train was about to start, the guard used to cry out along the train, 'Hold Hard! We're going to start.' And 'twas well he did, for sometimes, if unprepared, you might find your own nose brought into collision with that of your opposite neighbour, accompanied by some painful sensations in that important part of your profile."

The train by which Mr Edwards travelled left London at 8.30pm and was due in Birmingham at 2am. Happily, some traveller making the same journey by the 7pm from Euston in about two hours and thirty-five minutes may glance over this account, after enjoying a pleasant time in the dining saloon, and be thankful that his lot is cast in the present time and not "sixty years since."

London & Birmingham Railway Passenger's note book for complaints.

Chapter 7

The Irish Mail and The Emerald Isle via Holyhead

With Details of the North Wall and Greenore Boat Services
by V.L. Whitechurch

One naturally begins by thinking of the Irish Mail when one glances at the above title, and for more than one reason one must bring the Irish Mail into the foreground, chiefly because it existed before the iron horse came plunging through the gorse on Holy Island. It was in the early part of the Victorian era that a certain personage named Castle, arrayed in a resplendent red coat and gold-banded top hat, stood on the little quay at Holyhead awaiting the arrival of the boat from Ireland. When this occurred, he received one bag – the Irish Mail bag of the period – which he threw over his arm, and then marched in solemn and solitary state up to the old Royal Hotel, where the mail bag was duly deposited into the care of the guard of a coach, which then started on its twenty-six hours' journey to London.

Today, of course, all this has changed, and the good boats and big vans which convey Her Majesty's Mail merit some little description. The "Wild Irishman" has for many years been a familiar train-title, and the trains themselves have, until recently, possessed a dignity and certain exclusiveness which belonged to the earlier days of railways rather than to these. The London and North Western Company has taken great pains to inform the travelling public that, these highly *élite* and respectable trains were by no means run for ordinary passengers. "Not available by Irish Mail" was not so very long since a familiar legend on their tickets. I have frequently taken a ticket from Willesden to Brondesbury and found myself strictly forbidden to perform the journey by the Irish Mail, and have often wondered how it *could* be performed by that train. In fact, the whole of the London and North Western system has been for years haunted by the ultra-respectability of these trains, and the ordinary passenger has constantly been reminded of it, and made to see that he is not *quite* up to the social status the Company required. Even the "Scotch Express," with all its glories, can never hope to be arrayed in the traditional exclusiveness and dignified superiority of the Irish Mail. It stands – runs, I should say – unique among English trains.

Before entering into details concerning the running of the trains it is necessary to mention a few facts concerning the boats by which the mails – and passengers – are carried between Holyhead and Kingstown. They are the property of the City of Dublin Steam Packet Company, which is one of the oldest in the Kingdom, and from which the great Peninsular and Oriental Company sprang. This Company holds the Government contract for carrying the mails between the two islands; there is no doubt that the London and North Western Railway would have secured it years ago, but that the "Irish Nationalists" strongly protested against the privilege being granted to an English Railway; so the Company, for pacific purposes, wisely withdrew any application, not wishing to create any disturbance, and, I suppose one might say, having a strong dislike to the system of

Britannia Tubular Bridge crossing the Menai Straits to Anglesey (for Holyhead) Designed and built by Robert Stephenson and opened in 1850.

boycotting. The old contract, about which the fuss was made, expired a couple of years ago, and the present one has 18 more years to run.

October 1st, 1860, was the date which inaugurated the old service, and the boats, which were called after the four Irish provinces, were considered to be far ahead of their time.

Before this date the mails were carried by Government packets. They were capable of carrying all the passengers up to the time of their withdrawal last year, when they were replaced by four new boats, with the same names, built by Messrs. Laird Bros. of Birkenhead.

These boats are most comfortably fitted, and are the fastest and largest steamers engaged in any cross-Channel service. The mail steamers are the "Ulster," "Munster," "Leinster," and "Connaught." They are 372ft. in length, 41ft. 6in. in breadth, 3,000 tons gross tonnage, and are capable of travelling at a speed of 24 knots an hour. The ventilation is most perfect, and there is no unpleasant smell to remind one of the presence of the powerful engines. The saloon and second-class cabin are fitted up in the most luxurious manner, while the first-class dining saloon, the ladies' drawing room, and the smoking room have evoked

TSS "Scotia" at speed. Built in 1902 for the Holyhead to Dublin service. Twin screw 1,872 tons, 330ft in length, speed 21 knots. Also served in WWI and renamed Menevia in 1920.

the highest admiration from those accustomed to travel on our large ocean liners.

It is in connection with them that the Irish Mail trains run. There are two crossings each way per day and, consequently, two trains each way but those running by night are, *par excellence*, Irish Mails. Originally, they were called the "limited" mail, the number of passengers taken being dependent upon the mails, but this usage is now obsolete and on special occasions, such as the Dublin Horse Show, the train is run in two portions. The spring of last year marks the great epoch in the running of the Irish Mail. True, it was slightly accelerated some 14 years ago, but the changes made in 1897 were considerable. Up to that period only first and second-class coaches were run and the fares by these were slightly higher than by the ordinary trains. Now they have been reduced to the ordinary level and third-class coaches provided. Before then the night mail left Euston at 8.20pm, arriving at Holyhead at 2.25am; now these figures are changed to 8.45pm and 2.17am respectively, *while* there is a gain of 28 minutes on the up journey. But the very best comparison I can give of the "Wild Irishman's" speed is a 10 years' one, and I will proceed to do this accordingly. The down day mail in those days made five stops between Euston and Holyhead; now it stops at Rugby, Crewe and Chester only.

DOWN IRISH DAY MAIL, 1888

Miles		Time	Speed per hr
-	Euston	dep. 7.15	
46	Bletchley	arr. 8.14. dep. 8.16	47¼
82¼	Rugby	arr. 9.0. dep. 9.5	49
97	Nuneaton	arr. 9.24. dep. 9.26	45
158	Crewe	arr. 10.45. dep.10.55	46¼
179	Chester	arr. 11.23. dep. 11.33	45
263¾	Holyhead	arr. 1.20	47½

Total time on journey – 6 hrs. 5 mins
Average speed throughout – 43¼ miles per hour
Average running speed – 46 miles per hour

DOWN IRISH NIGHT MAIL, 1888

Miles		Time	Speed per hr
	Euston	dep. 8.20	
82¼	Rugby	arr. 10.0. dep.10.10	47¼
133¼	Stafford	arr. 11.18. dep. 11.20	44¾
158	Crewe	arr. 11.54. dep. 12.04	43¼
179	Chester	arr. 12.31. dep. 12.41	46¼
263¾	Holyhead	arr. 2.21	48

Total time on journeys – 6 hrs. 1 min.
Average speed throughout – 43 miles per hour
Average running speed – 46 miles per hour

DOWN IRISH DAY MAIL, 1898

Miles		Time	Speed per hr
	Euston	dep. 8.30	
82¼	Rugby	arr. 10.03. dep. 10.13	50¼
158	Crewe	arr. 11.42. dep. 11.48	50½
179	Chester	arr. 12.14. dep. 12.23	46¼
263¾	Holyhead	arr. 2.5	49¾

Total time on journey – 5 hrs. 35 mins
Average speed throughout – 47½ miles per hour
Average running speed – 48½ miles per hour

DOWN IRISH NIGHT MAIL, 1898

Miles		Time	Speed per hr
	Euston	dep. 8.45	
82¼	Rugby	arr. 10.25. dep. 10.30	49
158	Crewe	arr. 12.01. dep. 12.07	50
179	Chester	arr. 12.34. dep. 12.41	46¼
263¾	Holyhead	arr. 2.17	52¾

Total time on journey – 5 hrs. 32 mins
Average speed throughout – 47½ miles per hour
Average running speed – 49½ miles per hour

Irish Mail arrived in Platform 2 at Euston. Jubilee class No.1920 "Flying Fox" with 50 ft. brake van leading followed by a 32 ft. TPO. Part of the overhead signalbox can be seen on the left.

It will be seen that even now the running of the "Wild Irishman" is nothing so very much out of the ordinary, though of course, it satisfies the Government requirements. In 1888 the 84¾ miles run from Chester to Holyhead at an average speed of 47½ miles per hour was described as being "very fine for a scamper along the coast line" and it is still the best bit of the run and shows the greatest improvement in speed; in fact, it may be called a very fair piece of running indeed, considering one or two sharp curves and the gradients it encounters. The whole run is done, each way, with two engines, one working between Euston and Crewe and the other between Crewe and Holyhead, sometimes an extra engine being required out of Euston and put off at Rugby. Small shunting tank engines work the train between Holyhead Station and the landing stage, a distance of half a mile, although the road is now a "first-class" one.

The following scheduled running of the "up" mail may be interesting: -

	arr. am	dep. am
Holyhead		12.22
Bangor (passes)	–	12.53
Chester	2.10	2.17
Crewe	2.45	2.51
Stafford (passes)		3.21
Rugby	4.22	4.25
Bletchley	5.15	5.17
Willesden	5.57	6.0
Euston	6.16	–

The down Irish Mail formerly carried the whole of the mails from Euston. Now, however, two postal vans only are usually run right through, a special postal train working as under:-

	arr. pm	dep. pm
Euston		8.30
Rugby	10.08	10.12
Tamworth*	10.45	10.51
Crewe	11.49	

* Here mail from the Midland districts is picked up

The vans for Ireland are then attached to the passenger train at Crewe, and so taken on to Holyhead.

The "up" Irish Mail as a rule brings letters only, though sometimes a departure is made from this regulation, the parcels post being conveyed from Holyhead by a postal train running through as follows:-

	arr. pm	dep. pm
Holyhead		8.5
Crewe		12.41
Stafford	1.13	1.19
Tamworth	1.48	1.52
Rugby	2.25	2.30
Bletchley	3.15	3.18
Euston	4.16	

Leaving these somewhat Bradshaw-like details, we will return to the "Wild Irishman" itself, and make a cursory examination of the train. I recently performed the "run" one night and the train was a very fair specimen of the Irish Mail, consisting of 13 vehicles (nominally 16½), as follows:-

1. Six-wheel brake
2. and 3. Postal vans
4. Six-wheel brake
5. Composite 1st, 2nd and 3rd class: lavatories
7, 8, 9, and 10. Sleeping saloons, two 6 wheels, and 2 bogies
11 and 12. Composite 1st, 2nd and 3rd class fitted with lavatories
13. Composite brake

The compound "Teutonic" drew us as far as Crewe and this type of engine is usually employed. The train was pretty full, all the berths being engaged. There is no third class on board the boat, but third-class rail combined with second-class or saloon boat tickets are now issued. The down Irish night mail is still very select, no passengers being taken short of Chester, except on Saturday and Sunday nights, when a train leaves Crewe for Manchester at 12.15, and passengers to the *latter* place make use of the Mail from Euston to Crewe. The composition of the "up" night mail is similar to the above. If, by any chance, the train is run in two portions the "sleepers" proceed first and the mail follows. On the day trains breakfast, luncheon, and dining cars are provided for all classes. The new second and third-class dining car merits a brief notice. It is in reality a corridor third-class coach, with little tables placed in the compartments. The second-class is made slightly different by the addition of a rug and white head-rests. It must, however, be *borne* in mind that the recent great reduction in second-class fares on the London and North Western Railway has brought the second class to a position which it occupies on more than one line – that of a "superior third," for which the passenger pays a

I.

IMPROVED AND ACCELERATED
Train and Steamboat Services
BETWEEN
ENGLAND & IRELAND
Via Holyhead and Dublin, and via Holyhead and Greenore.
1st, 2nd, & 3rd Class by all Trains to and from Holyhead, including the Irish Mails.

TO IRELAND	Week Days.						Sundays.			FROM IRELAND.	Week Days.						Sundays	
	a.m.	noon	a.m.	p.m.	p.m.	p.m.	a.m.	p.m.	p.m.		p.m.	a.m.	p.m.	p.m.	p.m.	p.m.	a.m.	p.m.
LONDON (Euston) dep	8 30	11 0 noon	4 10	6 30	8 45	10 15	...	8 45	8 45	QUEENSTOWN ...dep	9 15	...	3 0	3 0	...	3 0	...	1 30
BIRMINGHAM (N. St.) ,,	9 55	...	12 30	5 50	8 40	10 15	11 42	8 45	10 15	10 15	CORK ,,	10 6	...	3 30	3 30	...	3 30	...	2 15
LIVERPOOL (Lime St.) ,,	11 0	12 50	...	7 15	9 45	11 10	11 55	...	10 45	10 45	KILLARNEY ,,	8 43	...	2 41	2 41	...	2 41	...	9 53
MANCHESTER (Ex.) ,,	10 45	12 40	...	5 10	9 20	10 40	...	9 50	10 40	10 40	WATERFORD ,,	9 0	...	3 40	3 40	...	3 40	...	11 0
,, (Lon. Rd.) ,,	10 45	...	...	6 25	...	10 50	12 0 night	9 0	10 50	10 50	LIMERICK ,,	11 0	...	4 0	4 0	...	4 0	...	12 0
CREWE ,,	11 48	1 0	...	7 49	10 22	12 7	1 25	10 45	12 7	12 7	LONDONDERRY ,,	9 30	...	3 53	5 3	5 3	5 3	5	...
CHESTER ,,	12 23	2 5	...	8 25	11 10	12 41	...	11 25	12 41	12 41	BELFAST ,,	10 0	...	4 50	4 50	5 30	4 50	5 30	2 0
HOLYHEAD arr	2 5 p.m	4 10	4 35	10 10	1 20 a.m.	2 17	3 30 a.m.	1 48 p.m.	2 17	2 17	GREENORE ,,	...	...	...	...	8 0	...	8 0	...
,, (Steamer) dep.	2 13		5 0	10 15	1†40 a.m.	2 25	3 55	2 13	2 25	2 30	DUBLIN (W. R.) ,,	8 0	...	7 45	...	...	...	8 0	7 45
DUBLIN (Nor. Wall) arr	...		8 30	2 0	...	...	7 30	...	...	...	,, (N.W.) ,,	...	10 15	...	9 10	...	9 10	...	...
,, (Wes. Row) ,,	5 30			...	...	6 0	...	5 30	6 0	...	HOLYHEAD arr. about	11 50 p.m	2 35 a.m.	12 01 p.m	1 25 a.m	1 30 p.m	1 25 a.m	1 30 p.m	11 50 a.m	12 10 p.m
GREENORE ,,	...		American Mail, Saturdays only.	6†15	...	...	...	...	...	6 55	,, (Train) dep	12 03 p.m	0	12 22	2 10	...	2 25	1 0	12 22
BELFAST ,,	9 0 a.m.			8†50	8 50	12 15 noon	...	2 25	8 50	9 50	CHESTER arr	1 42	4 40	2 12	...	4 22	4 10	2 12	
LONDONDERRY ,,	3 15			10†30	10 30	2 50 p.m.	...	3 15	10 30	2 50	CREWE ,,	2 18	5 20	2 45	4 15	...	4 50	2 45	
LIMERICK ,,	10 25		†Not on Sunday mornings.	...	9 55	1 25	...	1 50	9 55	...	MANCHESTER (Ex.) ,,	3 26	8	3 55	...	5 50	8 37	3 25	
WATERFORD ,,	...			...	10 20	2 0	...	3 45	10 20	...	LIVERPOOL (L. S.) ,,	2 50	5 38	3 35	...	5 40	5E30	5 25	
KILLARNEY ,,	...			...	11 58	3 15	...	4 18	11 58	...	BIRMINGHAM (N. S.)	4 25	7 5	4 35	6 10	...	7 30	5 45	
CORK ,,	11 25			...	10 35	2 15	...	2 50	10 35	...	LONDON (Euston)	5 45	8 45	6 10	7 45	...	8 20	6 10	
QUEENSTOWN ,,	12 3			6 15	...	11 a 5	2 51	...	11 5	...									

a—On Thursdays First and Second Class Passengers arrive Queenstown at 10.15 a.m. E—Landing Stage.

Passengers from the Interior of Ireland by the Night Express Services, leaving Dublin (North Wall) at 9.10 p.m., and Greenore at 8.0 p.m. respectively, will be able to dine at the Company's Hotels at Dublin and Greenore before embarking on the Steamer. Dinner may also be obtained on board the Steamers.

BREAKFAST, LUNCHEON, and DINING CARS for First, Second, and Third Class Passengers, and **SLEEPING CARS** for First Class Passengers are run on the undermentioned Trains:—

LONDON (EUSTON) TO HOLYHEAD—
8 30 a.m., Day Mail—Breakfast and Luncheon Cars.
11 0 a.m., Day Express—Luncheon Cars.
6 30 p.m., Greenore Boat Express—Dining Cars.
8 45 p.m., Night Mail—Sleeping Cars for 1st Class Passengers.
10 15 p.m., Night Express—Sleeping Cars for 1st Class Passengers.

HOLYHEAD TO LONDON (EUSTON)—
12 0 noon, Day Mail—Luncheon Cars.
3 0 p.m., Day Express—Luncheon and Dining Cars.
12 22 a.m., Night Mail—Sleeping Cars for 1st Class Passengers.
2 10 a.m., Night Express—Sleeping Cars for 1st Class Passengers.

HOLYHEAD TO MANCHESTER (EXCHANGE)—
2.25 a.m., Night Express—Sleeping Accommodation for 1st Class Passengers.

Return Halves of Saloon and Second Cabin Tickets issued for the Mail Boats will be available by the Boats between Holyhead and North Wall.

Return Halves of Saloon Tickets issued for the North Wall Boats will be available in the Saloon of the Mail Boats between Holyhead and Kingstown upon payment of the additional fare, or in the Second Cabin without additional charge. Holders of North Wall Deck Tickets must pay full fare if they travel by the Mail Boats.

Return Halves of Tickets to, from, and via Dublin (North Wall) and Greenore.

Passengers holding Ordinary Return Tickets to or from Dublin (North Wall) or Stations in the interior of Ireland via Dublin (North Wall), will be allowed to travel on the RETURN Journey via Greenore, and in like manner, Passengers holding Ordinary Return Tickets to or from Greenore or Stations in the interior of Ireland via Greenore, will be allowed to travel on the RETURN Journey via Dublin (North Wall).

This interchange arrangement does not include free conveyance by rail over any of the Irish Lines except the Dundalk Newry and Greenore Railway.

A

Irish Boat Service Time Table in 1898.

slightly extra charge and benefits, not so much, in springs and upholstery as in more privacy or more select travelling companions. The additional fare for the whole 263¾ miles from Euston to Holyhead is only half-a-crown now and the modern distinction between second and third class at a time when the latter is luxurious enough for the most fastidious passenger is entirely different to the distinction of 10 years ago. In August of the present year, the down day train was timed to leave Euston at 8.30am, the train and boat journey being accelerated by three-quarters of an hour. A passenger by this train can arrive in Dublin at 5.27pm, Belfast 9pm, and Cork 11.25pm. The hour of departure from Dublin (Westland Row) has been altered to 8am and with the same acceleration as in the down day service, passengers arrive at Euston at the same hour as previous to August – viz. 5.45pm.

The following scale of passenger fares between Euston and Dublin (Westland Row) by the Irish Mail and the City of Dublin Steam Packet Company's boats may be of interest: -

	1st and Saloon	2nd and Saloon	2nd and 2nd Cabin	3rd and Saloon	3rd and 2nd Cabin
Single	53s 6d	35s 6d	32s 6d	32s 6d	29s 6d
Return	93s 0d	55s 6d	51s 0d	51s 6d	47s 0d

In conclusion, one may say of the celebrated Irish Mail trains that, in their fittings and running, they are well worthy of the great Company to which they belong. They contain everything "up-to-date" in the way of accommodation both by day and by night; their sleeping saloons especially are beautifully fitted and comfortable. Then again, their running average is decidedly good. No one can make any great complaint against the speed of a train averaging almost 50 miles an hour on a run of 263¾ miles. That it *could* be done in a shorter time nobody will deny, but the necessity does not exist. If the Government and the bulk of the passengers are satisfied there can be no adequate reason for increasing expenditure – and increasing speed always means this. Ten years have brought about an improvement in the "Wild Irishman" that certainly forbids one applying to it a term that report says more than once *used* to be heard – that of "The Irish Snail."

Having, then, given a few jottings concerning this famous and select train, I propose entering into some more details concerning the connection of the London and North Western Railway with the Sister Isle.

The Dublin North-Wall Service

We now have to deal with the London and North Western Company's own route to Ireland; first of all, a little description of their harbour at Holyhead will not be out of place. Snugly sheltered from the "Wild Irish" waves, under the little town and protected by massive breakwaters, lies Holyhead Harbour and the snuggest and innermost portion of it is the property of the London and North Western Railway. The harbour, roughly speaking, is in the form of a triangle, at the apex of which stand the Company's hotel and station, the former facing the harbour. The side of the triangle is formed by the station platforms, which run alongside the harbour. Formerly there were about 12 acres of water space, but in the year 1874 the Company began enlarging the harbour, building a new goods shed and the hotel above mentioned, with passenger station attached. On June 17th 1880, the new harbour, now covering 24 acres of water space and station, were opened by the Prince of Wales. The station, with its fine harbour, is certainly one of the most important, not only on the Company's system but also on the West Coast. I shall presently try to show something of the hugeness of the traffic which passes through.

The next item that deserves attention is the "Fleet," and a little historical sketch may here be of interest. It was in 1848 that the Chester and Holyhead Railway Company, subsequently absorbed by the London and North Western, commenced running passenger boats between Holyhead and Kingstown. The four earliest vessels, the "Anglia," "Scotia," "Hibernia" and "Cambria," conveying passengers only, were about 200ft in length and attained a speed of about 15 knots an hour. Then came the "Ocean" and "Hercules," built for goods traffic only and afterwards (commencing in 1863), a series of cargo boats with saloon accommodation (in which second-class passengers were allowed to travel) came into existence and ran to North Wall, Dublin. The "Sea Nymph," "Cambria," "Admiral Moorsom," "Alexandra," "Stanley," "Telegraph," "Countess of Erie," "Duke of Sutherland," "Duchess of Sutherland" and the "Edith." The two latter are still running as cargo boats only, having been converted from paddle-boats to twin-screws. In the old days they berthed alongside the goods shed and passengers were taken in there.

The year 1876 ushered in a new era in the Irish traffic, an express passenger service in each direction between Holyhead and North Wall being inaugurated. For this purpose, the "Rose" and "Shamrock" were built, their tonnage being nearly double that of the old boats (i.e. 1,200 tons). These boats were far superior to anything that had before been running and passengers were chiefly their cargo. In 1880, it was decided to maintain a night express each way; in addition to the above-mentioned day expresses and two new steamers, the "Lily" and the "Violet" were built. They were 310ft. long, 1,035 tons and travelled at 19 knots an hour. It was on the "Lily" that the Prince

Holyhead – inside Cambria Class Steamer Saloon.

Dublin North Wall Station Concourse.

of Wales opened the new harbour. Subsequently, the "Banshee," a boat similar to the "Lily," but 10ft. longer, was built and is still running.

But the latest and finest addition to the North Wall fleet is the "Cambria," a ship of which the Company is exceedingly proud. She is 337½ft. long, 1,842 tons gross tonnage, attains a speed of 22 knots per hour and has accommodation for 1,378 passengers. Captain W.H. Binney, the energetic Marine Superintendent at Holyhead, who kindly accompanied me over several vessels under his charge, is enthusiastic when the "Cambria" is mentioned.* *The greatest pains have been taken to secure the comfort of every class of passenger; the lavatory arrangements are (?)and North Western Railway(?), under Mr F.W.Webb adoption of balanced engines on the Yarrow, Schlick and Tweedy system*; there is a system of electrically-driven mechanical ventilation throughout the boat, which constantly expels all foul air and Denny's patent spark and ash catcher prevents the fall of dust on the decks. The dining saloon, private and deck cabins and smoke-room are luxurious and the third-class accommodation is also very good. This is situated aft, fitted with two dining tables and contains seats divided into 2ft spaces to prevent selfish passengers taking up too much room. There is also a special ladies' cabin in the third class. The engines have been built by Denny and Co., from designs by Mr W. Brock. They are triple expansion, supplied with steam at 160lb. pressure from eight boilers. Size of cylinders, HP. 26in., MP. 40in., LP. 43ins. The lighting arrangements have been carried out by the Electrical Department of the London and North Western Railway, under Mr F.W. Webb, the machinery being made at Crewe.

The entire fleet plying between Holyhead and North Wall is as follows:

PASSENGER BOATS	CARGO BOATS
(Holyhead to North Wall, etc)	
1. Shamrock Used as an emergency	1. Holyhead
	2. North Wall
2. Lily	3. Irene
3. Violet	4. Olga
4. Banshee	5. Anglesey
5. Cambria	6. Edith
	7. Duchess of Sutherland

Now for a word or two about the trains which run in connection with the passenger boats. The reader must not confuse them with the Irish Mail. I have purposely dealt with that separately. It must be mentioned in giving hours of arrival and departure that the boats are in the habit of coming in long before 'scheduled time'. For instance, I saw the "Lily" come in at 1.40 when she was due at 2.10.

On July 1st 1898, the London and North Western introduced considerable improvements in the North Wall service and a portion of the Daily press, as usual, had paragraphs about the Wild Irishman, and in other ways mixed up the new running with the Irish Mail, which had not been altered in any way. It may be of interest to contrast the old running with the new and this is best done as follows: -

---

* As printed in original article – something missed out here – Ed.

1. The Day Service

(a) Down

	OLD		NEW
Euston	dep. 9.30	Euston	dep. 11.0
Willesden	dep. 9.42	Bletchley	arr. 11.58 dep. 12.3
Northampton	arr. 10.55 dep. 10.57	Stafford	arr. 1.45 dep. 1.53
Rugby	arr. 11.25 dep. 11.30	Holyhead	arr. 4.35 dep. 5.00
Stafford	arr. 12.30 dep. 12.43	North Wall	arr. 8.30
Chester	arr. 1.50 dep. 2.00		
Llandudno Junc.	arr. 3.7 dep. 3.10		
Banger	- 3.36		
Holyhead	arr. 4.10 dep. 4.55		
North Wall	arr. 8.30		

It will be at once seen that a very considerable acceleration both in trains and boat service was made. As regards to the former, the acceleration in actual running was 1 hour 5 minutes, while the gain to the passenger was 1½ hours. The run from Stafford to Holyhead, 130¼ miles without a stop, must be added to the list of long distance runs in this country during the summer; while it was the longest distance performed without a stop between Holyhead and any other point in the entire Irish service. The speed, however, was not so remarkable as one of the leading dailies would make out, for it did not quite come up to a 48½ mile average between Stafford and Holyhead. This train has been slightly altered since October and now calls at Chester instead of Bletchley, arriving at Holyhead at 4.40.

Up to October 1st the old train, leaving Chester at 2.05 and arriving at Holyhead at 4.10, still ran but not from London. It brought in passengers from the North and Midlands. The following is the up service: -

(b) Up

	OLD	NEW
North Wall	dep. 9.15am	10.15 am
Holyhead	arr. 2.10pm	2.35pm
	dep. 2.40pm	2.50pm
Euston	arr. 8.45pm	8.45pm
Stopping at Bangor, Chester, Crewe, Stafford and Willesden		Stopping at Bangor, Chester, Crewe, Stafford and Willesden

Before October 1st this train left Holyhead at 3.0 and did not call at Bangor. This was a very curious piece of acceleration, the extra 20 minutes being entirely gained between Holyhead and Chester, the run of 84¾ miles being performed in exactly 100 minutes.

2. The Night Service
This is especially worthy of notice

(a) Down

(No alteration)	
Euston	dep. 10.15pm
Crewe	arr. 1.20am dep. 1.25am
Holyhead	arr. 3.30am dep. 3.55am
North Wall	arr. 7.30am

(b) Up

	OLD		NEW
North Wall	dep. 8.50pm	North Wall	dep. 9.10pm
Holyhead	arr. 1.15am dep. 1.50am	Holyhead	arr. 1.25am dep. 2.10am
Crewe	arr. 3.55am dep. 4.00am	Crewe	arr. 4.15am dep. 4.20am
Northampton	arr. 5.51am dep. 5.53am	Northampton	arr. 6.13am dep. 6.15am
Willesden	arr. 7.12am dep. 7.15am	Willesden	arr. 7.31am dep. 7.35am
Euston	arr. 7.25am	Euston	arr. 7.45am

There is also a service of cargo boats between Holyhead and North Wall having no saloon accommodation but carrying third class passengers.

From the above it will be seen that the very fastest train running between Euston and Holyhead is the 10.15 down Irish Night Express, which also performs the "longest distance run," stopping only at Crewe and which may be analysed and compared with the Irish Mail as follows:

Time occupied on total journey – 5hrs 15min.
Average speed for total journey 50¼ miles per hour
Running average, Euston to Crewe 51¼ miles per hour
Running average, Crewe to Holyhead 50¼ miles per hour
Total journey – 51 miles per hour

From this it will be seen that the Irish Night Express deserves to rank very high among the long-distance trains of the country, 158 miles being a very fair journey without a stop. This and the "up" express are provided with "sleepers," while the day trains have luncheon and dining cars attached with accommodation for all classes. It might be mentioned that a certain number of passengers prefer to break the night journey at Holyhead and sleep in the hotel.

Once a week, on Saturdays, the London and North Western run a mail service via Holyhead and North Wall, leaving Euston at 4.10pm, stopping at Rugby, Tamworth, Crewe and Chester, arriving at Holyhead at 10.10, and at Dublin at 2am. The mails and passengers are then conveyed across Ireland to Queenstown, where they catch the Cunard liner leaving Liverpool at 4.30 on Saturday afternoon. Occasionally there is an inward mail landed at Queenstown, brought by special train and boat to Holyhead and thence transferred by special train to London.

The Express Route to North Wall is becoming an exceedingly popular one. The tourist especially has been turning his attention to Ireland of late and special tourist tickets at cheap fares are issued via this route to all parts of the Emerald Isle in the summer season. I give a list of ordinary fares from Euston to North Wall.

	1st and Saloon	2nd and Saloon	3rd and Saloon	3rd and Deck
Single	50s.0d	32s.6d	29s.6d	24s.6d
Return	87s.0d	51s.0d	47s.0d	40s.6d

Now for a time I will direct the reader's attention from this North Wall route and bring before him another important undertaking of the London and North Western Railway in connection with their port of Holyhead.

The Greenore Service

The route of Greenore was opened on May 2nd, 1873, the first boat used being the "Countess of Erne." This was followed by the "Earl Spencer," named after the Lord Lieutenant of Ireland at that time, and subsequently the "Eleanor" and "Isabella," vessels of 900 tons, 250ft. in length and of 15 knots speed, carried on this service until 1895, when it was determined to employ twin-screw steamers. The "Rosstrevor" and her sister ship the "Connemara" were then built for the Greenore service. I had the opportunity of going over the latter vessel, which may be described as a "miniature Atlantic liner," so complete is it in every modern convenience and comfort. The saloons are spacious and the cabins exceedingly comfortable and what strikes one most is the "neatness" and cleanliness of decorations and fittings, there being no unnecessary "gaudiness" aboard. These vessels are 280ft. in length and attain a speed of 18 knots; they are fitted throughout with electric light – a light that is carried to the bridge, where tiny lamps in front of the officer of the watch "repeat" the starboard, port and masthead lights, so that he is at once aware of an accident to them. Captain Binney, who of course, directs all these details also pointed out to me a novelty in the shape of an "automatic steam whistle," by which in foggy weather, the whistle may be set to blow at desired intervals. I also noted a clever arrangement for launching the boats, the withdrawal of a pin, the pressure of the foot on a little lever, a slight push at the bows and in less time than it takes to tell it the lifeboat is out on the davits ready for lowering.

This is the invention of one of the employees in the Marine Department at Holyhead. The system of electric ventilation obtains all over the boat.

The latest addition, however, to the Greenore Fleet is the "Galtee More," which was launched on May 24th 1898, at the Leven Shipyard, Dumbarton, where she was built by Messrs. Wm. Denny and Bros. She is 284ft in length, 35ft beam and 23ft deep, has large accommodation for saloon and steerage passengers and also for cattle, an important feature in the Greenore traffic. Needless to say, she is fitted with the latest improvements and will be as popular as her sister ships. She commenced running in August. It has been said that no cross-Channel steamers cater better for third class passengers than those on the Greenore service and Captain Binney informs me that this has been made a special feature of the Company's Irish traffic, down to the minutest details of ventilation and lavatory accommodation. They get some third-class passengers by this route, too, very rum ones some of them – "Wild Irishmen" at sea.

The passenger fleet, therefore, in the Greenore service is as follows:-

1. The "Rosstrevor"
2. The "Connemara"
3. The "GalteeMore"

There is one service a day each way between London and Greenore, except on Sunday mornings

Holyhead Custom House Pier with George IV Memorial Arch of 1824 designed by Thomas Harrison which also marks the end of Thomas Telford's A5 road. LNWR distant signal on left.

from Holyhead to Greenore, the trains being as follows:-

Passengers who travel by the 8pm boat from Greenore, arriving at Holyhead at 1.20am, take the 2.10 train, already described in connections with the North Wall service. A train at 2.5am conveys passengers to Manchester and the North. On the other hand, the Company runs a special "Greenore Boat Express," with dining cars attached, leaving Euston at 6.30pm and arriving at Holyhead at 1.20, after stopping at Willesden, Rugby, Nuneaton, Stafford, Crewe, Chester and Bangor. This train, as will be seen, does nothing extraordinary in its running.

Passengers to Greenore holding return tickets can travel back on the North Wall route and vice versa. This is a very handy arrangement for the tourist. A through coach is run from Greenore to Belfast by the Great Northern Railway of Ireland in connection with this service.

A Few Traffic Items

Mr William Guest, who for many years has been Stationmaster and Goods Superintendent at Holyhead and who was only too delighted to conduct a representative of the RAILWAY MAGAZINE on a tour of inspection, informs me that his predecessor, Mr Massingberd, who retired in 1879, could remember very well the time when all the goods for Ireland came down in one vehicle once a week! Now one train a day would not nearly suffice for all the traffic between Euston and that "famine-stricken" sister island of ours. A very large amount of this goods traffic consists of cattle and fish and statistics show a general increase of such traffic between England and Ireland via Holyhead for many years past.

The fish traffic varies, the great pressure of it coming in the April and May mackerel season, but all the year round it is being brought in. Some of the fish are caught in the Irish Sea and landed from small boats, but the majority are taken off the West and South-West coast of Ireland, brought across the Emerald Isle to North Wall, shipped thence to Holyhead and quickly despatched in a "fish special" to London, where possibly, the innocent Cockney imagines that the "fresh mackerel!" bawled in his ears by the coster were taken out of the Thames a few hours previously.

But the "Port of Holyhead" is not opened to Irish traffic only. It may be news to the reader to hear that for several weeks in the year a little fleet of small boats is constantly engaged in bringing cargoes of new potatoes *not* from Ireland, but from Jersey – these potatoes being intended for Liverpool, Manchester and the North. The seven weeks these boats are running are a time of joy to certain Holyhead boys, who are employed to help in the unloading thereof.

It is obvious that such a station as Holyhead, with its harbour combined, requires a very large staff to work the passenger and goods traffic. The total number employed in the former department is 79, those in the goods department numbering 330 in round numbers.

This of course, does not include any of the marine staff, which is probably double that engaged in handling the traffic. Possibly the diver belongs to the latter. At any rate, there is a diver, for I saw him at work in the harbour and also heard a very funny story about him. Recently he had come up from his task, and was resting in the boat with his helmet off, when a severe shower began to fall, whereupon he remarked to his mates, "There, put on my helmet again and let me get down out of the wet!"

And perhaps by this time I ought to be getting down out of sight of the reader, for he has probably had enough of Holyhead and its traffic. If he wants any more let him go for himself and he will find plenty to interest him between Euston and Kingstown or North Wall – or Greenore.

Chapter 8

"Precedents"
Some Wonderful Little Engines
by Charles Rous-Marten

To avoid the risk of misconception at starting, I may as well say at once that the engines I am going to write about are those designed and built by Mr F.W. Webb for the London and North Western Railway, having 6 ft. 6 in. coupled wheels and 17 in. by 24 in. cylinders, and being generally known as "Precedents", that being the name of one of the first built – or "Jumbos" – for no clearly ascertainable or conjecturable reason at all.

Up to the year 1866 all, or nearly all, of the express work on the London and North Western Railway – as, indeed, on most other lines – was performed by single-wheel engines. Not to mention a variety of types introduced in the early days of Messrs. Trevithick, Allen, Bury, Crampton, and others, the "Problems" of Mr Ramsbottom, with 7 ft. 6 in. wheels and 16 in. by 24 in. cylinders, and the "Bloomers" of Mr McConnell continued to run express trains, the former up to the present day and the latter up to 1885. Both of these types were admirably designed for the work they were originally required to do and many brilliant feats are on record to their credit. But just as even at the present day certain classes of express traffic have outgrown the capabilities of very fine single-driver locomotives and compelled recourse to coupling as affording larger adhesion weight, so as long ago as 1866 some of the London and North Western express work had become too much for the "Problems" and "Bloomers."

Mr John Ramsbottom, then the Chief Mechanical Engineer at Crewe, set himself to provide the requisite increase in power. The feasibleness of employing coupled engines for express work had already been demonstrated by Sir Daniel (Then Mr) Gooch on the Great Western in 1855, by Mr J. Cudworth on the South Eastern in 1858, and by Mr W. Kirtley on the Midland in 1863. And so Mr Ramsbottom turned out at Crewe in May, 1866, "Newton," No. 1480, the first of his coupled express engines. The coupled wheels were 6 ft. 6 in. in diameter, and the cylinders (placed inside) were 16 in. by 24 in. The new locomotive worked so well that no fewer than 96 in all were built – some, indeed, in 1873, after Mr Webb had succeeded Mr Ramsbottom in the Crewe chieftainship – and, proportionately to their power, they have always done excellent work. I believe that some of those latest built had their cylinder diameter enlarged to 17 in. and during the last dozen years or so all have been rebuilt by Mr Webb, with that cylinder diameter and larger boilers, and have, in fact, been converted into the "Precedent" class.

While it has been necessary, in elucidating the genesis of the "Precedent" engine, to refer to these forerunners of the type, I desire to give my absolute dissent from the view which I have heard expressed that the "Precedents" are merely a slight enlargement of the "Newtons," and that therefore to Mr Ramsbottom, not Mr Webb, belongs the credit of the later engine's excellence. That both have certain points in common is, of course, self-evident; but, if that alone be taken into account, then all modern engines are merely improvements of earlier types. The point here is that Mr Webb's modifications of the original 6 ft.

No.512 "Lazonby" on Hest Bank troughs. Known as 'Jumbos' or 'Improved Precedents' they were a development of John Ramsbottom's 'Newton' class and FW Webb built a total of 158 between 1887 and 1901.

6 in. coupled design were of sufficient importance to constitute the "Precedent" class a virtually new one, and to change what had been simply a good ordinary engine into one which has proved itself quite exceptional in its relative capacity. Anyone who has seen the "Newtons" in their original shape – not in their later forms as changed for the first and second time by Mr Webb – will readily appreciate the accuracy of my view.

Again, I have travelled many times behind the Ramsbottom engines before their rebuilding into "Precedents," and I have no record of such remarkable performances on their part as the Webb engines have given me in perfect "heaps," nor have I been able to glean any of the authentic character from other sources. They simply did the work ordinarily done by locomotives of the same dimensions, but no more. It may be rejoined that the Ramsbottom engines had not the same opportunities of distinguishing themselves as the Webb engines always have had, and that therefore this comparison is unfair. That, no doubt, is true to some extent. But it is not the whole truth. I personally have had opportunities of comparing the work of both classes on similar trains, and the superiority of the Webb engines was unquestionable. I say this in no disrespect to Mr Ramsbottom, for whom I have always cherished the warmest admiration, and whose engines, when they were built, were unsurpassed anywhere. All I say is that Mr Webb introduced a new type which was still better.

Nor were the "Newtons" the actual immediate precursors of the "Precedents." When Mr Webb came to the conclusion that a new and stronger engine was needed, he first tried the experiment of obtaining this increased tractive power by reducing the diameter of the driving wheels. I believe it is a fact, although I do not know it from himself, that he was impressed with the good work done in America with express engines having driving wheels only 5 ft. or 5 ft. 6.in in diameter, and that, to test the suitableness of small wheels to British express duty, he first tried a goods engine which had 5 ft. 2 in. drivers and cylinders 17 in. by 24 in., removing the side rods from the leading wheels, and so converting it into a 5 ft. 2 in. four coupled engine; and I believe that this engine, when employed in running the best London and North Western expresses of that day, kept perfect time, but that the desideratum of that period – "fifteen coaches on the level at a mile a minute" – could not be attained, because the small size of the wheels required the cylinders to be so frequently filled that the boiler could not supply sufficient steam. I do not vouch for all this, but "I tell the tale as it was told to me," and I have every reason to deem it accurate.

I have often regretted that the moral lesson deduced from this experiment was not – bigger boiler. If the boiler would not furnish enough steam with the small wheels which gave such enhanced power, there were two courses open – either the boiler or the wheels might be enlarged. It would have been interesting to see what results could have been attained on the Lancaster – Carlisle road with a large boiler and 5 ft. 2in. wheels. Mr Webb, however, thought it might be preferable to use a slightly larger wheel, and adopted the diameter of 5 ft. 6 in. He named the pioneer of this class "Precursor," and constructed altogether forty of that type. With cylinders 17 in. by 24 in., they possessed a tractive force of as much as 105lb. for every pound of effective steam pressure in the cylinders. That is to say, although they weighed only about 31 tons, they had the same nominal tractive effort per pound of cylinder pressure as the large new Great Western engines which weigh over 52 tons. And they did capital work, pulling up steep banks loads with which the "Newtons" had required pilot assistance, and running under favourable conditions, quite as swiftly as the 6 ft. 6 in. class. I have myself timed one of these "Precursors" at 74 miles an hour at a period when 75 was deemed the maximum possible in ordinary circumstances. In fact, when both the "Precedents" were sharing the same work I found no difference in the speed of the two types. That is to say, I found the "Precursors" run just as fast on the level and downhill as the 6 ft. 6 in. engines, while uphill they possessed a manifest advantage.

But soon after they had been placed on the road Mr Webb decided that a larger wheel was desirable for the fastest express work, and so he took his "Precursor" type as a standard and simply gave it a 6 ft. 6 in. wheel, instead of 5 ft. 6 in., and a slightly enlarged fire-box, which made the total heating surface 1,083 square feet for the 6 ft. 6 in. engine, instead of 1,074 as in the 5 ft. 6 in. coupled type.

And so we got the "Precedent" or "Jumbo" class of express locomotive, which, in my experience, has done heavier work than any other engine, present or past, of similar small weight. I have no personal enthusiasm or even predilection for any

No.1141 "S.R. Graves" at Penrith piloting a Greater Britain on an up express made up of a clerestory roof bogie van followed by arc roof bogie carriages.

No.2187 "Penrith Beacon" at Crewe North Shed.

particular engineer or designer or railway or type of locomotive. I simply judge the tree by its fruits, the engine by its work. I have styled these North Western locomotives of the "Precedent" class "wonderful little engines" and I have done so advisedly, in no spirit of partisan enthusiasm, but in calm view of their actual performances. When a cheaply built little engine, weighing only about 32¾ tons, can and does perform satisfactorily the same work as is allotted on other lines to large and costly locomotives, weighing from 47 to 52 tons, it is surely warrantable to attribute to the smaller engines exceptional merit in respect of design and construction. I am open to correction, but so it seems to me. Later on I shall produce abundant proof that I have not over-rated either the capacity or the performances of these engines.

Seventy of the "Precedent" type were built between the years 1875 and 1882 inclusive. No more were constructed; the "compound" era was setting in. But in 1885 or 1886 Mr Webb took in hand the rebuilding of the Ramsbottom or "Newton" class of 6 ft. 6 in. coupled, including those of that type which he himself had built on his first accession to the chief post at Crewe. All of them, 96 in all, have now been rebuilt, with larger and higher pitched boilers and the other improvements characterising the "Precedent" order have, in fact, been entirely transformed into brand new "Precedents," thus bringing up the total numerical strength of that class to 166. All are now at work, and, as I shall show, are doing wonders, considering their small size and weight.

Now have to be recorded two other metamorphoses on a large scale. Soon after the first advent of the "Precedents," the "Precursors" were taken off the best express services, even on such lengths of line as that between Preston and Carlisle, the newer 6 ft. 6 in. coupled taking their place. They continued, however, to run some of the expresses which were timed less fast, and did all sorts of duty on both the Carlisle and the Leeds

No.308 "Booth" at Colwyn Bay with down train of 6-wheel stock.

sections, besides sometimes piloting the faster expresses. And they appeared to me always to do it very efficiently, for in my opinion they, too, were "wonderful little engines" in view of what they could do with their weight of only 31½ tons. It would have been most interesting to see what they could have done with larger boilers and higher steam pressure. But apparently the 5 ft. 6 in. wheel was condemned as too small for express running, and so the fiat went forth that all forty of the "Precursor" engines were to be transmogrified into passenger "Tanks." This was done by degrees as the "Precursors" came in for heavy repairs, and by the time twenty years had elapsed since their first appearance all had been thus altered, the tenders and name-plates being taken off, the frames lengthened, and a pair of radial trailing wheels added. They make excellent tank engines for suburban work, but their admirers - of whom I avow myself one – may be permitted to drop a silent tear of regret over their disappearance from the higher class of service.

And now came another curious transformation scene. We have just seen forty main line express engines converted into suburban "tanks"; we have now to behold the conversion of ninety feeble little tender engines, originally built for the inferior classes of train service now far better performed by tank engines, into a new and excellent race of main line express locomotives, almost exactly resembling the "Precedents," save in having 6ft. coupled wheels, and so possessing 96lb. of tractive force for each pound of cylinder pressure, instead of 88lb as in the case of the 6ft. 6in. engine.

How those scrubby little 6ft. coupled tender engines, as they formerly were, came originally to be built I have never been able to understand. When such a man as John Ramsbottom could build sixty of them, and such another as Mr Webb some thirty more many years after the first came out, it must be presumed that they possessed, or appeared to possess, some capacity for usefulness. All the same, I frankly confess that I have never been able to detect it. To me they always seemed feeble and unsatisfactory. No one nowadays would dream of building a tiny 6ft. coupled engine, with Lilliputian boiler and cylinders 16 in. by 20 in., to do the work to which those small machines were put. The prototype of the class which came out in 1863 was named with obvious irony, "Samson." Similar irony seems to have been maintained in the description of operation they have undergone a "rebuilding." So far as I can make out, all

No.1522 "Pitt" on the up fast line at Harrow with an express of 6 and 8-wheeled stock.

that remains of the original engine may be said to be the wheels and nameplates, not even the crank-axles, for the throw of the cranks has been lengthened from 10 to 12 inches, with a 24 in. piston stroke instead of 20 in., so evidently the later opinion at Crewe agrees with mine.

In plain terms they may now be designated as very efficient, though small, new engines, slightly heavier than the "Precedents" and more powerful through having coupled wheels 6in. smaller. But they seem able to do anything that a 6ft. 6in. engine can do, and with heavy loads or on steep banks a little more. Practically, they are interchangeable with the 6ft. 6in. class in any express work, and may be regarded as bringing up the total number of non-compound coupled express engines now running on the London and North Western line to 266. They are chiefly used on the Carlisle and Leeds portions of the North Western system, where the gradients are most severe. They have thus replaced the "Precursors," and outnumber them by more than two to one.

Before I proceed to give instances of work done by the locomotives whose genesis and history I have been setting forth, it may perhaps be interesting to many readers who have not the means of access to the official records if I furnish a complete list of the "Precedent" class. The following are the names of the seventy engines originally built by Mr F. W. Webb of the "Precedent" type, together with the years in which they came out:-

1874	Precedent	1875	Caradoc	1877	Wizard
1875	Robert Benson		Salopian		Phantom
	Edward Tootal		Cambrian		Sir Hardman Earle
	Pluck	1877	Prince Leopold		Hercules
	Patience		Sir Salar Jung		Princess Louise
	Perseverance		Merrie Carlisle		Stewart
	Buffalo		Amazon	1878	Chandos
	Giraffe		Balmoral		Joshua Radcliffe
	Antelope		Meteor		Miranda
	Reynard		Pilot		General
	Alma		Envoy		Auditor
	Lowther		Courier		Plynlimmon
	Penrith Beacon		Disraeli		Nasmyth
	Chillington		Condor		Mercury
	Avon		Llewellyn		Marathon
	Princess Beatrice		Fairbairn		Rocket
	Snowdon		Proserpine		

1880	Caratacus	1882	Charles Dickens		
	Commodore		Henry Pease		
	Duchess of Lancaster		President Garfield		
	Pegasus		President Lincoln		
	Sir Alexander Cockburn		President Washington		
	Laxonby		Duke of Albany		
	Lawrence		Duke of Connaught		
	Mabel		Wheatstone		
	Breadalbane		Buckland		
	Humphrey Davy		Thomas Carlisle		

The following is a list of the 6ft. 6in. coupled engines originally designed by Mr John Ramsbottom or built to the same design by his successor, Mr F.W. Webb, before the advent of the "Precursor" class, and subsequently rebuilt by Mr Webb as practically new engines of the "Precedent" type:-

Minotaur	Isabella	Herschel	Corunna	John Bright
Penmaenmawr	Clarendon	Newcomen	Dagmar	Bevere
Booth	Hardwicke	Telford	Ilion	John Mayall
Sedgwick	Blenkinsop	Smeaton	Ganymede	(formerly -
Quernmore	Shah of Persia	Faraday	Shamrock	Tennyson)
Buckingham	Richard Cobden	Murdoch	Talavera	Britannia
Brougham	Wordsworth	Brindley	Lucknow	Hibernia
Eamont	North Western	Duke of Edinburgh	Delhi	Henry Crosfield
Tennyson	S. R. Graves	Shakespeare	Vimiera	Madge
(formerly Dunrobin)	John Ramsbottom	Scott	Nile	Alecto
Pitt	Pioneer	Milton	Badajos	Witch
Marlborough	Queen	Byron	Airey	Lynx
Wolfe	Prince Albert	Princess Helena	Bunsen	Princess
Abercrombie	Albion	Countess	Livingstone	Patterdale
Drake	Premier	Duchess	Minerva	Vulcan
Raleigh	Florence	Franklin	Novelty	Pluto
Frobisher	Phaeton	Gladstone	Sisyphus	Hector
Cook	Lightning	Cromwell	Speke	Director
Columbus	Belted Will	Hampden	Gladiator	
Scotia	Newton	Ariadne	Magdala	

Their dates range from May, 1866, to 1873. They have inside cylinders, 17 in. by 24 in.; driving and trailing wheels coupled, 6ft. 6in. or 6ft. 7½ in., with new tyres; 150 lb steam pressure; 1,083 square feet total heating surface – viz. tubes, 980 square feet, fire-box, 103. The following is the distribution of their weight in working order: – Leading Wheels, 10 tons 5 cwt.; driving wheels, 11 tons 10 cwt.; trailing wheels, 11 tons; total 31 tons 15 cwt. The weight available for adhesion is 22½ tons. The tender, which has the scoop for picking up water while running, weighs 25 tons. The boiler and wheels are of steel. The leading wheels are 3ft. 9in. in diameter.

It will be noticed from these dimensions how well the weight is balanced through its very even distribution among the three pairs of wheels; while the illustration appended brings out into strong relief the remarkable neatness and compactness of the general design. It may be added that the "Precedent" engines are constructed at a cost which seems extraordinarily small when compared with that of many other engines possessing no greater efficiency.

In the next few pages I shall give a number of striking instances of the splendid work done by these "wonderful little engines" under my own observation. I may remark here in passing that one of this class won the average speed record in each of the great races from London to Scotland. In the race to Edinburgh in 1888, No. 275 "Vulcan" ran from Crewe to Preston, 52 miles, in 50 minutes, and then from Preston to Carlisle, 90 miles 10 chains, in 90 minutes. The load was 76 tons. In the race to Aberdeen in 1895, No. 790 "Hardwicke" with 70½ tons, ran from Crewe to Carlisle, 141¼ miles,

No.1177 "Princess Louise" at Llanfairfechan with a down express.

in 126, 126½, or 127 minutes, according to the different timekeepers, thus averaging about 67 miles an hour, including the ascent of Shap bank, 4½ miles of 1 in 75. The loads, of course, were very light, but the average start to stop speed remains quite without parallel in this country, with loads however small, and was not equalled by any of the various classes of fine express engines which took part in these memorable "races". But I venture to think that some of my own experiences of them with heavy loads are still more remarkable.

Coming now to my own personal experiences of the work done by these 6ft. 6in. coupled engines – "Precedent" class – on the London and North Western Railway, I may remark that even my earliest acquaintance with them afforded excellent promise of the good things that were to come later.

Returning to England early in 1884, after an absence of some years, I found the number of original "Precedents," viz. 70 complete, and the locomotives themselves an established success. My initial trip behind "Hercules" No. 1105, which at the time usually ran the 12 noon Manchester Express from Euston to Rugby then timed to make the Willesden to Rugby run in 91 minutes for the 77 miles. "Hercules" did it easily in 88 min. 35 sec., easing down toward the end. The load, it is true, was only ten six-wheelers, but the work was very creditable throughout. Subsequently the same engine did this run with eight coaches in 86½ minutes, with eleven in 87, when the booked time had been quickened to 88 minutes. Returning from Rugby on the first occasion another engine of the same class, "Sir Hardman Earle," No. 890, on the up Manchester Express, ran to Willesden in

93 minutes with the enormous load of 20 coaches, weighing fully 240 tons, behind the tender. What was especially noteworthy about this performance was that it was not accomplished by extreme speed downhill. In no case did the maximum rate exceed 60 miles an hour down either down the Roade or Tring bank, while the 15¼ miles from Bletchley to Tring summit occupied only 19½ minutes. This struck me as a singularly fine achievement for so small an engine, having only 88 lbs. of tractive effort for each lb. of steam pressure on the pistons, and weighing only 32¾ tons.

Later, in 1884, "Stewart" No. 1189, with the Birmingham Express, timed to reach Bletchley in exactly one hour from Euston, with a three minute stop at Willesden, did reach Bletchley, 41¾ miles, in 46½ minutes from the latter station, and after a fresh start, ran to Northampton, 19 miles, in 21½ minutes with a bad slack over the crossing at Roade Junction. Thus the running time from Willesden to Northampton, 60¼ miles, with a midway stop and a bad slack, was only 68 minutes. This, too, was an exceptional feat in those days, although the train had not more than ten coaches.

Yet another run of what I may term the earlier "Precedent" period was that of the most widely famous member of the fraternity, "Charles Dickens," No. 955, which is renowned for having run more miles since her birth, in 1882, than any other locomotive that the world has ever seen. Up to Jan 1st, 1899, "Charles Dickens" had travelled the amazing distance of 1,718,564 miles! Her daily duty has been to run from Manchester to London by the morning express and back again by the corresponding afternoon train. This was a much harder task, so far as speed goes, in 1884 than now, as the up train was then allowed only 4¼ hours for its journey, while the run from Blisworth to Willesden – start to stop – the

No.506 "Sir Alexander Cockburn" on Bushey Troughs with up express of mixed stock. 27ft brake leading followed by arc roof centre brake and two four wheeled carriage trucks carrying vans.

allowance was but 65 minutes, the distance being 58¼ miles, an average speed of nearly 53 miles an hour being thus demanded. The trains, however, were much lighter in those days, and "Charles Dickens" accomplished the task with ease. Indeed, on the first occasion of my travelling by that train, the journey of 58¼ miles was performed in 62 minutes, or 3 minutes under time, but with a train of only seven vehicles.

In those days the timing over the Crewe – Carlisle length was very slow as compared with what existed during the last ten years. The quickest time between Crewe and Preston (51 miles) was 63 min., and between Preston and Carlisle (90¼ miles) 2 hr. 12 min. So there was not much scope for good work on that interesting section of the London and North Western, except occasionally when lost time had to be made up. In one instance, with the up Scottish Express, "Commodore" No. 478, covered the 37½ miles from Shap Summit to Lancaster (passing) in 35¾ min., attaining 74 miles an hour down the bank; the load was 13 coaches. This was smart work, but I found it rare in 1884, in what we now look on as the benighted and laggard days before the "Race to Edinburgh" had shown us what could be done with ease and safety in the way of rapid travelling.

But when it was discovered that the 51 miles from Crewe to Preston could be run in 50 min. and the 90¼ from Preston to Carlisle in 90 min., notwithstanding the Shap Bank, then the clever little "Precedents" had a clear chance of displaying their true powers. With a timing at the rate of 53 miles an hour from Carlisle to Preston, and 52.7 in the opposite direction, plenty of opportunities for fast running were afforded and were duly taken advantage of. Thus, when after another absence of several years I again returned to England at the beginning of 1893, I found most remarkable progress in respect of swift locomotion to the north of London, at any rate. Further, the "Precedents" had mostly been given new boilers with 150 or 160 lbs. of steam. I usually found the latter point reached before blowing-off occurred, and most of the Ramsbottom 6ft. 6in. coupled had been converted into "Precedents" while the 5ft. 6in. "Precursors" were undergoing conversion into tank engines and the 6ft. "Samsons" into express locomotives.

No.955 "Charles Dickens" in a shed yard. 955 regularly worked the 8.30am express from Manchester to Euston and 4pm return for 20 years covering more than two million miles – a record that has never been broken by any steam locomotive.

No.868 "Condor" approaching Bescot with a down train of mixed 6-wheel and arc roof bogie stock c1903.

I found the "Precedents" taking their turn on the best expresses and keeping time at very high booked speeds with heavy loads, while under favourable conditions they gave me instances of maximum velocities which were not surpassed by any of the "crack" single-wheelers of other lines, and indeed were very rarely equalled. In fact, in one of my earliest journeys over the Crewe to Carlisle line after my last return to England, I obtained figures which long constituted a record in my own experience. Two or three trips had been unmarred by signal checks or relaying slacks, but even so there were indications of the enhanced smartness. Twice, with the down train which leaves Euston at 10am, I noted a speed of 80 miles an hour between Penrith and Carlisle, and the distance of 17¾ miles from passing Penrith to the stop at Carlisle was done in 16¼ and 16½ min. respectively. But one of the up journeys proved in several respects most remarkable. It is true that two engines were employed from Carlisle to Crewe, but the load was fully 230 tons, exclusive of the engines and their tenders.

Starting from Carlisle two minutes late with two engines on, both of the "Precedent " class, we had done some good uphill work when we experienced our first stroke of ill-luck in a signal stop at Penrith, 22 min. 53 sec. for the 17¾ miles from start to stop, nearly all up a steep grade. Getting away again, we reached Shap Summit, 14 miles mostly 1 in 125 up, in 17¾ min., and then made a phenomenal descent of the Shap incline, the first 4½ miles of which are at 1 in 75, the last 2 miles before Tebay being run in 42 sec. each, or at the rate of 85.7 miles per hour. The next 6 miles of level and slight rise to Grayrigg were got over in 5¾ min. and then came another swift descent; the speed down Grayrigg Bank – which averages 1 in 130 for 15 miles – steadily increasing until 82 miles per hour was touched as Milnthorpe was neared. But then came another mishap. The Milnthorpe home signal said "Stop!" and this we had to do, much to my disgust, as there was a good chance of the Shap maximum being again reached before we lost the help of the long falling gradient. However there was no help for it; but when we got away again we had no further check before we stopped at Preston. The time for the 37¾ miles from Penrith to Milnthorpe, start to stop, including the 14 miles ascent of Shap was 38 min. 33 sec.; and that from Milnthorpe start to Preston stop, 34½ miles, including the climb from Lancaster to Galgate, was 34 min. 56 sec.

An analysis of this trip gives some very remarkable figures. The entire journey of 90 miles 10 chains from Carlisle to Preston occupied exactly 98 min., to a second. But out of this total we were standing 1 min. 38 sec. at Penrith and Milnthorpe respectively. Thus the actual time in motion was only 96 min. 22 sec. This allows nothing for the loss by two stops. If this loss, carefully ascertained, be deducted, it leaves the net time of only 90½ min., a sufficiently remarkable achievement when the gradients are taken into consideration. But our feats were not yet at an end. Leaving Preston we ran to Crewe, 52 miles, in 56 min. 2 sec., actual travelling time with two intermediate stops and two bad slacks by signals! Deducting these losses, the net time from Preston to Crewe was 49½ min., and from Carlisle to Crewe, 141¼, 140 min. Comparatively few smarter performances have ever come under my notice.

From Crewe we had only one engine of the same type, "Cromwell" No. 1531, but our load was reduced to about 210 tons, still a highly respectable weight to be hauled by one engine at such a speed. Indeed from the technical viewpoint of locomotive work, the Crewe-London length was even more praiseworthy than the other. After climbing the 10½ miles of 1 in 177, 1 in 250, and 1 in 330, to the Whitmore summit in 15 min. 28 sec., and passing Stafford 24½ miles in 28 min. 35 sec. from the start. We were making good progress when another adverse signal brought us to a dead stand at Elmhurst Crossing, 43 min. 10 sec. from Crewe, the distance being 39¼ miles. After a stand of 3 min. 4 sec. we obtained "road clear" again and ran the remaining 36¼ miles to the regular stop at Rugby in 40 min. 34 sec.; the actual running time from Crewe, 75½ miles, being thus 83 min. 44 sec. and the net time 81 min. The following length of 77 miles from Rugby to the Willesden stop was done in exactly 83½ min., the engine having eased down after Tring, as the train, notwithstanding all these delays, was before its time. Euston was reached finally at 6.42, or three minutes early, in spite of a start from Carlisle two minutes late, five extra stops – amounting to 6½ min. – and 9½ stay overtime at the regular stopping places, while the larger half of the journey was run with only one engine, and the loss of time through signal delays, exclusive of the actual dead stand, was fully 17 min.

On another occasion two of these engines, "Chillington" No. 2188, and "S.R. Graves" No. 1141, ran with 14 coaches from Preston to Crewe in 53 min. 4 sec., and "Marathon" No. 517, unaided, took a 15 coach train from Bletchley to Willesden, 41¾ miles, in 44 min. 23 sec.; while "Snowdon" No. 2191, with 15 coaches, ran from Rugby to Willesden in 87 min., the load in each of the latter two cases being fully 220 tons. Also "Buffalo" No. 2181, took 14 coaches from Rugby to Crewe, 75½ miles in 83 min. 58 sec., with an intermediate slack; and "Fairbairn" No. 870, ran the Dining-Car train of 13 coaches from Nuneaton to Willesden, 91¼ miles, in

No.867 "Disraeli" on Shrewsbury shed.

103 min. 10 sec. easing down after Tring to avoid a too early arrival.

I now come to more recent achievements which approach the marvellous, when the size and nominal power of the engines are considered. As an illustration of fast work with a light load on a course largely uphill, I may quote the performance of "Mercury" No. 749, which with 112 tons ran the first 58½ miles from Euston in 60 minutes, ascending the 14¼ miles, averaging 1 in 330, from Watford to Tring in 14 min. 28 sec., passing Tring Summit 31¾ miles, in 35 min. 17 sec. from the start; Bletchley 46¾ miles, in 48 min. 58 sec., easing down at Roade, but nevertheless, passing Rugby, 82½ miles, in 88½ minutes, Tamworth, 110 miles, in 1 hr. 59 min. 59 sec., and reaching Crewe, 158 miles, without a stop in 2 hr. 57 min. 35 sec. The same engine on the Irish Mail did equally good work in hauling a huge load of 245 tons from Euston to Rugby in 101½ minutes, and "Lazonby" No. 512, in taking an even heavier one of 264 tons from Rugby to Willesden in 92 min.

Just a week after the run of "Mercury" from Euston to Crewe, which I described just now, "Eamont" No.394, accomplished one even more meritorious, the load being 195 tons; in spite of which the speed never fell below 53 miles an hour up the bank from Watford to Tring, that station being passed in 37½ minutes from Euston; Bletchley in 51½ minutes; Rugby in 90 min. 11 sec.; Tamworth, 1 hr. 59 min. 15 sec.;

No.861 "Amazon" at Crewe Works, one of a line of newly painted engines. Gleaming coal tank No.1004 stands alongside.

Stafford, 2 hr. 35 min. 4 sec.; while Crewe was reached with that substantial load in 2 hr. 55 min. 4 sec. Clearly this was a very noteworthy piece of work.

More recently "Caractacus" No. 477, with 170 tons, did the journey, London – Crewe in 2 hr. 54 min. 24 sec. passing Tring in 37 min. 14 sec.; Bletchley, 50 min. 39 sec.; Rugby, 94 min. 8 sec.; Tamworth, 1 hr. 59 min. 28 sec.; Stafford, 2 hr. 24 min. 24 sec.

With loads of 112 to 120 tons "Hardwicke" No. 790 and "Queen" No. 1213, each passed Wigan from Crewe, 36 miles in 36 minutes, as timed by myself. "Dagmar" No.1668 took a train weighing 187 tons from Crewe to Rugby, start to stop, in 80 min. 30 sec. for the 75½ miles, in spite of 1 min. 50 sec. being lost by a bad relaying slack, which left the net time 78 min. 40 sec. The final length of 51 miles from Stafford to the stop in Rugby was covered in 49 min. 36 sec. The same journey was continued by "Disraeli" No. 867 from Rugby to Willesden in 82 min. 9 sec.

I now come to three cases which in some respects stand alone. They comprise one of the best start to stop runs I have ever had on a British line, and two instances of the highest speed I have ever recorded, with the single exception of my 90 miles an hour record for three quarters of a mile with a Midland single-wheeler.

Starting from Penrith 50 minutes late, a 6ft. 6in. coupled and a 'rebuilt' 6ft. coupled, actually made up 16½ minutes on the run to Preston, covering the 72½ miles in 69 min. 30 secs. from start to stop, with a load of 194 tons. The heavy ascent of the 14 miles to Shap Summit was mounted in 17½ minutes, and then the remaining distance of 58½ miles to Preston was run in 52 minutes to a dead stop. Of this total one length of 35 miles was done in 29 min. 53 sec. or at an average rate of 70.3 miles an hour and maxima of 81.8 and

85.7 miles an hour were attained at two different points. Such work is manifestly most exceptional.

In the other two cases still greater speeds were reached, although, owing to checks, the total journeys did not show such high averages. The 11.50pm from Euston, which weighed 304 tons, had been delayed by signal stops, and, making up time subsequently, was run by two 6ft. 6in. coupled engines of the "Precedent" class, from Shap Summit (passing at 15 miles an hour) to the stop at Carlisle, 31½ miles, in 28 min. 12 sec., with slacks past Eamont Junction and Penrith curve. From the last named station the run of nearly 18 miles to the Carlisle stop was done in 15 min. 10 sec., two miles being run in 41 seconds each, or at a rate of 87.9 miles an hour, an absolute record in all my experience up to that date.

Strangely enough that record was broken on the very next day, and by one of the same pair of engines going in the opposite direction. The load was 211 tons, and a pilot (of the "Samson" class) was taken from Carlisle to Shap Summit, the 31½ miles, mostly up – 1 in 125 and 1 in 132 – being climbed in 37 min. 36 sec. from start to stop. Dropping the pilot the train engine ran the next 31¼ miles to a signal slack at Carnforth in 28 min. 26 sec. and attained a maximum speed of 88.2 miles an hour, several successive miles being done in 10.2 seconds each. That, with the one exception noted above, is the highest speed which I have ever recorded, or of which I have any authentic record. It may interest those who regard such velocities as the peculiar prerogative of single-wheelers and large-wheeled engines to note that these rates of 88.2 and 87.9 respectively were attained by coupled engines with wheels only 6ft. 6in. in diameter.

But here I must stop for the present although my list is by no means exhausted. I think it will be admitted that I have justified my claim to regard these 6ft. 6in. coupled "Precedents" of Mr Webb's design and construction as emphatically "wonderful little engines."

Chapter 9
The Grand Junction Railway
by Gilbert J. Stoker
Late of the London and North Western Railway

Of the railways in operation at the commencement of 1836 many were for the transport of minerals only, whilst others, such as the Leicester and Swannington, condescended to allow some exceedingly uncomfortable vehicles for passengers to be attached to the tail of their trains of coal and stone wagons. This line was 16 miles long, and carried about 400 passengers per week, and is probably a favourable specimen of the extent to which the travelling public availed themselves of the accommodation afforded by such railways.

Mr Thomas Cook, the originator of public excursion trains, relates that he made his first railway journey between two of its stations. The Newcastle and Carlisle Railway, 64 miles long, at this time had only 17 miles completed for traffic; the remaining portion was not ready for use until later that year. The Liverpool and Manchester, and the group of smaller lines connected with it, formed practically the only railways on which the passenger was considered of equal importance with the goods.

Following the first proposal for a railway between Liverpool and Manchester in 1822, a scheme was got out in 1823 for one from Birkenhead to Birmingham and another from Birmingham to London. The time was not ripe, however, for such extensive projects. The public had still to be educated as to the advantages of railways, and the teachers being almost as deficient in practical knowledge of the subject as those whom they tried to instruct, the process was rather slow. How dimly even the most far-seeing of projectors realised the possibilities of the system they were recommending may be gathered from the prospectus of the proposed line from Birkenhead (Liverpool) to Birmingham issued in 1824.

After expressing the hope that by means of either stationary or locomotive steam engines, goods would be transported at the rate of eight miles, and passengers at twelve miles an hour, it proceeds, "but as no experiments have been made on a large scale, we will not pledge ourselves to this." Considering the large amount of capital required, and the unknown risk enveloped, these proposals did not offer much inducement to speculators to encourage, or to Parliament to sanction, a scheme put forward in such a timid and hesitating manner. The work of education went on, however, the perception of all classes of society being quickened by the inconvenience felt in consequence of the uncertainty and tardiness of the means of communication. This was very serious with passengers but was perhaps felt more severely by the general public with regard to the transport of goods, which was slow and laborious to a degree hardly to be realised by the present generation.

The quickest time, under the most favourable circumstances, for goods from Birmingham to Liverpool by "fly boat" was 66 to 70 hours; the average time 4½ days, and even this ample allowance was frequently exceeded. A gentleman writes, in November 1827: "Saw the Duke of Bridgewater's agent (at Liverpool), who says that from the quantity of grain to go into Staffordshire he cannot take any for myself or others for fourteen days. I have just sent some away that had waited for weeks." We can readily see what an effect such delays might have, in the days before free trade, through causing a scarcity, and raising the price of the most absolute necessities of life, and how far-reaching would be their influence.

Motives of humanity and mercy towards overworked and overtaxed beasts of burden were urged by powerful pens, but it is to be feared that if the introduction of railways depended upon considerations such as these, it would have remained a long time in abeyance. When, however, it was pointed out that Birmingham Canal Shares which cost £140 stood at £2,800, and that other canals were almost as prosperous, a more tender chord was touched. Men of capital saw sweet visions of their £50 railway shares becoming equally valuable. "Why should they not," suggests a writer in the *Birmingham Chronicle*, in December 1824, "become worth £1,500?" "Why not?" echoed the man with money lying idle in the bank, or earning only a modest 5 per cent, and straightway he prepared his bill, and knocked at the door of Parliament. He was there in 1824, in 1826, and in 1830; but the men with canal shares worth twenty times their nominal value, and all the other vested interests, were too much for him, and each time succeeded in keeping the door closed.

In 1830 the directors thought that if they converted their big bill into two little ones, they might perhaps slip through. Accordingly the line was divided into two sections, with a Board of Directors for each, at Liverpool and Birmingham, and bills submitted, one for a line from Liverpool to Chorlton, near Whitmore, and another for one from Birmingham to Chorlton.

The Bill for the Birmingham section was thrown out; the other passed the first reading, but was lost owing to the dissolution of Parliament in consequence of the rejection of the Reform Bill. No doubt there were reasons, but it is not easy to see why it should be supposed that two Bills could get through more readily than one, nor why one should be accepted and the other rejected; they seem to be the necessary complement of each other. If the Liverpool Bill had not been lost, by accident as it were, the Directors would have found themselves with a line ending in a field, far from any town of importance. The whole affair seems absurd, but it throws a little sidelight on the manner in which railway matters were dealt with in those days.

It was perhaps fortunate for the Company that their early efforts were not successful, because when they applied again they had a much better scheme to propose than any previously submitted. In the former Bills the line was to start from a point opposite Liverpool, on the Cheshire side of the Mersey, a most inconvenient arrangement for Liverpool, as, of course, all traffic would have to be ferried across the river; this route was chosen to serve Chester and pick up traffic from Wales and Ireland. Probably also the directors were influenced by the fact that many of the stage coaches and wagons took that route. A short line, about 4¾ miles in length, had been constructed by a separate company from Warrington to Newton, where it joined the Liverpool and Manchester Railway, and at a meeting held in Liverpool on 25th January 1832, it was proposed to abandon the Chester route, re-unite the two former companies, and purchase this short line and extend it to Birmingham. The advantages of this plan, by which a considerable saving would be effected in the length of the line to be constructed, and the inconvenience of crossing the Mersey at Liverpool avoided, were so obvious that it at once recommended itself to all concerned and was adopted. The new railway was to be called the "Grand Junction," because it was designed to join the Liverpool and Manchester, and London and Birmingham lines, and bring into direct railway communication the four greatest towns, and the most important manufacturing and trading communities, in the Kingdom.

The usual elaborate figures were got out as to the traffic through the districts affected, and a dividend of 14 per cent was confidently predicted. This estimate was higher than the experience of the Liverpool and Manchester Company warranted; their dividend had been just declared at the rate of 4½ per cent, for the past half year. It was not, however, so wide of the mark as some we have heard of lately in connection, say, with Cycle Companies. In 1841, 12 per cent was paid by the Grand Junction, and from that time until the Company ceased to be a separate corporation a dividend of 10 per cent was uniformly declared every year. At the same time the meeting was held the £100 shares in the local railways stood as follows:-

Liverpool and Manchester	£205
Bolton and Leigh	£105
Warrington and Newton	£108
Stockton and Darlington	£215

It was calculated that the number of passengers by coach between Birmingham and Liverpool and Manchester was about 220,000 per annum, including through and intermediate journeys. That there was large passenger traffic is evident from the fact that one firm alone, "P. Bretherton & Co," advertised ten coaches daily from Liverpool to Birmingham and the South Wales and West. Fares to London, 42s inside, 21s outside; to Birmingham, 21s inside, 10s.6d outside; to Bristol, 50s inside, 25s outside. In a note on the Bill the public are requested to observe that "these coaches go direct – the same guard and coach throughout – thus avoiding the unpleasantness of crossing the river, which unavoidably takes place in travelling via Chester."

An advertisement by another proprietor announces the "Albion" coach for London, via Chester, Whitchurch, Birmingham, Daventry, etc, performing the journey in 22 hours. A traveller leaving Liverpool by this coach, say on Monday morning at 7.45 – the advertised time – would, if punctual, arrive in London at 5.45 on Tuesday morning. Passengers had the option of sleeping in Birmingham and going on next day. These coaches travelled at the rate of about nine miles an hour. A much higher speed was attained by "Express" messengers conveying important news. We probably learn the utmost that could be done in this way from what was accomplished in connection with the passing of the Reform Bill on the morning of the 14th April 1832. The news was at once dispatched by Mr Wilmer's "Express," and reached his shop in Liverpool at 10.15 on the same night, having travelled 202 miles in 14 hours. Incidentally it may be mentioned that the streets were crowded with people waiting for the expresses, and on the result being announced a scene of the wildest excitement ensued. The next message arrived at Mr Arnold's shop at 11pm. It is not stated whether the messengers made use of any portion of the Liverpool and Manchester line, but it may, we think, be assumed that they made the journey throughout by road, via Chester and Birkenhead. On the same day (Saturday) Mr W.H. Smith's express, bearing supplies of all the morning papers for his country agents, left London at 11am, reached Birmingham in time for the Liverpool mail, and Mr Arnold, newspaper agent, received his papers in Liverpool on Sunday morning. The House of Lords adjourned at 7am and the newspapers must have been printed and ready for dispatch before 11 o'clock, which, considering the appliances at that period, seems pretty expeditious work.

We may note the progress that was being made even before railways came into use, by comparing the times just mentioned with that occupied in transporting a party of soldiers a quarter of a century earlier. In December, 1806, at a time of excitement in Ireland, troops for Dublin were dispatched by canal from London to Liverpool, and it was remarked as something special that the journey would occupy only seven days, as against 14 by road, this wonderful celerity being achieved by having relays of Irish horses in readiness at all the stations.

At the meeting in Liverpool already referred to, a committee composed of 12 gentlemen from Liverpool and 12 from Birmingham was appointed to manage the affairs of the Grand Junction Railway Company. Eventually the whole direction fell into the hands of the Liverpool men; either from want of interest on the part of the Birmingham representatives, or because the knowledge of railway matters possessed by the members who had been connected with the Liverpool and Manchester Railway enabled them to take the lead. The necessary levels, and other particulars, were got out by Mr Locke, under the direction of Mr George Stephenson for the Warrington section, and by Mr Rastrick for the Birmingham portion, and an Act applied for. And "soon a wonder came to light" : the Bill which had been repeatedly applied for and persistently refused during the previous 12 years, when now brought forward (with some important modifications, certainly), was passed practically without opposition, and received the Royal assent on 6th May 1833. It is said that although as a matter of prudence counsel was retained, not a single brief was delivered. This is perhaps the only instance of the kind on record in connection with a railway of such magnitude, and will explain the smallness of the expense of gaining the Act, which amounted to only £22,157. It cost the previous companies £26,225 to *lose* their bills.

The Grand Junction Railway was fortunate in other ways. The Warrington and Newton line, which formed just the link they wanted, was acquired on easy terms. Its share capital consisted of 518 shares of £100 each, fully paid up. On the amalgamation a corresponding number of Grand Junction shares were created, and issued to the Warrington Company in exchange for their shares; a loan of £40,000 raised by the latter Company had also to be taken over.

The new line, which (exclusive of the Warrington and Newton) was 78 miles long, passed through a country involving few engineering difficulties or expensive engineering works. The cost of making it was only at the rate of £18,846 per mile, a remarkably low figure compared with that of the other lines. In another important respect they were favoured; their contracts for iron were placed when the price was very low whilst the London and Birmingham Railway, about the same time, were hesitating as to the best form of rail to adopt; prices went up £4 per ton, causing an additional expense of upwards of £250,000, and their deliberations after all ended in the adoption of parallel rails of the same make as those of the Grand Junction – the only difference being that the latter were 62 lbs to the yard, whilst the London and Birmingham were 64 lbs.

There was but little trouble with unexpected quicksands and slippery clay, such as vexed the souls of the engineers on the sister line – at Kilsby tunnel, the London cuttings, and other places. A sort of Chat Moss on a very small scale was met at Penkridge; to form an embankment large quantities of material were tipped daily, and disappeared during the night. The engineers were puzzled to know what became of it, until the mystery was solved by the surface of a field near the work rising into a huge mound, not unlike in shape, as one writer puts it, an enormous mushroom; it was evident the "tip" had run away by some channel and got under the field, or the pressure on the adjacent soil had caused the upheaval.

Except a very short one, scarcely longer than an ordinary bridge, near Preston Brook, the only tunnel is at Wednesfield, near Wolverhampton. It is 200 yards long, and passes underneath a canal and a public highway through good solid material, including a thin seam of coal from which the poorer inhabitants helped themselves freely whilst the excavation was being made.

The most important work on the route is a viaduct over the river Weaver near Dutton, which is 1,400 feet long, and 28 feet wide, and consists of 20 arches, each 63 feet span, and 65 feet in height above the level of the water. The completion of the bridge was made an occasion of great rejoicing. The last keystone was laid by Mr Heyworth in the presence of a party of his fellow Directors, the Chief Engineer and other officers, and the workmen. Mr Heyworth congratulated those connected with the work on the fact that in the two years during which it was in progress, there was no accident causing loss of life or limb; in the evening a grand display of fireworks terminated the proceedings.

Vale Royal Viaduct is a somewhat extensive work, notable for an *unfulfilled* prediction "that when the rocks near Warrington should visit Vale Royal the sun of the Cholmondeley family would set." The stone of which the viaduct is built came from the High Cliff quarry near Warrington, which caused the good people on the neighbouring estate of Lord Delamere, who is of the Cholmondeley family, very ominous thoughts; when what appeared to be the fulfilment of the first part of the prophecy took place, wiseacres shook their heads.

"But what gave rise to no little surprise,
Nobody seemed one penny the worse!"

The heaviest earthworks in cuttings and embankments are probably near Madeley on the borders of Staffordshire and Cheshire, where there is a long incline rising almost from Crewe to Whitmore, in the course of which, between Basford and Madeley, occurs the steepest gradient of the line; in a distance of about six miles it varies from 1 in 260 to 1 in 180. This would not be considered very formidable for one of Mr Webb's big engines, but it was evidently with a sense of relief that the directors mentioned in their report, soon after the opening of the line, that "the engines can surmount Madeley summit, with a train of more than 200 passengers, and their luggage (a load far exceeding the average), without any material diminution of speed." Even now drivers tell you that "Madeley Bank" is a "stiff bit of road." On reaching the summit near Whitmore, 390 feet above the level of the sea, the line is flat for about half a mile, and then falls with a comparatively easy descent until within about three miles of Stafford. The highest elevation on the line, 440 feet above sea level, is attained at Wednesfield, near Wolverhampton.

With the view of mitigating the effect of an engine or vehicle running off the rails on high embankments, a small bank or ledge of earth about a foot high was run along the edge at each side, in which it was expected the wheels would become embedded instead of going over and down the bank. Between Penkridge and Spread Eagle (or Gailey as the station is now called) an ingenious use was made of the spare material taken from cuttings. The railway runs for about three quarters of a mile alongside the high road, and the spoil was so disposed between the rail and the road as to form a screen to prevent horses being frightened by the engines.

According to the original plans the stations for the lines from London and Liverpool were to be in Broad Street, Birmingham; subsequently, to avoid the heavy work and tunnels this would entail, it was arranged to erect them at Curzon Street, where the ground was on a lower level and the approaches much easier. To get to Curzon Street from Vauxhall, the valley of the Reay had to be spanned by what is called the Lawley Street Viaduct. At the time this was considered a very magnificent structure, and no doubt it looked striking and imposing before the graceful curve formed by its twenty-eight massive arches was hidden from view by buildings.

A few years ago when the line was widened, another viaduct was erected on the top of the original one, which bears the superincumbent weight with perfect safety, from which we may conclude that the "jerry builder" had no hand in its construction. With the happy knack railwaymen have of applying descriptive epithets, the new work, which rises very sharply at one end to descend as rapidly at the other, has been dubbed the "switchback."

The Grand Junction directors were more mindful of the comfort of their passengers than other early railway companies; their carriages were far in advance of those of the Liverpool and Manchester, and were much superior to corresponding vehicles at first placed on most of the lines opened later, which it might be supposed would have profited from their example. Even the second-class carriages, the lowest priced at the time, were covered in and closed at the sides, and some pains were taken to give all the coaches a handsome appearance outside.

By an Act passed in 1837 a company was incorporated to construct a railway from Manchester to Birmingham through the Potteries, but opposition and lack of support caused the scheme to be curtailed, and a shorter line was made, to join the Grand Junction at Crewe. A through carriage of a rather peculiar pattern was run once a day from Manchester to Liverpool via Crewe. In the middle was a covered compartment for those who were willing to pay for the luxury, and at each end an open compartment, unprotected from wind or weather, for more economical passengers.

Before proceeding to the opening of the new line we will notice an opposition scheme started in 1833. In that year a prospectus was issued for making a granite road from London to Birmingham, and from Birmingham to Holyhead and Liverpool. The name of the company was to be "The London, Holyhead, and Liverpool Steam Coach and Road Company," the capital £350,000, in £20 shares. Consulting Engineer, Thomas Telford, President of the Institute of Civil Engineers; Acting Engineer, John MacNeil.

The line was to consist of two rows of pavement, composed of stones six or eight feet long and one or two feet square, laid endways along each side of the road. This would form a track along which, whether hilly or level, it was anticipated engines would easily travel at the rate of 20 miles an hour, including stoppages. "The road being on a level with the long stones the carriages could easily quit the stones for any momentary necessity." For repairs it would only be necessary to turn the blocks over, so as to present a new side to the surface and after another lapse in time do the same, until all the four sides were worn in their turn. After this the "parallelopipedons" might be submitted to the mason's chisel. The rate of speed was "to be limited only by due regard to the safety of the passengers."

If the scheme had been put forward by an inexperienced amateur, it might be excused on the ground of want of knowledge, but that it should be supported by engineers of such eminence as Telford and MacNeil is very surprising. The practice of laying down stone wheel tracks was not new; roads laid in this manner had been in use for ages; what we find difficult to understand is that their obvious unsuitability for being worked by steam power, under the conditions described, were not at once perceived by practical men such as these. The reason perhaps is not far to seek, both were famous road-makers, and it was another exemplification of the old adage, "there is nothing like leather." In connection with this proposal a sort of trial trip to show what could be done by road carriages was made in Col. Dance's steam coach on the 1st November 1833. It was intended to proceed from London to Birmingham, but the engine was found not to be powerful enough for the load, and only got as far as Stony Stratford. The engine, with the coach and passengers, weighed six tons, average rate of travelling seven and a half miles an hour. Telford and MacNeil were of the party, and a report of the proceedings was signed by them.

As the Lawley Street Viaduct was still incomplete when the other portions of the Grand Junction Railway were finished, a temporary station was erected at Duddeston close to some public gardens called Vauxhall, after the famous grounds in London, and by this name it was generally known; this was the first station erected in Birmingham; it was here the first railway trains were seen in the town.

The line was opened on Tuesday, July 4th 1837. No official notice was taken of the event by the public authorities or the directors. Even the local newspapers had but slight references to it. We are indebted to a London paper for particulars.

Birmingham Vauxhall Station was the temporary terminus of the GJR in 1837 until transferred to Curzon Street in 1839 to link up with the London & Birmingham Railway.

The account brings the scene so vividly before us that it is worth transcribing:

"Birmingham, Wednesday, July 5th, 1837.

"At an early hour the town was in a state of great commotion and pleasurable excitement, owing to it being the day appointed for the general opening of the Grand Junction Railway from Birmingham to Liverpool and Manchester. Soon after five o'clock the streets leading in the direction of Vauxhall, where the Company's temporary station is situated, were crowded with persons of all ranks anxious to witness the first public travelling on this important line of railway communication.

"It was remarked, however, as somewhat singular, that there was, even throughout the day, a comparatively small attendance of the leading merchants and manufacturers of Birmingham, which has been attributed to none of the latter having been placed on the direction of the Grand Junction Railway. Indeed the Directors of the latter are entirely limited to bankers and merchants of Liverpool.

"By six o'clock yesterday morning the bridge which crosses the railway at its entrance to the station yard, and indeed every eminence that commanded the least view of the line, was covered with persons awaiting the starting of the carriages. But it was not in Birmingham, or its immediate vicinity only, that the public curiosity was unusually excited. The embankment of the several excavations, and even the valley

Birmingham Curzon Street c1859. This Jones & Potts 4-2-0 loco was ordered for the Chester and Holyhead Railway in 1847 but delivered new to the LNWR Southern Division in 1848 as No.189. Curzon Street, the original London & Birmingham terminus opened in 1838 and the Grand Junction arrived alongside in 1839 after building an extension from Vauxhall over a viaduct. The London and Birmingham Railway part of the station is on the left (Derby & Gloucester bays to the right). The former Grand Junction station is on the far right. It was used by passenger trains from 1838 to 1854 when they were transferred to New Street.

through which the railway alternately 'wends its way' between Birmingham and Wolverhampton, were literally covered with dense masses of admiring spectators. Indeed, in the neighbourhood of Bescot Bridge, James' Bridge, and Willenhale, contiguous to the iron and coal district, the crowd was, if possible, more formidable than in the suburbs of Birmingham.

"Upon entering the station yard about half past six o'clock, we were, however, much struck with the thinness of the company within the company's premises. It presented a striking contrast to the station yard on Olive Mount, at the opening of the Liverpool and Manchester Railway in 1830. It was evident, indeed, that no exertions had been made to give *éclat* to the proceedings of the day; there were no bands of music, no profuse display of banners, no attendance of distinguished visitors – in fact, within the precincts of the station there was scarcely anything to distinguish it from an ordinary day of business. The only display we observed was a small flag attached to the first carriage of the train, on which was emblazoned in small characters, with the Royal Arms, the letters 'W.R.' 'A.R.' and the words, 'The True Reformer.'

"At seven o'clock precisely the bell rang, when the opening train, preceded by the 'Wildfire' engine, commenced moving. The train consisted of eight carriages, all of the first class, and bearing the following names: The Triumph, the Greyhound, the Swallow, the Liverpool and Birmingham Mail, the Celerity, the Umpire, the Statesman, and the Birmingham and Manchester Mail. The train started slowly, but upon emerging from the yard speedily burst off at a rapid pace. To those who for the first time witnessed such a scene it was peculiarly exciting, and the immense multitude, as far as the eye could reach, gave expression to their admiration by loud and long continued huzzas, and the waving of hats and handkerchiefs.

"Having in some degree escaped the multitudes, power was laid on, and from Perry Bar in Newton Road the speed could not be less than 35 to 40 miles in the hour. The succession of trains which followed throughout the day served to keep up the popular excitement, and the crowd, instead of diminishing in number, hourly increased. At half past eight o'clock a train of the second class set out amidst similar demonstrations of admiration to those called forth by the first. The chief object of attention which now engaged the public attention was the arrival of the first train from Liverpool. The Directors in their published statement of arrivals and departures announced that this train would leave Liverpool at half past six in the morning, and arrive in Birmingham at five minutes past eleven, that is in four hours and a half. It was to be expected, however, that owing to the crowds which would assemble at the various stopping places, some interruptions would occur, and the arrival of the train at Birmingham be delayed beyond the appointed hour. In this respect the general expectation was in a small degree eventually confirmed.

At about twenty-seven minutes past eleven the cheering at a distance announced the approach of an arrival, and at exactly half past eleven o'clock the first train from Liverpool entered the station yard in Birmingham amidst the most vociferous applause. It was difficult to say which party appeared the most delighted – the astounded travellers, or the multitudinous wonder-struck company by whom they were received. Throughout the entire journey the opening train from Liverpool experienced the uninterrupted enjoyment of 'wind and weather.' It consisted of the Hibernia, the Chanticleer, the Patriot, the Delight, the Delamere, the Columbus, and the Birmingham and Manchester Mail.

"The train left the stations at Manchester and Liverpool at half past six. …. including stoppages, the train performed the journey at the rate of at least 20 miles per hour; being, as might be expected, about half an hour late on account of the interruptions incidental to the day.

The starting of the several trains which followed from Birmingham was remarkably regular, but owing to cause to which we have already alluded, the arrival of those from Liverpool was not equally well timed. The mixed train which ought to have arrived at two o'clock did not arrive until four. This delay was attributed chiefly to the obstreperous intrusion of the work people in the iron and coal districts. From Wolverhampton to James' Bridge, the carriages were literally besieged by the multitude, and the only way to avoid accident was to proceed slowly and surely, without regard to the published time of arrival in Birmingham. The first return train from Liverpool arrived at seven o'clock, and was loudly cheered upon its entrance into the station yard.

"So far the proceedings of the day passed off joyfully and without any mixture of alloy, but the non-arrival of the mixed train, which ought to have come in at ten o'clock, very soon gave rise to very considerable apprehension. The last first class return train was advertised to arrive in Birmingham at five minutes past eleven, but the hours passed away, and midnight succeeded, and still no tidings of it had been received. At three in the morning, however, both trains arrived, the delay having been occasioned by the breakage of one of the tubes of the engine by which the mixed train was worked."

The first train from Birmingham, 7am which was due in Liverpool at 11.30, did not arrive there until nearly 1 o'clock. Some delay was caused through the train having to stop for the luggage to be removed from the roof of several of the coaches and placed on others, in consequence of the weakness of the springs allowing the carriages to bump against the axles. A portion of the bottoms of some of the carriages was completely worn away by the friction.

A writer, who travelled from Birmingham to Wolverhampton in October 1837, describing the operation of booking says:

"I entered a moderate-sized room, shabbily fitted up with a few shelves and a deal counter, like a shop. Upon this counter, spread out, were a number of large open books, the pages of each being of different colour to the others. Each page contained a number of printed forms, with blank spaces to be filled up in writing. On applying to the clerk in attendance, I had to give my name and address, which he wrote in two places on the blue page of one of the books; he then took the money, tore out a ticket, some 4 inches by 3, and left a counterpart in the book. I was then shown to my seat in the train, and on inspecting at my leisure, the document I was favoured with, I found that in consideration of a sum of money therein mentioned, and in consideration, further, of my having impliedly undertaken to comply with certain rules and regulations, the Company granted me a pass in a first-class carriage to Wolverhampton."

The railway had not at this time, three months after opening, driven all the other conveyances off the road, for he mentions that he returned from Wolverhampton in the evening on an omnibus.

EARLY PASSENGER TICKETS – some examples from 1842

An ordinary return ticket issued in 1842 is not numbered, and has no date except the day of the week. The date appears to have been omitted from motives of economy, in order that the tickets might, after they were collected and checked, be returned to the stations from which they were issued, and used again on the corresponding day of the following week. The fare was printed at the foot. The practice of showing the fare on the ticket gradually fell into disuse, and was only recently revived after an interval of many years, by Act of Parliament. A very troublesome Act it is to the companies, and a cause of considerable expense. A slight alteration of fares may make it necessary to reprint many thousands of tickets, and printing these, and withdrawing the existing stock, involves an amount of labour only to be realised by those who have to carry out the work. It is understood that the object of the regulation was to protect the public against rapacious booking clerks, and no doubt the system is useful in this respect. Many clerks express a wish that something could be introduced to work the other way, and protect them against the public. It is singular, and not very flattering to the human nature, how readily the majority of passengers will detect an error against themselves, and how slow they are to perceive one made in their favour. Possibly railways share the depravity said by some cynical humourists to be inherent in umbrellas and horses, which tends to weaken the moral sense in certain people, otherwise of the most unimpeachable integrity.

An excursion ticket from the same time is extremely interesting. It is generally understood that the first publicly advertised excursion was run at the instance of Mr Thomas Cook on the 5th July, 1841. The idea must have "caught on" pretty quickly, as we have here, only twelve months later, an important excursion, evidently as much in the ordinary course as any of the thousand and one trips advertised during the season at the present time.

Soon after the opening of the line a singular difficulty arose. The Grand Junction Company wished to arrange trains at certain hours on Sunday, but this was objected to by the Liverpool and Manchester Company, which had a by-law prohibiting the running of trains over their line between 10 o'clock in the morning and 4 o'clock in the afternoon on that day. It so happened that the trains interfered with carried the mails, and on being appealed to, the Secretary of the Post Office put his foot down, and "declined being a party to an arrangement (for the suspension of any of the trains on that day) that will so vitally affect the public interest." Although it may as in this instance sometimes be carried too far, the Liverpool and Manchester Directors were actuated by a sound principle, and it is to the honour of the great company by which they succeeded that it has, whilst affording all necessary accommodation for the ordinary requirements of the public, adhered to the same lines thus preserving as far as possible the inestimable boon of a Sunday rest to its staff, and setting an example which has had a salutary and far-reaching effect.

The Grand Junction Railway never made any great display in the world; it passed very quietly through Parliament, the work of construction was carried out so silently that one writer says it seemed to have been forgotten for three years, and on completion it was opened without display or formality. Subsequently it went on in the same unobtrusive manner, subscribing additional capital to schemes that seemed for its advantage, such as £250,000 towards the Lancaster and Carlisle Railway, and absorbing little lines here and there in the vicinity. At the beginning it amalgamated with the Warrington and Newton Line, and subsequently, in 1840, the Chester and Crewe, and in 1845, the Bolton and Leigh, the Liverpool and Manchester, and the Kenyon and Leigh. Meanwhile its bigger neighbour, the London and Birmingham, with much flourish of trumpets, was progressing rapidly, and by construction, and amalgamation, and leasing, was enlarging its territory, and increasing its capital, until at length occurred what was foreseen from the first to be inevitable. On the 16th

Trevithick 'Crewe Goods' 2-4-0 No.3032 shown later at Buxton c1875 with Webb chimney. The first batch of these locos were built by the GJR at Crewe.

2-2-2 No.49 "Columbine" was one of the first locomotives to be built by the Grand Junction Railway in their newly opened Crewe Works in 1845. Designed by Alexander Allan it had 6ft driving wheels, weighed 18 tons and had a 120psi boiler pressure. The two outside cylinders were 15in x 20in. Renumbered to 1868 by the LNWR in 1872 it was later modified and used by the Engineer at Bangor (North Wales) from 1877 to 1902. The "Columbine" design was widely copied in the UK and abroad during the 1850s/60s. Seen here on display in the London Science Museum.

July 1846, a grand amalgamation took place. By Act of Parliament, 9&10 Vict. c.204, the London and Birmingham, the Grand Junction (of which the Liverpool and Manchester already formed a part) and the Manchester and Birmingham were united into one great Company, henceforth to be known as the "London and North Western Railway." The capital of the new company was declared by the Act to be £17,242,310, contributed as under the respective companies:- London and Birmingham £8,653,750; Grand Junction £5,788,560; Manchester and Birmingham £2,800,000.

How the London and North Western has been built up, step by step, since its incorporation, fifty-two years ago, until it has become the greatest railway company in the kingdom, it is unnecessary to enter upon here. Although ours is but a sober, common-place history, we will take example from the novelists, who usually conclude when their most interesting characters change their names. Having brought the Grand Junction Railway to the point where it starts afresh, under a new title, we will follow its fortunes no further for the present.

Grand Junction Railway 2-2-2 No.10 "Dragon" with a down train at a level crossing near Penkridge (between Wolverhampton and Stafford) about 1840. The two leading coaches are named "Antelope" and "Despatch". Also note a stage coach loaded on a flat wagon and train staff on outside seats at roof level. Luggage was regularly carried on the roof in the early days. From a painting by Gerald Broom GRA.

Chapter 10
Crewe – The Result of Railway Enterprise
by Gilbert J. Stoker
Late of the London and North Western Railway

The busy town of Crewe may be considered the heart of the London and North Western system. Whosoever would travel any considerable distance thereon must pass through Crewe. London and Birmingham in the southern parts, Wales and Ireland westerly, and Liverpool, Manchester, Leeds, and Scotland northwards are the extremities, between which trains are constantly running to and from this central point, as the blood circulates through the body. How many out of the millions who travel by these trains, have any knowledge or conception of the place, beyond a vague and general idea that here the company's engines are made? The town being situated on a dead level, no glimpse of it is obtained by a passing traveller. When approaching from the south he sees on either hand only an expanse of converging railway tracks, and sidings ornamented by strings of goods and coal wagons; at the northern end the view is much the same, varied, but scarcely improved, by the blank walls of the works.

In the station, after the first announcement on arrival of the train, the last place one hears of is Crewe; the talk of the officials is of the Liverpool "portion," the Holyhead "portion," the North "portion," and so on. It is fortunate that in most cases through carriages are provided, thus obviating the necessity for changing, otherwise the bewildered passenger would find it difficult to assure himself of which *portion* he formed a small atom. And yet few places are more full of interest to those who reflect that here is to be seen one of the most striking results of the growth of the railway system, and the finest example this country can show of what may be effected by the wise and beneficent administration of a great industrial community. Especially interesting is the present time when so many railway companies are ordering locomotives from America, to know what has been done on the most important line in the kingdom, and what is to be seen may well reassure any who have fears for the future of our mechanical and scientific progress. There is no danger of the London and North Western Railway having to call in foreign aid. Not only have they met every requirement of an immensely increased traffic up to the present, but their mechanical resources are such that they can without difficulty supply any demand likely to arise in the future.

From the point of view of the ordinary tourist, the traveller does not lose much by not seeing Crewe. If he is in search of fine streets or handsome buildings, or of monuments of art, ancient or modern, he will not find them here. What he will find is a prosperous town consisting mainly of well laid out streets of clean, respectable-looking artizans' dwellings, supplied with all things necessary for health and comfort.

In this article we propose to give a brief account of the origin and progress of the town, reserving for a future occasion a description of the works.

Somewhere about 70 years ago a solicitor, residing in Nantwich, purchased for £35 per acre,

Crewe Station North End looking south. In the siding are three TPO vans, a horse box and two carriage trucks. Lord Crewe's private siding is on the left with three Madeley Coal & Iron wagons. The main signal gantry has three slotted post signals whilst the smaller signal on the left has an old slotted post and signals with rings. Crewe Arms Hotel is on the left of the station platforms.

Crewe – The Result of Railway Enterprise • 133

Crewe North Junction Box in 1883.

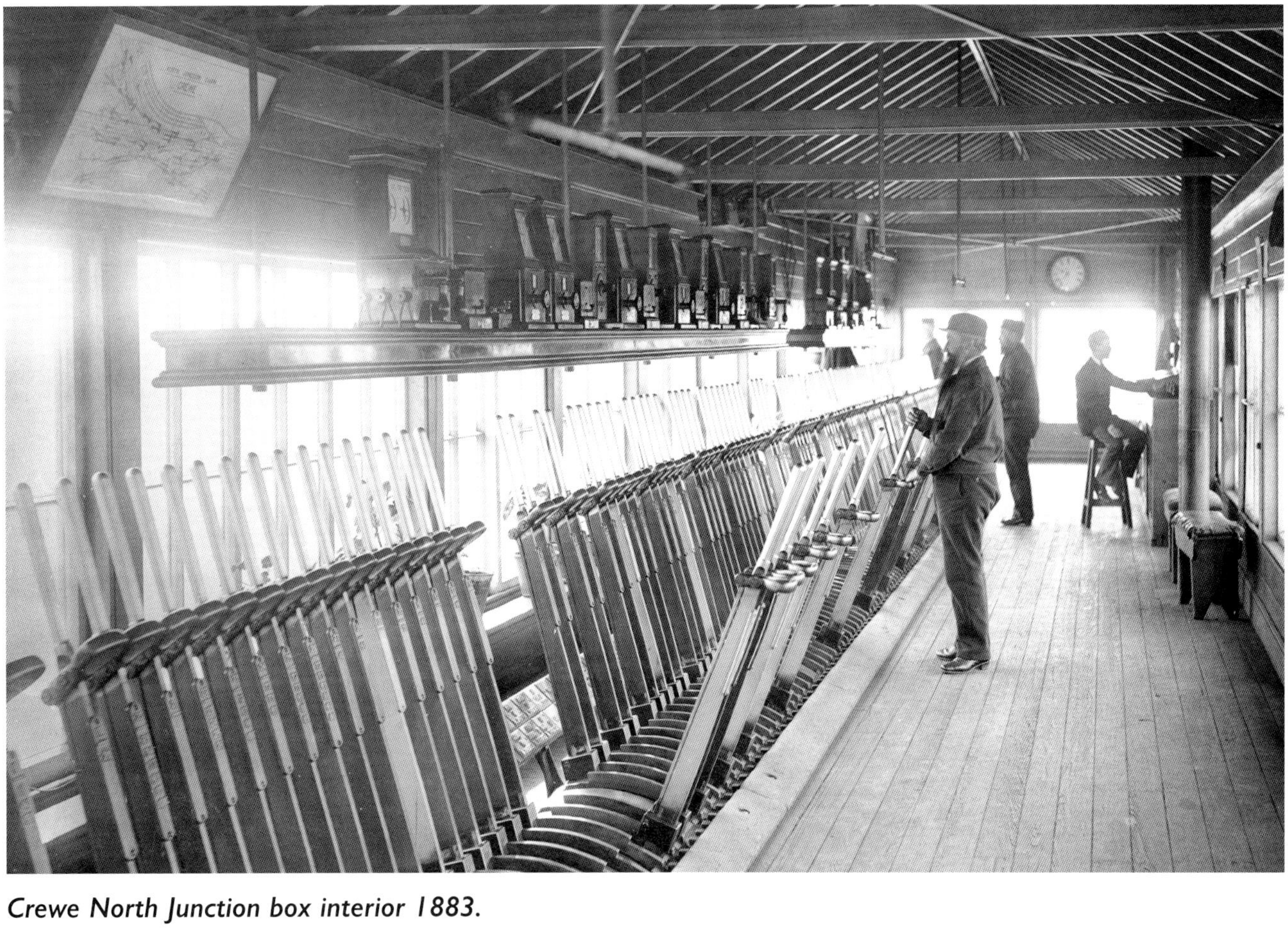

Crewe North Junction box interior 1883.

a piece of land 60 acres in extent, called the Oak Farm, situated near the village of Coppenhall in Cheshire. It did not appear to be a very desirable acquisition, the soil was poor and marshy, the farmhouse old and dilapidated, and the nearest market town (Nantwich) four miles distant. The society in the neighbourhood was not particularly lively, there were no houses very near – the whole township only contained 27, inhabited by 140 persons, amongst whom the man who could write his own name, especially if it could be read after he had written it, was accounted a learned individual. The lawyer's friends were amazed that so good a man should have made so bad a bargain, and each strongly advised him to pass it on to some other friend as soon as possible. He took no heed of their advice – possibly from professional prejudice, as no charge was made for it – but as opportunity offered purchased additional land, until the estate was enlarged to about 200 Cheshire acres – not the degenerate statute acre of the present time – in those days the people of Cheshire had spacious ideas, their acre contained 10,240 square yards. Probably the astute lawyer knew more of what was going on in the great world, and could see further ahead than the friends who were so concerned about his rash speculations. There was talk in the air of railways running through the county to connect the manufacturing districts of the North with London and the Midlands.

Before long a portion of the land was required for the Grand Junction from Birmingham to Liverpool; then another slice for the line from Manchester; and yet another for the one from Chester, which all united on the Oak Farm. Later, when the Grand Junction Railway commenced to build their works at the convenient centre formed by the junction of the three lines, and a town began to spring up on the erstwhile silent and solitary moorland, the property acquired a value never dreamt of even by the far-seeing and fortunate purchaser of the lucky farm. The memory of the farm still lingers in the names of "Oak Street" and the "Oak Inn"; but it is as Crewe the town is known, and has become famous throughout the world. The works and the chief part of the town are in the parish of Coppenhall.

The name Crewe was taken from that of a small township in the adjacent parish of Barthomley, which in 1837 contained a population of about 20* and was probably given to distinguish it from the one, long since discontinued, at the village of Coppenhall, and out of compliment to Lord Crewe, whose seat, Crewe Hall, is in the neighbourhood. The station was built at the bridge carrying the turnpike road from Nantwich to Sandbach over the railway, and was designed for the accommodation of these towns, and of other places in the district. It was a station of the first class – i.e. one at which all trains stopped, and had an engine shed in which *one* spare engine was kept. Lord Crewe built a handsome hotel, a good service of omnibuses and cars was established with the neighbouring towns and Crewe started in life on quite a respectable scale.

In 1840 the Grand Junction amalgamated with the Chester and Crewe, and in August 1842 the so-called Manchester and Birmingham line was opened, and also joined the Grand Junction at Crewe, the nearest point to Birmingham it ever attained; for some years it had a separate station, with its own staff, consisting of one man, named Frost, who was something more than "three single gentlemen rolled into one," being stationmaster, clerk, porter, pointsman, and general utility man. In a rail–fence between the two stations there was a gate through which passed a single line crossing connecting the two railways. It was Mr Frost's duty on arrival of a

---

* The township of Crewe was severed from the parish of Barthomley in 1857, and assigned as a district to a new church, to which Lord Crewe presented the rectorial tithes, value £180 per annum, and in 1877 the small tithes, value £30 per annum, were given by Mr Dunscombe, the rector of Barthomley. In old chronicles the name is spelt Creu, Criwa, and Crue.

train to open the gate and work the points for the engine to run round and back a through carriage, which ran from Manchester to Chester, into the Grand Junction station. When he turned the first pair of points he inserted a wedge to keep them in position; then jumped on the engine and went to the other end to work the points there. It is not surprising that with such clumsy arrangements the poor fellow eventually met with an accident. One day attempting to jump on the engine step, he slipped and got under the wheels, with the result that his toes were cut off.

There were only two lines of rails through the main line station. The stationmaster's house stood on what is now the centre of the present station. The contrast between the state of things now and as they existed then is sufficiently striking, but will be still greater when the extensions in progress, which will make Crewe one of the largest stations for passengers and goods in the kingdom, are completed. The first stationmaster, Captain Winby, was a retired sea captain, bluff and hearty, who brought to his new duties the sense of discipline acquired in the rough school in which he had been brought up, and was endowed with a native humour, the recollection of which still keeps his memory green amongst some old travellers and officials.

The great event in the history of Crewe occurred six years after the opening of the railway. In the summer of 1843 the Grand Junction Company removed their works for the construction and repair of engines, carriages, and goods wagons from Edge Hill, near Liverpool, to Crewe. This is the era from which the creation of the town may be dated. Before the "flitting" took place, care was taken to have everything ready in the new premises. In addition to the buildings for the works, houses for the workmen had to be erected. This was not left to private speculation; the

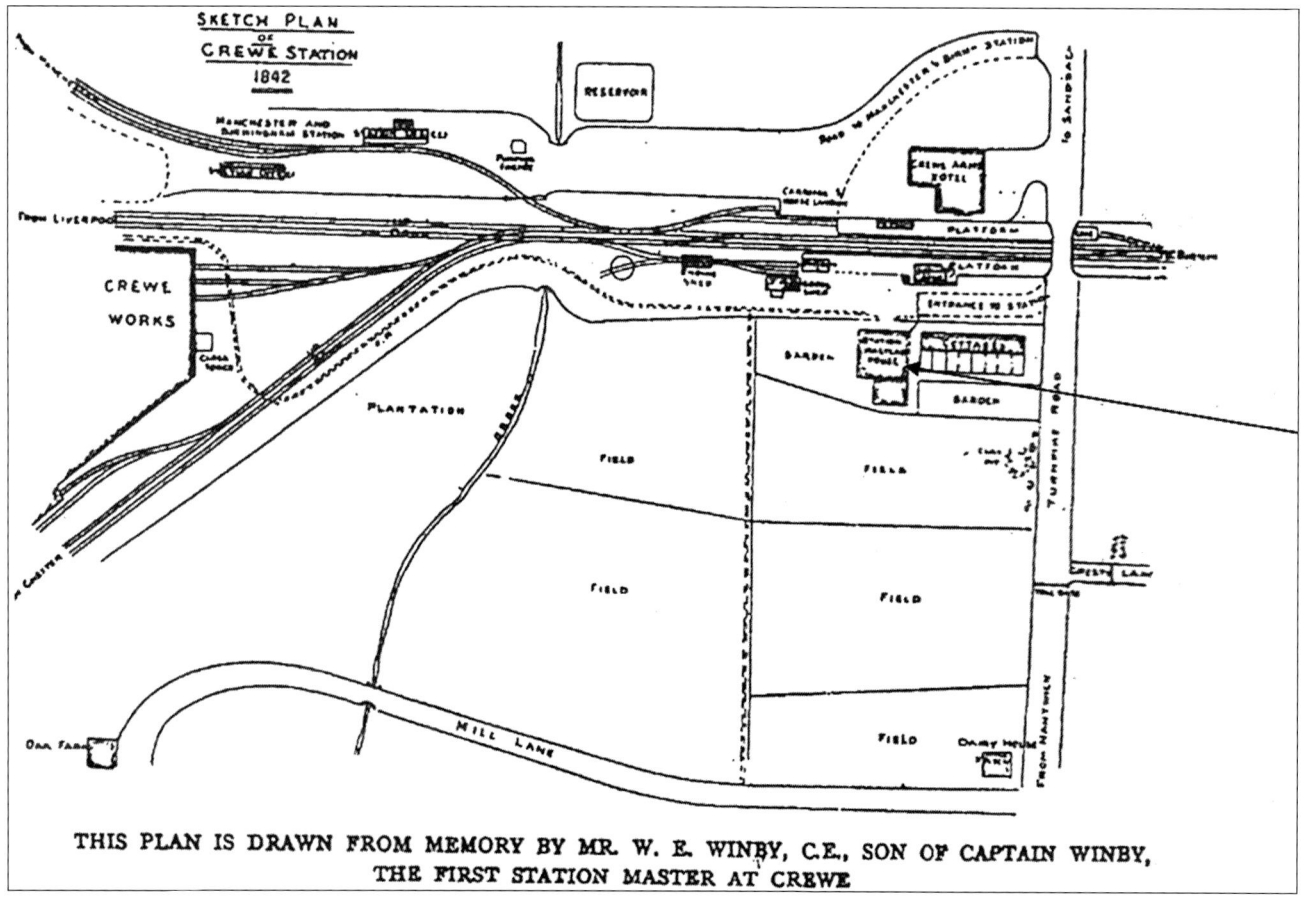

Crewe station plan 1842 drawn by son of the Stationmaster.

Company purchased thirty acres of land for the works, and fifty on which to erect houses.

The land taken was far in excess of the immediate requirements, but the directors considered it desirable to make ample provision for the future. How far their anticipations fell short of the reality may be judged from the fact that the works, which at first stood on 3½ acres of land, are today a mile and a half long, and occupy an area of 116 acres, of which 36 (more than three times the space on which the Crystal Palace stands) are covered in. The 50 acres taken for houses was soon used up. In 1843 the number of men employed was 161; in 1846 it had risen to 600, and inhabitants of the town to two thousand. In the next three years the population doubled; in the ten years following it doubled again. At the present time it is over 30,000 of whom 8,000 are employed in the works, and some 2,000 more at the Steam Shed, in the Permanent Way Department, and in the Passenger and Goods Departments. It will be seen from this that the railway absorbs practically the whole of the working population. The only other manufactory in the place is indirectly connected with it.

In 1865 Mr Compton, of London, established a works for making up uniform clothing for railwaymen; this is very useful in giving employment to some of the female members of the community, there being but little work suitable for the superior sex in the construction of locomotives. The expansion of the town and works would have been still more marked were it not that in 1853 the Wagon Department was removed to Earlestown, and in 1859 the Carriage Department was transferred to Saltley, Birmingham. A few years later the locomotive establishment at Wolverton was drafted to Crewe, and the Carriage Department concentrated at Wolverton. In the Carriage and Wagon Department over 5,000 men are employed.

The houses were built by Messrs. Samuel and James Holme of Liverpool, from the designs of Mr Cunningham. They were, of course, of different types to suit the positions in the service of those for whom they were intended – villas for the higher officials; for the mechanics, separate houses, each accommodating four families; for the labourers, cottages on a smaller scale. Every house had a garden, the advantage of which is apparent even now, when the conditions have changed considerably, in the amount of air and space secured. The company have built additional cottages from time to time, and now possess about 900. The mechanics were paid 3s.6d per week, the labourers 2s; water was to be had free from pumps in the street; for gas, 2d per week was paid for each burner.

Schools were provided, at which the rising generation were educated at a charge of 2d per week for each child. A surgeon (Mr Edwards) was appointed, who agreed to physic the community for the modest charge of 3d per week for each family, in addition to a small subsidy from the Company. It was noted as a proof of the wisdom of this arrangement, that for some time after his appointment there were no deaths, although previously there had been several. Perhaps the erection of baths, for the use of which the charge was very small, had something to do with the improved health standard.

For a time a service was held in the works by a clergyman paid by the Directors. A sum of £1,000 was voted for the erection of a church, but this proved insufficient; part of the required amount was made up from a very appropriate source. Some of the shareholders declined to accept the portion of their dividends earned by Sunday working, and about £500 standing to their credit in the books was handed over to the church fund, together with £391, balance of the Director's fees which remained unpaid in February 1843.

Having thus paid for the physical, moral, and religious wants of their people, the next thing was to meet the intellectual requirements. Accordingly an institute was built, containing a library and reading-rooms. Classes in connection were established for instruction in various branches of practical knowledge. From this institution, it is said, more Whitworth scholarships have been gained than from any other of a similar kind in the country, which speaks well for the efficiency of the teaching, and the intelligence and application of the students. It also shows that the scientific training of our engineers is not neglected to such an extent as some of our critics would have us believe.

A rather original arrangement was adopted for the government of the new settlement. Twenty names were submitted to the Directors, who selected twelve, from whom nine were to be elected; this done, the Directors added three. For public purposes the district was under the jurisdiction of the Nantwich Rural Sanitary Authority and the Nantwich Highway board. In 1860 it was felt that the town had grown sufficiently to be able to stand alone and govern itself, and in that year the Crewe Local Board was formed. It was not an extravagant body. The clerk, surveyor, and Treasurer received £35 per annum between them. A determined effort was made to secure a Sanitary Inspector for £8 per annum, but the Police Sergeant, who was considered most suitable for the post, was firm, as became a man in his position, and rather than lose his services the Board sadly "sprung" another £2, raising the pay to the magnificent sum of £10 per annum. The Board did good work in its day and generation; when in 1877 the town arrived at the dignity of incorporation, with a real live Mayor, Aldermen, and town Councillors, its condition was such as to do no discredit to the body by which it had been governed for 18 years. The first Mayor, Dr Atkinson, was elected July 9th, 1877.

Municipal matters are somewhat simplified by some remains of paternal government still to be traced. By arrangement with the corporation the railway supplies the town with water and gas. In the early days water was drawn from a brook near the station and purified by being passed through filtering beds; for many years past it had been obtained from Whitmore, where it is pumped from the red sandstone, and is of such purity that no filtering is required – it contains only 5 grains per gallon of inorganic impurity, and is entirely free from organic matter. Where such water is to be had temperance should flourish. Whitmore being 580 feet higher than Crewe, the water descends by gravitation through pipes laid along the railway.

The loyalty of the people is evinced by the splendid Volunteer (Railway) Engineer corps, six hundred strong, a body of men whose training, skill, and fine physique entitle them to a place amongst the most effective of our citizen soldiers. The uniform always has charm for the ladies, and no doubt many bright eyes grow brighter as they rest on their own particular Tom or Harry marching with his comrades to the inspiring strains of the regimental band to the deadly drill hall, or preparing to serve his country through all the rigours of a week in camp at midsummer.

There is also a well organised Fire Brigade, composed of men connected with the works, which has the perhaps unique advantage of having the residence of each member in electrical communication with one of the offices, so that in case of an alarm of fire no time is lost in calling them into action.

In dealing with Crewe it is impossible to avoid reference to the works. In the words of one who wrote of Crewe a generation ago, "There is only one town, one great town that has been conceived for the locomotive, wet nursed for the locomotive, breeched for the locomotive, birched for the locomotive, apprenticed for the locomotive." Every improvement in the works, every stage advanced, means a corresponding improvement and advance in the town. Had the managers been ordinary men, content to go with the stream and obtain what they required from outside sources, neither works nor town would have stood in the position they occupy today.

The first manager, Mr F. Trevithick, was the son of the man who first showed the possibilities of the locomotive engine, and himself produced engines which in their day were considered models of the most perfect type of locomotive. The writer well remembers the most affectionate way in which drivers nearly half a century ago spoke of Trevithick's engines, and expatiated on their excellencies, much as a groom dwells on the *points* of a favourite horse. Fifty years after the opening of the works it was written of him that "he was a man much admired and esteemed in Crewe, and his memory will always be revered by its inhabitants."

Mr Trevithick was succeeded by Mr Ramsbottom, by whom several changes were introduced, which had a most important bearing on the progress of the town. The first steel rails were rolled at Crewe in 1861, and exhibited at the Great Exhibition in 1862. The first locomotive boiler, made of Bessemer steel, was built in Crewe in 1863; in 1864 the Bessemer steel works were erected, and in consequence a large number of additional workmen employed. In 1868 Siemens-Martin furnaces for the conversion of steel were constructed.

A short time ago an article went the rounds of the papers in which it was claimed that the alleged superiority of American works arises to a great extent from the early and general adaption of steel to purposes for which iron was generally used. As a matter of fact, Crewe was

Crewe Works Wheel Lathe.

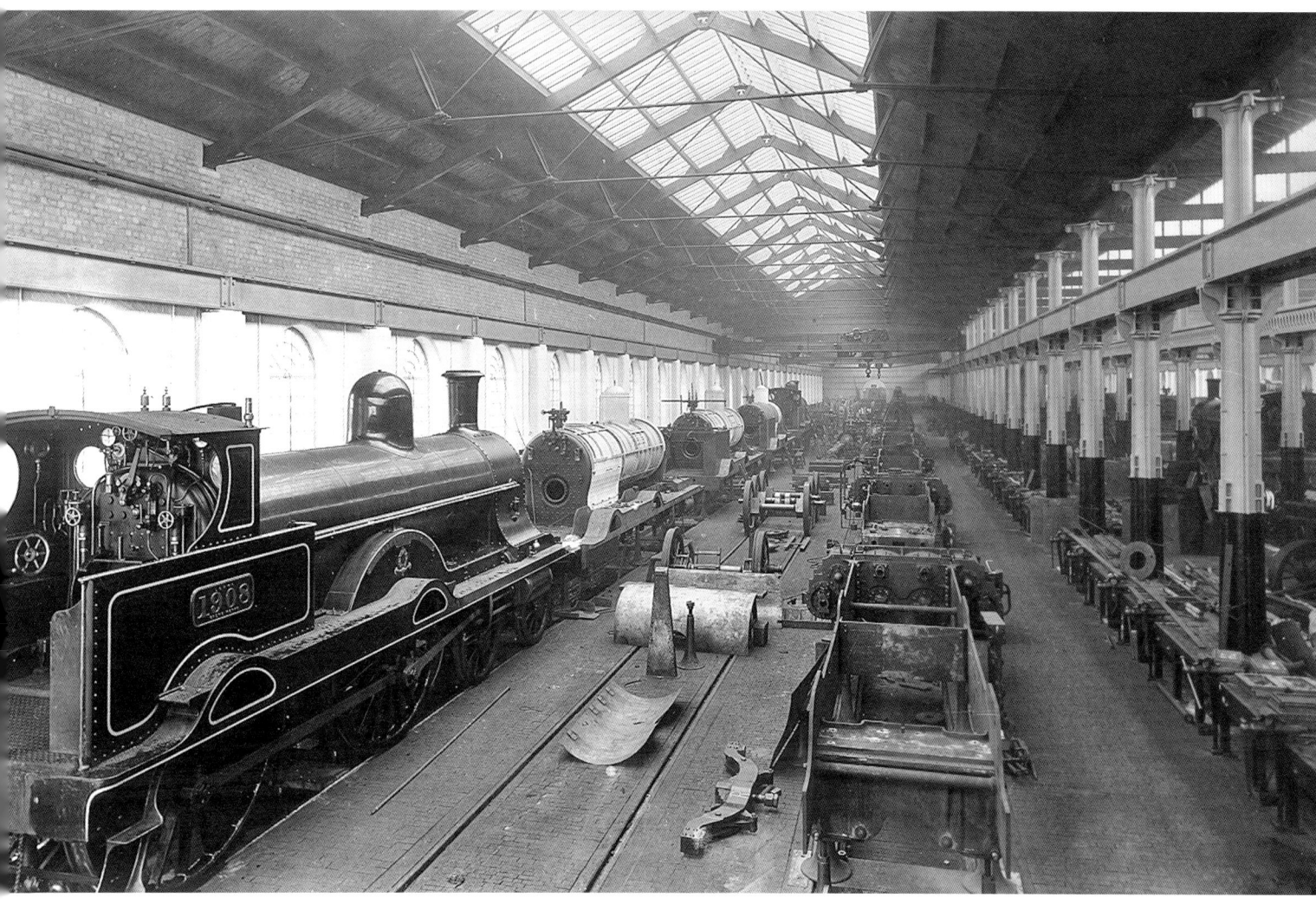

Crewe Works No.8 Erecting Shop in 1899 with several Jubilee Class 4-cylinder compounds under construction. On the left is No.1908 "Royal George" (which had already been completed).

the first place to take up the making of steel on a manufacturing scale, both by the Bessemer and Siemens-Martin processes. So fully was the encouragement given to the invention by the management at Crewe recognised by those most interested, that when the freedom of the City of London was presented to Sir Henry Bessemer in 1882, the gold casket in which it was enclosed had on the cover a vignette in *repoussé* work of a London and North Western locomotive, entirely constructed of steel and standing on steel rails.

Mr F.W. Webb, who succeeded Mr Ramsbottom on his retirement from the service of the Company in 1871, has increased the use of steel to such an extent, that it has practically superseded iron for every purpose to which it can be applied. In 1874 the Company commenced making their own signals on a system devised by Mr Webb, causing another large accession of workpeople. The making of many other articles has been introduced from time to time, until the works have become a great assemblage of workshops for the manufacture of almost every article required on a railway. We have alluded to these matters merely to show the effect the broad and progressive policy of the management has had on the fortunes of the town, the interests of which are indissolubly united with those of the works.

In 1868 Sir Cusack Roney wrote respecting Mr Ramsbottom:-

"At the head of the mighty establishment at Crewe ... is one man, who if it had been in Egypt, with works not a quarter the size and not half so ably carried out, would have been at least a Bey, or more probably a Pacha; in Austria a Count of the Holy Empire; in any other country in the world, except England, with crosses and decorations, the ribbons of which would easily make a charming bonnet of existing dimensions. But in England, the earnest, persevering, never tiring, JOHN RAMSBOTTOM is – John Ramsbottom."

If for John Ramsbottom we substitute the name of F.W. Webb, who is at the head of establishments mightier than Ramsbottom ever knew, not only in extent, but in that scientific importance, which a writer in the *Engineer* says, Crewe Works possess to a degree much greater than can be measured by their mere size. Many royal and distinguished persons have visited Crewe, and expressed their admiration at what they have seen, but the British Government is apparently as slow today to recognise the incalculable services to the nation of the great captains of industry as was the case 30 years ago. The importance of services rendered by Crewe who can estimate? From it have gone forth (and will no doubt continue to go) ideas and inventions that have enriched the world. It has trained and sent out men who have carried with them the knowledge, skill, and the enthusiasm that have given English engineers the foremost place amongst the great army of workers by whom the cause of science and civilisation has advanced in all quarters of the earth.

The town received an unexpected visit from the Queen in 1848. On her return from Balmoral on the 28th September 1848, she embarked at Aberdeen, in her yacht the "Victoria and Albert," with the intention of proceeding by sea to London, but the weather was so bad, owing to a strong wind, with drizzling, misty rain, and a high sea running, that it was not considered safe to take the voyage. The party, consisting of the Queen, Prince Albert, the Princess Royal, and the Prince of Wales, with their attendants, proceeded by road to Perth, whence they took a train at 9.30 on Saturday morning. A telegraph message was sent to the stationmaster at Crewe, with instructions to engage the hotel, and a special messenger was despatched in advance to make the necessary preparations. Lord Crewe being away from home, the party could not be entertained at Crewe Hall. They arrived at 7pm on Saturday evening in the midst of a furious downpour of rain, and were made as comfortable as possible at the Crewe Arms Hotel, Her Majesty and the Prince taking everything with the utmost good humour, and appearing much amused at the whole affair. Notwithstanding the fatiguing journey on the previous day, they left Crewe by special train at 6 o'clock on Sunday morning, arriving at Euston at 10.10am – not a bad run in the days when troughs and "pick-ups" were unknown.

It must not be thought that life at Crewe is "all work and no play." We have to record several events of what may be termed social importance, which shows that on occasion the inhabitants can take their pleasure, not "sadly," as the libellous old chronicler hath it, but with a gusto and abandon which indicates that a little joviality is not at all foreign to them, but is very much in their way indeed. In December, 1843, before the machinery was put in, a grand ball was given by the Directors to the work-people, their wives, sweethearts, and friends in one of the new shops, by way of housewarming. The dining-room, in which about 500 sat down to dinner, was about 250 feet in length by 100 feet in breadth. At 5 o'clock the company retired to the tea-room, where about 1,200 sat down to tea. The refreshment tables occupied only half the room, the remaining space being left for dancing. Although 1,500 were present at times, there was ample room for all. Several Directors and their families joined in the dance. Outside there was a grand display of fireworks. A full account of the proceedings appeared in the *Illustrated London News*. The writer concluded "All appeared to be delighted, and the whole fete will long be remembered, and doubtless, stand recorded as one of the first remarkable events in the annals of the juvenile city of Crewe."

On the 24th May 1876, the completion of the two thousandth engine was made an occasion of much rejoicing, but the greatest demonstration ever witnessed in Crewe was on the completion of the three thousandth engine in 1887, which happily synchronised with the celebration of two other events of great importance – the jubilee of Her Majesty and the completion of the fiftieth year of the existence of the Grand Junction Railway.

The Railway Company and the town rose to the occasion. Mr F.W. Webb, the Chief Mechanical Engineer and Locomotive Superintendent of the London and North Western Railway, was Mayor, and in his dual capacity was able to take a leading part in all the arrangements. The proceedings commenced on the 21st June. In order to be in touch with the country in general the town was decorated on that day and various sports and amusements provided, including a free dinner given by the Mayor to about 700 poor people. A fund was raised from which £302 2s was given to the Imperial Institute and £277 to the Local Celebration Fund.

The great doings were on Monday the 4th July, the date on which the Grand Junction Railway was opened fifty years before. Some preliminary skirmishing took place on the previous Saturday when the town was crowded with people attracted by the Alexandra club sports, and a desire to witness the decorations to which finishing touches were being given. On Sunday the Mayor and Corporation, with the Volunteer Corps and the Fire Brigade, attended Divine service at St. Paul's Church. On Monday the town was *en fete*. So profuse were the decorations, that the local

Problem Class No.1428 "Eleanor" at Crewe south end.

historian declared it would be utterly impossible to describe them. We will not attempt to do so. It requires the genius of a Macaulay to resuscitate the ashes of a dead enthusiasm, or to revive the glories of a show that has passed.

The official proceedings commenced with the presentation, by the Mayor, of the freedom of the Borough to Sir Richard Moon, the Chairman of the Company, on whom a baronetcy had been conferred at the distribution of the Jubilee honours. The scroll was enclosed in a handsome gold casket, designed by Mr J. Blackhurst, of Crewe. The officials and invited guests then proceeded by a circuitous route, in order to view the decorations, to the Drawing Office at the works, where luncheon was served to a company numbering about 400.

Amongst the many noble and distinguished guests, Sir Richard Moon specially referred to the presence amongst them of Mr W. Patchett, who was appointed Goods Agent at Crewe when the station was first opened, 50 years before. Whilst the luncheon was being partaken of, a grand procession of trades, friendly societies, children, etc, was traversing the streets, and was joined at the Town Hall by the Chairman and directors of the London and North Western Railway and their guests. From there they proceeded to the new park presented to the town by the Railway Company in commemoration of the day which Sir Richard Moon, on behalf of the Railway Company, dedicated to the service of the inhabitants of the town. The Mayor having accepted the park, and returned thanks, the Bishop of Chester offered a dedicatory prayer, a hymn was sung, and the town Clerk presented an address to Sir Richard Moon from the Mayor and Corporation. Along with the address the Mayor handed him a gold medal, struck from the same die as a large number of medals distributed amongst the employees of the Company. Sir Richard Moon having made a suitable reply, nine of the oldest workmen were presented to him, with each of whom he cordially shook hands. A poem, composed by Mr David Atkinson, a fitter, was then read by the Mayor.

After a few more remarks from Sir Richard Moon, Mr Webb introduced Mr James Middleton, who, he explained, was the first man to drive an engine from Liverpool to Crewe, to announce the birth of the Prince of Wales. This brought the dedicatory service to a close. We have dwelt rather long – possibly our readers may think too long – on these proceedings, because they bring out in sharp relief the contrast between the lonely little township of 1837 and the energetic, world-famous borough of 1887. A contrast well expressed in the rugged, virile lines of Mr Atkinson, already referred to, of which we give a few stanzas:-

Clay to the right of them,
Clay to the left of them,
Clay fore and aft of them;
'Twas a dirty and gross land –
Obstacles everywhere,
Trouble, and toil and care,
Still they did persevere-
For they had come to build
Engines - Three Thousand!

High rose the curling smoke
Quick went the hammer stroke,
Which the long silence broke,
Over the bleak land;
And on the twentieth day,
October 'forty-three,'
'Tamerlane' cleared the way,
First of Three Thousand!

Now to the right of them,
Now to the left of them,
Now to the front of them,
All o'er the townland;
Bands play triumphantly,
Flags waving gallantly,
From near and far we see
Enormous crowds gather
To join in the 'Jubilee'-
And hail the completion of
Engine – Three Thousand!

Crewe South Junction. 2pm Euston to Glasgow Corridor Express pulled by an 'Alfred the Great' compound. A 3-cylinder compound coal engine is departing from sidings on the right. New bracket signals on the main line and slotted post signals on North Stafford Junction on the left.

The park on its completion was formally opened by HRH the Duke of Cambridge on 9th June 1888. A clock tower erected by the subscriptions of the staff on the line forms a conspicuous ornament in the grounds.

Although Crewe is the creation of the London and North Western Railway, and in the early stage of its existence was necessarily dependent on the Company for most of the conveniences of life, it must not be thought that the inhabitants were "dry-nursed" and "coddled" until they lost their self-reliance and ceased to depend on themselves in public matters. That was not the spirit the Company wished to cultivate; at the beginning they entrusted a certain amount of self-government to the people, and as the town grew the leading strings were withdrawn, and this broad and enlightened policy has borne fruit in the development of an independent, self-respecting community, holding their own opinions without interference, and at the same time appreciating fully, and gladly acknowledging, the benefits conferred on them by the Railway. This feeling is embodied in a sentence in the address presented to Sir Richard Moon: "The Board of Directors of the London and North Western Company have always shown a generous desire to promote and foster the well-being of the inhabitants of this town." Speaking a little later, Sir Richard Moon said: "he wanted them to take a pride in their town and park and Company, and to maintain a right and independent character in everything they did."

Greater Britain Class No.525 "Princess May" at south end of Crewe with safety valves blowing.

Crewe North Junction c1892. View from the "spider" bridge of train running off the Chester line hauled by a Dreadnought class loco. (? Irish Mail).

Webb 2-4-0 No.1045 "Whitworth" at Crewe. 90 Whitworth class locos were built between 1889 and 1896.

There is an admirable hospital for the sick and injured. For those who are disposed to be saving and thrifty there is no lack of friendly and other societies prepared to take care of their spare cash, and to turn it to the best advantage. Ably-conducted newspapers dispense news and opinions, and direct the people in the way they should go in political and municipal matters. In short, as the house agents say, the place is fully supplied with "all modern improvements."

The head offices of the Permanent Way Department, of which Mr H. Footner is Chief Engineer, are at Crewe; also the offices of Mr Sharpe, the District Goods Manager – altogether it is about the "railwayest" place in the world.

When the town was incorporated, someone suggested as a suitable moto, "In the van," but it was felt that, from a railway point of view, this was liable to misconstruction, railwaymen usually thinking of the van as being in the rear. By a happy inspiration, the converse, "Never Behind," was hit upon.

We will close with the wish that works and Town live up to their motto, and like their locomotives, be always in front. To again quote friend Atkinson-

> "May they live long and see
>   Increased prosperity."

Chapter 11

To Manchester via Ashbourne

The London and North Western New Line from Parsley Hay to Ashbourne

by D.T. Timins, B.A.

The iron horse is for ever seeking out new country, penetrating fresh districts, and giving access to hitherto inaccessible spots. Each fresh advance excites corresponding opposition on the part of conservative landowners and all those selfish people who would fain exclude the many from a participation in the pleasures of the few. But notwithstanding the efforts of the anti-progressivists, that which makes for the ultimate good of the greatest number invariably triumphs, and hence comes about that each year witnesses the opening up of some new beauty spot in the British Isles, the gift of some new lung to England's gasping cities of toil.

Of such a nature is the London and North Western Railway Company's new line from Parsley Hay to Ashbourne, though no doubt it will eventually prove to be a blessing to the company as well as the public, for it will provide the former with an alternative route between Manchester and London, which may one day be of great utility.

Derbyshire has hitherto been the special preserve of the Midland, the North Staffordshire alone among the railway companies venturing to dispute its sway, though dispute is perhaps hardly the word, seeing the North Staffordshire line makes no attempt to compete with any of the Midland Company's iron roads.

But now the North Western are making a bold incursion into this Midland demesne, and by their new line from Parsley Hay to Ashbourne, inserting the thin end of the competitive wedge. Before proceeding to a more detailed description of the new line itself, let us review the North Western's position in regard to Derbyshire, with a view to estimating the true strategical value of this new link in their system. The only really

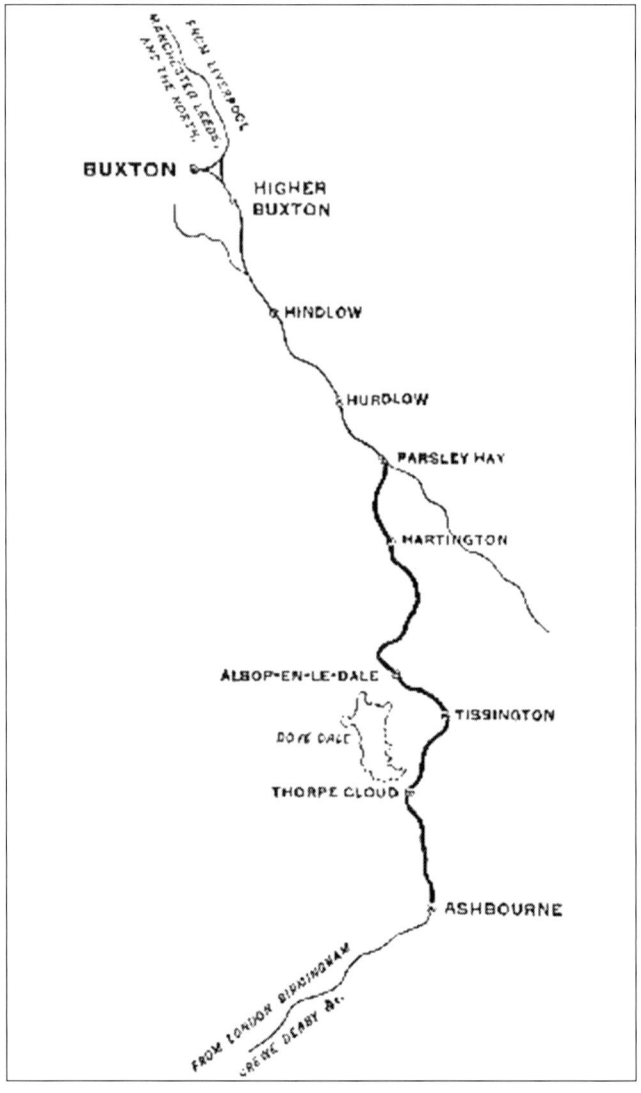

Buxton to Ashbourne Map.

competitive point in the Peak county hitherto has been Buxton, and that town enjoys the benefit of a double rivalry between the Midland and the North Western, firstly, in regard to the London traffic; and secondly, in regard to the local traffic to and from Manchester. For a long time the Midland route from St. Pancras via Derby and Miller's Dale was the only one between London and Buxton, the distance being 163 miles. But later on the London and North Western Railway, with the co-operation of the North Staffordshire, also started a service of through coaches between Euston and Buxton via the Potteries and Macclesfield, the route being 33½ miles longer than that of the Midland.

But although the Midland undoubtedly win over the Metropolitan course, the North Western hold the trump card in regard to the increasingly large Manchester – Buxton residential traffic. Possessing the shorter route they are able to accomplish the journey in a best time of 37 minutes as against their rival's 70; indeed, the service between Buxton and Manchester (London Road) is a very good one, as a gentleman took occasion to mention at the opening ceremony of the new Ashbourne line.

Buxton itself may be regarded as the gate of the Peak District, for it has hitherto been the best centre from which to make excursions into the lovely surrounding country, and as such has been duly patronised. Therefore the opening of the new line, which is sure to attract a large volume of tourist traffic, will make the Midland look to their laurels, for it will bring Buxton within exactly the same distance of Euston as it is of St. Pancras, viz. 163 miles, besides taking in the most interesting part of the Peak District *en route*. Here then, at a single bound, Buxton leaps from the comparatively humble position of a branch line station to that of being an important town on a new through route between North and South, into which traffic can pour direct from London and the Midlands on the one hand, and from Yorkshire and the North thereof on the other. In making this connecting link through a very inhospitable county at a cost of one and a half millions, it seems more than probable that the North Western are looking far into the future to a time when their present main line shall at last become so crowded as to make the provision of an alternative route between London and Lancashire an imperative necessity. To take a single example; the distance from Euston to Manchester via Buxton and the North Staffordshire Railway (over which the North Western possess running powers), Ashbourne and Buxton would be about 194 miles, as against 183½ by the existing routes *via* Crewe or Macclesfield.

It will be gathered from the foregoing that what might at first sight seem to be a somewhat unimportant matter, viz. the opening of a short length of line in the wilds of Derbyshire, is in reality an event which is destined to produce far-reaching results. The new line, therefore, deserves to be described on this account alone; but there is another reason for so doing, and one more likely to weigh with the ordinary reader viz. the extreme beauty of the country adjacent thereto. We will accordingly proceed to give some account of the line itself and of its construction, for it passes through a very wild piece of country and one teeming with engineering difficulties.

Though the present extension is only from Parsley Hay to Ashbourne (the line from Buxton to Parsley Hay having been opened 4½ years ago), we propose to give a brief description of the entire route between Buxton and Ashbourne, for its every yard is full of interest.

The Peak District of Derbyshire, wherein lies Buxton, is really the southern termination of the Pennine Chain which forms the watershed between the rivers that flow east to west. It has hitherto been but little explored by tourists owing to the comparative inaccessibility of its loveliest parts. Buxton itself, however, is a very flourishing town, largely patronised as a health resort and inland watering place. Moreover, its residential population is enormously on the increase, very few towns in England boasting of such rapid growth as Buxton has shown during the last few years.

The town is finely laid out, boasts of many handsome buildings, and also of some splendid pleasure gardens. The Ashbourne Railway starts from the north-west corner, and after passing through Higher Buxton is carried on a very lofty viaduct towards Hindlow, the first station.

The track as far as Parsley Hay was principally constructed out of the bed of the old High Peak Railway, a very ancient and peculiar bit of line, built in 1825, and finally closed for passenger traffic in 1876. One of its small branches – viz. that to Ladmanlow – still exists in the neighbourhood of Buxton. From Ladmanlow onwards the rails have been removed, but the former course is still enclosed and plainly marked as far as Whaley Bridge.

At Parsley Hay the High Peak Railway reappears again as a branch on the left hand side of the present line, and is still worked for goods and mineral traffic between Parsley Hay and Cromford, a distance of 16 miles.

Originally the gradients on this railway were so severe that it was necessary to use stationary engines at certain points to raise and lower the trains on the inclined planes of 1 in 8½ by means of ropes. On the section to Hopton, which is worked by ordinary locomotives, a very stiff bank of 1 in 14½ is still negotiated.

The nine miles from Buxton to Parsley Hay are somewhat dreary and uninteresting, for the country is merely a succession of low hills and dales, which are almost uninhabited. Indeed, the two daily passenger trains hitherto run between Buxton and Parsley Hay seem to be more than sufficient for the requirements of the traffic.

But the intermediate stations, if offering no particular attraction in themselves, at any rate give access to some most interesting spots. Within an easy walking distance of Hindlow is Chelmsford, famous because it contains the "highest church in England," the word "highest" being here used simply in its physical sense.

Near Hindlow, the next station is Monyash, which was an important town in Saxon times and boasted of a three day's fair. Later still it was the centre of the lead-mining industry, but nowadays has fallen from its high estate, and is merely a well-kept but rather desolate village. The lovely Lathkill Dale, however, is within a few minutes' walk of Monyash, and teems with fantastically carved boulders and massive rocks.

Parsley Hay is a very dreary-looking spot; but here, again, in the close proximity of Arbor Low, it possesses an enormous attraction for the antiquarian, and, indeed, for the public at large, seeing that Arbor Low is one of the most perfect Druidical circles in existence. Some authorities believe that this circle of stones marks the resting place of the great chieftains who fell in a battle between Britons and Romans, as such an engagement is known to have taken place on Hartington Moor. A discussion of the arguments for and against these conflicting theories would, however, be obviously out of place in the present article.

From Parsley Hay to Ashbourne the line was built in two sections, the first or northern section being five miles in length, and the second, or southern, eight. Work was commenced simultaneously at each end. The construction of this line had long been in contemplation, and was, in fact, one of the cherished schemes of the late Sir George Findlay, the necessary parliamentary powers having been obtained as long ago as 1890.

The work, however, was not, for various reasons, at once put in hand, and when the bad times of 1893-4 came it was still further delayed. A start was finally made in January 1896, and the line was then pushed forward with all speed. An extension of time was obtained; but so anxious were the directors that it should be in readiness for the tourist traffic of the present year, that at one period as many as 500 men were employed upon it, and the work was carried on very rapidly indeed. The northern section, though the shorter of the two, cost almost as much as the southern, owing, as we shall presently show, to the very heavy nature of the work which it entailed. Labour was very difficult to obtain, for the modern navvy, whose wages would make the mouth of a gentleman farmer water, will not, if he can help it, work at any great distance from a big town, for he hopes to find some amusement therein when his day's toil is over.

The 500 labourers employed on the Ashbourne extension nearly swamped both Buxton and Ashbourne; indeed in the case of the latter village a great number of them were absolutely unable to find accommodation of any sort, and were therefore compelled to sleep wherever they could – in the half-finished stations, in sheds, and elsewhere. But then the pay was very good, and, moreover, the men were taken to and from their work in special trains every day.

At Parsley Hay the line is 1,107 ft. above sea level, and shortly after leaving the station the limestone has been trenched through for half a mile, forming a cutting 60 ft. deep. Meres, which are artificial circular tanks cut in the hill-sides to catch the rain and the dew, gave the water supply for the engines of the contractors.

All excavations and blastings were made by the use of gelignite, a very powerful explosive gelatine, and, indeed, without its help the workmen would have been quite unable to secure a level track.

The next point of interest is a large three-arched viaduct at Hand Dale, where a gigantic "spoil" bank of excavated limestone will by-and-by be sent to Crewe for fluxing the steel. In making the foundations of this bridge, an old mine, in which the miners had been suddenly overtaken by disaster, was discovered.

A fine view is obtained from this point over the ranges of the Staffordshire hills, with the Dove at their foot, and beyond it the mysterious Manyfold, which loses itself in the rock near Ecton for five or six miles, to reappear at the picturesque village of Ilam, near Ashbourne.

Within a short distance of Hartington station is Beresford Dale, a most beautiful spot, flanked by perpendicular cliffs and graced with the foliage of the mountain-ash and birch. A very fine view of it is gained from a commanding rock, reached by a footpath from the brink of the River Dove, which separates Derbyshire from Staffordshire. Hard by are the ruins of Prospect Tower ("Cotton's Hole"), one of the hiding places of the friend of Izaak Walton and the site of Beresford Hall.

Izaak Walton's fishing house itself is on the Staffordshire bank, and was erected by Charles Cotton, as a mark of the friendship existing between himself and the author of the "Complete Angler". It still bears the dedication "Piscatoribus Sacrum, 1764," with the initials of the two worthies in a monogram. Pikes Pool, a bend or two further on, is remarkable for a needle rock rearing itself up in the midst thereof.

Between Hartington and Alsop-en-le-Dale, one of the most expensive and troublesome works was carried out. We refer to the making of Coldeaton Cutting, in which the solid rock is pierced for a distance of three-quarters of a mile by a trough 600 feet in depth. Here 314,000 cubic yards of solid stone were excavated with the help of 200 men, eight steam cranes, and four locomotives, the latter of course being employed to help carry away the *debris*. Notwithstanding the extremely arduous nature of the work it was carried out most successfully and rapidly, and reflects the greatest credit on all concerned.

Alsop-en-le-Dale Station is only two thirds of a mile from Dove Dale, and offers to the tourist the chance of traversing that lovely stretch of sylvan beauty with its fairy-like combinations of wood, rock and water by a very little known route. The end of the dale boasts Ilam Rock, a singular object with a verdant base, towering above the trees and shrubs that border a murmuring stream. A little further on we come to the Doveholes, two splendidly formed caverns at the base of a tall precipice, the largest showing a span of 60 feet, and an elevation of 30 feet. They have a symmetrical central column and vaulted roofs, and were no doubt at one time actually inhabited.

Hartington – excavation of wide cutting through fractured rock south of station. 3 steam shovels are at work in the background and a contractor's saddle tank pulls several wagons laden with spoil c1898.

Returning to the railway, after leaving Alsop the line enters a stiff series of cuttings, which begin at Newton Grange. It is evident to the geologist that nature has here experienced great convulsions in past ages. The trial shafts were completely at fault, so variable is the formation, which is a curious mixture of red, yellow, and blue clay – very brilliant when first exposed to the air – with limestone and some suggestion of iron and lead. In Tissington Cutting, five-eighths of a mile in length, the strata of shale, limestone, coloured clays, and green sand become most curiously distorted, often tilted in the form of a letter V.

Tissington itself (the next station) is well known by reason of a most curious and interesting ceremony call "Well Dressing" which takes place there on Ascension Day each year. There are five wells in the village, called respectively the Yew Tree (or "Goodness"), the Hall, the Hands, the Town, and the Coffin, the last named, which is at the east end of the village, near the post office, being so christened on account of its shape. They are all tastefully decorated with flowers on Holy Thursday, and a special service is held in the church, after which the inhabitants of the village go in procession to the different wells, where the collects for the day are said and psalms and hymns sung. The decorating of the wells has lately been revived or introduced at many other places, but the religious service in connection with the ceremony at Tissington gives solemn character to the proceedings which is lacking to them elsewhere. In fact Tissington is the Mecca of the "well dressers."

After leaving Tissington the railway crosses Buxton Road at Bentley Hill, by means of a very large bridge 90 feet on the skew. There is to be a goods station at this point. Close by lies the village of Fenny Bentley, containing a curious church dedicated to St. Edmund, wherein, north of the chancel, is a remarkable altar-tomb of Thomas Beresford, 1473, and his wife Agnes, 1463. The style, however, shows that it must have been erected about a century after their death.

The line next crosses a ridge from one valley to another, which caused much cutting, for the contractors were obliged to remove no less than 210,000 cubic yards of boulder clay. Another feature is the well-built viaduct of seven arches – 25 openings – of blue brickwork.

The last station before Ashton is Thorpe Cloud, one mile from Dove Dale. A very fine tunnel cut in the dry red sandstone burrows under the old town of Ashbourne for 390 yards, and emerges where the London and North Western and North Staffordshire Railway Companies are building a new joint station.

One very lovely bit of country adjacent to the new line is the hitherto little known valley of the Manyfold. It derives its name from the river flowing through it, which is a tributary of the Dove.

Ashbourne itself, the terminus of the new line, is situated in a rich and well-wooded valley, and boasts a population of 1,900 souls. It is divided into two parts by the Schoo or Heunne, a small tributary of the Dove, and as early as the

Entrance to Ashbourne Tunnel looking towards Buxton. In the foreground the approach cutting is being excavated and abutments for the bridge lined with stone blocks. Part of a temporary wooden crane is seen mounted on side of cutting. c1898.

Ashbourne Tunnel northern entrance during construction c1897. Contractor's track still in place.

13th century was a market town and one of the most populous places in the Midlands.

It is now destined to become an important railway junction, and will no doubt be called upon to deal with a large traffic in the near future. A great deal of milk already finds its way from Derbyshire to the Metropolis, as milk from a limestone district is especially good. The opening of the line will see a great development of this trade. Those who know well the neighbourhood through which the Buxton-Ashbourne line passes, prophesy an enormous increase in local traffic, both goods and passenger.

With a view to anticipating this state of affairs, all works (with the exception of a few steel bridges, and of course the permanent way) have been built double, so as to allow of a second track being laid as soon as it may be necessary to do so. Moreover the line has been built with a view to fast running, the steepest gradient, in spite of the drop of 700 ft. between Hartington and Ashbourne, being only 1 in 59, whilst the radius of the sharpest curve is but 20 chains. The building of the line was by no means all plain sailing, for snowstorms were sometimes encountered of such severity as to cause

Ashbourne Station. View from Uttoxeter direction showing station buildings and signalbox. LNW train in the bay platform. Two dark coloured LNW signal posts – one with ringed arms. Large station hotel in the background.

a suspension of all operations. Upon one occasion it took a whole week to clear away the snow sufficiently to enable the work to be proceeded with.

At present a service of four stopping trains run each way between Buxton and Ashbourne, with the addition of an extra one on Saturdays. Commencing October 2nd, a service of two through expresses each way daily between Euston and Buxton *via* Ashbourne, by means of slip carriages off existing trains, will be run. It is not proposed, however, to attempt to improve very much on existing times until the track shall have become thoroughly consolidated and settled, though no doubt the through expresses will be accelerated later on.

Meantime extra facilities are to be granted to tourists in the shape of cheap week-end and excursion tickets from Manchester to stations on the new line. It might incidentally be mentioned that prior to the opening of the Buxton-Ashbourne extension to the general public, the company conveyed all the inhabitants of Hartington to Ashbourne and back in a special train, free of charge, an outing which was much appreciated, seeing that the majority of villagers had certainly never travelled by train before in their lives!

We must heartily thank Mr Linaker, the District Superintendent of the London and North Western Railway Company, and Mr Hull, the Resident Engineer of the northern section of the Ashbourne-Buxton line, for the courteous manner in which they placed all information at our disposal.

Hartington: Opening of Ashbourne branch. View looking north along platform. Trevithick single "Locomotion" with Engineer's Inspection Saloon has stopped and Mr Webb is posed on the platform beside it along with station staff. Signal box on the right 1.8.1899.

Hartington. The western face of the three arch bridge over Hand Dale seen from the southern side of the valley up from Hartington village. The inaugural train from Buxton to Ashbourne is crossing headed by Cauliflower No.930 piloting an Improved Precedent No.2004 "Witch" made up of 6 and 8 wheeled carriages. 1.8.1899.

Chapter 12
Euston Station in 1899
Notable Railway Stations
by S.M. Philip LNWR

Euston may certainly claim to be ranked amongst "Notable Railway Stations," for if it boasted of no other distinction, it is unique in being the head-quarters and principal terminus of the greatest railway undertaking in this country. The London and North Western, with its hundred and seventeen millions of paid-up capital, its thirteen millions of annual receipts, and its yearly train mileage of nearly forty-eight million miles, has an undoubted right to rank as the greatest railway company in the United Kingdom, and Euston, its largest and most important station, is the fountain-head of its whole vast system.

The first thing that would naturally occur to anyone who saw Euston Station for the first time, and had it explained to him that this was the London terminus of a great railway company, would be to wonder how it came to be located where it is, amongst a congeries of mean streets in St. Pancras, remote from the centres of commercial

Euston Doric Arch. Built by the London & Birmingham Railway in 1837. 72 feet high. Designed by Philip Hardwick and inspired by Roman architecture. It was built with stone from Bramley in Yorkshire at a cost of £35,000.

activity in the city, and from the classic precincts of the West End, its fine proportions and handsome frontage hidden from view, and its access rendered difficult by reason of the narrow and congested thoroughfares by which it must be approached. The explanation of this is an old story, with which students of the history of early railway enterprise are tolerably familiar; and it affords a striking illustration of the want of foresight displayed by the legislators of a past generation. Euston, as most people know, was originally the terminus of the London and Birmingham Railway, one of the first, although not absolutely the first, of the railways constructed in this country, it having been authorised by Parliament as early as 1833, and opened in 1838, the year after Her Majesty ascended the throne. The promotors of railways in those early days had an up-hill task in contending against the forces of ignorance and prejudice, especially on the part of the landowners, whose property they had to acquire; and one result of this was that in constructing their terminal stations, particularly in London, they were debarred from approaching the sacred precincts of the City and West End, and the "accursed thing" was rigidly kept at a distance on what were then almost the outskirts of civilisation. Thus we find the London and North Western at Euston, the Great Northern in the wilds of Pentonville, and the Great Western at Paddington.

It is a fact, indeed, not generally known, that as originally projected and authorised by Parliament, the London and Birmingham had their London terminus at Chalk Farm, near the south end of Primrose Hill tunnel; but while the railway was under construction, the directors obtained supplementary powers to construct the Euston extension, a short branch from Chalk Farm, to what was then known as "Euston Grove." The directors say in their report, dated 13th February, 1835:-

"The directors, believing that it would be for the interest of the company that passengers by the railway should have nearer access to the Metropolis than is afforded by the station at Camden town, caused surveys and estimates to be made of a line, which the Engineer recommends, about a mile length, and without a tunnel, from the present terminus to Euston Grove."

Euston differs widely from its rival "St. Pancras," inasmuch as instead of, like the latter, springing up like Aladdin's Palace, complete, as we see it today, Euston was a plant of slow and gradual growth, and only step by step has it attained its present colossal proportions. In fact, it might also be likened to "Paddy's breeches," which had been patched so often that there was nothing of the original fabric left.

The station was first erected as the terminus of the "Euston extension," although it possessed an imposing frontage, was of modest dimensions, occupying only a couple of acres of ground; but naturally it grew with the growth of the railway, and thirty years ago, in the year 1870, we find that by successive additions it had reached the respectable dimensions of 50,000 square yards, or upwards of ten acres. In that year, a very important enlargement of the station was determined upon and commenced, although it was not until five years later, in 1874, that the whole works were completed and brought into use. These comprised the widening of the station on the eastern, or Seymour Street side, to provide additional lines and platforms, a large extension of the roofing, the making of a new approach from Euston Road by cutting through the gardens in Euston Square, and many other improvements, adding nearly three acres to the area of the station.

Only about 12 years had elapsed before once more the cup was found to be full to overflowing, and again the directors had to face the enormous expenditure for enlarging the station, this time on the west side. Cardington Street, which formed the western boundary, had to be diverted, and what was at first almost a distinct station with several new platforms and separate booking offices, waiting-rooms, and conveniences, was constructed on that side. It was soon found, however, that the separate stations had been somewhat of a mistake, as they proved inconvenient to work and confusing to the public, and a further alteration was carried out by which all the lines and platforms were thrown into one homogeneous station, with a single continuous frontage to the courtyard and central booking offices.

These alterations, begun in 1887, were completed in 1894, and added upwards of five acres, or, to be exact, 88,000 square yards, thus exceeding by about two acres the area of Liverpool Street, which is by many people supposed to be the largest railway station in the Metropolis.

To make an end of statistics, let it be said at once that Euston boasts of 13 separate platforms, having a superficial area of 16,150 square yards, and a total length of 9,180 feet, so that if they were placed end to end they would extend for a distance of nearly a mile and three quarters. There are within the precincts of the station just six miles of lines of rails. The courtyard in front of the station, which on busy days is so packed with a struggling crowd of vehicles that it is difficult to enter it or leave it, nevertheless contains 5,500 square yards, or considerably more than an acre of ground.

With regard to the roofing of the station, there is a curious fact worth mentioning, which is, that the present roof contains two spans, each 40 feet in width, which formed part of the original station roof erected in 1836, and the whole of the present roofing, measuring 465,000 superficial feet, has been from time to time constructed on the lines of the original design. It may not boast the magnificent span of St. Pancras, but it is claimed by its architect to be the cheapest to construct, the most economical and easiest to maintain, and the best adapted for its purpose which has ever been designed for the covering of a railway station.

It has been admitted that the approach to Euston station is not all that could be desired, and many schemes, more or less imperial in their character, have from time to time been suggested for improving it; one such scheme, which has much to recommend it, being to close Drummond Street, and carry the front of the station bodily out to the Euston Road, but it may be contended boldly that when the difficulties of the approach have been surmounted, Euston station is the most convenient railway station in London, both for the public who use it, and for the officials who have to work in it.

To begin with, it is possible for no less than eighteen trains to be dealt with simultaneously within the station, that is to say that seven incoming trains may be received, while simultaneously eleven trains are being loaded up with passengers and luggage ready for departure. This rather than mere acreage is the true test of the capacity of a station, and there are not many stations in Europe which can approach Euston in this way. Again, the construction of the station is so admirable that there can be no confusion on the part of passengers as to where their trains start from.

All vehicles drive into the central courtyard, with its long line of frontage to the vestibule, or great hall. In the hall, where the passenger first finds himself, there are indicators showing the numbers of the platforms from which the trains depart, either right or left of the main entrance, and in either case the passenger must pass the booking-office to reach the train. The station is well supplied with waiting rooms, four refreshment rooms, and a handsome and commodious dining-room, a post office, telegraph office, bookstalls everywhere, and every modern convenience, the latest addition being a first class tea room, in which ladies especially are glad to take tea and light refreshments quietly and in comfort without struggling at the bars amongst the male passengers.

There are several architectural features of Euston Station which are of interest, and some which are quite unique, and of these not the least striking is the noble portico, composed of massive stone columns in the Doric style, which forms the entrance to the station. This fine erection, which was the work of the celebrated architect Philip Hardwick, measures no less than 72 ft. to its apex, and no one can behold it without a feeling of regret that its imposing proportions should be dwarfed, and to a great extent neutralised, by the want of a more extended perspective, and by its surroundings of mean streets.

Another feature which, as regards railway stations in the Metropolis or elsewhere may be considered entirely unique, is the vestibule, or great hall, another of the masterpieces of Hardwick, in which the passenger finds himself on entering the station from the courtyard. This noble chamber, which measures 137 ft. by 62 ft. and rises to a height of 62 ft. from floor to ceiling, is constructed in the form of what architects know as double cube. It possesses what is believed to be the largest panelled and coffered ceiling in the world, being a reproduction of the celebrated ceiling of St. Paul's, Extra Muras, at Rome, this ceiling being supported by bold consols carried down between the continuous rows of windows, which latter are placed high above the cornice. A balcony with a handsome bronze balustrade

Euston Station Great Hall with George Stephenson statue.

runs round three sides of the hall and adds greatly to its appearance. At the four corners above the cornice are groups of statutory emblematic of the principal cities of the empire. At the north end is a colossal statue, executed in Carrara marble by the celebrated sculptor Baily, of George Stephenson, the great engineer, to whose genius the world is indebted for improvements in the locomotive engine, and who may be, the writer considers, be justly named the "father of railways."

At the back of this statue rises the grand staircase which leads to the board rooms, committee rooms, and the vast range of offices, in which upwards of eleven hundred clerks are employed, representing the headquarters staff of the Company.

One fact not suspected by the general public is that beneath Euston Station, as they are familiar with it, is an under-world of which they see nothing. To a great extent, the whole station is built upon arches, and the vaults below, comprising an area of 40,000 square feet, are utilised for a multitude of purposes, such as storage for coals, wines, and the provisions for the hotel, engine rooms, strong rooms, and workshops. The shareholders' meeting room is a fine chamber, in the Palladian, or modern Italian style, 76 feet by 45 feet, and 38 feet in height, and by the kindness of the Directors, is frequently made use of by the staff as a ballroom, and for concerts, for which purposes it is admirably adapted.

The Euston hotel, which fronts the courtyard of the station, while not possessing any very striking architectural features, is a fine and commodious building containing 225 rooms. It was originally built in 1840, but in 1881 it was greatly enlarged, and the east and west wings were united, so as to convert what were originally two distinct buildings into one.

In connection with the offices at Euston, there is one very useful institution which is worthy of

Euston LNWR Directors' Board Room (or Traffic Room) 1897.

Euston Station Hotel in 1884.

mention, and which is known as the "Inter-office Telephone Exchange." The offices, having been built at various times in the last fifty years, and in detached blocks, are much scattered, and in some cases widely apart. The introduction of telephone exchanges in towns caused the Company's electrician to have a happy thought. "Euston is a town in itself, why not have a telephone exchange?" No sooner said than done. One room on the station was converted into an "exchange," with a clerk always in attendance, every one of the 100 offices on the station was connected up to it, and now it may be said that every officer and clerk in the scattered range of offices is brought within speaking distance of every other. The immense saving of time, and the facilities for conducting the business which this affords, can readily be imagined.

The trains which leave Euston daily, and equally, of course, those that run into it, divide themselves naturally into four classes. There are first, the important West Coast trains, running in conjunction with the Caledonian Railway, via Carlisle to and from Edinburgh, Glasgow, Aberdeen, and the far north; secondly, the Irish trains running to and from Holyhead to connect with the mail steamers, or the fine fleet of steamers owned by the London and North Western Railway plying between Holyhead and North Wall; thirdly the not less important services of expresses between

'Alfred the Great' class No.1973 "Hood" at Euston Arrival Platform. Webb built 40 of these 4-cylinder compounds between 1901-03).

London, Birmingham, Liverpool, Manchester, Leeds, North and South Wales, and a host of other important towns, served by the ubiquitous North Western system; and last, but not least, the admirable service of local or suburban trains plying between Euston and Watford, and calling at all intermediate stations, with such clockwork regularity, that one might almost set their watch by them. There are others, of course, for instance, there are trains running to Bletchley, Tring, and Rugby, and others which only run as far as Willesden Junction, but the majority fall within the above categories.

In all there are, on a busy day in the summer, upwards of 200 loaded passenger trains in and out of the station during the 24 hours, but even this takes no account of empty trains and engines without trains, and on any given day during, say, the month of August, when the tourist traffic is at its height, the total number of trains of all descriptions, and engines, passing the signal box at the entrance to the station in both directions is upwards of 400. As the station is practically closed from midnight until the departure of the newspaper train at 5.15am, this gives for nineteen hours during which it is open, an average of 22 trains per hour, or more than one every three minutes during the working day.

Amongst the large number of trains leaving Euston daily, there are some which for one reason or another stand out prominently from the rest, and their making up and departure constitute quite a series of epochs in the life of the station during the 24 hours.

First, and literally first, since it is the earliest to depart, is the newspaper train which leaves Euston every morning throughout the year at 5.15am. Although widely known as the newspaper train, it conveys, in addition to newspapers, mails, parcel post hampers, and a few passengers, and to an early riser, who finds himself in the neighbourhood, the departure of this train forms a spectacle not without interest. It is a long and heavy train, made up of newspaper vans, parcel vans, with a couple of passenger carriages. It conveys daily about 28 tons of newspapers, 3½ tons of letters, and 6 tons of parcel post hampers, and it is the running of this train which admits of the London morning papers being on sale at Birmingham soon after 8am, at Manchester, Liverpool and Chester soon after 10am, and even at Carlisle soon after 1pm.

The train, with its connections, covers practically the entire London and North Western system, the newspapers being sorted by Messrs. Smith and Son's men *en route*, and handed out in bundles at the various stations and junctions. It is a scene of great animation and intense activity when, as the hour approaches 5am, some 30 to 40 newspaper and Post Office vans dash up in hot haste, and disgorge their loads, at once to be pounced upon by a small army of about 70 men including railway porters, Post Office officials, and Messrs. Smith and Son's men, who with incredible quickness, but with perfect order and method, bestow them in the train.

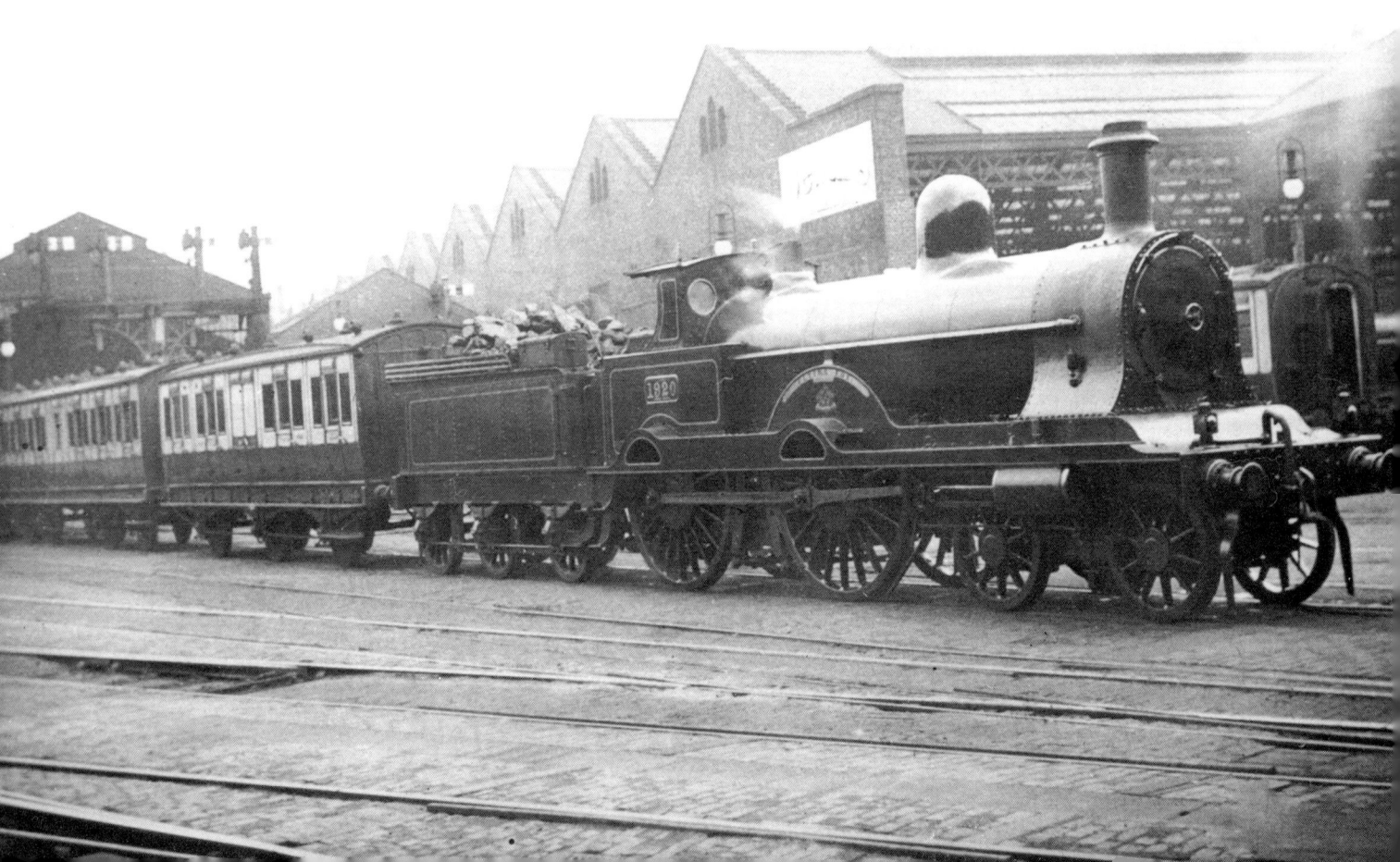

Jubilee class No.1920 "Flying Fox" waiting to depart from Euston with a train of mixed arc roof stock, 6 wheel centre brake leading followed by an 8 wheel radial. A good view of the transverse pitched roof sections on the west side of the station. The track area is paved with setts.

Passing over the north express at 7.10, the next train of first importance to leave is the Irish day mail, departing at 8.30 to catch the mail boat which lands her passengers at Kingstown (Dun Laoghaire) at half past five in the afternoon. This train has corridor throughout by means of which both first and third class passengers have access to the saloons in which breakfast is served soon after departure, and luncheon about mid-day. The 8.45 is the morning train for North Wales Coast towns, and 9.20 sees the departure of the first of a fine series of Birmingham expresses which run at intervals during the day, performing the journey on the average in about 150 minutes, and with the utmost punctuality, running into New Street Station five times out of six on the stroke of the big clock which overhangs the bridge, and rarely more than a minute or two behind time. The 10am train is one of the most important in the day, being, perhaps, the most convenient train for Scotland, inasmuch as, without leaving at an unreasonable early hour, the passengers can reach either Edinburgh or Glasgow in good time for dinner, after having had luncheon, and tea if desired, served on the train. The train is only available for passengers going to Carlisle and beyond, of whom there are sufficient to monopolise the whole of the seats provided.

The 10.15am, which also contains a luncheon car, is the convenient morning train for Liverpool, Manchester, and Central Wales, and then follow in quick succession the 10.25am, which is a Scotch train, with through carriages for Whitehaven, and the 11 o'clock, which is the Irish day express, connecting with the Company's own steamer at Holyhead. 12 o'clock sees the departure of one of the most important Manchester expresses, running through the Potteries, and performing the journey in 4 hours and 20 minutes, and close upon it follows, at 12.15, the drawing-room car express train to Liverpool, with connections to North Wales, Preston, and Fleetwood. The 1.30 is

Problem Class No.827 "Victoria" arriving at Euston in 1902 with train of mixed 6 and 8 wheel stock. Circular smokebox door and vacuum pump.

one of the most useful and patronised trains of the day, for it is a sort of "maid of all work"; it is not only a good train for Birmingham, but it serves Manchester, Leeds, North Wales, Central Wales, and the Cambrian line.

This brings us to the 2 o'clock, one of the most notable trains which leave Euston during the day; in fact, its departure usually collects quite a little crowd of interested lookers on, apart from those who come in considerable numbers to see their friends off. It is the last day train for Scotland, and conveys no passengers for places south of Preston, being made up of through carriages for Glasgow, Edinburgh, and Aberdeen. It is corridored throughout, has dining saloons for first and third class passengers, is steam heated, well lighted, and replete with every modern convenience. Even in quiet times it is nothing unusual for every seat to be occupied, and at busy seasons the train has to be strengthened, and often divided and run in two or more portions. Close on its heels follows the 2.15 which is known as the Liverpool, Manchester, Southport, and Windermere express, and then comes another Birmingham express at 2.35. The 2.45 is a useful train, running as far as Stafford, but serving a certain number of intermediate stations, and after this there is a little breathing space, for the next departure of consequence is at 4 o'clock, when the Manchester express via Stoke leaves, having a tea car attached. A quarter of an hour later at 4.15 sees the departure of the corridor train with dining carriages for Liverpool, while at 4.30 there is another Birmingham express, one of the best in the day.

An interval of an hour is filled up by the despatch of four or five less important trains, and then, at 5.30, a long and heavy train composed of corridor carriages, with dining saloons, starts for Liverpool, Manchester, and Fleetwood, this being known as the Belfast boat express, because it connects at Fleetwood with the steamer for Belfast. This train has a splendid run to Crewe, 158 miles without a stop. The 5.35, five minutes later, is also a dining train to Manchester, but makes more stoppages and has connections with Birmingham, Chester, and Birkenhead. At 6.40 the Greenore boat express leaves, carrying passengers for the north of Ireland by the company's steamer, which sails from Holyhead for Greenore at 1.40am daily. The 7 o'clock is the last of the Birmingham expresses, properly so called, and has a dining car for Birmingham and Wolverhampton.

The next train of note is the 8 o'clock, which is a heavy Scotch train chiefly made up of sleeping saloons for Glasgow and the far North, Dundee, Inverness, and Stranraer. Next follows the Irish night mail at 8.45, and five minutes later, at 8.50, this is followed in its turn by another heavy Scotch train, taking through carriages for Glasgow, Edinburgh, Inverness, and Perth. This train travels via Birmingham, so that the belated Birmingham passenger who missed the 7 o'clock still has a last string to his bow, to say nothing of the midnight train, of which more hereafter. The 10 o'clock is a kind of "general utility" train, for it calls at nearly all the important junctions between London and Carlisle, and has connections for Manchester, Liverpool, North Wales, the Furness line, Windermere, Keswick, Wigan, Preston, and Carlisle. The train which follows a quarter of an hour later, at 10.15, is the Irish night express, which runs straight away to Holyhead with only one brief stoppage at Crewe. The passengers reach Holyhead at 3.30am, go straight on board one of the London and North Western Railway's own steamers in the inner harbour, and four hours later are landed at North Wall.

Now we are approaching the close of the long day's work. About 11 o'clock a long train consisting almost entirely of sleeping saloons is placed in position at No.9 platform with the beds all made up for their intending occupants, who can retire to them as soon as they like, after that hour. The train actually starts 10 minutes before midnight, and has a fine run to Carlisle with only one five minute stoppage at Crewe, conveying passengers for Edinburgh, Glasgow,

Crewe Special Tank No. 3192 shunting at eastern side of Euston coupled to clerestory roof bogie van. Lined black with drop down smokebox door. A horse and cart and milk churns are in the left background.

Perth, Aberdeen, and Inverness. But even now the tired-out porters must rouse themselves to one more effort, for there is still the midnight train, one of the most useful trains of the day, landing its passengers at Birmingham, Liverpool, Manchester, Chester, Holyhead, and all the principal places in the North of England at various times in the early morning, with the whole day before them for business or pleasure.

Such is a day's work at Euston. Nothing has been said of the numerous and less important trains, and to analyse in the same way the long list of trains arriving from different destinations, which must be received and dealt with, would be tedious; but enough has been said to give an idea of the enormous amount of work which has to be got through by the staff, even on an ordinary day in the least busy season of the year. In the height of the tourist season, in the middle of August, many of the trains which have been mentioned are duplicated, and in some cases, the Scotch trains especially, are run as three or even four trains, instead of one.

Perhaps the absolutely busiest day in the year at Euston station is the 10th August, the day which sees the climax of the great exodus to the Scotch moors for the commencement of the grouse shooting on the 12th, and anyone who has ever

Improved Precedent No. 1678 "Airey" in Euston arrival platform with train of arc roof stock of suburban carriages.

watched the animated, and, in fact, to an outsider, bewitching scene, is hardly likely to forget it. The late Sir George Findlay, in his well-known work entitled, "The working and management of an English Railway," has given a description of the scene in language which is perhaps worthy of quotation:-

"The spacious courtyard blocked with cabs and carriages incessantly arriving and departing, the long lines of people waiting their turn at the numerous booking-offices, the extensive platforms crowded with passengers from end to end, and so blocked with mountains of heavy luggage that it is difficult to move a yard, the great engines noisily blowing off steam as if they were bellowing their impatience to set off upon their long journey, and, to make confusion worse confounded, the Post Office mail vans dashing up every five minutes and discharging into the thick of the fray tons of parcels and mail bags – all go to make up a scene which might well daunt the courage of the perspiring officials, who know that they are responsible for getting all these excited and bewildered passengers, those mountains of luggage and those tons of mails and parcels, into the right trains, the right carriages, and the right vans; in short, for evolving ultimate order out of this chaos, and all within a short space of time. The task would appear to be an almost impossible one;

but such is the power of the system, and of careful organisation of means to an end, that after all it is triumphantly accomplished, and soon after 10 o'clock at night the vast station is again silent and all but deserted, while the huge crowd that lately thronged it is packed into the many heavily loaded trains speeding fast through the darkness to their destination in the distant North."

On a busy day in the summer, it is no unusual thing for upwards of 7,000 passengers to be booked at Euston between morning and evening, and, counting the long distance passengers who arrive and the season ticket holders who arrive and depart by the local trains, the number of passengers coming in or going out on such a day is not less than 25,000. There are no less than 4,000 season ticket holders alone, who on the average use the station twice a day.

The record day's takings over the counter at Euston are enough to make a needy man gasp with envy. On the 10th August 1899, one of the busiest days ever known at the station, the constantly flowing stream of notes, gold, and silver mounted up to the magnificent total of nearly £6,500. This represented an average of 17s for every passenger booked, showing that it was not the short distance excursion passenger that swelled the company's money bags that day, but the prosperous long distance tourist for Scotland and the North.

There are no chamber maids at Euston except at the hotel, but bed-making is practised as the fine art on a grand scale. On a busy night in August it is not uncommon for as many as 500 beds to be made up in the sleeping compartments of the various trains, and for most of these to be specially reserved, and labelled with the names of the intending occupants. Indeed, the reservation of the berths, compartments, and seats is the work of one very important department at a large railway station, and at Euston upwards of a thousand such commissions are sometimes executed in one day.

No.1563 Webb 18in 0-6-2 'Watford' tank in Euston Engine siding – 80 were built between 1898 and 1902. Bracket starting signals on the left.

The reader, having grasped some idea of the vast amount of work which is carried on day by day at Euston, will be prepared to believe that the staff employed is a very large one; but even those who are familiar with the heavy wages bills which have to be paid at important railway stations may be surprised to learn that the total number of men on the wages staff at Euston, comprising inspectors, porters, shunters, cleaners, and others, and quite exclusive of clerks, amounts to close upon a thousand men, sufficient, if they were armed and drilled, to furnish a complete regiment to the British Army. In fact, these men, with their wives and families, would represent the population of many a fair-sized town.

A description of Euston Station would hardly be complete without some reference to the great signal cabin which controls all the points and signals at the entrance to the station, and which is claimed to be one of the largest ever constructed. This cabin is 80 ft. in length by 27 ft. in width, and contains 288 point and signal levers, and 73 telegraphic instruments of various kinds. No less than 11 signalmen are required to man this cabin throughout the 24 hours, working in 8-hour shifts; and it will suffice to give some idea of the magnitude of the operations conducted by these men, to say that on a very quiet day in February last, when for some purpose a record was taken during the 24 hours,

Improved Precedent No.480 "Duchess of Lancaster" standing at Euston in 1901/2 waiting to depart with safety valves blowing. Bracket of starting signals behind and end of station roofs beyond.

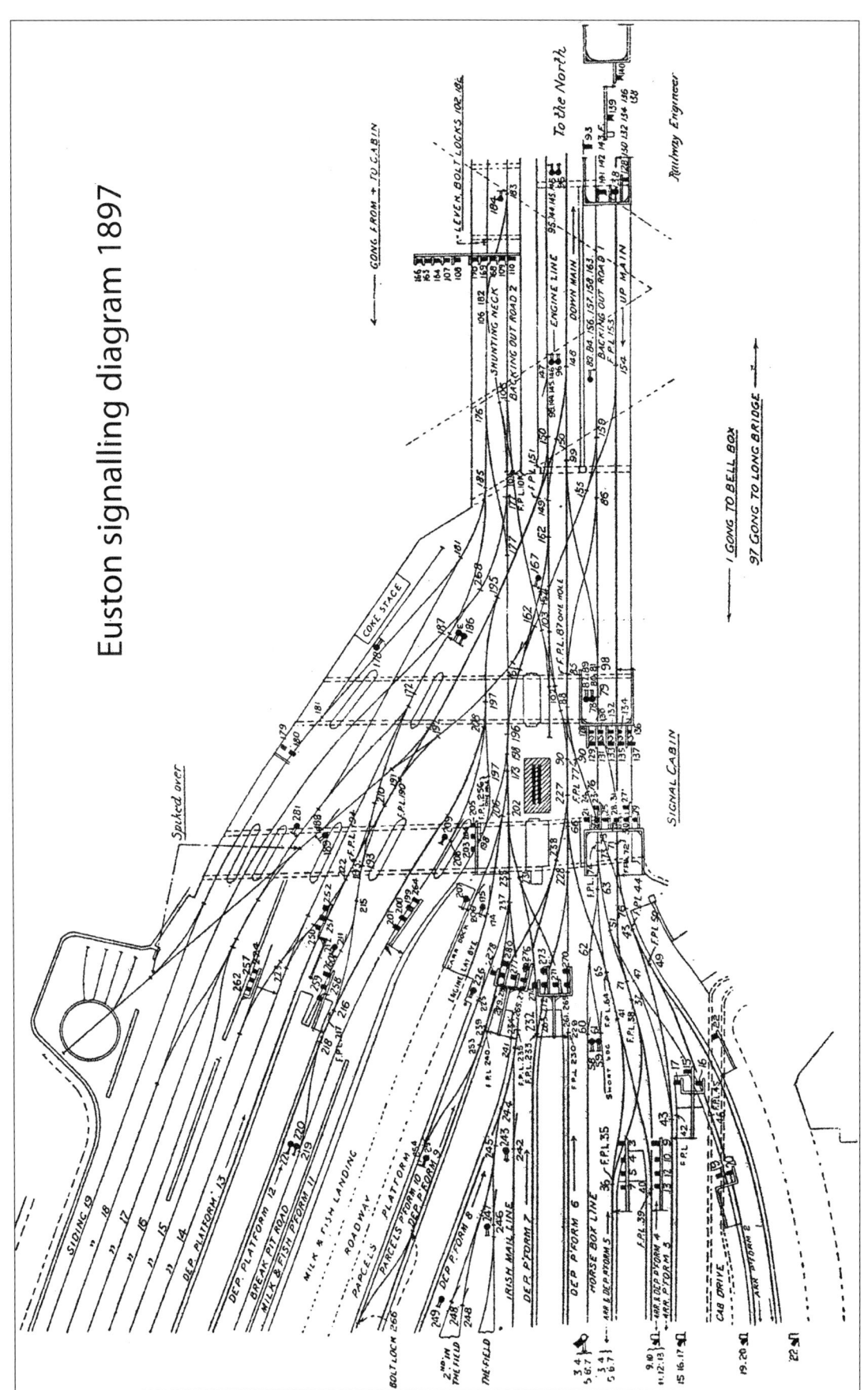

Euston Station Signalling diagram 1897 – showing platforms and sidings together with signal and point numbers.

there were close on 10,000 movements of the levers, and nearly 3,000 block telegraph signals were received or forwarded.

In improvements and alterations at Euston there appears to be no finality, and at the present time extensive works are going on at the north end with the object of improving the curves of the lines approaching the platforms, and widening the exit lines from the station. Another great work is in contemplation, and may shortly be undertaken. Hitherto, one of the difficulties of working the station at busy times has been that there is little space available for storage of empty carriages, and the stock of vehicles has had to be kept at Willesden, 5½ miles distant, and the trains made up there, and sent down to Euston empty for loading. To obviate this, there is a scheme for laying down a great park of carriage sidings at a point on the incline not far from the station, where a large stock of carriages could be kept, and the trains marshalled and sent into Euston as required, without the present loss of time. This, if carried out, would effect an incalculable improvement in the working of the station, especially at busy times, such as bank holidays, and at the height of the tourist season.

No.610 "Princess Royal" Problem Class in Euston arrival platform – as train engine in rear of pilot (just seen on left). Round smokebox door.

Chapter 13
Francis William Webb M.I.M.E.
Chief Mechanical Engineer, London and North Western Railway
A Personal Interview

"The Railway Magazine is about to publish a series of 'Illustrated Interviews' with the Locomotive Engineers of the principal railways of this country, and I have called upon you, Mr Webb, as the Chief Mechanical Engineer of one of the greatest of our railways, to obtain from you anything you may be willing to tell me respecting the history and work of your department and your connection with it."

"I have a great disinclination," said Mr Webb, "to being made the subject of an interview, but I will make an exception in the present instance, if you think anything I may say will interest your

FW Webb (with hat) and family group in his Chester Place garden in Crewe – seated from the left Mary (sister), Walter (younger brother), William (father), William (elder brother), Maria (mother), Standing FWW and an unknown man – possibly his younger brother Henry who was vicar of St. Pauls (one of the two LNWR built churches in Crewe).

Railway Magazine readers. You must, however, please be as brief as you can, for I am a busy man, as you know."

"First then, may I ask, without seeming unduly inquisitive, when you entered the railway service, and what positions you have filled in it. I understand you have been a very long time with the London and North Western Railway Company?"

"I entered Crewe works nearly fifty years ago; to be exact, on the 11th August, 1851, as a pupil of the late Mr Francis Trevithick, the first Locomotive Superintendent at Crewe. He was the son of Mr Richard Trevithick, the 'father of the locomotive,' who, in 1805 exhibited his wonderful 'steam coach' on a portion of the site now occupied by Euston Station. At the termination of my pupillage, I was placed on the Drawing Office staff, and on 1st March, 1859, was appointed Chief Draughtsman. On 1st September, 1861, I was promoted to the position of Works Manager, but resigned on 30th June, 1866, in order to take the management of the Bolton Iron and Steel Company's works. Five years later I left Bolton, and after visiting some of the principal railways and works in the United States of America, on behalf of the London and North Western Railway Company, I returned to Crewe on 1st October, 1871, as the late Mr Ramsbottom's successor in my present office."

"If I understand rightly, there used to be more than one locomotive superintendent on the North Western?"

"Yes. The department was formerly divided into three sections, each with a superintendent, who was responsible to the directors for the working of his division. In August, 1857, upon the retirement of Mr Trevithick – in fact on the very day I completed my pupillage – Mr John Ramsbottom, who was then at the Longsight works,

FW Webb with his 4-cylinder compound 'Jubilee' class 4-4-0 loco No.1903 "Iron Duke".

Manchester, and had charge of what was known as the North Eastern Division, was transferred to Crewe, and the Northern and North Eastern divisions combined and designated the Northern division. In March 1862, upon the retirement of Mr J.E. McConnell, who was at Wolverton, and had charge of the Southern Division, the Northern and Southern Divisions were amalgamated, and Mr Ramsbottom was appointed Chief Mechanical Engineer and Locomotive Superintendent of the whole line."

"I take it there is a great difference between Crewe as it is today and as you knew it in its early days?"

"When I came in 1851, there were less than 5,000 inhabitants; when I returned in 1871 there were 18,000, and since then the number has increased to about 40,000."

"I believe you filled the office of Mayor and Chief Magistrate during the Queen's Jubilee period?"

F.W. Webb when Mayor of Crewe 1887/88.

"Yes: I was elected Mayor for two successive years, viz., from 9th November 1886, to 9th November, 1888."

"Did not the Jubilee of the railway and the Queen's Jubilee happen about the same time?"

"Yes, the 4th July, 1887, was the fiftieth anniversary of the opening of the Grand Junction Railway, which railway, by connecting the Liverpool and Manchester Railway with the London and Birmingham Railway, laid the foundation of the present London and North Western system, and that date was selected to commemorate the Queen's Jubilee as well as the opening of the line through Crewe, by dedicating the park given by the London and North Western Railway Company for the use of the town. The corporation on the same date conferred upon Sir Richard Moon the honorary freedom of the borough in acknowledgement of the munificent generosity of the Company."

"Crewe works must have grown considerably in the extent to keep pace with the increased work of the department?"

"Naturally they have done so, for the advantages of Crewe as a locomotive centre were seen to be so great, owing to its central position in the North Western system, that first one addition was made and then another, until now no less than 116 acres of ground, with a covered area of 36 acres, are devoted entirely to the work of the locomotive department. The extent of the works is so great, that to save time and facilitate the transport of materials, we have about 5 miles of narrow gauge railway within the works worked by engines of a special type. We also have district workshops at Carlisle, Longsight (Manchester), and Rugby, where small repairs can be done to engines without bringing them to Crewe."

"How many engines have you built in Crewe works?"

"Nearly 4,000. The celebration, on the Queen's birthday in 1876, of the completion of the 2,000th engine built in these works marked an epoch in the history of Crewe. The completion of the

Crewe Works. A cylinder boring machine seen in place within the inside cylinder of a 'Class A' 3-cylinder compound 0-8-0. 1890s.

Crewe Works Group of workmen with No.759 a new 18in 'Cauliflower' 0-6-0 goods loco which they built in 1901.

3,000th engine was celebrated on July 4th, 1887, in connection with our celebration of the Queen's Jubilee, and the Jubilee of the opening of the railway through Crewe, and, if the Company send an engine to the next Paris Exhibition, it will be the 4,000th engine built in the works."

"That is rather a big record. Having regard to the present high speed and heavy weight of the trains running on the London and North Western Railway, I suppose there is a vast difference between the engines built nowadays and those which were in use when you first came to Crewe? Have you anything you can give me in the nature of a record of work done by one of these modern engines?"

"Yes: in connection with the Engineering Conference of the Institution of Civil Engineers, a visit to Crewe was arranged to take place on the 8th June last, when I conveyed a party of about 200 from Euston to Crewe and back by a special train drawn by the 'Iron Duke.' The weight of the engine and tender was 81 tons, and the weight of the train it had to draw was 339 tons 5 cwt. The weight of the coal used on the down journey to Crewe was 3 tons 2 cwt.; but on the return journey to Euston it was only 2 tons 16¼ cwt. Being new stock, the engine ran rather stiffly on the journey down, but was easier going back, as shown by the less consumption of fuel. The train travelled the whole distance (159 miles) in three hours and ten minutes, but I am not so much concerned in excessively high speed as in getting a very heavy train along the line with one engine at a reasonable speed."

"Can you give me a rough idea of the number of London and North Western engines running on the railway in 1871, when you took charge of the Loco Department, and at the present time?"

"We had 1,894 engines in November, 1871, compared with 2,959 in November 1899."

"But is not the increase in engines small compared with the increased work you have to do?"

"Yes: but you must remember the engines of today are much bigger and stronger than those of even a few years ago, as the weight of trains they have to haul is always on the increase, and it was the working out of the problem of dealing with increased weight, combined with my desire to economise the quantity of fuel used, that caused me to go so exhaustively into the question of compound engines, and to adopt that system as no doubt you are aware I have done extensively."

"Can you give me the number of hands employed in the Locomotive Department when you took charge in 1871 compared to the number at the present time?"

"The total number in the department in February 1871 was 10,610, of whom 4,668 were employed in Crewe Works. In December last year the total number was 21,705, of whom 7,600 were employed in Crewe Works. To give you an idea of the work which is done in providing for the running of engines, I may tell you that, including drivers, firemen, cleaners, mechanics, and fuelmen, close upon 21,000 persons are employed at the various steam sheds up and down the line."

"I suppose the fitting and erecting shops are the principal shops in the works? Can you give me any particulars about them?"

"In the fitting shop we employ 700 hands and 388 machines. We have eight erecting shops, and turn out annually 110 new engines; but we have, in busy times, turned out as many as 146 new engines in one year, in addition to keeping in repair the whole of the engine stock. The boiler shop is also an important department of the works. It is 672 feet long by 107 feet wide, and is fitted up with electric cranes and motors, and with pneumatic caulking and riveting machines. Nine hundred and eighty-six men are attached to the shop, and 452 boilers (new and repaired) are turned out annually."

"Perhaps it is a comparatively small matter, but I think that the London and North Western Railway has a place for washing their own enginemen's cloths; and I have been told that there are some interesting figures with regard to the work done there."

"We have a wash house in which about 10,224,000 enginemen's cloths and 90 tons weight of waste are cleansed every year, the refuse grease extracted being made into soap for cleaning purposes. Upwards of 2,300,000 new cloths are supplied to the men annually."

"What other matters are dealt with in your department, besides the building and running of engines?"

"I deal with all signal work, and we have 1,500 signal-cabins and about 17,000 signals; the lighting of our railway's premises all over the system; the provision of water and coal for all purposes; the supply of weighing machines, and all other machinery used for traffic purposes, in fact, with anything which can be considered the business of the mechanical engineer, or comes within the category of locomotive work. We make all sorts of things in Crewe Works – down to artificial legs and arms for the poor fellows who lose their limbs by accident in the service of the London and North Western Railway."

"What is the distance run by engines of the London and North Western Railway Company in the course of twelve months?"

"Last year we ran nearly 75,000,000 miles, of which 38,000,000 have been run during the last six months. Of course, you will understand that this is engine mileage, and not train mileage, pure and simple, and if your readers are curious in such matters, you can tell them we run the distance to the moon in about 28 hours and to the sun in about 15 months."

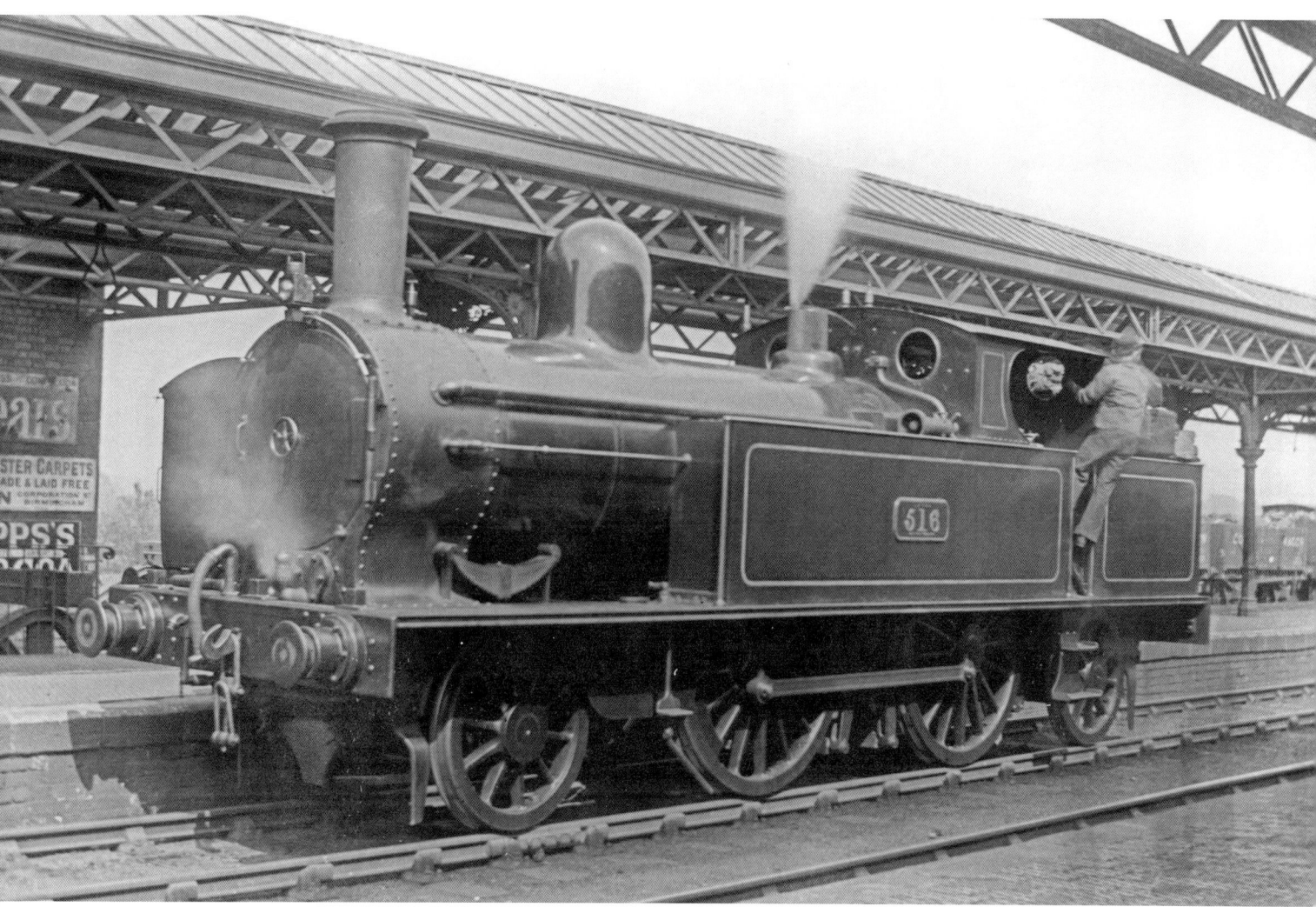

No.516 2-4-2 5ft 6in tank in Bescot station c1904. 160 were built between 1890 and 1897. They were effectively a tank version of the 'Precursor' class.

"What is the longest run you have made without a stop?"

"299¼ miles – the distance from Euston to Carlisle – which was run by 'Ionic,' one of my compounds, on 8th September, 1895, in 5 hrs.53 min. The weight of the train, exclusive of engine and tender, was 150 tons 14 cwt., and the speed averaged 51 miles an hour."

"What is the greatest average speed at which a London and North Western engine has travelled any considerable distance in working an ordinary train?"

"67.2 miles an hour. This was done by the engine 'Hardwicke' when working the North express from Crewe to Carlisle on the 22nd August 1895, the distance run being 141¼ miles."

"As a matter of public interest, could you give me an idea of the quantity of raw material used in the construction of a locomotive?"

"138 tons 18cwt. 2qrs.2½ lb. of raw materials are used for building an engine, which when completed and in working order, weighs 49 tons 5 cwt. Of course, this includes coal, coke, and limestone, which explains what would otherwise appear somewhat of a mystery."

"How long does it take to build an engine?"

"We usually reckon on 25 days, but, as an experiment, to show what could be done in an emergency, we once built one in 25½ working hours."

"I presume, Mr Webb, in an engineering works on such a vast scale as yours, there is ample

Whitworth 2-4-0 No.795 "Falstaff" about to depart from Buxton. Webb built 90 of this class between 1889 and 1896.

No.3248 0-4-2 4ft Crane Tank Shunter with 3 ton steam powered crane (built 1894) at Crewe North coupled to a NSR medium sided wagon and LNWR high sided wagon No.44828.

scope, as well as great necessity, for the exercise of considerable inventive ability in order to keep pace with the times?"

"Yes: as you are aware, this is the age of invention, and the immense advantage of increased production and economy derived from labour-saving devices is more apparent in the mechanical world than anywhere else, and this we have done at Crewe to a very large extent. But there is no such thing as finality."

"Has the London and North Western Railway a hospital in Crewe for the treatment of accidents arising to its servants?"

"Yes: and the Company's surgeon attends to all accidents befalling the men while on duty, whether in the works or on the railway, in the neighbourhood of Crewe."

"But did you not personally originate a hospital for the use of persons not employed by the Company?"

"Yes: there was no place nearer than Chester, Manchester or Liverpool, where, in case of accident, the townspeople not connected with the Company, or servants of the Company injured whilst off duty, could be taken for treatment, and I thought it only right that a great centre like Crewe should have an institution of the kind at which persons could be treated who were suffering from other than infectious diseases, or who, being infirm or convalescent, would be likely to recover more quickly than at their own homes. I had the idea in my mind for some time, when one day I met Mr Henry Yates Thompson, the son of an old director of the London and North Western Railway, and he said he should like to give me £1,000 for some purpose that would serve to perpetuate his father's memory and be some memento of his long connection with the company. I accepted his offer; the London and North Western Railway gave the land required,

No. 1745 "John Bright" at Ordsall Lane Shed with Webb cab and boiler mountings c1890.

and with what I was enabled to give myself, and the assistance afforded by residents in the town and neighbourhood, and the work people, I was able to accomplish my purpose."

"There is another institution in the town, I believe, which is indebted to you for a good deal of its success. I refer to the Mechanic's Institution."

"I am the president, and am, of course, very much interested in it, and have altered it from time to time so as to adapt it to modern requirements, and they have converted it into what is practically a technical institute of a high order."

"Can you suggest any reason why Crewe should win a larger proportion of Whitworth Scholarships than falls to the lot of most towns, as I believe is the case?"

"I can only suppose it arises from the fact that our students, being engaged in the works, in the nature of things and in the course of their daily employment, acquire a technical education and practical training in the very subjects dealt with at the examinations. This, of course, must be a great advantage to them in competing with others."

"Have you a laboratory or practical workshop attached to the institution?"

"Yes, we have a chemical laboratory, also a mechanics' shop fitted up with a gas engine and the necessary machinery to enable students to acquire a technical knowledge of mechanical engineering and tools. A practical mechanic is in attendance to give any advice or assistance that may be required by those using the shop, and the members generally can make use of it for making and repairing articles for themselves."

"Has the London and North Western Railway anything to do with the elementary day schools in Crewe?"

"Yes, there are twelve schools in the town, and the Company built seven of them. Altogether provision is made for about 7,000 scholars, the schools built by the Company providing upwards of 4,000 of them. In fact, Crewe may almost

Webb 17 inch coal engine No.433 on passenger train at Heaton Chapel. Drop down smokebox door, no brakes on engine. A total of 499 were built between 1873 and 1892.

be termed a railway colony. For instance, the Company supplies the whole town with gas, made at the works, and water, pumped at Whitmore, about 12 miles distant. Upwards of a thousand of the houses in the town belong to the Company, having been built by them for their work people, and they have also built and endowed a church in the town, and subscribed towards the erection of several other places of worship."

"I am afraid I have already trespassed too much upon your valuable time, but, as some of your workmen connected with the 2nd Cheshire Royal Engineer Railway Volunteers are now out in South Africa, and as the war is uppermost in all our minds just now, may I ask you for some particulars of the corps, which I understand was originated by you?"

"Seeing that Crewe has become a great centre of railway industry, and that the working and maintenance of railways must form a most important feature in times of war, I spoke to the late Mr W.H. Smith, then Secretary of War, on the subject of the advisability of having a volunteer engineer corps composed exclusively of railway men, with a view to their being ready for active service if required. He agreed with me, and I named the matter to the late Sir Richard Moon, then Chairman of the London and North Western Railway, who approved of the scheme. The result was that a corps, consisting of six companies, was embodied on 1st April 1887. The corps had the honour of being inspected on 9th July, 1888, on the occasion of the opening of the 'Queen's Park,' Crewe, by the then Commander-in-Chief of the Army, H.R.H. the Duke of Cambridge, who complimented them very highly on their appearance and steadiness on parade. The corps is expected to furnish 245 men to the Royal Engineers, as a railway reserve, and these men are selected from efficient members of the corps. They receive reserve pay and are liable to be called up for service at any time, and it is a portion of these men who are now serving with the Army in South Africa. Although classed with the first-class Army Reserve, they are really volunteers who have enlisted in the Royal Engineers for one day, as a matter of form, and then have been transferred to the reserve. The present strength of the corps is about 760 including the reserves to whom I have referred."

"How many of the men have been called up for service?"

"126 left Crewe on 16th October. A further 104 have now been ordered to report themselves, and to hold themselves in readiness for active service. In addition to these, upwards of 300 members of the corps not in the reserves have volunteered for active service; and the War Office have notified their acceptance of two sections, each consisting of one officer and 25 rank and file."

The Boer War Memorial in Queen's Park Crewe for the Cheshire Engineers (Railway Volunteers). The tall column surmounted by soldier in khaki. A model of a Webb Jubilee is mounted on the plinth. A large pavilion and tea room in typical LNWR black and white is situated at the rear.

Chapter 14

Birmingham New Street

Notable Railway Stations
by S.M. Philip, London and North Western Railway

The claim of New Street Station, Birmingham, to rank amongst the "Notable Railway Stations" of this country rests on more grounds than one. Its fine proportions alone would entitle it to this distinction, for it is admittedly one of the largest railway stations in the kingdom; but in addition it is, or was, the terminus of one of the earliest passenger railways in the country – The London and Birmingham; and it is the most important station in one of the busiest and most important cities in England, sheltering under its ample roof two of the three great companies who between them provide all the train service to and from Birmingham. But apart from all this anyone to whom the station is familiar is aware of one distinctive characteristic pertaining to it, and that is its intense all-pervading bustle and activity. Birmingham, as most people are aware, is one of the busiest and most thriving commercial centres in the country, and it would seem as if its great railway station had imbibed and partaken of its spirit, and become as eager, as restless, and as bustling as the city itself. At other railway stations there are times of pressure, and times of comparative stagnation; at New Street there seems to be pressure all day long. At other stations people walk; at New Street they almost run, for everyone seems to be in a hurry. To stand on the bridge which dominates the station and look around is like gazing on a panorama, for almost every minute a train is running in and disgorging its hurrying stream of passengers; or a train is about to depart, and passengers are hurrying to join it. Everywhere people are crowding up one staircase or down another, and every one of them seems pressed for time. This is the distinguishing note of New Street Station – ceaseless bustle and activity.

New Street is, no doubt, by many people still looked upon as a station of the London and North Western Railway; and they are right in so far as that the freehold of the station is still vested in that Company; yet to all intents and purposes, it is now, and has been since 1897, a joint station of the London and North Western and Midland Companies. The story of the Midland Company's connection with New Street belongs to the early history of railways in this country, and may be worth recalling.

The London and Birmingham Railway, as many people know, was one of the earliest passenger railways ever projected, Parliament having sanctioned its construction in 1833; but its original terminus in Birmingham was not at New Street, but at Curzon Street, where the London and North Western Company's principal goods station in Birmingham is now situated; indeed, in the Curzon Street Goods yard there stands today, in good preservation, the old portico, with its massive Doric columns, which formed the frontage of the original passenger station. In 1828 powers were obtained for constructing a "railway or tramway" from Bristol to Gloucester, and in 1836 another Act authorised the making of a railway from Gloucester to Birmingham, forming a junction with the London and Birmingham, and having running powers over the latter railway to its then terminus at Curzon Street. In 1846 when

Birmingham New Street 1890 view through station looking towards the Stour Valley line with Queen's Hotel on the right, platform 2 in the centre with train of 6-wheel stock. 4ft.6in. tanks Nos. 522 and 894 in platform 1 on the right.

the Stour Valley Railway between Wolverhampton and Birmingham was authorised, powers were given for the making of a central station in Birmingham, at first known as Navigation Street, but now familiar to us as New Street Station, and this, when constructed, became the terminus of the London and Birmingham Railway instead of Curzon Street. To revert for a moment to the Acts of 1828 and 1836, which, in conjunction with the amending Acts, authorised the railways between Bristol and Birmingham, the promoters of those Acts, as was not uncommon with railway promoters in the early days, appear to have found that when they had obtained their Parliamentary powers they were only at the beginning of their troubles, and that before the necessary capital could be raised, and the railways constructed, it would be necessary for a dividend on the shares to be guaranteed by some established railway company. The powers were, of course, valuable and it was distinctly in the interest of the London and North Western Company that the railway should be made, as it opened up the way to an important exchange of traffic between the West of England and the North over their line by way of Birmingham.

The Midland Company were interested in the same way, and thus it came about that these two Companies, the North Western and the Midland, were induced to guarantee a fixed rate of dividend on the capital of the Bristol and Birmingham Railways, another deciding factor being that there was some apprehension that the required guarantee might be furnished by the Great Western

Birmingham New Street in Sept 1885. View from east end along platform 2 looking west towards footbridge. The light engine on the through road is a McConnell 'Bloomer' 2-2-2 No.1816 in excellent condition (built at Wolverton works in 1861). The 6 wheel carriage on the right is 3rd class No.1523. Note the double gas lamps along the platform.

Company, who were then committed to the broad gauge. In that case, of course, the Bristol and Birmingham Railway would have been made in conjunction with the Great Western, and upon the broad gauge instead of the normal 4ft. 8½ in. gauge, which a large number of railways in this country had adopted.

A few years passed, and in 1846, the Midland Company, who had meanwhile tightened their hold upon the Bristol and Birmingham, obtained powers to absorb it altogether. The North Western guarantee of half the share capital remained, but by an agreement entered into in 1847, this was got rid of, and a bargain was struck which was thought to be mutually advantageous to both parties. Briefly put, the nature of the bargain was that the Midland Company released the North Western from their share of the Bristol and Birmingham guarantee, taking it on their own shoulders, while on the other hand, the North Western gave the Midland the use of their fine station at New Street, subject to a merely nominal rent, and the payment of a certain share of the working expenses. It was in this way that the Midland first gained a footing in the station, but at that time, they stood purely in the light of a tenant company.

Even at that time (1847) it was a fine station, with a grand roof span, covering seven and a quarter acres of ground, but in course of time, it became manifest that the rapid growth of the two Companies' traffic had rendered an extensive enlargement necessary. This raised rather a nice question of policy as between the Boards of the two Companies; the extension was obviously necessary, but who was to pay for it? The station belonged to the North Western Company, and the Midland Company were entitled to the use of it for a nominal sum; but, on the other hand, the North Western could plead that it was the growth of the Midland Company's traffic, as well as their own, that had necessitated the enlargement. To do the Midland Company justice, they met the question very fairly and reasonably, and, without any undue haggling, it was agreed that the enlargement should be carried out, and that they should bear a fair share of the cost, based on the relative user of the two Companies. The extension, which was carried out on the south side, had the effect of making the station just double its original size, increasing the area from 7¼ acres to 14½ acres, or upwards of 70,000 square yards. What was done, in fact, was that the thoroughfare known as Great Queen Street, which formerly bounded the station on its south side, became a central carriage drive, and the old station was virtually reproduced on the south side of this roadway.

The alterations, first mooted in 1880, were commenced in 1882, and completed and brought into use in 1885, and since that time, as a matter of convenient arrangement, the Midland Company's trains have been accommodated in the new part of the station, the old station being restricted to the North Western Company's use for their own trains, although both Companies, as a matter of right, are entitled to use the entire station.

New Street June 1905. view across the station from the hotel next to platform 1. The Stour Valley route is on the right and London on the left. In the Stour Valley bay in the foreground are 6-wheeled 28ft brake 2nd No.12 and 1st/2nd composite No.717. In the through platform are 50ft. 3rd No.1762 and 1st No.101.

Only five years had elapsed when an almost equally serious expenditure became inevitable in connection with New Street Station. The station is peculiarly situated inasmuch as it lies in a hollow, and is approached both from the east and the west in tunnels, the mouths of which are actually within the confines of the station, but the trouble arose in connection with the east (commonly, though rather incorrectly, termed the "south") tunnel, and the lines leading to it. It must be understood that the Rugby and Birmingham Railway, at a point rather more than a mile from its terminus at New Street, was joined by the Midland Company's line from Bristol to Gloucester coming from the south-west, while a quarter of a mile further on it was joined by the line from Derby coming from the north-east, and still a quarter of a mile further on, the London and North Western line from Lichfield and Aston whipped in, crossing the intersecting lines running into the Curzon Street goods yard.

Thus in the last mile of the run into Birmingham, four busy railways all practically ran into a kind of "bottle-neck," and served to obstruct each other, so that the line from Gloucester Junction to New Street, and the single pair of rails through the east tunnel, over which the whole of the trains from both Companies from whatever direction must run, became for passengers, it must be admitted, a veritable *via dolorosa* with a carefully arranged timetable, if every train ran punctually, and nothing happened out of course, all might be well, but timetables are sometimes counsels of perfection, and in foggy, or otherwise bad weather, or at holiday times, when ordinary traffic was duplicated or trebled, passengers often enjoyed ample opportunities of studying the interesting features of one of the latest suburbs of Birmingham while seated in the trains waiting the welcome "Line Clear."

Few diseases are so desperate that they admit of no remedy, and a remedy was found for this one. A scheme was devised for widening the east tunnel, laying down two additional lines of rails between Gloucester Junction and Birmingham, diverting the Derby line so as to take it under the London and Birmingham to the south side, and prolonging the Gloucester line alongside it to the point where the new widened lines were reached, thus doing away with the junctions altogether, and giving all trains, whether from Gloucester, Derby, London, or Lichfield, a free run in and out of New Street independent of all others. The intersection at Curzon Street had been got rid of about three years earlier, the Lichfield line being carried over the goods lines by a viaduct. It was a fine scheme, but the cost involved was, of course, very large, and again the question arose as to how it should be borne. Once more the Midland Company loyally rose to the occasion, and recognised their obligation to share the burden by paying their fair quota of the outlay, but this time they sought to impose a condition. They thought that as they would now have invested so considerable a stake in the New Street Station, they were morally entitled to a voice in the management, and as the North Western Company could hardly deny this to be a reasonable contention, they conceded the point, and New Street, since the year 1897, has been, to all intents and purposes, a joint station, managed by a Joint Committee, and worked by a joint staff under a Joint Superintendent.

The writer has thought it worthwhile to recall the history of these negotiations because they form a good illustration of the methods by which railway companies, by the exercise of common sense and a reasonable spirit of compromise, frequently deal amicably with negotiations involving the expenditure of very large sums, instead of wasting time, temper, and money in obstinate disputes and expensive litigation.

The widening of the eastern approach lines to New Street, and the diversion of the Gloucester and Derby lines, were duly carried out and brought into use in May 1896, since which there has been a great and most gratifying improvement in the working of trains in and out of the station.

One of the most remarkable and striking features about New Street Station is the bridge, which is in

New Street in June 1905. View through station from Coffee Tavern at the Stour Valley end of platform 3 looking towards Coventry. In the centre Watford Tank No. 2037 heads long train of 6-wheeled stock - indicator shows 'Walsall Express'.

fact the key to the whole station, besides being the busiest public thoroughfare in the City of Birmingham. When, in 1846, powers were granted by Parliament for the construction of the station, it was foreseen that this would absorb a huge slice of land in the very heart of the city, and that to get from north to south of the station, or vice versa, would involve a very long *detour* for foot passengers between two busy neighbourhoods, unless some special provisions were made for them. Accordingly a clause was inserted in the Act rendering it obligatory upon the Company to provide, and at all times to maintain and keep open, a footbridge across the station for the use of the public. Being under this obligation, the Company, making a merit of necessity, so laid out the station, and so constructed the bridge that the latter should serve as the means – and the only means - of access between the town and the various platforms on the station.

The bridge thus "contrives a double debt to pay." It extends completely across the station, the new portion as well as the old, from New Street on the north side to Station Street on the south side, with staircases leading down right and left at intervals to all the various platforms.

Thus every passenger who alights from or enters any train at New Street must pass over the footbridge, and in addition it is one of the main arteries of the city from north to south for the general public. The result is that an extraordinary tide of humanity is passing over this bridge in both directions all through the day, from morning till near midnight, without ceasing; in one endless procession and the spectacle is really a most impressive one. All classes are represented in the motley throng – the aristocrat and the barefooted newspaper boy, merchants, clerks, workmen, factory lads, and lasses – the bridge serves them all.

"Laughing, weeping, hurrying ever,
 Hour by hour they crowd along."

Midway on the bridge, a widely known firm of tobacconists, with their usual acuteness and foresight have, by arrangement with the Company, established a shop, and probably in all Europe it would be difficult to find a more splendid site for such a business.

It has already been said that New Street is one of the leviathan railway stations in the country as regards size, and truly its proportions need to be ample to cope with the enormous traffic which flows in and out of it every day throughout the year. Nominally there are six platforms, Nos.1,2, and 3, being reserved for the North Western Company's trains and Nos. 4,5, and 6 for the Midland trains; but as a matter of fact, these six platforms, which have an aggregate area of 146,520 square feet, and a total length of 2,850

Birmingham New Street. View along cab road, Queen's Drive, looking east with the new part of the station on the right. Two storey Midland Railway Booking Office in centre. LNWR cabs and horse omnibus on cab road. Sept 1885.

yards, or more than a mile and a half, are of such great extent, that, being constructed on the island principle, and some of them worked in both directions, each one is able to accommodate three or four trains simultaneously. The station has a very fine roof, extending over upwards of 41,000 square yards, or 8½ acres, one span of this roof alone, that which covers the old or original station, having a span of 210 feet.

Some idea of the business done at New Street may be gathered from the fact that on any ordinary day of 24 hours, there are close upon 700 trains in and out of the station, exclusive of shunting operations and the movements of engines and trains of empty carriages. This is an average of one train in and out every two minutes, but if it be borne in mind that during certain hours of the night, say between midnight and 5am, the trains are very few in number, it will be evident that during the more busy parts of the day the number must greatly exceed the average. Here are the arrivals and departures during some of the more crowded "business" hours:-

	Trains Arriving	Trains Departing	Total
Between 8 and 9am	26	21	47
" 9 " 10am	26	27	53
" 10 " 11am	16	16	32
" 11 " 12noon	19	15	34
" 4 " 5pm	17	18	35
" 5 " 6pm	25	24	49
" 6 " 7pm	17	21	38
" 7 " 8pm	18	20	38

(this is an average of over 40 an hour during 8 hours)

No.1713 Special DX Class 0-6-0 at New Street. 857 DXs were built by John Ramsbottom between 1858 and 1872 as goods engines making them the largest class to be built in the UK (a further 86 were built for the L&Y Railway). Many were later rebuilt by FW Webb with new boilers and vacuum brakes allowing them to be used on passenger trains and were reclassified as "Special DXs".

These figures represent the ordinary average working of the station, but at holiday seasons, of course, they are largely exceeded, and on the August Bank Holiday, for example, it is no unusual experience for the staff at New Street to have to deal with as many as 900 trains in a day of 24 hours, this number, of course, including ordinary passenger trains, excursions, and relief trains, and trains of empty carriages.

These are large figures, but probably only a railway official can effectively grasp them, and realise the task of dealing with 900, or even 700, trains in and out of one station in a day.

What will convey perhaps more forcibly to those of my readers who are not railway experts the enormous business which is conducted at New Street Station will be to inform them that the number of passengers carried in and out of the station by both companies during the past year, including the journeys of season ticket holders, considerably exceeded *Fifteen Millions and a half.* Leaving out Sundays, when traffic is comparatively light, this would give an average of nearly 50,000 per day, and this mighty army must pass day by day over the bridge, in addition to the general public, not being railway passengers, who make a highway of it.

To deal with the immense business, the two companies employ at New Street Station, either on the joint staff, or on their separate account, about 560 porters, ticket collectors, guards, parcel men, and others.

For the working of the complicated system of points and signals regulating access to the station at both ends, six signal cabins are required, which contain in aggregate 382 levers. The largest of these is No.5, situated at the north end of the station, which contains 145 levers, and requires three men night and day to work it, so that a staff of nine signalmen is employed to man it on three 8-hour shifts.

The footbridge, spacious and convenient as it is, would be found lamentably deficient for its purpose if, in addition to the foot passengers, there had to be carried over it the vast quantities of luggage and parcels traffic which is brought to and from the station, but this is otherwise provided for. To the right and left of the bridge, near the two ends of the station, are commodious subways, passing under the whole of the lines and platforms from one side of the station to the other, with inclined slopes to each platform, and lifts for heavy luggage and parcels. These subways are available for foot passengers who choose to make use of them, primarily they are intended for luggage. Leading out of the subway at the west end of the station is another underground passage connecting the platforms with the General Post Office buildings in Hill Street, a facility which is of incalculable advantage in the conduct of the Post Office work in connection with the railways. During the Christmas week of 1899, there were nearly 17,000 Post Office receptacles containing postal parcels sent away from New Street, and this was independent of the mails and of the Parcel Post Hampers exchanged at Birmingham between the two railways amounting to many thousands. The exchange of postal matter between the railways at Birmingham is always a very important feature in the working of the station, Birmingham being a sort of handing-over point for mails coming from the West of England, and going to the Midland Counties and to the North, or vice versa.

In connection with the subway at the eastern or London end of the station, there is an underground passage leading to the parcels office in Worcester Street, and another debouching in Station Street, with an entrance contiguous to the Market Hall, and very convenient for the market folk who bring produce to the trains.

There are eight booking offices, four for each company, and the intending passenger enters these from the street, passing through them onto the bridge. As soon as he sets foot on the bridge, which, as already stated, is the sole access to the platforms, he is faced by a huge board informing him generally from which platforms the various trains start, for instance, "London and the South,

18in. Cauliflower 0-6-0 No.195 with passenger train at Birmingham New Street.

No.1," "Sutton and Lichfield, No.2," and so on, each staircase being numbered. At the head of each staircase is a list of all the trains that start from that particular platform throughout the day, and the passenger, having thus verified the fact that the particular train he is seeking will be found somewhere at the foot of this particular staircase, on descending, will be confronted at the bottom by an indicator pointing plainly to the train, right or left, as the case may be.

There are, of course, times of stress and emergency when all this admirable order and method have to a certain extent to be cast to the winds, and the best has to be done under the circumstances, and such a time is the evening of a fine Bank Holiday, when the scene at New Street Station is one which, once beheld, will not readily be forgotten. The writer has seen late at night on a Whit Monday every one of the vast platforms, and the bridge itself, packed from edge to edge, and from end to end, with one seething, swaying mass of people, so dense that it was difficult for an individual to move a yard, and the officials themselves had the greatest difficulty in forcing a passage through the crowds.

It would manifestly be an almost impossible task to give any detailed account of the many hundreds of trains which arrive at or depart from New Street Station in the course of a day. It must suffice to say that the train service is made up of several distinct elements. Not the least important of these is the local or suburban traffic, which is a very extensive one.

One of the most important services of this kind is the one between Birmingham and Sutton Coldfield, which accommodates Gravelly Hill, Erdington, Wylde Green, and Sutton Coldfield itself, some of the trains being extended to Four Oaks, a growing suburb, while others run as far as Lichfield. There are about 30 trains per day in each direction between Birmingham and Sutton, and the service is so good and so well arranged that it is not uncommon for those who reside on the branch, and have their business in the city, to go to and fro for their meals. These are season ticket holders, who get good value for their money!

The Midland Railway also have a line between Birmingham and Sutton Coldfield by another route passing by way of Saltley, Castle Bromwich, and Penns, and thence beyond to Walsall and Wolverhampton. Most of the trains they run on this line stop at all stations, and constitute a good local service between Birmingham and Sutton Coldfield.

Another great residential district is that served by the Harborne branch, and, between New Street and Harborne, the London and North Western company run a frequent service of trains throughout the day, performing the journey in a quarter of an hour, while they have a circular service starting from Birmingham and running out of the north end of the station, round by Soho, Handsworth, and Perry Barr, and into New Street at the south end, and vice versa. The round trip is performed in about half an hour. Another London and North Western service is between Birmingham and Coventry, serving what is becoming a growing neighbourhood around Stechford, Yardley, and Marston Green, in addition to which numerous trains throughout the day ply to and from between New Street and the densely populated suburb of Aston. On the south side the Midland have two services running out in the direction of Barnt Green, Redditch, and Droitwich, one running by way of Moseley and King's Heath, and the other by way of Selly Oak and Bourneville, and both these are available for residential purposes.

But in addition to the suburban traffic, New Street has to deal with numerous and important through services, and it is also a terminal station for the services of trains which run between Birmingham and Wolverhampton and Stafford. On the other hand, it is merely a calling place for the splendid service of trains which exists by the London and North Western route between London, Birmingham and Wolverhampton. All these trains originate in Wolverhampton on the up journey, and terminate there on the down journey, there being usually ten minutes' stop at New Street. Some very fine trains run between Birmingham and Liverpool and Manchester, stopping only at Wolverhampton and Crewe and performing the journey in about two hours and a quarter, and for these Birmingham is the terminal station.

Turning to the Midland side, we find again that New Street is a terminal station for some services, and a passing place for others. It is merely a calling place for the admirable service of trains which runs from Bristol, Gloucester, Cheltenham and other places in the west of England, through Birmingham northwards to Tamworth, Burton, and Derby. Some of these are very fine trains, running the distance between Bristol and Derby in just over three hours, and only stopping at Cheltenham and Birmingham. Yet, for many Midland trains running in the direction of Worcester, Gloucester, and Derby, Birmingham is the starting point.

Land in great cities is far too valuable to be occupied as carriage sheds, and as a rule the next best thing is done by providing carriage depots away from the stations, but as near to them as possible, and with convenient access to and fro. In the case of New Street, the ample proportions of the station admit of a certain number of carriages standing within it, but not by any means the whole of those required, and accordingly, it has been found necessary to erect extensive carriage sheds on the outskirts of the city. The London and North Western Company have done this at Monument Lane on the north side and at Vauxhall on the south, while the Midland Company's depot is at Saltley. There the vehicles not only are stored, but are cleaned, examined, charged with gas, and made ready for use, by a large staff of men specially employed for the purpose.

The Queen's Hotel, which is under the management of the London and North Western Railway, forms the frontage to the station, and there is direct access from the platforms to the

Birmingham New Street entry to station and the Queen's and North Western Hotels viewed from Stephenson Square. Shows the Hardwick Gates which were originally from Curzon Street. LNWR Enquiry and Tourist Office at the front. 1904.

hotel, with lifts for the passengers' luggage, while there are commodious refreshment rooms on every platform except No.2, which is only used for local trains. There are cloak rooms on Nos. 1,3,4, and 6 platforms, and three postal telegraph offices, so that all the needs of passengers are well supplied.

A quaint old writer (Roscoe) who published a book on certain railway matters as long ago as 1839, seems to have been very much impressed by the bustle and activity displayed at the terminus of the London and Birmingham Railway which was then at Curzon Street. He says:-

"The scene at this place immediately before the starting of the train is irresistibly striking, and greatly resembles the bustle and variety which give so much animation to the piers and promenades of the fashionable watering places on the coast. Indeed, the perpetual succession of trains *arriving and departing nearly every hour* with the stream of passengers pursuing their way to and from the station bids fair to assimilate the towns in the very centre of England to the liveliness and ever-shifting variety of its Ports."

If this ancient writer could but "re-visit the glimpses of the moon," and behold New Street Station with its 700 trains and 50,000 passengers a day, one can only vaguely wonder what he would think of it! [Ed: now 170,000 passengers a day!]

Chapter 15
LNWR Liverpool Express
World-famous Trains
by Victor L. Whitechurch

When I began to think of my choice of subject in connection with a "world–famous train" a vision passed my mind of many splendid expresses. Two – the "American Special" and the "Irish Mail" – were struck out of the list at once, however, partly because I have already described each of these runs pretty fully, and partly because I wanted a train that should run between two termini purely and simply, and in connection with no steam boats. The "Scotch Express" claimed my thoughts, only to be dismissed, because I wanted, again, a train that ran over the London and North Western system only, and not consisting of joint stock. Then there naturally followed a choice of trains between Euston and Liverpool, or Manchester or Birmingham. The first of these seemed so very much the best, for many reasons, that I wrote to Mr Turnbull, and suggested it, receiving a reply that I had made an excellent choice, and enclosing an exchange order for a ticket.

Just a few words of introduction before I begin the actual details. Here are, perhaps, the two most important cities in England. At all events, there

'Problem' Class No.117 "Tiger" piloting a 'Teutonic' with a down Liverpool Express at Weedon c1900.

can be no question about London, though perhaps the "Manchester man" who reads these lines may bristle up at the idea of placing Liverpool before his metropolis of cotton, and may reply to the mild suggestion that Liverpool possesses one of the finest harbours in England, "Pooh! Haven't we got the Ship Canal?" But putting the vexed question aside, here are, as I say, two of our very greatest commercial centres, a couple of hundred miles apart, but brought into very close connection with each other by means of the shining lines of metals between them – brought into such constant and easy connection that even the season-ticket holder from London to Liverpool is to be met in nearly every express train. Now, no route comes up to that of the London and North Western Railway. Of course, there is the Great Western route, via Birkenhead and Woodside Ferry, and that of the Midland; but neither of these is to be compared with the "4½ hour service" of the London and North Western. And even this is not by any means the "quickest" journey between the two towns, for, as I have shown before, the "American Special" does the trip from Euston to Edge Hill in 3¾ hours without a stop; and, tell it not to the "railwayae," for he knows it already, every good four-coupled "Jumbo" knows within her pulsating heart and expansion cylinder that if only she were allowed to run as she could run, that 4¼ hours would tumble down, while as for No. 1919 – that new creation with four cylinders and a bogie, who ran us from Crewe to Euston on the return journey – she only played with the heavy train, and snorted contemptuously when she saw me entering notes of the speed at the end of the journey.

No.234 "Mazeppa" Ramsbottom Problem Class 7ft 6in single 2-2-2 with Webb cab and boiler mounting, closed splasher and drop down smokebox door with train of 6-wheel stock. Liverpool Lime Street c1900.

Liverpool Lime Street departure platforms with good view of interior in 1901.

In 1846 the London and Birmingham, the Liverpool and Manchester, the Grand Junction and the Manchester and Birmingham Railways were amalgamated, under the title of the London and North Western Railway, and a route to Liverpool, via Birmingham, was available for the adventurous traveller on the one system. "At that time," says a writer, "it was possible, without delay of a night in Birmingham, to get through from London to Liverpool in 14¾ hours." Since then they have knocked 10½ hours off this time, and varied the route considerably. Today there are thirteen regular trains each way between Euston and Lime Street every weekday, and five on Sundays. That the comfort of the passengers is well studied will be found from the following:-

In the course of each day, from London to Liverpool, there is one train with luncheon cars, one with drawing-room cars, three with dining-room cars, and one with sleeping-room cars; while, running from Liverpool to London, we have one train with breakfast car, one with luncheon car, one with dining-room car, and one with sleeping-room car. Of these thirteen trains, there are two each way, that may, *par excellence*, be characterised as the "crack" expresses between the two great cities, the only trains which do the journey in 4¼ hours. They are:-

Down – The 10.15am express, stopping at Willesden Junction and Stafford only.
The 5.30pm express from Euston, stopping at Crewe only.

Up – The 9.45am express from Lime Street (Liverpool), stopping at Stafford and Willesden only.

The 4.5pm express from Lime Street, stopping at Crewe and Willesden only.

It is my intention to give a few notes concerning two of these four trains – namely, the 10.15am down, and the 4.5pm up.

The 10.15 train from Euston to Liverpool is the old 10.10am which ran for some fifteen or sixteen years until about two years ago, when the hour of departure was delayed until 10.15, the reason being that the 10am Scotch express has grown into such a heavy train that it is frequently necessary to run it in two portions, and, naturally, three express trains despatched on the main line within ten minutes meant a little too close work. The original train used to occupy 4½ hours on the journey, and stopped at Willesden, Bletchley, Nuneaton, Crewe and Runcorn.

The 10.15am express from Euston is, as it starts, a composite train, the first part going to Liverpool, the second, taken off at Stafford, having Manchester for its destination with a stop at Stoke, besides which there are some through coaches for the "Central Wales" system which ultimately reach their respective destinations of Aberystwyth and Swansea. The average number of vehicles on the whole train is seventeen or eighteen, and, in most cases, an extra engine is required as far as Willesden only; but on Monday morning, the day I happened to travel, the passenger traffic between London and Liverpool is always heavier, and the train generally has two engines to Stafford. The particular morning in question I found the train consisted of 20½ vehicles made up as follows:-

A – The Liverpool Portion
 1. Six-wheel brake
 2. Bogie, "compo" third and second class and luggage compartment
 3. Bogie, second and third class dining car
 4. Bogie, second and third class dining car
 5. Bogie, (twelve-wheeled) first class dining car
 6. Bogie, first and third class "compo"
 7. Bogie, "compo," brake and third class

B – The Manchester Portion
 1. Bogie, first and third "compo"
 2. Bogie, first and second "compo"
 3. Bogie, third
 4. Bogie, second and third, and brake compartment, "compo"
 5. Six-wheeled brake

C – For Central Wales
 1. Bogie, "compo" for Aberystwyth
 2. Bogie, "compo" for Llangammarch, Llanwrtyd Wells, etc. Two trucks (braked)
 3. Six-wheeled brake.

A and B sections are vestibuled throughout. The "second and third class dining cars" are, in reality, ordinary corridor coaches, with a folding table made to let down in each compartment. This is a very favourite device of the London and North Western Railway, as I have already shown when describing the Irish service. The two engines which were to pull us as far as Stafford were the "Oceanic" and the "Alma," the former being the type generally used on this train.

In addition to the guard, the train staff of the Liverpool portion consists of the following: One train attendant, four waiters, one chef, one assistant cook. And they have all their work cut out, too, for the lunches are served en route, one before and the other after the stop at Stafford. The train is beautifully appointed throughout, and the journey is excellent as regards comfort.

Punctually at 10.15 we were off, and I settled down to study the working timetable with a view to working out the speed and comparing it with the actual running. I append a carefully compiled log of the latter, compared with the scheduled timing, and a few deductions from the running will be, I think, most interesting to the lover of express trains.

Euston to Liverpool is 193½ miles, so the average speed works out at 45.52 miles per hour for the whole journey. Deduct from this the few minutes allowed for stopping at Willesden and Stafford, and we have a running average of 47.19 miles per hour. Not an extra high speed, perhaps, but one that is splendidly maintained from year's end to year's end by the drivers who know that they are really allowed too much time, and often have to hold their engines in. The best bit of long-distance running is that between Willesden and Stafford, the 127¾ miles being covered in 2hrs. 32mins, at an average speed of 50.4 miles per hour. Allowing for several minutes lost in the reduction of speed at Atherstone Crossing, this average works out very well. When running with two engines it is necessary to stop at Nuneaton for water, the reason being that it is practically impossible for the locomotives to make use of the picking-up troughs at the same time, as the first engine debars the second from scooping up water. Notice how easily the three minutes were made up in the down gradient between Tring and Blisworth, and how a minute ahead of time was kept till beyond Rugby. Again, although two minutes were lost at Stafford through a tight coupling, the time was easily regained beyond Crewe, and the arrival was punctual. The thing that struck one most, both going and returning, was the ease in running in less than scheduled time when necessary. The following is the "log":-

Station		Scheduled Time	Actual Time
Euston	dep	10.15	10.15
Willesden	arr	10.25	10.25
Willesden	dep	10.28	10.29
Harrow	pass		10.33
Watford	"	10.42	10.45
Berkhampstead	"		10.58
Tring	"	10.59	11.2
Cheddington	"		11.6½
Bletchley	"	11.16	11.16
Wolverton	"		11.21
Roade	"	11.31	11.30
Blisworth	"		11.33
Weedon	"		11.42½
Rugby	"	11.58	11.57
Brinklow	"		12.5pm
Bulkington	"		12.11
Nuneaton	"	12.15	12.15*
Atherstone	"		12.28
Polesworth	"		12.31½
Tamworth	"	12.31	12.35
Lichfield	"		12.43
Rugeley	"	12.49	12.49
Colwich	"		12.53

Station		Scheduled Time	Actual Time
Stafford	arr	1.0	1.0
Stafford	dep	1.5	1.7
Norton Bridge	pass		1.17
Standon Bridge	"		1.23
Madeley	"		1.31
Crewe	"	1.37	1.40
Winsford	"		1.52
Acton Bridge	"		1.59
Runcorn	"		2.9
Ditton Junction	"		2.13
Liverpool Edge Hill	"		2.25
Liverpool Lime Street	arr	2.30	2.30

* Stopped at Nuneaton 3½ minutes for water

At Stafford the train is broken up. The front portion proceeds at once to Liverpool, with one engine only (The "Lord Herschell") in our case. The Manchester portion goes forward five minutes later, while the Welsh coaches proceed at 1.14, via Shrewsbury.

A few notes on the number of passengers, etc, may prove of interest. On this particular Monday the following was the total of London to Liverpool passengers: - First class, 18; second class, 23, third class, 100; total 141.

In the old days this number would not have necessitated the running of so many coaches, but, under modern circumstances, the corridor coach presents a serious problem on account of the immense waste of space and subsequent additional weight. We see the result in the number of trains that have to be run in two parts, or with two engines, during a busy season, and what passengers gain in comfort and safety the railway undoubtedly has to sacrifice in increased outlay and working expenses.

The number of luncheons served on the run to Liverpool was as follows:- first class,18, at 2s 6d each; second class,16 and third class, 32, at 2s each. These luncheons are cheap, and admirably served. They and the diners constitute one of the chief features on the London and Liverpool service, and there are many regular passengers who look upon the train very much in the light of a hotel, and where idiosyncrasies are studied by and known to the attendants as carefully as the waiter in a City restaurant looks after his regular customers.

After a very pleasant run, we drew up at Lime Street terminus punctually to time. In five minutes the passengers had dispersed, the luggage was out, and the train was in the hands of a little army of cleaners, being furbished up and swept ready for the return journey at 4.5.

I had time for a little stroll, and shortly before 4 o'clock found myself back again at the station, watching the bustling scene at the departure platform, a scene that is ever full of new interest whenever one of our crack expresses leaves its terminus. The train, of course, consisted of the same number of vehicles as on the down journey (10½), but with the addition of three bogie coaches and a six-wheeled brake at the front, designed to separate at Crewe and proceed to Birmingham, arriving there at 6.38. With such a load a couple

3-horse bus from Liverpool Lime Street to Landing Stage labelled 'Isle of Man Steamers'.

Lime Street exterior showing end screen of the South East arch of roof. Royal Hotel on right. Electric tram on right for Pier Head. c1905.

of engines were necessary as far as Crewe, and "President Washington" and "Abercrombie" came backing up a few minutes before the start. Crewe could have been reached some minutes before time, but we ran in slowly only a minute ahead. Then ensued a bustling scene. Five minutes only was allowed to take off the Birmingham portion, couple on a new engine, and attach a couple of carriages to the rear of the train, which carriages start from Birkenhead at 3.38, and are "Through" to Euston. No. 1919, the "Resolution", was waiting, in all her magnificence, to take us on, and though she had a load of 13½ behind her, as I stated in the beginning of this article, she only played with this train, and could have done the run in far under the scheduled time if the "powers that be" had allowed her. She simply crawled from Harrow to Willesden in order not to arrive too early and get a scolding.

I append another carefully compiled log of the up journey, which I trust will prove of interest to my readers. Of course, the average throughout is the same as the down train, but the average from Crewe to Willesden, a run of 152½ miles without a stop, works out at just about 49.4 miles per hour. But a glance at the running log will show that a very much higher speed is attained at certain points, notably on the down gradient from Tring to Watford.

Precursor No.2023 "Helvellyn" waiting to depart from Lime Street.

Station		Scheduled Time	Actual Time
Liverpool Lime Street	dep	4.5pm	4.5
Ditton Junction	pass		4.23
Runcorn	"		4.26
Acton Bridge	"		4.37
Winsford	pass		4.45
Crewe	arr	4.57	4.56
Crewe	dep	5.2	5.2
Madeley	pass		5.15
Norton Bridge	"		5.28
Stafford	"	5.32	5.33
Colwich	"		5.40
Rugeley	"	5.43	5.43
Lichfield	"		5.51
Tamworth	"	5.59	5.58
Polesworth	"		6.2
Atherstone	"		6.7
Nuneaton	"	6.18	6.15
Bulkington	"		6.20
Brinklow	"		6.25
Rugby	"	6.30	6.31
Weedon	"		6.47
Blisworth	"		6.55
Roade	"	6.59	6.59
Wolverton	"		7.6
Bletchley	"	7.15	7.14
Cheddington	"		7.28
Tring	"	7.31	7.31
Berkhampstead	"		7.40
Watford	"	7.52	7.49
Harrow	"		7.57
Willesden	arr	8.7	8.5
Willesden	dep	8.10	8.10
Euston	arr	8.20	8.20

We had a fair number of passengers on the return journey, namely: first class, 18, second class, 19, third class, 62; total 99. While dinners were served as follows: first class, 14, at 3s.6d each; second and third class, 34, at 2s.6d each.

Finally, I stepped out of the train, after my run of 387 miles, impressed with the extreme comfort and easy travelling of the whole route. The trains are certainly allowed too much time, and the 4¼ hours could easily be reduced to 4 hours; but the very lack of the necessity to hurry, combined with the splendid management of the company, has turned out a service of trains between these two great centres which it would be hard to beat for punctuality and comfort.

Chapter 16
Carlisle Citadel
Notable Railway Stations
by H.V. French

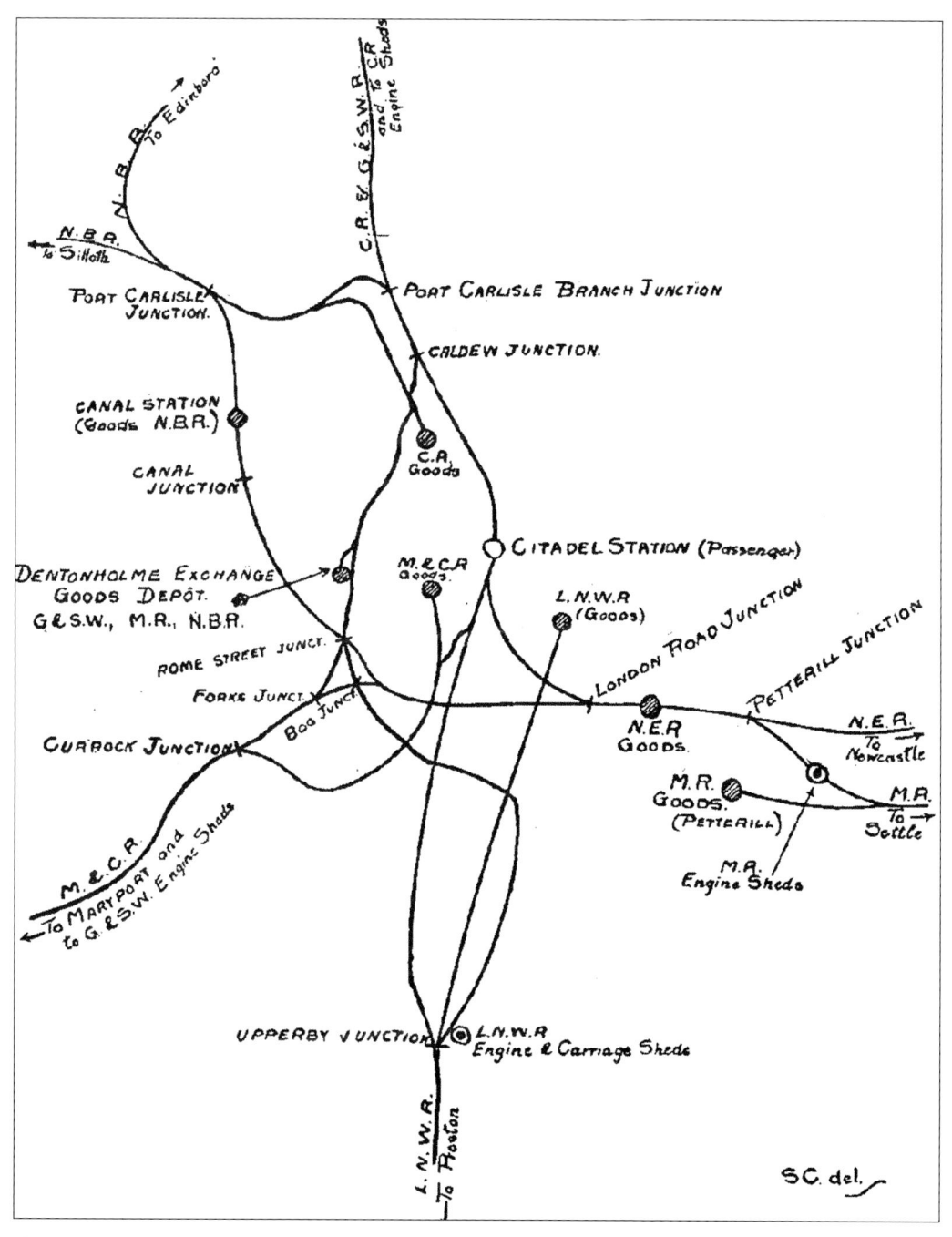

Carlisle Area Map.

It is not an exaggeration to describe Carlisle Citadel Station as one of the best known, best managed, and most important railway centres in the United Kingdom. Situated near the site of the Citadel, which at one time formed the southern bulwark, or English gate of the defences of the ancient fortified city of Carlisle, the railway station has, after several enlargements, assumed gigantic proportions. Even now, in the height of the tourist season, its large area, covered with a glass roof seven acres in extent, is inadequate to the strain put upon its platform resources, and the reason for this congestion of traffic becomes obvious when it is remembered that Carlisle is the terminus of no fewer than seven railway systems, while it is the connecting link between two kingdoms of two out of the three great trunk lines from London giving connection with Scotland. Every through passenger train which leaves either Euston or St. Pancras for "the land of the mountain and the flood," must draw up at one or other of the numerous platforms of Carlisle Citadel Station; and, in addition, to this pressure of express traffic, accommodation has to be found for the ordinary trains of the London and North Western, the Midland, the Caledonian, the North British, the Glasgow and South Western, the North Eastern, and the Maryport and Carlisle lines.

Geographically speaking, the railways converge upon Carlisle as follows: The London and North Western from Euston via Crewe and Preston, from the south; the Midland from St. Pancras, via Leicester, Normanton and Skipton, also from the south; the Maryport and Carlisle, from west Cumberland; the North Eastern (Newcastle and Carlisle) from Newcastle, from the east; the Caledonian, from Aberdeen, Edinburgh (Princes Street) and Glasgow (Central), via Carstairs, from the north; the North British (Waverley route), from Edinburgh (Waverley), via Galashiels and the "Land of Scott" from the north-east; the Glasgow and South Western from Glasgow, via

Carlisle Citadel platform 5 with Whitworth Class No.36 "Thaliba" piloting a 'Jubilee' on an up express. A Midland train is on the left.

Kilmarnock, Dumfries and the "Land of Burns" from the north-west; and the Silloth section of the North British Railway, from the west. It will, therefore, be seen that Carlisle Citadel Station has to provide for the passenger trains of seven distinct railway companies, which enter the station from eight points of the compass. Long ago it was found necessary to exclude all goods and mineral trains from the Citadel Station. Each of the companies named above have their separate goods depots situated at various points, some of which are a considerable distance from the centre of the town. Railway lines circumvent the city, by means of which goods, minerals and other merchandise can be transferred from one company's system to another, so that the Citadel Station is left free for passenger and express fish traffic only. And it is fortunate that this excellent arrangement, necessitated by circumstances years ago, was wisely effected in 1877 by the Joint Board under which the Citadel Station is controlled.

An idea of the animated scenes witnessed in Carlisle Station, at all hours of the day and night, can best be gathered from the following graphic details, which appeared in the "Carlisle Journal" on August 17th, this year:

"HEAVY RAILWAY TRAFFIC THROUGH CARLISLE"

A RECORD TRAIN

"The officials at the Citadel Station have just experienced a period of almost unparalleled pressure, owing to the "rush" to Scotland, which year by year shows a tendency to increase rather than diminish. In spite of some fears that the war and other events might have a depressing effect on the travelling public at the present time, this August has been ushered in on the Royal West Coast route extending from London (Euston) through Carlisle to Edinburgh, Glasgow, Oban and Aberdeen by the most enormous amount of passenger traffic on record. The night of August 10th, and the morning of the 11th, is always a memorable period in regard to long distance traffic on the trunk lines. This year the fact that the 12th August fell on a Sunday tended to spread the pressure over a little longer interval, but officials of the London and North Western Railway at Euston, the Citadel Station staff, and the Caledonian officials northwards have had a busy time. Some idea of the amount of traffic can be gathered from the fact that on the night of August 10th, thirteen Scotch expresses left Euston, and over 300 beds were made up in the trains for first-class tourists only. The first portion of the 7.45pm was filled with first class passengers, all for the Highland Railway, via Dunkeld. The second portion was also for the Highland line only. The next train to leave was the first portion of the 8pm, all of which was for Aberdeen. This express created a record by reaching Carlisle at 2.12am, exactly on time- a feat never before accomplished on any August 10th. The second portion of the same train was for Aberdeen and Oban. Ten minutes later followed the Stranraer boat express, close on the heels of which ran a special horse and carriage train for all parts of Scotland. The express leaving at 8.50pm was for Glasgow (Central) only. Ten minutes afterwards followed a heavy train for Edinburgh only, with a second portion labelled for the north. Last of all came the fastest train on the West Coast route, the 11.50pm in two portions, the first bound for Glasgow and the second for Edinburgh and the north. Nearly all these trains were made up equal to 19½ vehicles, but although the weight was so great and the time between each none too long, wonderful time was kept to Carlisle. As stated above, the train due in Carlisle at 2.12am with a load of 19½ vehicles, was in at "time" and none of the rest were more than six minutes late.

All the running was done without hitch or accident of any kind, so that the perfection of the arrangements over 300 miles of line was unquestionable. Under the direction of Mr Haythornthwaite, the Superintendent of the Citadel Station, the traffic was worked smoothly through Carlisle, excellent assistance being given by Mr Killin, the night stationmaster, and the staff of inspectors. It may be of interest to add that under ordinary circumstances, and exclusive of special trains, the number of trains dealt with each weekday at Citadel Station is as follows: London and North Western 61; Caledonian 45; Midland 35; Glasgow and South Western 32; North British 34; North Eastern 36; Maryport and Carlisle 16; total 259. The London and North Western Company bring thirteen trains to Carlisle, which do not proceed further northwards, while the Caledonian run five trains to Carlisle which end there. Of the sixty-one London and North Western trains, no fewer than forty-three are expresses, and of these ten run over 150 miles each without a stop. The Caledonian have thirty-five expresses on the list, the Midland twenty-three, the Glasgow and South Western seventeen, and the North British fifteen."

The Citadel Station was built by and belongs to the London and North Western and the Caledonian Railways, which together form the West Coast (Royal Mail) route. When, however, the Midland, the North Eastern, the North British, and other companies obtained access, it was deemed advisable to transfer the management to a committee, which was composed of four directors of the London and North Western, and four directors of the Caledonian, elected annually. The station, of course, has existed since the time when the London and North Western was constructed over Shap Fells, but after one enlargement in 1861 it was opened in its present form in 1880, three years after the goods relief lines of the London and North Western, Caledonian, Midland, and the

Whitworth class No.263 "Pheasant" on through road at Carlisle Citadel at the head of a line of engines, the second is No.777 "Richard Trevithick" (Greater Britain) in 1896.

Webb 3-cylinder compound No.1301 "Teutonic" on Carlisle Upperby Shed. 10 Teutonics were built 1889/90.

Glasgow and South Western had been successfully constructed round the city.

The following particulars of the present staff of the station will be of interest to railwaymen: One secretary, one superintendent, one night stationmaster, seven inspectors, seven foremen, twenty signalmen, eighteen ticket-examiners, four luggage-room attendants, four lavatory attendants, eight ladies' room attendants, eleven shunters, six shacklers, seven policemen, thirty-six porters, four lampmen, two engine-men, ten platelayers, eight painters, joiners, plumbers, etc., one chief booking clerk, nine booking clerks, one chief parcels clerk, and sixteen parcels clerks. There are three platforms and five bays in the station; the total length of the covered area is 750 yards, and though the station is "bottle-necked" at both ends, there is ample scope for future development and extensions.

Carlisle is situated exactly 299¼ miles from Euston, and the station has been the scene of many exciting incidents connected with the "race" to Edinburgh between the East and West Coast routes in the summer of 1888, and the still more recent "race" to Aberdeen, between the same routes, in July and August, 1895. The results of these struggles were watched with keen interest all over the country, but in the 1895 race the enthusiasm of the railwaymen of Carlisle reached a high pitch as each night the performances of the West Coast train from Euston to Aberdeen excelled the previous record. On the final night of the competition the "racer" from Euston actually reached Carlisle 4 hours 36 minutes after leaving the Metropolis, a great crowd present on the platform at 12.30 (midnight) to raise a hearty cheer for the intrepid driver of the engine, "Hardwicke." The writer of this article was one of those present on that memorable occasion, and, fired with enthusiasm, lost no time in obtaining the official statistics of the run, from which the following analysis was carefully prepared and published in the columns of the "Carlisle Journal" in August 1895:

"THE WORLD'S RECORD RAILWAY RUN"
"The following table gives the official details of the running of the West Coast Express

from Euston to Aberdeen on the night of August 22nd and morning of August 23rd last. To this train belongs the credit of having established the world's record in all respects – as regards speed, distance run, and time occupied. It left Euston at 8pm, reached Crewe at 10.27, leaving at 10.30; passed Preston at 11.16; reached Carlisle at 12.36am, leaving for the north at 12.38; reached Perth at 3.7½, leaving at 3.9½; and drew up at Aberdeen ticket platform at 4.30, leaving there at 4.31; and finally stopped in Aberdeen Station at 4.32. The total time spent on the whole journey in stoppages was only eight minutes, viz: three minutes at Crewe for change of engines, two minutes at Carlisle, and two minutes at Perth, also for change of engines, and one minute for collection of tickets at Aberdeen ticket platform. The 299¼ miles to Carlisle were consequently run in 273 minutes, and the whole journey of 540 miles in 504 minutes. The West Coast route includes two very heavy gradients – namely, at Shap Summit and at Beattock Summit, each of which is about 1,000 ft. above sea level.

	Miles from Euston	Distance between stations miles. chains	Time Running minutes	Speed per hour miles. chains
London (Euston)	–	–	–	–
Crewe	158	158.0	147	64.39
Preston	209	51.0	46	66.42
Shap Summit	268	59.0	54	65.44
Penrith	281¼	13¼	11	72.22
Carlisle	299¼	18.0	15	72.0
Lockerbie	325	25.63	27	57.24
Beattock	339	13.75	12½	66.72
Summit	349	10.1	13½	44.40
Symington	366¼	17.10	15	68.40
Carstairs	372¼	6.53	6	66.50
Holytown	389	16.27	15½	63.19
Greenhill	405½	16.23	16	61.6
Stirling	417	11.18	11	63.22
Perth	450	33.2	33	60.4
Forfar	482½	32.40	29½	66.8
Kinnaber Jn	501¾	19.25	18	64.30
Stonehaven	523¾	21.68	19½	67.18
Aberdeen ticket platform	540	16.12	13½	71.62

Average speed between Euston and Carlisle, 65 miles 59 chains per hour

Average speed between Carlisle and Aberdeen, 62 miles 59 chains per hour

Average speed on the whole journey (including stoppages) just over 53¼ miles per hour

London and North Western engine "Adriatic" from London to Crewe, P. Clow, driver

London and North Western engine "Hardwicke" from Crewe to Carlisle, B. Robinson, driver

Caledonian engine No. 90 from Carlisle to Perth, A. Crooks, driver

Caledonian engine No. 17 from Perth to Aberdeen, John Soutar, driver

It is interesting to add that a month later – on September 8, 1895 (Sunday) – the train which has run the longest distance in the world without stoppage reached Carlisle. It was an experimental train, which left Euston that morning, drawn by the London and North Western engine "Ionic" and traversed the 299¼ miles to Carlisle without a stop in just under 6 hours.

Ben Robinson of Crewe, who had helped to win the race to Aberdeen, was the driver, and the experiment proved so successful that ever since the London and North Western company have run their chief Scotch expresses between London and Carlisle with only one stoppage on the way – at Crewe, which is 158 miles from Euston and 141 miles from Carlisle.

Carlisle station is unique, inasmuch as no express train has ever run through it. Each through express has to stop at Carlisle for change of engines, and the difficulty of working the traffic is increased by the varying gradients over the different lines to the city, and the various brakes in use. Three out of seven companies' trains are fitted with the Westinghouse brake, while the other four use the vacuum brake. Hence, every through west coast train has to be altered from Westinghouse to vacuum or vice versa while the train is standing in the station. The Midland trains have to be divided between the North British and the Glasgow and South Western Railways, and the trains of these two Scottish lines are made into trains for the Midland Railway. Through coaches run from various points on the several systems, that have to be transferred at Carlisle, so that the amount of shunting and marshalling that daily takes place at the Citadel station is enormous. Numerous improvements have recently been effected at the station, which is fitted throughout with electric light, the installation comprising sixty-three arc lamps and 700 incandescent lamps. The "clock" system of indicators has also been established with success, platforms have been numbered, and other desirable things are now being done.

This article must not be closed without reference to the management. Mr W. Haythornthwaite, the genial Superintendent, has won the respect and esteem of all classes since he took over the appointment held by Mr Jamieson, who retired on pension nearly four years ago, after a service extending over just fifty years. Mr Haythornthwaite is forty-eight years of age, and was born near Lancaster. He entered the railway service in 1870, and, like his predecessor, Mr Jamieson, has risen through well-nigh all grades by his perseverance, integrity and tact. For the first four years he worked as a yard-man and goods and passenger guard. After that he was, for a similar period, the joint foreman at Tebay for the London and North Western and the North Eastern. He spent the next two years at Carnforth as joint inspector for the London and North Western and the Furness Railways. Mr Haythornthwaite, after this, held the appointment of stationmaster at Kendal for three years, at Tebay for two years, and at Carnforth for ten years, the last named being for the London and North Western, Furness and Midland Railways conjointly. In April 1895

Ben Robinson the famous Crewe Driver who was involved in the 1895 "Race to the North".

No.20 "John Hick" Webb 3-cylinder compound on through road at Carlisle Citadel. Built in 1894 – the first of a class of 10. Caledonian Loco No.71 in platform on left.

he was transferred to Carlisle as Mr Jamieson's assistant, and was appointed superintendent when Mr Jamieson retired, on completion of his jubilee, with a present of £200, a pension of £100 a year, and a handsome sum of money subscribed by the public of Carlisle and the country generally. On leaving Carnforth to take up his responsible duties at Carlisle, Mr William Haythornthwaite was presented, on June 8, 1895, with a purse of gold and an illuminated address from the public and railway employees of the district. The first three signatures to the address were those of the Earl of Derby, Lord Henry Bentinck, and the Hon. Victor Cavendish, M.P. Mr Thomson, the secretary of the Citadel Station Committee, is now in his sixty-third year. He joined the railway service in Carlisle as a telegraph clerk as far back as January 1852, so that in fourteen months' time he will, like Mr Jamieson, be able to look back over fifty years of honourable service in the same place. By his assiduity, his patience, and his perseverance, Mr Thomson rose through many grades of the service until he was appointed secretary in the Citadel Station committee in 1875. He also holds the secretaryship for the goods relief lines round the city; for the Portpatrick and Wigtownshire Joint Railway since its amalgamation in 1885, the head office of the company being at the Citadel station; and for the Larne and Stranraer Steamship Company, which also has its head office in Carlisle, Mr Thomson being registered as the managing owner of the boats.

Thus we end our account of the headquarters of perhaps the biggest railway centre of its kind in the world, for it is computed that the "railway population" of Carlisle is something like 2,000. The London and North Western Company alone have "stables" for about 100 engines at their Carlisle sheds, together with extensive repair shops and carriage sheds. The Midland Railway keep no fewer than seventy engines at their sheds at Durran Hill, a mile from Carlisle, while the other railways keep a proportionate number at Kingmoor, the Canal, London Road and Redbank respectively. It is also worthy of mention that many of the Crowned Heads of Europe have seen the Citadel Station, while Her Most Gracious Majesty the Queen passed through Carlisle from Balmoral to celebrate her Diamond Jubilee in London in 1897, most elaborate preparations were made on the West Coast route, and Mr Webb's great engine, "Queen Empress" from Crewe, which drew the Royal train from Carlisle southward, was painted in cream colour, in imitation of the horses used with Her Majesty's State coach. By way of coincidence, the pilot engine run in front of the Royal train from Carlisle on that occasion was named the "Prince of Wales."

Carlisle Citadel Station exterior c1905. Showing ornate façade and clock tower with train shed roof beyond. Fountain in centre with canon from Crimean war nearby. Horse drawn 4-wheel cart near station entrance.

Chapter 17

Webb Compounds

What Mr Webb's Compounds have done
by Charles Rous-Marten

At this period of railway history it is necessary that I should tell over again the oft-told tale of the genesis and development of the two different systems of compounding which Mr F.W. Webb has successfully designed and introduced for the engines employed in the express services of the London and North Western Railway. I may, at least, take it for granted that everyone who is interested in locomotive engineering knows how Mr Webb first came to build compound engines at all, and how he gradually advanced from his original "Experiment" to his latest "Jubilee" or "Black Prince "or "Polyphemus" type, which at present represents his "last word" on the subject, but which I fully expect to see succeeded sooner or later by a still more powerful class.

My present purpose is rather to give an account of some of the work done under my own observation by these engines during the several years past, in compliance with requests that have frequently been addressed to me through the editor of this magazine, and in accordance with a promise which I made some months ago, Let me say , however, that the work I am about to describe will be the actual practical work performed by these engines, not the technical diagrams they have given or theoretical horse power they have indicated. It has proved more than once in actual experiment that an engine which indicated larger horse power than another did inferior in work practice, and as my viewpoint is the practical one I make the actual work my touchstone of locomotive merit. It has never seemed to me valuable that an engine should exhibit immense "horse power" if she cannot pull a heavy train so well as another which presents inferior theoretical figures. Therefore I shut my eyes and ears and memory to all questions of diagram

Webb 4-cylinder compound No. 1901 "Jubilee" was the first of 40 Jubilee Class locos built between 1897 and 1901.

and horse power records, as doubtless interesting and, perhaps, useful in their place, but purely irrelevant in the present connection. My subject is "What Mr Webb's Compounds Have Done."

Up to the time I am writing, Mr Webb has, I believe, built exactly 150 compound express engines for the London and North Western Railway during a period of just under twenty years. Of these, 100 are of the three cylinder type, while the other fifty are four cylinder compounds. But while the fifty four cylinder compounds are all of one class, the 100 of the three cylinder type are subdivided into no fewer than five different classes, each with its separate and distinctive features. Thus, the engines of the earliest "Experiment" class have 13in. high pressure cylinders and a 26in. low pressure cylinder with 6ft. 6in. driving-wheels, and 160lbs. steam pressure. The "Dreadnoughts" have 14in. high pressure cylinders, 30in. low pressure, 6ft. driving-wheels, with larger boilers, and 175lbs. steam pressure. The "Teutonics" have 7ft. wheels, but otherwise are virtually the same as the "Dreadnoughts". The "Greater Britains" have 15in. high pressure cylinders and larger boilers with midway combustion chambers, but with the same wheels and low-pressure cylinders as the "Teutonics". Finally, the "John Hicks" are "Greater Britains" with 6ft. wheels. All the 100 three cylinder compounds have 24in. piston stroke, and in each case two high pressure cylinders placed outside and one low pressure inside. There are thirty of the "Experiments" and forty of the "Dreadnoughts" but only ten each of the other three classes. And now all have been succeeded by four cylinder compounds, each of which has two 15in. highpressure cylinders placed outside, two 20½in. low pressure inside, 24in. piston strokes, four 7ft. driving-wheels coupled, and 200lbs. steam pressure. And of them there are fifty.

Experiment No.1113 "Hecate" pilots No.1304 "Jeanie Deans"(Teutonic) on a down express with 6-wheeled stock over Whitmore Troughs.

When I began my experimental trips with the Webb Compounds in the year 1884, most of the original batch had already been built. These engines were designed simply as a compounded version of Mr Webb's standard 6ft. 6in. coupled type, which had proved so remarkably efficient in express work; but it was calculated that through being able to use their steam twice over they would develop increased power, as well as economy in fuel consumption, and that, as the four driving-wheels were not coupled, they would run with the freedom of a single- wheeler, while possessing the adhesion of a coupled engine. These three advantages are, of course, claimed on behalf of all the three-cylinder compounds. The first I at once recognise. The second can only be verified by official records, which can seldom be utilised satisfactorily for purposes of comparison in the absence of the opportunity of detailed analysis, but I see no reason to doubt that fuel economy is obtained. As to the third my experience is adverse, as I have observed indications that the high pressure and low pressure engines for these are virtually two on one frame – do not always work absolutely together in practice as in theory as they ought to do, the result being occasional interludes of inferior performance. Were their driving wheels coupled there would, I believe, be few, if any, more efficient locomotives in this country, proportionately to their size, than these three-cylinder compounds, and, as they are, I have usually found them to do excellent service. But the advisableness of coupling the wheels has been recognised by Mr Webb in his later four-cylinder type. So that point may be regarded as conceded.

The "Experiment" batch suffered from another drawback, that of inadequate steam pressure. When they came out 140lbs. was the standard pressure throughout Britain, and so when Mr Webb gave his "Experiments" 160lbs. he was adding 20lbs. to the pressure in general use, as did Mr T.W. Worsdell when he brought out *his* first

Experiment Class No. 1116 "Friar" waiting at Stockport Edgeley coupled to GWR clerestory carriage. These 3-cylinder engines were Webb's first large-scale experiment with express compounds and thirty were built between 1882 and 1884.

compounds on the Great Eastern Railway. But in each instance the pressure was insufficient to enable the compound to be fully satisfactory in the case of express engines, and so the "Experiments" were soon withdrawn from first-class express duty, while the Great Eastern compounds were all converted into non compounds.

It was somewhat unlucky for the "Experiments" that in 1884, just after they came out, there was a sudden and marked acceleration of the express services. This brought, as acceleration always has done and does, a substantial increase of traffic. That meant heavier trains, and so the new engines, which would have performed well enough the work required when they were designed, proved unable to fulfil the fresh and more onerous conditions. Mr Webb promptly recognised the fact, by bringing out in 1884 his second and greatly-enlarged design, the "Dreadnought" type, of which forty were built with all convenient despatch. The first engine of the pioneer class, No.66 "Experiment", has lately been rebuilt with a new boiler and 180lbs. steam pressure, and is, I am informed, doing well, but I have as yet had no opportunity of testing her under the new conditions. However, the thirty "Experiments", after being entrusted with most of the important express duty in 1884 and 1885, were quickly taken off as the "Dreadnoughts" came in, and were relegated to work of an inferior class.

It has always been the fashion to speak of the "Experiment" engines as failures, and I am aware that many people so regard them. But I have always protested against so sweeping a verdict as in some degree unjust as, at any rate, not setting forth "the whole truth". Assuredly, they were not equal to the best express work which had to be done in the summer of 1884 and thence-forward. They could pull good loads and climb hills. But they *were* sluggish. There is no doubt at all about that. It took a tremendous lot of hard flogging to get much over 50 or 55 miles an hour out of them. Anything over 60, even down the most tempting descent, was most rare. At least, that is my experience, which forms the sole basis of my remarks. Other people may have had better or worse luck than I had with the "Experiments" but that is not *my* business. My function is simply to record what I myself have observed. I tried them with all sorts of expresses, sometimes travelling on the footplate, sometimes behind them. Setting aside one failure through a slight mishap to the machinery, I found the work consistently respectable, but never brilliant. Had, however, the timings and loads of 1883 remained in force in 1884 and 1885 the "Experiments" would certainly have acquitted themselves quite satisfactorily. They would have kept time, and probably saved coal.

Perhaps what has done so much to give their class a bad name is the fact that although they could not rise to the requirements of the situation, Mr Webb's older non-compound 6ft. 6in. coupled engines did so in a most surprising and noteworthy manner. I have discoursed before in these pages on "some wonderful Little Engines" of the London and North Western "Precedent" type, and any reader who desires to know what *they* did under the fresh conditions can ascertain that by referring back to the RAILWAY MAGAZINE Vol. IV, pp 260 and 370. My present business is with their successors, the 6ft.6in. wheeled compounds, and I simply remark that these latter undoubtedly suffered by comparison with the "Precedents" and the brilliant way in which those non-compounds rose to the occasion.

When the Irish Day Mail was accelerated in July 1881 to reach Rugby in 1 hr.45min. from Euston, with a stop at Bletchley, the times being Euston – Bletchley 47¾ miles, 59min.; Bletchley-Rugby, 36 miles, 44min. – fairly smart timing – the "Experiments" were put to work on it. I tested it with "Experiment" herself, which exactly kept time all the way to Crewe; with "Velocipede" which dropped a minute to Bletchley; and with "Compound" which lost 2 min. to Bletchley, but kept time thence to Rugby. The load in each case was twelve six-wheelers. Then "Britannic" took on the train, reduced to five coaches, to Chester, 21 miles, in 25 min., and thence to Holyhead, 84¾ miles in 1 hr. 42 min., while "Empress" ran from Holyhead to Chester with twelve coaches, in 1 hr. 47min. net. Making up several minutes, and "Victor" performed very similarly on another occasion. "Trentham", with nine coaches, ran from Northampton to Euston, 65¾ miles in 84 min., stopping 4 min. at Willesden. The time from Northampton to Willesden was 72 min. net. And the run thence to Euston was the smartest I have ever noted – exactly 7 min. from start to stop for 5½ miles, a speed of 60 miles an hour being maintained all the way from Queen's Park to Chalk Farm. One more journey worth noting, behind these engines, was by the day Scottish express from Crewe to Euston. The engine was "Knowsley" and the load twelve six-wheelers. The time for 61 miles to Nuneaton was 77¼ min., a loss of 2¼ min. and from Nuneaton to Willesden, 1 hr.56½ min., a gain of 1½ min., there was a gain of 45 sec. on the entire journey from Crewe to Euston, but, of course, on the relatively slow timing of that day 3 hr. 35 min., before the "race" of 1888 enlivened matters. One more performance of fair merit was to run from Crewe to Edge Hill, 33 miles, in 40½ min. with seven coaches. This was done by No.1111 "Messenger".

Now all these runs, although not brilliant, are quite respectable for the period at which they were done, but naturally they seem feeble when compared with the splendid feats achieved up to the present day by the small coupled engines, which preceded the compounds on London and North Western metals. I never attained a higher speed than 65 miles an hour with one of the 6 ft. 6 in. "Experiment" compounds, whereas, as my readers will remember, I have several times recorded over 87 with the coupled class, and once 88.2. Perhaps the "Experiments" developed greater haulage and gradient climbing power than the coupled "Precedents" had exhibited up to that date, but not more than the latter have shown in more recent times. So, on the whole, I cannot wax very enthusiastic over the type as it was. But I believe that with larger boilers, higher pressure, and coupled wheels, they would surprise many of their detractors.

However, they were brand new locomotives in 1884-1885, and there was no question then of rebuilding to meet the novel necessities of the London and North Western express services. For their noses were promptly put out of joint by their successors, the "Dreadnoughts", of which I am able to write in terms of warm praise. True, they have the drawback of non-coupled driving wheels, and so suffer at times from temporary interruption of synchronous working between the high pressure and low pressure machinery. But their bigger boilers – very large for 1884, when they first came out, having 1,400 square feet of heating-surface – and their higher pressure, 175lbs. unprecedented in those days – gave them an enormous advantage. And thus, although they too were and are somewhat sluggish starters, they did, and do, some very fine work.

At the beginning of 1885 only two were at work, "Dreadnought" 503, and "Titan" 508. Each showed me that the new type possessed remarkable capacity in respect of haulage power, but the Scottish Expresses of that time were not what they became three years later, and so the new locomotives were as much *under*weighted with the work cut out for them as their predecessors were *overweighted*. But with the accelerations of 1888 came their chance.

I was, unfortunately, at the Antipodes in that "impetuous year" as one writer has termed it, and so cannot record from my own experience the share taken by the 6ft. compounds in its fast running. The statement has often been made – quite truly – that they took no part in the "Race to Edinburgh" and it has been added – quite inaccurately – that the reason was their inability to run at the speeds required. It is hardly necessary to contradict so obvious an error, but as some people may have been misled by it, I may say, briefly, that the compounds were not used in the "Race" proper of 1888, simply because such powerful engines were not needed to pull the light 76-ton trains which the little 7ft. 6in.of the "Problem" class, brought out in 1859, were able to run with ease, there being an abundance of work for the big compounds in hauling the other fast, but far heavier, trains, which the stimulation of traffic, due to acceleration, had brought about. As to the compounds being unable to run fast enough for a timing which only involved a maximum rate of 65 miles an hour, that is disposed of by the fact that more recently they have done much faster time with really heavy loads, and have often attained and maintained speeds of 76 miles an hour and upward.

Nevertheless, these fine engines were not exempt from attack. That they are sometimes sluggish starters I have already admitted. But the figurative language of poetic hyperbole has been freely used to express their shortcomings in this particular respect. A friend of mine once assured me that one of these engines, on an express in which he was travelling to London, could not get away from Rugby until it had *"backed nearly half way to Crewe!"* Now Crewe is distant 75½ miles from Rugby! Therefore, I suspect my friend of "dropping into poetry" in a friendly Silas-Weggian way! Again, there have doubtless been times when the "Dreadnoughts" have fallen short of their normal efficiency and of their timetable requirements. I have heard of many such cases, but my own experience has furnished very few genuine instances. Glancing over my notes of the last eight years, I cannot find among my very numerous journeys with these engines more than two or three cases of definite shortcoming. If an engine keeps the time set down for it in its official schedule it cannot be blamed for not doing *more* than that. Its driver perhaps, may be, if, for the sake of his coal premium he has deliberately abstained from making up time, or his superior may be blameable for instructing him so to abstain, but it would not be the engine's fault. And, on the whole, I say frankly that whatever any other people's experience may have been, my own has been decisively favourable as regards Mr. Webb's "Dreadnoughts" and that, too, as much when the drivers had no knowledge that I was observing as when I was on the footplate or taking notes, with their cognisance. I do not mean for one moment to imply that any allegations as to inferior performance on their part are untrue or erroneous. I am well aware that travellers may have times of good and bad luck with locomotives which can hardly be satisfactorily explained. I myself have had such experiences of both kinds. But in view of the remarkable variety of my experiences with the "Dreadnoughts" during the past eight years, I think I am warranted in accepting the results to which experiences conclusively point. As the results are, on the whole, emphatically favourable, while in some cases they are of quite exceptional merit as specimens of locomotive work.

In reviewing the performances of the "Dreadnought" compounds it will, I think, be convenient to take in their order of sequence the trains worked by them under my own observation, rather than attempt to place their achievements in the relative order of merit.

Beginning, then, with the Irish Day Mail, then booked to leave Euston at 7.15am and reach Rugby at 9.0, stopping two minutes at Bletchley, a train of ten coaches was merely played with by "Leviathan" 510, which ran under easy steam all the way, and had a signal slack at Kilburn, yet reached Bletchley in 57 min. 40 sec., and ran thence to Rugby in 42 min. 56 sec. arriving before time. Next comes the 10am Scotch express, which on one occasion was taken by "Raven" 643, one of the same class. The load was reckoned as twelve coaches and weighed about 190 tons, including passengers and luggage. This proved to be one of the smartest performances I have ever noted with the "Dreadnought" compounds. After starting from Willesden, Tring was passed in 30 min.17 sec., a distance of 26¼ miles, almost all uphill, mostly at 1 in 330. A bad check was encountered at Hillmorton, yet Rugby was reached in 85 min.

Dreadnought Class No.2063 "Huskisson" picking up water on Bushey Troughs with an up Belfast Boat Express in 1899.

20 sec. from Willesden, or 83 min. net for the 77 miles. This was very good, but what followed was even better. When the express was ready to move on from Rugby to run the 75½ miles thence to Crewe in 85 min., or at 53.3 miles an hour, the starting signal was adverse and it did not get away until 3 min. late, but "Raven" made such remarkable progress that Stafford, 51 miles, was passed in 53 min. 9 sec.; the 14 miles moderate climb to Whitmore summit was done in 15 min. 2 sec., in spite of a check, and after a descent of the Madeley bank at 72 miles an hour, and another check at Betley, Crewe was reached in 78 min. 56 sec. from Rugby, or 77 min. net. The arrival at Crewe was 4 min. early, in spite of 18 min. 5 sec. being occupied at a dead stand, and of total delays which left the net time from Euston to Crewe only 2 hr. 50 min. for the 158 miles. Considering that the load was equal to nineteen South of England coaches, and that although the road is not a hard one, it includes several considerable lengths of steady collar-work, I do not hesitate to express the opinion that the performance was an extremely good one and creditable to any engine. Even a single performance such as this would suffice to establish the character of the "Dreadnoughts" for smartness and efficiency.

Another instance of very good work was furnished by the down Perth express which left Euston at 10.30am and observed much the same intermediate times as the 10am. In this case the run was from Crewe to Carlisle, and the engine was "Achilles" 511. The load was fifteen coaches, representing a total weight of about 220 tons behind the tender. A bad check was met with just after starting from Crewe, so that the first two miles occupied more than 6 min., and this, with a second signal check near Leyland, spoiled the first stage to Preston, in spite of some fast running near Warrington. The net time for the 52 miles was 59 min. For the 90⅛ miles to Carlisle, including the ascent of Grayrigg and Shap banks, the time allowed was 105min., representing an average speed of 51.5 miles an hour from start to stop. The load was reduced to about 160 tons, equivalent to sixteen ten ton coaches. But even so, it was a capital performance for "Achilles" to cover the 90 miles and 10 chains in 100 min. 3 sec., especially as the speed was eased all the way down the bank after Shap summit, the 31½ miles descent thence to Carlisle occupying the same number of minutes. The distance of 58½ miles from the Preston start to the summit, including the ascent of the long Grayrigg bank, 5 miles at about 1 in 130, and of the Shap incline, of which the last 4½ miles are at 1 in 75, was covered in 69 min. 22 sec., averaging 50.2 miles an hour and the 5½ miles from Tebay to the Summit, mostly up 1 in 75, in 9 min. 8 sec., averaging 38 miles an hour. On another occasion "City of Carlisle" No.2, with a load of 202 tons, climbed the Shap incline at an average rate of 30.5 miles an hour. When a train was put on at 1.45pm, booked to run from Euston to Rugby without stopping at Willesden in 1 hr. 40 min. "Harpy" 2061, started with 165 tons and covered the first 81 miles in 93 min., in spite of two bad slacks, and had to do the last 1½ miles dead slow so as not to arrive too early, that 1½ miles occupying nearly 5 min., and the total run from Euston to Rugby 97 min. 49 sec., of which the delays accounted for quite 5 min.

Two runs with the evening up express due Euston at 9.45pm are worth noting on account of the steady evenness of the work done. In the early case "Autocrat" 2064, the last ever built of the "Dreadnoughts", took a train of 200 tons from Rugby to Willesden, 77 miles, in 86½ min. and reached Euston 4 min. early. In fact the driver had to ease down after Tring to avoid getting in too soon. In the second instance the engine was

Dreadnought No.659 "Rowland Hill" waiting departure in the old part of Stafford Station.

"City of Chester" 437, and the load 207 tons; the run from Rugby to Willesden, occupied 88¾ min. Another case is worthy of mention, owing to the heaviness of the load which was very nearly 270 tons. The engine, "City of London" 639, took that load from Northampton to Bletchley, 19 miles, in 27 min. 3 sec., almost the whole distance being a continuous climb, several miles after the start at 1 in 200. The next stage Bletchley – Willesden, 41¼ miles, was done in 50 min. 5 sec., the first 15 miles uphill to Tring being covered in 21 min. 11 sec., and the downhill descent thence being made under easy steam as the train was in good time. "Stork" 1379, with 203 tons, ran from Crewe to Nuneaton, 61 miles in 69 min., climbing the 10½ mile bank at 1 in 177, 1 in 250, and 1 in 330 to Whitmore in 15 min. 50 sec.; next ran from Nuneaton to Bletchley, 49¼ miles, in 58 min.; and, finally, Bletchley to Willesden, 41¼ miles, in 46 min. 3 sec. "Mammoth" 513, took seventeen coaches, 249 tons, from Rugby to Willesden in 88 min., doing the 15 miles uphill, Bletchley to Tring, in 18 min. 29 sec., while the speed did not fall below 45 miles an hour up the last 6 miles of 1 in 330, or exceed 60 miles an hour downhill, very even and steady work. "Marchioness of Stafford," "Tamerlane," "Niagara," "City of Glasgow" and other "Dreadnoughts" have also given me some excellent experiences, but not differing materially from those already recorded, so that it is not necessary that I should unduly extend these remarks by producing them in detail. I have said enough to show that the 6 ft. wheeled compounds can, and do, acquit themselves very creditably, and I may say that the same will appear in the case of the "Teutonics," "Greater Britains," and "Jubilees" when I come to them in their turn.

At this point I desire to impress the facts (1) that in *none* of the cases I have quoted was a pilot taken, and (2) that all the loads mentioned are those of the *trains* – that is to say, *exclusive* of the engines and tenders.

Before leaving Mr Webb's 6ft. compounds of the "Dreadnought" class, I must refer to one performance by an engine of that type, which I should be disposed to consider the best in all my experiences with them, could I be certain upon a particular point, which I fear must now remain for ever doubtful.

During the summer of 1895 – in fact, while the "Race to Aberdeen", for which that year is famous, was in full progress I returned from Aberdeen several times by the 10.5am corridor-diner, due Euston at 10.45pm. On one occasion this train, when it arrived at Carlisle, was estimated to weigh 312 tons, exclusive of engine and tender. When it reached Euston behind "Jeanie Deans" its weight was set down as practically the same. I did not see any reduction made at Carlisle but most unfortunately I omitted to examine the train personally, either after the London and North Western engine came on at Carlisle or on arrival at Preston. Therefore I feel unable to vouch for the load being the same weight on arrival at both Carlisle and Euston. I can only say that it did not apparently undergo any natural reduction, but I suspect that some reduction must have taken place. Several Caledonian coaches usually come off with the Caledonian engine at Carlisle. Nevertheless, the load was unquestionably a heavy one, and No.515 "Niagara" kept exact time with it from Carlisle to Preston – viz. 1 hour 55 minutes, with an intermediate stop at Tebay. The speed did not fall below 35 miles an hour up the long banks of 1 in 125 approaching Shap Summit from the north, and it rose to 76.3 miles an hour down the subsequent descent. *No pilot was used.* The distance from Tebay to Preston (53 miles) was covered in 59 minutes 59 seconds.

I greatly regret the uncertainty which attaches to the load on this occasion, and have endeavoured to verify it by reference to Crewe, but, unluckily, the entry has not been preserved.

Approaching Tamworth station about 1900 with a down express hauled by two Webb compound locos – a Dreadnought class 3-cylinder No.645 "Alchymist" piloting a 4-4-0 Jubilee 4-cylinder. (This could be the 2pm Scotch express from Euston) On the left is an up Trent Valley local (probably Stafford to Rugby) with a Webb 5ft. 6in 2-4-2 tank taking refreshment from the water column. Large water tank behind the express. From a painting by Gerald Broom GRA (based on an original black and white photo).

After the "Race to Edinburgh" of 1888, in which the compounds were not employed owing to the extreme lightness (76 tons) of the racing trains, which were taken easily by the small 7ft. 6in. single-wheelers, Mr Webb decided not to adopt a larger diameter for the driving wheels of his express compounds; and accordingly the next ten constructed were given driving wheels 7ft. in diameter – 7ft. 2 in. with new tyres – the other dimensions being virtually unchanged. Ten of these were built at Crewe, their numbers running from 1301 to 1312 – omitting 1308 and 1310 and their names being "Teutonic," "Pacific," "Oceanic," "Jeanie Deans," "Doric," "Ionic," "Celtic," "Gaelic," "Coptic" and "Adriatic" – all after Liverpool steamers of the White Star fleet, excepting "Jeanie Deans," which was specially named after one of Sir Walter Scott's favourite heroines, with a view to her appearance at the Edinburgh Exhibition.

Comparisons we all know are "odious", or, at least, invidious; but I may perhaps be permitted to say that these ten engines have always seemed to me the most successful of all Mr Webb's three –cylinder express compounds. Certainly, they have given me a long list of performances singularly uniform in their excellence. Three engines of the class are better known than the rest; "Jeanie Deans" deservedly enjoys distinguished renown on the score of her remarkable runs daily for several years between Euston and Crewe with the afternoon Scottish corridor diner, which usually weighed 300 tons and upward. "Adriatic" is famed as having made the "record" run with the Aberdeen racing train in August 1895, from Euston to Crewe – viz. 2 hours 28 minutes for the 158 miles. "Ionic" is noted as having made the record long run without a stop – viz. Euston to Carlisle (299 miles) also in 1895.

With each of these three locomotives I have had some striking experiences. Over and over again I have travelled behind No. 1304 "Jeanie Deans" in the Scottish corridor- diner, and in no case did she ever lose a minute of time either way between Euston and Crewe when I was in the train; although the absolutely smallest loads I noted were 256 and 264 tons, respectively, each on one occasion only, while in all other cases the loads equalled or excelled 300 tons. Yet in all these cases the speed from start to stop for the 91½ miles from Nuneaton to Willesden averaged over 53 miles an hour, ever a road which has as nearly as possible equal proportions of rising and falling gradients, mostly at 1 in 330 to 1 in 365. Curiously enough, the fastest run of all on that length – viz. 101¾ minutes for the 91½ miles – was made with the heaviest load of all, 326 tons behind the tender. A mean rate of virtually 54 miles an hour with such a load, and without any balance of aid from gravitation, must be admitted to be extremely good work, especially when it is remembered that on the south of England lines the load would be reckoned as "32½ coaches".

With No. 1309 "Adriatic" and 224 tons, I timed the run from Euston to Crewe in 2 hours 52 minutes 2 seconds; and with No. 1307 "Coptic" and 207 tons in 2 hours 52 minutes 20 seconds. In the latter instance Rugby (82½ miles) was passed in 90 minutes 20 seconds from Euston.

To No. 1306 "Ionic" belongs a large share of the credit for a very fine run from Crewe to Carlisle in September 1895, when the booked time for that run of 141¼ miles was only 2 hours 28 minutes, representing an average speed of 57.4 miles an hour from start to stop. This being the highest ever publically booked by the London and North Western, I was curious to see whether time would be kept over such a heavy road, including as it did the Grayrigg and Shap banks and the Preston slack, with a load of 225 tons. With such a load, on such a road, booked at such a speed, there was no discredit in taking a pilot; but of course, the use of an assistant engine made it impracticable to appraise with precision the work done by "Ionic" herself. Still, the run, even with a pilot, was a remarkable one. The distance of 141¼ miles from Crewe to Carlisle, was covered in exactly 143 minutes, or at an average rate

Teutonic Class No. 1306 "Ionic" at Crewe Works in 1895 following a non-stop run from Euston to Carlisle. Crewe Driver Ben Robinson and Fireman Bill Wolstencroft with the guard on the footplate.

of 59.3 miles an hour, in spite of the regulation slack – duly observed – through Preston Station and Yard. Warrington (24¼ miles) was passed in 21 minutes 51 seconds, Wigan (36 miles) in 33 minutes 52 seconds, Preston (51 miles) in 49 minutes 38 seconds, and Shap (109¾ miles) – including the Grayrigg and Shap banks of 1 in 130 for 15 miles and 1 in 75 for nearly 5 miles, respectively – in 116 minutes 43 seconds. The ascent of the Shap incline (5¾ miles, including 4½ at 1 in 75) occupied 8 minutes 24 seconds, and the subsequent descent of the 31½ miles to the stop in Carlisle was done in 26 minutes 17 seconds; the final 18 miles from passing Penrith to stopping at Carlisle, occupying only 14 minutes 57 seconds, while a maximum speed of 85.7 miles an hour was attained and maintained for some miles. The pilot was one of Mr Webb's 6ft. 6in. coupled class.

In another case, "Ionic" with 220 tons ran from Rugby to Crewe, start to stop in 82½ minutes for the 75½ miles after doing the 77 miles from Willesden to Rugby in 88 minutes 54 seconds, and maintaining a very even rate of speed up and down hill. No. 1313 "Gaelic" with a much heavier load – 255 tons and a severe side gale blowing all the way, managed to accomplish the run from Rugby to Crewe in just 7 seconds under the fast time allowed – 85 minutes for the 75½ miles. In the circumstances this was, perhaps, a better performance even than the one previously noted. With "Doric," "Celtic," "Pacific," "Oceanic," and "Teutonic" I have recorded work of very similar merit.

In the year 1892 Mr Webb brought out the first of his new and enlarged type of three-cylinder compounds, "Greater Britain", which differed from the "Teutonics" in having 15in. high pressure cylinders instead of 14in. and a much larger boiler with a midway combustion chamber – giving 1,505 square feet of the heating surface in all – also an additional pair of carrying wheels behind the firebox. A sister engine, built simultaneously, was named "Queen Empress" and was sent to the Chicago Exhibition. I may observe here that all the stories current then and since about her having been "run against" American engines *are* "stories" in the juvenile application of the term. That is to say they are without the slightest vestige of truth or foundation. But thus is current history written especially as to railway matters.

While "Queen Empress" was "showing off" at Chicago, "Greater Britain" was doing some excellent work at home. One of her achievements was remarkable, consisting of running daily both ways the entire distance between Euston and Carlisle for the whole working week of six consecutive days. In that period she covered a distance of some 3,600 miles at express speed with considerable loads. That was in the spring of 1893. I published at the time such full details of the performance of the best day's work, which I noted from the footplate, that it is unnecessary to give them now. It may suffice to state that "Greater Britain" took the down day Anglo-Scottish express from Euston to Crewe, and ran from Willesden to Rugby (77 miles) in 89 minutes 57 seconds, easing down after Welton so as not to arrive too early. The speed down the bank after Tring reached 78.2 miles an hour, which was maintained for 2 miles. The load was 212 tons behind the tender. Proceeding from Rugby "Greater Britain" ran to Crewe (75½ miles) in 82 minutes 27 seconds start to stop, but was delayed 4 minutes by relaying slacks in the Trent Valley; speed in each case being reduced to 10 miles an hour for a considerable distance. Thus the actual start to stop time from Rugby to Crewe was only 78½ minutes, a very smart performance. In this case also a maximum speed of 78.2 miles an hour was attained; it was done down Madeley Bank. The steam pressure was only 160lbs. per square inch at starting from Euston, but then rapidly rose, the needle pointing to 190lbs. before the safety valves blew off.

On another occasion "Greater Britain" took the Manchester dining-car train from Euston. It weighed 250 tons, but was hauled with ease from Willesden to a signal stop near Hillmorton, 76 miles in 87½ minutes start to stop. In each of these cases the ascent to Tring was made at a sustained good speed.

A fine run was made by No. 527 "Henry Bessemer" of the same class, with the 8.0pm down "Tourist" train, whilst it ran from Euston to Crewe without stopping. The load, it is true, was not a heavy one, 161 tons behind the tender; but that was equal to sixteen South of England coaches, and the booking too was fast – viz., Euston to Crewe in 2 hours 55 minutes for the 158 miles, or an average rate of 54.1 miles an hour. After passing Willesden at full speed in 8 minutes 27 seconds from the start, "Henry Bessemer" covered the next 26 uphill miles to Tring summit in 27 minutes 38 seconds, passing Tring (31½ miles) in 36 minutes 5 seconds from Euston. The speed never fell below 56 miles an hour, and was maintained at that point with remarkable evenness all the way up the ascent, which is chiefly 1 in 330 and 1 in 400. Downhill the rate was not allowed to exceed 72 miles an hour, and Bletchley (46¾ miles) was passed in 49 minutes 57 seconds; Blisworth (62¾ miles) in 66 minutes; Rugby (82½ miles) in 86 minutes 10 seconds, at reduced speed – 25 miles an hour; Stafford (133¼ miles) also at reduced speed, in 2 hours 22 minutes 1 second; and Crewe was reached in 2 hours 51 minutes 56 seconds. The rate was eased down all the way after Rugby as the train was before its time. Undoubtedly, the time could have been materially shortened, but as it was an average of 55.1 miles an hour was maintained throughout.

From Crewe to Carlisle the train was taken by No. 525 "Princess May" of the same type, the load increased to 170 tons. In this case the engine was badly handicapped by the length of time allowed for the run for the 141¼ miles; but the Preston accident had sounded a note of warning against the danger of running through such a station and maze of junctions, over a labyrinth of points and crossings, and round a 7-chain curve without check

Greater Britain class No.525 "Princess May" at Crewe.

rails or adequate cant, at a speed of 40 or 50 miles an hour. Hence, in this instance, the train actually took 3 minutes to crawl through Preston station, beside slowing for some distance approaching the entrance. Even with this delay, however, the time allowed was excessive, and difficulty was found in filling it up. A good start was made, and Warrington (24¼ miles) was passed in 24 minutes 56 seconds; but then a bad relaying slack caused delay, and Preston was not passed till 56 minutes 34 seconds after leaving Crewe. Thence the driver did not hurry, having abundant time in hand, but a minimum of 36 miles an hour was maintained up the Grayrigg Bank – 1 in 125 – and 25.7 up the 1 in 75 of Shap Summit. Some high speeds were run down the descent to Carlisle, 80.3 miles an hour being reached at one point; but the approach to Carlisle was made so gradually that the final mile occupied nearly 5 minutes.

On another occasion No. 526 "Scottish Chief" was on the "Perth Express" from Crewe to Euston. The load was 163 tons, and the actual running time was 2 hours 58 minutes 54 seconds with *three* stops – viz. Nuneaton, Bletchley and Willesden. The time from Crewe to Nuneaton (61 miles) was 67 minutes 41 seconds, and the 10½ mile bank to Whitmore, including 3 miles at 1 in 171, 3 miles at 1 in 250, and the rest at 1 in 330, was climbed in 15 minutes 24 seconds. From Nuneaton to Bletchley (50¼ miles) the time was 57 minutes 17 seconds, with a slack through Rugby; from Bletchley to Willesden (41¼ miles) 45 minutes 13 seconds; Tring being passed in 18 minutes 37 seconds. The actual running time from Nuneaton to Willesden (91½ miles) was 102 minutes 30 seconds, with a dead stop at Bletchley and a slack through Rugby. Making due allowance for these delays, the net time would be 99 minutes. This, although not equal to the performances just previously quoted, is, nevertheless, very creditable work. Certainly, the achievements of "Henry Bessemer" and "Princess May" conclusively disprove the oft-heard allegation that the "Greater Britains" are unable to attain high speeds. They have always seemed to me to run very freely and swiftly, and even when going at such rates as those I have mentioned – 78.2, 80 and 80.3 miles an hour – appeared to be well within their means, and capable of still faster work if this were required of them.

It will be observed that I am not now expressing any opinions to the relative merits of Mr Webb's system compared with any other, or even as to the positive merits of his system itself. I am simply offering an absolutely impartial and unprejudiced statement of what his three-cylinder compounds have done in a few particular cases under my own personal observation. What they could do then, it is reasonable to assume that they could do always *under identical conditions*. Therefore, in cases where the same engines have not reached so high a level of merit, it is but fair, as well as scientific, to assume that the conditions have in some respects differed. I may say, however, that the cases cited above are, on the whole, fair specimens of the general work noted by me in the case of these engines.

After building only ten of these "Greater Britains" Mr Webb discontinued their construction, as he did in the case of their predecessors the "Teutonics" and next brought out ten of a class known as the "John Hicks" which were virtually identical save in having 6ft. driving wheels instead of 7ft. The ten are numbered and named as follows:

No.	Name
20	John Hick
1505	Richard Arkwright
1512	Henry Cort
1534	William Froude
1535	Henry Maudsley
1536	Hugh Myddelton
1548	John Penn
1549	John Rennie
1557	Thomas Savory
1559	William Siemens

I may mention, by the way, the ten "Greater Britains" are as follows:

No.	Name
2053	Greater Britain
2054	Queen Empress
525	Princess May
526	Scottish Chief
527	Henry Bessemer
528	Richard Moon
767	William Cawkwell
772	Richard Trevithick
2051	George Findlay
2052	Prince George

As to the performances of the locomotives of the "John Hick" class I am unable to say anything, for the simple reason that I have never been so fortunate as to travel behind one of them unassisted by a pilot engine. In these circumstances it is impossible to attempt any comparison between them and the other three-cylinder compounds, and so I merely mention them in passing. Should I in any future journeys have the luck to test one unaided by a pilot, I shall be happy to record my experiences. At present no experiences exist, so far as I am concerned.

Finally – for the present – Mr Webb brought out in 1897 his present standard express type, the four-cylinder compound of the "Jubilee" or "Black Prince" class. This differed in several prominent respects from its three-cylinder predecessors. The 7ft. driving-wheels and the 15in. high pressure cylinders were retained, as also was the outside position of the latter. But they were moved forward to a position abreast of the smokebox, and drove the front pair of driving-wheels. Instead of one 30in. low-pressure cylinder placed inside and under the smokebox, two low-pressure cylinders, originally 19½in. but subsequently 20½in. in diameter, occupied the same position; and by means of a double crank axle propelled the front pair of driving-wheels which were coupled to the

No.1548 "John Penn" (John Hick Class) at Shrewsbury Shed.

trailing pair by fluted side rods 10ft. 7in. in length. The "Teutonic" boiler with 1,400 square feet of heating surface was practically reverted to but the steam pressure was increased to 200lbs. per square inch. One important difference between the three-cylinder and the four-cylinder type consists in the latter engines having their two pairs of driving-wheels coupled instead of running independently as did those of the three-cylinder engines. Also all four cylinders drive a single axle owing by which plan Mr Webb holds that a smaller strain is placed upon the axle owing to the stress being better distributed. I am bound to admit the force of this contention so far as it goes, but, personally, I prefer the plan adopted by Monsieur de Glehn of driving each pair of wheels with a different pair of cylinders. The matter is purely one of individual opinion.

A further change in method has consisted in the adoption of what Mr Webb styles a "double-radial truck" under the leading bogie of the locomotive. This appears to be simply a pivotless bogie, but, as the other term is preferred at Crewe, I am quite willing to accept it.

The main point is that the front end of the engine can accommodate itself to curves, instead of being rigid, or nearly so. This is a distinct advantage.

No fewer than fifty of these four-cylinder compounds have already been constructed at Crewe, and so far as my own experience of them has gone, they have proved themselves very efficient. In one instance No.1903 "Iron Duke" drew a load of 339 tons from Euston to Crewe (158 miles) in 3 hours 4 minutes net, ascending with entire ease and readiness the bank at 1 in 70 for half a mile approaching Chalk Farm, without pilot assistance; and sustaining a rate of 45 to 48 miles an hour up the ascent at 1 in 330 to Tring, while nothing faster than 72 miles an hour was done downhill. In the opposite direction No.1919 "Resolution" ran with the Perth express, weighing 215 tons, from Crewe to Euston, in exactly

Jubilee class No.1905 "Black Diamond" with Up Express of mixed stock at Harrow.

3 hours net. No.1902 "Black Prince" took the day Scottish express, weighing 244 tons, from Rugby to Willesden (77 miles) in 83 minutes 39 seconds, without exceeding 65 miles an hour downhill, or falling below 50 miles an hour up the rising gradients of 1 in 330. Yet another performance consisted in hauling a train of 339 tons from Crewe to Willesden (152½ miles) in 2 hours 53 minutes start to stop, representing an average rate of 52.8 miles an hour. Three points specially suggested themselves in this run. In the first place, the engine, with that heavy load, attained and sustained a speed of 37.5 miles an hour up the Madeley Bank at 1 in 177 for 3 miles, 1 in 280 for 4 miles, and 1 in 330 for 3½ miles. Secondly it kept up to 47 miles an hour ascending the 6 miles of 1 in 330 to Tring summit. Thirdly, in descending the Tring Bank to Willesden the speed was kept down to 65.2 miles an hour, but for which restriction still faster time could have been accomplished between terminal points.

All these performances which I have quoted are so distinctly good, and some of them so exceptional, that, even in themselves, they establish the character of the "Jubilees" as capable and successful engines. As weight-pullers they are undoubtedly very efficient. In respect of swiftness, I have not yet had the opportunity of testing their full capabilities. But I see no reason to doubt that they can run at least as fast as their predecessors, in whose credit there stand in my notes several instances of over 80 miles

The unique No.777, 2-2-4-0T 3-cylinder compound tank – the only one of its type (built in 1887) Fitted with water pick-up scoop.

an hour, and one of 85.7. But they are designed mainly to carry out the policy of maintaining as even and uniform velocity as possible uphill and downhill alike. This they do in a large degree, as shown by my experiences above related with the "Iron Duke" drawing 339 tons. With such a load many locomotives would have dropped to 30 or 25 miles an hour uphill, and rushed, perhaps, at 80 to 85 miles an hour downhill to make up for the time lost in the ascent. "Iron Duke" ascended at 47 and descended at 65, far more even work.

Personally, I see no reason why an engine should burn an extra quantity of coal in ascending gradients at high speed, in order to be able to run down them at only 50 or 55 miles an hour. But it is an unquestionable advantage to an engine to be capable of a rapid ascent, because then she has all the extra time in hand, and can either make any that may have been previously lost or can run in advance of booked time, should this be required for any particular reason, as in such a case as that of the first portion of the East Coast day express to Scotland, which has to arrive at Edinburgh, if possible, a few minutes before time so as to keep clear of the accelerated Midland-North British express, which might otherwise engross the platform and block it out. Should any similar necessity arise on the West Coast the advantage of having engines which can pull big loads and get uphill quickly will become evident.

I may add that the four cylinder compounds weigh slightly over 51 tons, or about 2 tons more than the "Greater Britains". Also I should like to remind my readers that all the train weights given are *exclusive* of engine and tender; that all the runs quoted are from start to stop, unless where explicitly stated to be otherwise; and with a like qualification – that in none of the cases noted was a pilot or assistant engine employed. I append a log of the run made by No.527 "Henry Bessemer" from London to Crewe:-

Miles	Station		Actual times
	Euston	dep.	8.0.44
1¼	Chalk Farm	pass	4.24
3	Kilburn	"	6.41
5½	Willesden	"	9.11
11½	Harrow	"	15.23
16	Bushey	"	20.15
17½	Watford	"	21.45
21	Kings Langley	"	25.14
24½	Boxmoor	"	28.59
28	Berkhampstead	"	32.44
31½	Tring	"	36.49
36	Cheddington	"	41.10
40¼	Leighton	"	44.35
46¾	Bletchley	"	50.41
52¼	Wolverton	"	56.4
54¾	Castlethorpe	"	58.20
59¾	Roade	"	9.3.45
62¾	Blisworth	"	6.48
69¼	Weedon	"	13.18
75¼	Welton	"	19.14
82½	Rugby (slack)	"	27.24
93½	Bulkington	"	41.25
97	Nuneaton	"	44.54
102¼	Atherstone	"	50.6
106½	Polesworth	"	54.4
110	Tamworth	"	57.45
116½	Lichfield	"	10.3.53
121	Armitage	"	9.10
124	Rugeley	"	12.30
127	Colwich	"	15.38
133½	Stafford (slack)	"	22.45
143½	Standon Bridge	"	35.40
147½	Whitmore	"	40.47
150	Madeley	"	43.49
153½	Betley	"	46.51
158	Crewe	arr.	10.52.40

Note: eased down after Stafford

Chapter 18
Cross Country Train Services of the LNWR in 1901
by S.M. Philip LNWR

Certain articles having appeared in previous numbers of the RAILWAY MAGAZINE relating to the crosscountry train services of some of the railway companies, possibly a descriptive account of some of the most important services of this character on the London and North Western system may prove to be not without interest.

In point of fact, cross country train services have, or should have, a more absorbing interest for the ordinary railway traveller than he is at first prepared to realise. Of the splendid trains made up of dining or sleeping saloon carriages, running at phenomenal rates of speed on the great trunk routes from South to North, or vice versa, we hear a great deal, and the man who desires to travel, say from London to Glasgow, from Manchester or Liverpool to Edinburgh, or from London to Plymouth, has only to choose his route, and his train, and take his seat or his sleeping berth, as the case may be, and rely with confidence on a comfortable journey, and a speedy arrival at his destination. But for the man who has, for his sins, to perform an awkward cross country railway journey, say from a station in Westmoreland to a station in Suffolk or Dorsetshire, the case is far different. He will find that, after progressing some

Llandrindod Wells looking south from Down Platform. Two 4ft 6in tanks with a Euston express train of mixed arc roof stock is arriving in the Up Platform.

distance on his journey, he arrives at a junction where he must wait for some hours, and proceed by a slow train, stopping at every station, only to find another long "wait" at the next junction.

Indignant correspondents of the newspapers have often pointed out, quite truthfully, cases in which a long summer's day has been occupied in a journey of less than 100 miles, and such instances could be multiplied indefinitely, their explanation and their justification being, of course, that it would not pay the companies concerned to establish and maintain a special through service to accommodate an occasional passenger. There are, however, cases in which, for various reasons, there is a steady flow of traffic across country between one given point and another, and where this state of things exists, it will usually be found that the companies are ready to rise to the occasion and provide the necessary facilities. The trouble is that the casual indignant correspondent of the newspapers is multiplied in his own eyes into an important stream of traffic which ought to have been provided for, but has been reprehensibly neglected by the companies concerned.

Enough has, however, been said to show that "cross country services" properly so called, that it is good and fairly speedy through services, say, from east to west, west to north, east to north-west, and so on, where such do exist, form a very important element in the railway system of this country.

One of the most important Cross Country Services on the London and North Western is also one of the oldest, in fact, the oldest of all, being the service between Liverpool and Manchester. Indeed, it is said to have been the urgent need of improved means of communication between the Manchester district, one of the greatest manufacturing centres of the kingdom, and Liverpool, one of our greatest seaports, that led, in a measure, to the construction of the first passenger railway. The original service of trains by the Liverpool and Manchester Railway (which line is now an integral part of the North Western system) was started as long ago as 1830, and was of a very meagre and intermittent character; in fact, the trains were despatched at no stated times, but as and when they could be got ready to start, and the passengers patiently waited for the exciting moment of departure!

Twenty years later in 1851 there was a regular timetable showing ten trains from Liverpool to Manchester in a day, and twelve in the opposite direction, the time occupied varying from one hour to two hours. At the present time, there are twenty-five trains in each direction, including what is practically a regular hourly service throughout the day, performing the journey in 40 minutes, and with the utmost regularity. Most of these trains have only a single stoppage for taking tickets, but a few of them, which occupy a few minutes longer on the journey, are timed to stop at such places as St. Helens Junction, Earlestown, Newton-le-Willows, or Eccles.

The trains are made up of six "bogie" carriages, each 50ft. in length, fitted with steam heating apparatus and electric lighting; and, in fact, are thoroughly up to date in every respect. Those who desire to travel between Liverpool and Manchester suffer, indeed, from almost an *embarrass de riches* in the matter of train service, for in addition to the numerous trains run by the London and North Western, the Lancashire and Yorkshire Railway, and the Cheshire Lines Committee each have a frequent service of trains between the same points; but as if all this was not enough to meet the demands of the travelling public, the existing companies are now threatened with a new and formidable competitor by Mr Behr's Mono-Rail Electric Railway, which is to perform the journey in 18 minutes.

From Manchester to Leeds, a distance of 48 miles, the North Western afford by their route a frequent service of quick trains passing over the Lancashire and Yorkshire Railway between Manchester and Stalybridge (where they make connections with the trains coming from the south by way of Stockport), thence through the Standedge Tunnel, one of the longest tunnels

Saddleworth viaduct on the Leeds to Manchester line with an improved Precedent on a southbound train of five cove-roofed carriages. Saddleworth station is at the far end of the viaduct (from LNWR postcard).

in this country, and so by way of Huddersfield, Dewsbury, and Batley, to the fine new station at Leeds, which is the joint property of the London and North Western and North Eastern Railways. The journey occupies from one hour to an hour and a quarter, which may not appear to involve a high rate of speed; but it is to be borne in mind that the gradients for the first 15 miles after leaving Manchester are severe and continuous, while the line is a very crowded one. The trains, which perform the journey exactly in an hour, calling only at Huddersfield, form an admirable service between these two important towns.

In 1884, in conjunction with the North Eastern Railway, a valuable and convenient through service was established between Liverpool and Newcastle, via Manchester and Leeds. Originally, only two trains were run in each direction, but these proved to be so popular, and were so well patronised, that a third has been added, and there are now three trains in each direction, leaving Liverpool at 8.35am, 2pm, and 5.35pm, and Newcastle at 7.30am, 10am, and 4.20pm, the journey occupying 5½ hours. These trains incidentally afford a convenient service between Liverpool and Manchester, and York, Scarborough, the Hartlepools, Harrogate, and other places on the North-East coast. Of course, there are several other trains in the day by which a fairly convenient connection is given between Liverpool and the North Eastern district by changing at Leeds, but the popularity of the six trains in question rests upon the fact that they run straight through at a good rate of speed from Liverpool on the west to Newcastle on the east, and so form a substantial link between the two seaports.

In addition to the Newcastle trains, there are some five or six trains a day in each direction running through between Liverpool and Manchester, on the one hand, and Hull and York, on the other, without a change at Leeds. The journey to Hull from Liverpool occupies from 3 hours and 20 minutes to 3½ hours and from Manchester about an hour less. To go from Liverpool to York takes just under 3 hours, or from Manchester 2 hours. This service is continued all the year round, but in the summer, when the needs of the holiday seekers have to be consulted, at least two of the York trains in each direction are extended to Scarborough, which is reached in a little under 4 hours from Liverpool, or 3 hours from Manchester.

From the foregoing it will be seen that the wants of travellers between the great industrial centres of Lancashire and the important seaports, and the large towns on the East Coast have been well provided for by friendly cooperation on the part of the two great railways concerned, but one special facility which is afforded remains to be mentioned. For the benefit of the merchants of Hull and the district attending the Manchester Corn Market, a train is specially run, leaving Hull on Thursdays at 09.15am. Running through with only one stoppage, and reaching Manchester at 11.38am. At 2.53pm the train returns from Manchester to Hull, arriving at the latter station at 5.23pm. This train is quite an institution amongst the corn merchants of the district it serves, and is much appreciated.

There has always existed a large and important traffic between the North of England and Bristol and the West of England, and up to the year 1888 this was left almost entirely in the hands of the Midland Railway, who carried it via Birmingham and by their own route to Bristol; but the construction of that great engineering work, the Severn Tunnel, by the Great Western Railway, opened up a possibility to the North Western and Great Western Railways which they were not slow to take advantage of. By means of the tunnel, an admirably direct route was at once established between North and West by the lines of the two companies, and in the year mentioned they established an entirely new and most valuable train service, and made a big effort to secure a fair share of this important traffic, which effort has undoubtedly proved successful.

The service is composed of through carriages starting from Manchester and Liverpool, respectively, joined together at Crewe, and thence run through Shrewsbury, Hereford, Pontypool Road, and the Severn Tunnel to Bristol. At the outset, three trains in each direction proved sufficient, but as the business increased these were added to, and there are now five trains running from the North to Bristol, and six from Bristol to the North, while at Bristol there are convenient train connections by the Great Western Railway to the extreme West of England, including Bath, Exeter, Torquay, Plymouth and Penzance. The journey from Liverpool or Manchester to Bristol occupies, on the average, about five hours, some of the trains performing it in a little less than this, while others take a little longer, but it is, on the whole, a good and convenient through service with but few stoppages, and well maintained. Its value to the public is enhanced by the fact that by several of the trains, through carriages are run between places other than Liverpool and Manchester, and places beyond Bristol, thus avoiding any changing either at Crewe or at Bristol. For example, by two trains a day through carriages run between Manchester and Cardiff, and once a day from Manchester and Liverpool to Plymouth and Penzance, besides which a through carriage runs every evening from Glasgow to

Plymouth throughout, a most valuable facility. Similar through carriages are run in the opposite direction, while in the summer months the importance of Torquay, Dartmouth, and Weston-Super-Mare as tourist resorts is recognised by the running of through carriages between those places and Manchester, Liverpool, Leeds, and Scotland.

It will be seen that the opening of the Severn Tunnel route has conferred great advantages upon the travelling public, which the companies concerned have done their best to develop, both in their own interest and in that of their patrons, and not without a large measure of success.

Although perhaps not strictly germane to the subject of this article, it may not be without interest to state in connection with the Severn Tunnel route that the enormous traffic which has of late years grown up in flowers between Western France, the Channel Islands, and the Scilly Islands, and the industrial centres of this country, has justified the companies in establishing a special service of fast trains, which leave Penzance and Plymouth during the afternoon and enable the flowers to be delivered in time for the early markets the following morning at Manchester, Liverpool, and the principal towns in Yorkshire and Lancashire.

A useful service is afforded all the year round between Manchester and the favourite seaside town of Llandudno on the North Wales Coast. Every afternoon at 4.5pm an express train leaves Manchester, and after a fast run of only 2 hours and 20 min. reaches Llandudno at 6.25pm. The corresponding train in the opposite direction is even quicker, for it leaves Llandudno every morning at 8 o'clock and reaches Manchester at 10.10. The advantages of such a service are obvious, and are much appreciated, especially by Manchester merchants and others, who are by its means enabled to spend a few hours by the sea with the least possible loss of time taken from their business. In fact, it is quite feasible to leave Manchester after business hours, dine and sleep in Llandudno, and be back in Manchester for business the following morning.

Manchester folks, indeed, are well catered for in the matter of crosscountry services to places

Up express approaching Llandudno Junction with a Jubilee 4-cylinder compound . Site of old station and hotel on the right. Conway estuary on the left with castle in the distance.

of seaside resort. By a train leaving Manchester (London Road) at 11.50 every morning, through carriages are run to Tenby, arriving at the latter place at 8.20pm so that this somewhat awkward crosscountry journey, via Crewe, Shrewsbury, Craven Arms, Llandrindod, and Carmarthen is accomplished in 8½ hours. In the opposite direction, the passenger leaves Tenby at 8.20am and arrives in Manchester at 4.35pm, a journey of 8¼ hours. The same carriages are run to and from Pembroke Dock, and by changing once are available also for passengers from Leeds or Liverpool.

Seeing the wide ramifications of the North Western throughout the country – north, south, east, and west – it would be obviously impossible, without greatly exceeding our limits, to give an account of the whole of the numerous crosscountry services which they run, either within their own system or in conjunction with other companies; but one more may be mentioned in conclusion, and that is the Continental service to and from Birmingham and the Midland Counties. By a train leaving Wolverhampton at 3.35 in the afternoon, through carriages for Harwich are run, and on the train reaching Rugby on its way to London these carriages are detached, and run express to Peterborough, where the Great Eastern Railway takes charge of them, and runs them to Parkeston Quay alongside the Continental boat, which leaves at 10pm. The return service is at 7.0am by the same route, reaching Birmingham about noon, and Wolverhampton some 20 minutes later. In addition to this, during the summer months a through service is run between Birmingham and Yarmouth, with the object of fostering the tourist traffic between the Midlands and the Eastern Counties.

Chapter 19
Manchester London Road
Notable Railway Stations
by Thomas J. Matthews

In a former article I dealt at some length with Victoria Station, Manchester, from which it may be said without disparagement to the other notable railway terminals in that city, there is a continuous flow of traffic to the great manufacturing towns of Lancashire and Yorkshire. I don't mean to assert that other lines do not top that industrial hive which is responsible for the smoke and grime and wealth of the North where John Bright's humorous retort, "Get money honestly if you can, but get it,"

Manchester London Road approach showing LNWR side of frontage. Horse drawn cabs, some marked LNWR. Soldiers in dress uniform 16 July 1904.

is exemplified by the spelling of business with a capital B. Victoria Station, the headquarters of the Lancashire and Yorkshire system is, *par excellence,* the centre which thrives because of its close association with the commerce of the two counties; and in giving it the place of honour in a series of articles on the notable railway stations of Lancashire, one but pays tribute to the all-powered Moloch of trade and industry.

And yet Victoria is but one of four great arteries which play a very important part in the progress and development of Manchester. It has not altogether a monopoly of the manufacturing constituency of the North, and I know not whether, in strict justice, London Road Station, the terminus of one of several 'Royal Mail' routes from the South, has not the prior claim for consideration. Whereas Victoria stretches its talons over two counties, London Road takes one far away to that outer world whose only terminal is the ocean. East, west and south, as far as railways go, London Road has its connections, and frequently its through trains. The Continent is served direct, via Harwich; the Far East, represented by Grimsby and Cleethorpes, is a comparatively near neighbour; and right away in the West Country, Penzance sends us a carriage to join the confederacy of Railway stock, which daily pays its toll at London Road. Nor would it be London Road if it had not some immediate association with the metropolis. As there were many roads to Rome, so there are a fair number from Manchester to London. It would be a pity for Manchester if there were not, for the Manchester man likes nothing better than good, honest, healthy competition; and as London is the hub of the universe, so essential to him as trader and traveller, he would not be a Manchester man if he could not split ha'pence in his bargaining for the accommodation the iron road affords.

Of the four routes to the metropolis, London Road Station affords arrival and departure platforms for two, viz., that of the London and North Western – the aforesaid Royal Mail route from Euston – and that of the Great Central,

"Engineer" 2-4-0 at Manchester London Road Engineer's Yard coupled to an Inspection Saloon.

whose indomitable struggles to secure a grand trunk line to the capital were crowned with success two and a half years ago, when the then President of the Board of Trade, the Right Hon. C.T. Ritchie, first opened the line for passenger traffic. As was stated at the time, it is more than thirty years since such an important piece of railway as the Great Central's extension to London, only accomplished at a cost of millions, has been constructed and it seems likely to be the last great line to enter the metropolis. What an interesting line it is, as it forges its way through the industrial counties of the North and Midlands, leaving smoke and grime behind for the sylvan beauties of Nottinghamshire, Leicestershire and far–famed Buckinghamshire, before arriving once more at those scenes of life and activity in the wake of the world's commercial centre. Sir Edward Watkin did not live to see the fruition of his life's labour, but in part he was satisfied, for he was spared to see the line with which his name is inseparably associated, thrown open to the great travelling public.

Before Sir Edward's dream was realised, the traffic to London was conducted by arrangement with the Great Northern Railway, whose carriages came into London Road Station, but the motive power for which was supplied by the Manchester, Sheffield and Lincolnshire Railway, since known under its higher sounding title of the Great Central. A company with a direct trunk line to London could not but have aspirations in the direction which the very substantial curtailment of name implies. And yet the old Manchester, Sheffield and Lincolnshire Railway, with its headquarters at London Road Station, Manchester, has a history and a record for progress which justified the motto "Forward," so conspicuous today on the panels of its rolling stock.

I have by me a "Bradshaw" for 1853, which tells of the financial difficulties encountered in raising the necessary capital during the building of the

Improved Precedent No. 2190 "Princess Beatrice" standing in the Altrincham Platform at Manchester London Road.

line between Manchester and Sheffield, with a branch to Ashton-under-Lyne, involving a loss on the re-issue of forfeited shares of £105,216; but was "Forward", the motto of those days as it is today, under the metamorphosised or glorified title of Great Central? The fifties and the sixties were, in fact, the days of small beginnings; the struggling days which led step by step to the vast system controlled by the company today. From this same "Bradshaw" I gather that in the year 1853 there radiated from the Manchester, Sheffield and Lincolnshire side of the dingy, incommodious old London Road Station of that day, a meagre 167¾ miles of line and that Parliament had then authorised the construction of 74 miles.

Even in those pioneer days the directors had eyes on that vast traffic which has practically established the port of Grimsby, whose exports in coal during 1898, it is interesting to note, at a moment when we are hearing so much about a tax of one shilling per ton, ran up to the respectable figure of 1,644,415 tons, and whose dealing in fish – for Grimsby has been made into the largest fishing port in Great Britain – amounted, in the same year, to 103,771 tons, distributed by railway to all parts of the country. Although the Manchester, Sheffield and Lincolnshire Railway was not incorporated till 1846, it can claim 1837, the year of the late Queen's accession to the throne and of the opening of the London and Birmingham, and Birmingham to Manchester lines, as the birth year of the principal portion of its system, viz, the 41¼ miles of railway between Manchester and Sheffield. Between 1837 and 1852 extensions were made till we reach a total mileage of 167¾ miles; given by "Bradshaw"; today there is a total mileage of 453 miles, with canals and tramways in addition, the created capital for which, in 1898, was £40,665,030, as compared with £14,783,533 in the fifties.

The motive power – the brain – for the vast organisation which these figures imply is and has been concentrated for over half a century at London Road Station, Manchester, the station

No.3044 Special DX Class leaving Manchester London Road with train of arc roof bogie stock.

on the hill, or, as many of an older generation still describe it, "Bank Top." Half a century ago London Road Station was a diminutive building from which there was but one platform to accommodate the limited passenger traffic of the Manchester, Sheffield and Lincolnshire line, and that of the London and North Western Railway, who by amalgamating with the Manchester and Birmingham Railway, had in 1842 advanced their system from this southern outlet of Manchester as far as Crewe, the great railway metropolis of today.

For upwards of sixty years the London and North Western Railway and the company now known as the Great Central have been in possession of London Road Station, described in the official guidebooks of today as "a vast structure" with eight platforms, two carriage ways, telegraph offices, bookstalls, refreshment rooms, etc. The growth since the fifties has, indeed, been phenomenal. Even in those days it began to be seen that "Bank Top" Station would soon be utterly inadequate for the demands of the inhabitants of Cottonopolis, whose trade was developing east, west, north and south. The station, then a meagre structure, dull, dirty and deficient – was at that time in the joint occupation of the London and North Western Railway and the Manchester, Sheffield and Lincolnshire Railway; who, about the year 1860, formed a Committee of Directors, representing the interests of either side, to consider the advisability of erecting a station which should meet the growing requirements of the public. The late Mr Henry Morgan and the late Mr Edward Ross, two veterans of the railway world, acted as joint secretaries, with the net result that the London Road Railway Station Extension Act was passed in 1861, and three or four years later, the present station – since enlarged, reared itself above and around the remains of that woeful looking building which had performed its useful part and had passed out of date. In lieu of the highly inconvenient single platform of the fifties, the travelling public found, in 1864-5, four platforms for the arrival and departure of trains, with a spacious carriage way along the centre, marking, as it were, the dividing line of the interests of the two companies. The interior of the station was enclosed by a curved roof of glass, sustained by iron girders, while the approach from the road was carried along a series of arches having an easy gradient, culminating in a massive building of stone, with fine, bold architectural lines, whose clock face and handsome copings are today a landmark in the city of Manchester. One half of the interior of this spacious building, offering, as it does, so striking a contrast to the puny hut of the almost pre-historic period, is today used as the general headquarters of the Great Central system.

Up to the time of the erection of their Exchange Station, a few years ago, the London and North Western Railway also had their offices here, and indeed the District Goods Manager, Chief Telegraph Superintendent and District Cashier still have their offices at London Road Station. They are the landlords of the station, though the Great Central Railway have the right of user in perpetuity, and are not liable, as was reported quite recently, to be turned adrift in the course of a few years' time. That part of the building sacred to the administration of the Great Central is equipped with the necessary offices of administration and the Directors' board room, in which Sir Edward Watkin was wont to appease or to affright inquiring shareholders, who were appalled at the magnitude of the schemes his fertile brain formulated. It was here that the London extension scheme first took shape and was first explained to a wondering, doubting crowd of proprietors, who "swearing they would never consent, consented". It was here too, that there hangs a great oil painting by a well-known artist, of those famed Grimsby Docks, acquired by the company at a cost of 2½ millions of money, which have done so much for the fishing industry of the East Coast. In the immediate neighbourhood of the board room there are

No.3209 17in 0-6-0 Webb Coal engine (with wooden brake blocks) passing eastwards through Manchester London Road MSJ&A platforms with a goods train.

the offices of Sir William Pollitt, the General Manager, and his staff, the Secretary, Mr O.S. Holt, and the general offices, wherein, roughly speaking about 1,000 clerks are employed, one of their number at one time – and he is not ashamed to confess it – being one of the present Sheriffs of the City of London, Mr Joseph Lawrence MP. Beneath are the departments devoted to the use of the general public, Booking, Parcels, Telegraph and other accessories of a big railway station.

I am reminded, in connection with the parcels traffic, that a comparatively new source of revenue to the company, as it is a novelty in itself, is the parcel fish trade. Over and above that enormous fish traffic which comes daily over the Great Central system from the port of Grimsby to the port of Manchester, hundreds of parcels of fish arrive daily by express passenger trains. The size of each parcel or bass of fish varies from 7lb. to 14lb. It is ordered by postcard, at a nominal sum, from a dealer at Grimsby, who despatches a bass of fresh fish off by an early morning train and the Great Central Railway deliver it in Manchester, or the immediate neighbourhood, in time for tea the same evening.

Another branch of the company's traffic which has grown considerably within recent years is that of the Refreshment Department, whose headquarters are located at London Road Station. It was in 1893, I believe, that the Great Central Railway, in pursuance of their "forward" policy, took over from a private company the duty of supplying their passengers with dinner and refreshment generally. The new dining and buffet cars, six in number, now running to London, have made great inroads on the energies of the staff employed; but there are few more pleasant meals than dinner served aboard a Great Central

Whitworth Class No.773 "Centaur" at Manchester London Road Engineer's Yard with the overhead signal box behind.

dining car. From the kitchens in the basement of the London Road Station the dining cars, and the whole of the stations between Manchester, Guide Bridge, Penistone and Wigan, draw their supplies, under the watchful supervision of Mr W. Ingram, who for seventeen years acted as steward to the Salford Corporation. Mr Ingram has a staff of about eighty occupied in the various departments of the district assigned to him – for Mr G. Lassam, of Sheffield, is the supervising manager for the whole system – and in addition to the cooking, the storing of wines and the many other duties incidental to the working of the department, which are all conducted at London Road Station, he and his staff attend to the acquirements of close upon 100 diners at the station daily.

The London and North Western Railway also cater extremely well for travellers who like to take their meals *en route*, four express trains running to, and the same number from London having dining cars attached to them; the arrangements for these moving restaurants being under the superintendence of Mr A. F. Waters, of Euston.

One of the two stationmasters at London Road is Mr J.W. Hattee, a well-set Yorkshireman, who has been in the service of the company, now styled the Great Central, for over thirty-five years. Like the majority of railwaymen, Mr Hattee has worked himself up from the lowest rung of the ladder. Employed by the company when quite a youth, he graduated at a country station just outside Doncaster. After serving in various capacities, he was given charge of a station when twenty-one years of age, that of Gunness-and-Burringham, in Lincolnshire, and having subsequently gained experience at Ecclesfield, Mottram and Rotherham, he came to Manchester seven years ago. Mr Hattee tells you how, during those few years, the traffic on his section at London Road, and especially since the opening of the London line, has grown, and is growing, and statistics, gathered officially, show that whereas in 1856 there was a total of 28 trains in and out, the number had jumped to 72 in 1866 and 174 in 1901. These, it should be explained, are only the figures for what are known as "booked" trains.

Owing to the limited accommodation at the station, the "making up" of the trains has to be accomplished at Ardwick, nearly a mile away, and the labour of shunting these in and out of the station very materially adds to the traffic. So cramped for space was the Great Central Railway a few years ago that, taking advantage of a vast extension by the London and North Western Railway to which I am about to refer, they constructed another platform. There are now three arrival and departure platforms; A platform being 640ft. long, B 650ft. and C 530ft., the area of their portion of the station and buildings being 9,337 square yards. The spacious carriage way which divided the two stations originally has since been attenuated, owing to the exigencies of the rapidly increasing traffic, but as that, perhaps, forms part of another story, I will refer to it later.

So far, London Road Station has been described mainly as it deals with the headquarters of the Great Central system. By far the larger area, however, is the terminal station of the London and North Western Railway, who according to Lord Stalbridge, are the happy possessors of the "best permanent way in the world." Their interests at London Road are assiduously cared for by Mr James Hunter, a veteran in the service, whose wide and varied experience, dating over a period of thirty-three years, entitled him to the position of stationmaster of so important a centre of activity. Mr Hunter, who hails from the Lake District, had a thorough training in railway work on the North Lancashire and Westmoreland sections of the London and North Western system. He has passed through the mill of both Goods and Passenger Departments, and so far back as 1873 he was stationmaster at Kirkby Lonsdale. Later, we find

Newton class 2-4-0 No.1482 "Herschel" in Manchester London Road MSJ&A platform with the signal box and main station in the background. C1880. Designed by John Ramsbottom - 96 were built between 1866 and 1873.

him acting as Traffic Inspector at Lancaster for the Lancaster and Carlisle divisions of the system, and for a period he was General Inspector under Mr F. Harrison, formerly Assistant Manager, and now General Manager of the vast system of the London and North Western Railway. On the promotion of Mr Carley, in 1887, Mr Hunter, then stationmaster at Longsight, accustomed to deal with the great crowds who come during the summer months from all parts of the country to the far-famed Belle Vue Gardens, received the higher appointment of Chief at London Road, and judging from the smoothness with which the work is carried on there, a more discreet, a more shrewd, or a more capable stationmaster could not have been selected.

The through traffic to the South and West, so enormous in itself, has its counterpart in that huge suburban and residential service which may be divided again into two sections – the express service for season ticket holders, who solace themselves after the toil of the city amid the rural charms of Cheshire lying between Stockport and Crewe, or between Stockport and Macclesfield; and that other essentially suburban traffic between Manchester and Stockport. The London and North Western Railway also provides an excellent service of through express trains between London Road Station and Buxton, and the beautiful district around Buxton is rapidly becoming a favourite place of residence for Manchester business men. At a rough calculation there are in this important branch of the London and North Western traffic from London Road Station between 13,000 and 15,000 holders of season tickets who arrive in and depart from the city daily. The one complaint about the service is that the shorter distance passengers are too frequently delayed in order that their more favoured fellows from a distance may pass them on the way to the city.

These, however, are trifling matters in comparison with the multifarious duties incidental to a traffic, which, taken in conjunction with the normal business traffic, has to concern itself with the carriage of about 20,000 passengers outward, and another 20,000 inward daily. So as long ago as 1880, the London and North Western Railway Company recognised the utter inadequacy of their three platforms of that day, by taking in a vast area of land, several whole streets in fact, and covering them over with an extended station area, which more than doubled their portion of this notable terminus. They widened one and added two other spacious platforms to cope with the then growing business, and they constructed a concrete roadway along which vehicular traffic from outside might come to the aid of the travellers from a distance. But they did more during the great extension of 1880.

One of the most important considerations in the Commissariat Department of a great city is its milk supply. The dairy farmers of Derbyshire, Staffordshire and Cheshire find in the Manchester market a continuous outlet for their produce, and it was to meet the needs of this enormous traffic that the London and North Western Railway Company, when setting their hands to the work of extension in 1880, directed special attention. One of their five platforms at London Road is almost entirely set apart for the milk trade, which is brisk morning, noon and night – brisk by reason of the endless arrival of distributors with their "dandies" and milk floats, and brisk by reason of the frequent appearance of special trains bearing the churns from the farms at a distance. About 1,200 cans, each carrying about eighteen gallons of milk, roughly about 21,600 gallons of milk, are deposited at this platform daily, and removed for consumption. The collection of cans, varying in shape and colour – for each farmer seems to have a design of his own – is one which is difficult to describe, but that the whole trade is conducted in and out of the station with a minimum of confusion is testimony to the excellent system of organisation which prevails.

Then there is the strawberry season. The connection between strawberries and milk seems

Special DX No.3166 lined black with circular smokebox standing with tender under large overhead water tank in Manchester London Road Engineering Yard in 1902.

obvious, and London Road Station materially assists in adding to our enjoyment of these luxuries. During the month of July in each year, Kent and Cheshire send strawberries by the ton to London Road Station. Special trains arrive during the "wee sma' hours" from Kent carrying strawberries, whose total weight averages a ton a truck, and as there are frequently a dozen trucks attached to each special some idea of the yield of the strawberry grounds may be gathered. From Manchester many of these self-same strawberries are despatched without loss of time to the Potteries and the Sheffield and Buxton markets. Then there is the excursion traffic, which, with the close proximity of Belle Vue Gardens, is at times exceptionally heavy, and to divert which the company have special platforms at Longsight.

At the end of twenty years the London and North Western Railway is again moving in the direction of extensions. The vast alterations of 1880 no longer suffice to meet the demands of the city, and there is at this moment a gigantic scheme afoot which suggests dreamland. That it is to be something more than a dream is shown by the fact that plans have already been sanctioned for the widening of the three quarters of a mile of viaduct between Ardwick and London Road Station, now known as the "bottle neck," which has been the cause of more forcible language being used than perhaps any other length of line outside some of the London termini. Instead of four sets of metals as now, we are to have eight, and there is to be a new station erected on the site of an adjoining print works, for the accommodation of essentially local traffic. It is a gigantic undertaking to which the London and North Western Railway Company have set their hands, involving the demolition of hundreds of houses; and that business is intended is shown by the fact that the company have already entered into an arrangement to

Whitworth Class No.642 "Bee" at Manchester London Road with windshields on sand pipes. Adverts on platform behind.

erect compensation dwellings at Longsight, while they themselves intend to build others in the neighbourhood of Openshaw. When this project is carried out London Road Station will, indeed, be a "vast structure," of something more than the proportions mentioned in the present official guidebook. Perhaps the greatest boon to the travelling public will be the widening of the viaduct, which is responsible for so much delay at present.

Chapter 20
Earlestown Wagon Works of the LNWR
by S.M. Philips (LNWR)

The wagon stock of a railway company is not one of its least valuable assets, as will be readily understood if it is borne in mind that every wagon costs on the average at least £40 or £50 to build while the number of vehicles required to carry on the traffic of the country is enormous. Some statistics prepared nearly three years ago showed that at the time the number of goods wagons owned by the railway companies in the United Kingdom, exclusive of Ireland, was approximately 660,000, while, in addition there were about 550,000 wagons owned by private traders, such as colliery owners, quarry owners, and others; but as it is known that the stock is constantly increasing, the total number of wagons in use in the country today cannot be far short of 1,250,000, representing an invested capital of upwards of 62,000,000 sterling. And yet, whenever there is a period of commercial prosperity and the railway traffic is unusually heavy, the dolorous cry of the trader resounds through the land complaining of shortness of wagon supply everywhere and consequent loss of trade. The truth is that if the railways provided an ample wagon supply for any short period of inflation, they would, in periods of less prosperity, have thousands of wagons lying idle, and representing unproductive capital; but the question has always been admittedly a difficult one to deal with, and the companies can only do their best to please everybody, which is, after all, to their own interest as much as that of their customers. Enough has, however, been said to show that the question of wagon supply is an all-important one with railway companies who depend mainly, or even largely, upon the carriage of merchandise for their revenue.

The London and North Western Company, who have so many claims to priority amongst the railway companies in this country, do not reckon amongst these the claim to be the largest wagon owners. Rightly or wrongly, they have adhered in the principle of making the colliery proprietors who use their system largely provide their own wagons, while some other railways, and notably the Midland Company, have adopted the practice of extensively buying up the private wagons, and retaining them in their own hands, recouping themselves for the outlay by the charges for wagon hire; yet the London and North Western Railway possess nearly 73,000 wagons of their own, in addition to about 106,000 which run over their system, but are the property of traders.

Seeing the enormous number of wagons required to conduct the traffic of the country, it seems a natural question to ask, where and how, and by whom, are they all made? To this it may be answered that most of the large railway companies who have locomotive works build their own wagons, while the smaller companies and the private traders purchase theirs from various firms or private companies who undertake the business of carriage and wagon building throughout the country. The railways which build their own wagons maintain that they reap a substantial benefit thereby, not only directly by the saving of the manufacturers' profit, but indirectly by reason of the greater efficiency and reliability of the vehicles. Indeed, it is quite obvious that it is necessary for every vehicle that has to travel on a railway to be constructed with the most scrupulous care and attention to the smallest

7- Ton Covered Van No.12553.

4-plank 10 ton goods wagon No. 44597.

details, because the slightest weakness or fault in one of the most apparently insignificant parts, if it chanced to reveal itself while the wagon was travelling, and perhaps passing on the opposite line of rails another train filled with passengers, and moving at great speed, might cause an appalling catastrophe.

One of the greatest anxieties connected with railway management arises from the extent to which the traffic is worked by private wagons not built by the companies, but for the condition of which they are responsible whilst travelling on their railway, and with regard to which they have to exercise the most unceasing vigilance. For their mutual protection, the various companies, parties to the Railway Clearing House, have agreed between themselves upon a standard specification, with drawings, in accordance with which private owners are required to have their wagons built, down to the most minute details. Before the wagons are permitted to run upon the railway, they are carefully examined by the company's Wagon Superintendent, who, after satisfying himself that every requirement of the standard specification has been faithfully complied with, affixes to each wagon a plate, bearing a registered number, showing the date of registry and the maximum load. The wagon is then free to work over any line of railway, but it has to be efficiently maintained and kept up to the standard, and the railways reserve to themselves the right to stop any defective wagon, and refuse to allow it to run until it has been properly repaired or renewed, as the case may be.

It has been said that many of the large railway companies build their own wagons, and the London and North Western Railway has adopted this plan from the outset, and still adheres to it. In the very early days, they built wagons at Crewe and Liverpool, and later on at Ordsall Lane, near Manchester; but just half a century ago (1852) they purchased a small engineering works at

Goods Brake Van No. 197B lettered 'Crewe & Carlisle'.

Earlestown from a private firm and converted it into a wagon works. It was comparatively a small place, comprising an area of only about eight acres, but it was the nucleus of the present extensive and widely known "Earlestown Works." These works, if they do not claim to be one of the great show places of the world, like the Crewe Locomotive Works, are yet of vast extent and great importance, and the processes pursued in them are so interesting as to well repay a visit. They embrace now an area of about thirty-six acres, and employ nearly 2,000 skilled artisans, in addition to which there are about 750 men employed at various outlying repairing shops and examining stations but attached to the central department at Earlestown. The capacity of these works is very large, for they turn out ordinarily, in a busy year, as many as 4,000 finished wagons, in addition to repairing about 13,000, and building 200 or 300 carts, vans, lorries, etc., which are also constructed at the works. At a time of pressure, indeed, they are able to turn out eighteen finished wagons during a working day of 9 hours, *or at the rate of a wagon every half-hour!*

Such great results as these are, of course, only achieved by the perfection of system and organisation, and by the aid of the most powerful, ingenious and up to date machinery. The works comprise no less than eleven different "shops," devoted to the various processes which go to the building up of a wagon; for instance, in one shop the framework will be roughly put together, in another the wheels are made, in a third they are affixed, in another the wagon is painted; one shop is devoted to the making of springs, another to the removal of old tyres by hydraulic machinery, and another to the breaking up of old wagons which are worn out. In addition, there are three smithies, containing, in the aggregate, 130 smiths' fires, two iron foundries for the manufacture of the various castings used in the construction of a wagon, a forge fitted with gas furnaces for the conversion of old scrap into new iron, two saw mills, an extensive timber shed and yard, stores and other buildings. Some of the shops are of imposing dimensions; for example, the largest of the wagon shops, where the wagons are "laid down," as it would be called in the case of a boat or a ship, measures 163ft. in length by 291ft. in width, and thus contains an area of nearly 15,000 square yards. In this shop alone, 170 wagons can be "laid down" at one time, in addition to about fifty carts or lorries. Another wagon shop is the same length, but not so wide; but even in this, 138 wagons can be "laid down" simultaneously. The paint shop is 350ft. in length, and will hold 146 wagons, and the total length of the three smithies amounts to 821ft.

Altogether, the various shops, smithies, foundries, and mills cover an aggregate area of nearly fourteen acres out of the total area of thirty-six acres constituting what is known as "the works." It has been said that one shop is devoted entirely to the making of springs for the wagons, and here no less than 100 sets of new springs are turned out every week throughout the year, in addition to the whole of the existing stock being kept in repair. An imposing sight is the timber yard, measuring nearly 14,000 square yards, and containing vast stores of seasoned timber. English oak, pine, teak and elm, and other timber from abroad, sufficient to build London and North Western Railway wagons for years to come. Since George Stephenson's wonderful discovery of the power of steam, and its application to locomotion, how many thousands, how many millions, of tall trees have bowed their proud heads to be converted into wagons to run over the railways of the world!

A description of the machinery employed in such a works as Earlestown would in itself absorb the space assigned to this article, for there are upwards of 500 machines of one kind or another in use, including forty-three boring and drilling machines, seventeen for making bolts and nuts, sixty-three lathes of various descriptions, twenty-two steam hammers, fifty-two wood working machines and a host of others too

Earlestown in 1878: 7 ton 2 plank fixed side wagon No.42024 was built in 1 hour 41 minutes. The Foreman and joiners who built it are standing in the wagon holding their tools. Mr E.W. Emmett (The Superintendent) is at the front on the left.

numerous to mention, some being actuated by steam, some by hydraulic power and some by electricity, the latter as a motive power being of recent introduction at Earlestown.

It was once said that electricity might not inaptly be termed the "handmaid of steam," so important was the part it played in many of the operations connected with railway working; but even in these early days of the twentieth century, it begins to look as if the "handmaid" would ere long supplant her mistress altogether, like Hagar of old. Already we see electricity employed to draw trains where steam was formerly used, and now steam-driven machinery is beginning rapidly to be replaced by tools actuated by electricity as the motive power. Earlestown, thoroughly up to date in most respects, has not been behindhand in this, and already an electrical installation has been set up, consisting of two of Willan's Triple Expansion high-speed engines, one of 175 I.H.P., and the other of 75 I.H.P. with two Crewe dynamos, and not only by these means are the works lighted throughout by electricity, but a considerable portion of the lathes, drills, punching machines, and wagon traversers are driven by electric current. An extension of the electrical installation is under consideration at the time of writing, and there can be little doubt that before long the whole of the machinery in these works will be actuated by electricity, and the use of steam will be practically abolished, except for generating the electric current.

The electric lighting installation is of a very complete character, there being no less than thirty-six arc and 589 incandescent lamps in use in the various shops, stores, yards and other premises, with a total candle power of 63,728 candles. This system of lighting is found greatly to facilitate the carrying on of the works during the short winter days, and is no more costly than gas, although the result is so greatly superior. In point of fact, experience has shown that where the railway itself provides an electric lighting installation of any considerable magnitude, the cost, including interest on the first outlay, and depreciation works out at about the equivalent of gas at 2s.9d. per 1,000 cubic feet.

It has already been hinted that all the work connected with the wagon stock of the London and North Western Railway is not carried on at Earlestown. There are repairing shops scattered throughout the system, where minor repairs can be carried out without the necessity of sending the wagons long distances to be dealt with at Earlestown, and they only go there when the damage or deterioration is of a more serious character, requiring the use of the powerful machinery employed at the works. An ordinary wagon has a life of about 25 years, and in the course of its career it sometimes passes many times through the hands of the local repairers for every journey that it performs to Earlestown.

But besides small repairs, a most important duty devolves upon what is called the "outdoor staff" in connection with the examination and greasing of the wagons, with regard to which the most careful and minute precautions are taken. The company employs a staff of nearly 300 men, who are posted singly or in gangs at every station or junction of importance throughout the system. Their duty is to satisfy themselves that every wagon starting from or stopping at their particular station is in proper running condition. They test the wheels and the axles, and carefully examine the springs, buffers, draw gear, brakes, and all the working parts of the wagon, and if anything is found amiss, the wagon

Drop side ballast wagon No.820 with wooden brake shoe on one wheel only. 1885.

Single plank wagon with 9in sides No. 24945. Wooden brake shoe and long brake handle.

is promptly shunted out of the train, and a label is attached to it which indicates that it is not to travel until the defect has been remedied. Another of their duties is to see that the axle boxes are kept well supplied with grease for lubricating purposes, and it may be of interest to state that the London and North Western Railway Company alone in the course of a year, consumes nearly *a thousand tons* of grease for lubricating its wagon wheels.

It is hardly necessary to say that wagons built at Earlestown are constructed of the best materials, and with the utmost solidity and perfection of workmanship, without regard to cost where the question is between efficiency and economy; for a railway company who build their own wagons, knowing what may be the consequences of a broken axle or a faulty drawbar, have too much at stake to run any risk. The frames, as a rule, are constructed of well-seasoned English oak, but as this has of late years been getting rather scarce, it is beginning to be rather extensively superseded by a hard and tough Australian wood called "karri." The bodies are made of oak, "karri," teak, or pine, and the underframes of the best Staffordshire iron, the wheel tyres and axles being of Bessemer steel.

The London and North Western stock of 73,000 wagons is made up, roughly, of 42,000 open goods wagons, 7,000 covered goods wagons, 10,000 coal wagons, and 11,000 wagons of various descriptions for special kinds of traffic.

Of the open wagons, nearly 15,000 are low-sided, the sides being 9in. in height; about an equal number have sides 20ins. in height, and about 11,000 have high sides, 3ft. in height, with falling doors. All these have a carrying capacity of 7 tons, the tare of the wagons ranging from 4 tons 4 cwt. 2qr to 5 tons 6 cwt. 3qr.

Those who follow railway matters at all closely – and these are an increasing class in the community – are aware that much debate has recently arisen as to the proposal that British railway companies should in these bad times reduce their working expenses by adopting the American plan of carrying merchandise in wagons of 20, 30 or 50 tons capacity, instead of in our small 7 ton wagons, so as to reduce the haulage of dead weight. It would not come within the scope of an article descriptive of Earlestown Works to discuss the merits of this controversy, although there is plenty to be said on both sides; but one consideration that is quite obvious is that in this country our hoists, tips, turntables and other appliances have been constructed for our present small wagons, and to fit them to deal with the large vehicles in use in the United States would require an enormous initial outlay. At the same time, it is conceivable that between certain specified points, and for dealing with particular streams of coal, or other heavy traffic, the large wagons might be used in such a manner as to result in greater economy in working; and some of the English railway companies have not hesitated to initiate experiments in this direction.

The London and North Western Railway has not as yet proceeded very far on these lines, but it has built at Earlestown a few 20 ton open goods wagons, and it is now building a limited number of coal wagons of equal capacity, which, when ready, will be used experimentally, and the result will be carefully watched.

Another question which has been agitating the world of wagon builders during the last year is that of "either side brakes." Under the "Railway Employment (Prevention of Accidents) Act, 1900," the Board of Trade have power to make rules on certain subjects for the avoidance of accidents to railway servants in the execution of their duty, and, amongst other things, they have power to make an order that every wagon must be fitted with brake-levers on both sides, so as to admit of the shunters applying or releasing the brakes from either side of a wagon, and to prevent the necessity of the men going between, round, under, or over the wagons in order to put the brakes on or take them off. This order has not yet been promulgated, but it has been drafted, and, meanwhile, the wagon builders of the various railway companies are busily experimenting with various inventions for "either-side" brakes, with a view to decide upon the best for general adoption. When the decision has been arrived at, Earlestown and the other great wagon works will be busily engaged for the next few years in transforming the brakes on the million and a quarter wagons running upon our railways, for this operation alone will involve an outlay of at least £2,500,000, and only a limited time will be allowed to carry it out.

22ft Cattle Box No.72332 with compartment for cow man.

It cannot truthfully be alleged against the directors of the London and North Western Railway that at any of the great large works where bodies of men are employed, they have been unmindful of the moral and material welfare of their servants, and this is a reflection which is fully applicable to Earlestown. In connection with the works there is an admirable mechanics' institute, called the "Viaduct Institute," erected by the company at their own expense where the workmen and their families have the opportunity of attending, free of charge, lectures, both scientific and on general subjects, throughout the winter evenings. In addition, classes are held on five nights in the week, not only for the study of subjects forming the elements of a commercial education, such as book-keeping, shorthand, arithmetic, algebra, French, etc. but also for technical education in such branches as practical, plane and solid geometry, machine construction, building construction, applied mechanics, electricity, etc., in addition to which, for the female members of the families of the workmen, there are classes in cooking, laundry work, dressmaking and millinery. The commercial classes are open to both sexes, the fees are small, and there is no lack of incentives to study, for several scholarships are offered annually for competition by the Lancashire County Council, each of them worth £60 per annum for three years, besides exhibitions, value £10, for one year.

There is also a valuable scholarship, founded by the late Sir Richard Moon, who was for so many years Chairman of the London and North Western Railway, and there are numerous prizes offered, some by the committee, and some by the Union of Lancashire and Cheshire Institutes. The Institute, besides class-rooms, boasts of a comfortable reading room, a library, containing upwards of 5,000 volumes, and a cricket and recreation ground, covering an area of 6 acres, which is much appreciated. The Institute is in a flourishing condition and doing good work. The London and North Western Railway has also provided a large and commodious dining-room, capable of seating upwards of 400 persons, where the men and boys employed in the works can have their food cooked free of charge, and thus get their meals without leaving the premises, if they prefer to do so.

Any article descriptive of these works would be incomplete without mention of the man whose energy, sterling abilities and high character have so largely contributed to render them what they are – that is to say, one of the best disciplined, most efficient, and well-worked wagon works in the country. Mr J.W. Emmett, the Superintendent of the Wagon Department, may almost be said to have wagon building in the blood, for he served his apprenticeship partly under his father and partly under his uncle who was at that time the Wagon Superintendent of the Lancashire and Yorkshire Railway, subsequently working at the bench as an artisan for five years, and being then promoted to be foreman and draughtsman. On the death of his uncle, in 1865, he succeeded him as Wagon Superintendent of the Lancashire and Yorkshire Railway, which post he retained until, in 1867, he was selected to take charge of the Earlestown Works, succeeding the late Mr Owen Owens. He has thus spent thirty-five years in the service of the London and North Western Railway and is universally recognised as one of their oldest and most valued servants.

Chapter 21
The London and Birmingham Express Train Services – 1838–1901
by H.G. Archer

At the dawn of the twentieth century it may prove interesting to sketch the history of the express train services between London and Birmingham. The London and Birmingham Railway was opened for passenger traffic on September 17th 1838, the distance from Euston to the Birmingham terminus in Curzon Street being 112½ miles. The original through service consisted of one mail train in either direction – Euston, depart 9.30am; Birmingham depart 8.30am - taking 5 hours over the journey, and calling at Tring, Wolverton, Weedon and Coventry *en route;* five "mixed" trains in either direction, taking from 5 to 5½ hours; and one first class train in either direction, taking 6 hours. The running speed of the last named must have been higher than that of the mail, for it halted at Rugby, Blisworth, Leighton and Watford, in addition to calling at the mail stations. Practically all these trains were in connection with those of the Grand Junction Railway – Birmingham to Liverpool and

Alfred the Great class No.1949 "King Arthur" with the 1.35pm up Birmingham Express picking up water on Bushey Troughs. 40 of this class were built between 1901-03.

Manchester – whose station was side by side with the Curzon Street terminus and through passengers to or from the North were allowed sufficient time at Birmingham to partake of refreshments, served by "female attendants." Between London and Birmingham, the first-class trains consisted of first class and mail carriages, carrying four inside, one compartment of which was convertible into a bed carriage, if required, and of carriages conveying six inside. The "mixed" trains were composed of first-class carriages carrying six inside and of second-class carriages, open at the side, without linings, cushions or divisions in the compartments. The night mail trains consisted of first-class carriages carrying six inside, and of second-class carriages, closed and entirely protected from the weather.

Barely seven years had elapsed since the opening of their line ere the London and Birmingham directors were flabbergasted to find that a scheme was afoot for providing an alternative route on the broad-gauge principle via Oxford. The project crystallised in 1846, when the Rugby and Oxford Junction Railway obtained an Act to construct a line from Itchington, near Fenny Compton, on their system, to Birmingham, 42¾ miles in length; and by a special clause the shareholders were empowered to lease their line to the Great Western Railway, if three-fifths of them should be in favour of doing so. Whilst the Bill was passing through Parliament, the London and Birmingham and Grand Junction Railways were busy with an amalgamation scheme, hence the former found themselves with too much on their hands to make any active opposition; but directly the amalgamation was carried into effect, on July 16th of that year, under the title of the London and North Western Railway Company, war was declared in earnest.

The tactics employed consisted in buying up the shares of the invading association, so that in 1847 the North Western held 40,000 out of 50,000 shares, constituting the capital of the Rugby and Oxford Junction Railway. A special meeting was then summoned, at which it was proposed to raise the number of directors from twelve to eighteen, the six additional directors being North Western men, while four more were brought forward to take the place of four directors possessing Great Western sympathies, due to retire. The latter, however, refused to retire; nevertheless, the North Western got their six nominees appointed, and succeeded in passing a resolution rescinding the clause, already confirmed, for the transfer of the new line to the Great Western Railway. The Great Western directors appealed to Parliament, and at the same time commenced proceedings against the Rugby and Oxford Junction Railway for breach of contract.

The House of Lords appointed a Committee to inquire into the matter, but the committee withheld their decision on seeing that, in February, 1848, the Great Western obtained a judgement in their favour, confirming the original lease to them, and declaring the six North Western directors to have been illegally elected. Consequently, the extension of the broad gauge to Birmingham now became assured. Meanwhile, however, the narrow-gauge champions had gained a small victory by obtaining Parliamentary powers compelling the mixed gauge, that was, the narrow as well as the broad gauge, to be laid down between Birmingham and Oxford. At the threat of an invasion from the broad gauge, the London and North Western Railway increased the speed of their trains between Euston and Birmingham to about 37½ miles per hour, including stoppages; but that speed was only attained with comparatively light trains, and could not be maintained with heavy ones.

In August, 1848, the best down train, the Scotch express, left Euston at 9am and reached Birmingham at 12 noon, while the "crack" Birmingham express proper, due to depart from Euston at 5pm, took five minutes longer. The fastest of the ten up trains took 3 hours 15 minutes. Of course, these trains were confined to first-class and second-class passengers. On the down journey, the solitary third class connection left Euston at 6.45am and arrived at Birmingham at 2.45pm. No wonder the London and North Western Railway were uneasy, for on the Great Western system, although the broad-gauge route was not then completed to Birmingham, a speed of upwards of 44 miles per hour was constantly maintained, and with trains more than double the weight of those run between Euston and Birmingham.

Immediately after the creation in 1846 of the London and North Western Railway, that company decided to construct a large central station at New Street, and to close the old double terminus at Curzon Street for passenger traffic. The works were commenced in 1847, and as they progressed, the claim of the Midland to having running powers thither as well was allowed without demur, at a nominal rental of £100 per year, as a reward for the manner in which they had checkmated another threatened attack on the part of the feared broad-gauge by forestalling the latter in the acquirement of the Birmingham and Bristol Railway.

In 1853 the Grand Central Station in New Street was completed, and the journey between Euston and Birmingham increased by 1 mile.

In September, 1850, the Oxford and Banbury section of the new broad-gauge route was opened for traffic, and just two years later the extension to Birmingham was completed, thus furnishing a rival route 129¼ miles in length. On September 30th 1852, a trial train left Paddington for Birmingham, hauled by the magnificent locomotive "Lord of the Isles," and including in its make-up one of the earliest (in this country) eight-wheeled passenger-coaches on record 38ft. long, 9ft.9in. wide, and containing accommodation for twenty-four first-class and fifty-six second-class passengers. The trip, however, met with disaster, for at Aynho the special overtook and collided with a slow train; the "Lord of the Isles" was derailed, and many of the company's guests severely shaken. In consequence of this mishap, it was determined to proceed no further than Leamington, where a dinner was held, and the toast, "The Broad Gauge to the Mersey," drunk with enthusiasm.

Nothing daunted by the unpropitious omen, however, the Great Western Railway gave effect on October 1st to the following excellent express service; Paddington, depart 9.15am, 5.30pm; Birmingham, arrive 12 noon, 8.25pm; Birmingham, depart 8am, 7.30pm; Paddington, arrive 10.45am, 10.25pm. The trains stopped only at Oxford and Leamington, but by far the fastest running was made between London and Oxford, the 63½ miles being accomplished in 70 minutes, which was at the rate of speed of 54.4 miles per hour. The North Western responded to the challenge by issuing a revised time-table as follows: -

Euston, depart 6.0am, 9.15am, 5.15pm; Birmingham, arrive 8.50am, 12.0 noon, 8.05pm; Birmingham, depart 7.30am, 7.15pm; Euston, arrive 10.15am, 10.0pm.

The inclusive rate of speed by the broad-gauge 2¾ hour service was 47 miles per hour, and that by the narrow-gauge, 41.2 miles per hour. Tradition relates, however, that, whereas the former trains kept excellent time, the latter seldom achieved the journey under 3 hours. A statement in the "Times," announcing that the London and North Western Railway intended building new locomotives which would enable them to run to Birmingham in 2 hours, was never fulfilled, though there is reason to believe that the step was contemplated. However, the excellent Great Western trains slackened their speed before the close of the year, on account of the indifferent state of the permanent way north of Oxford, which was not safe for the heavy broad-gauge trains at much over 40 miles per hour.

In December, 1852, the fastest journey was lengthened to 3 hours 5 minutes, whereupon a similar "deceleration" took place by the North Western route. In 1858, the best down Great Western train still took 3 hours 5 minutes, but the best up one was scheduled at 3 hours 10 minutes, against which the North Western had one down in 2 hours 55 minutes, and one up in 3 hours. By this time, however, the Trent Valley line was open, and Birmingham no longer enjoyed the full blaze of North Western expresses serving Liverpool, Manchester and the North. The first chapter of one of the most unfortunate errors ever perpetrated in the history of our railway system, namely, the abandonment of the broad-gauge, was now rapidly approaching its consummation. During the fifties, the Midlands and North were entirely won over by the narrow-gauge exponents, so that in 1859 – the year of Brunel's death – the broad gauge had become an anachronism in those districts.

Two years later, the Great Western Railway found themselves compelled to make the best of the inevitable by transforming their Oxford and Birmingham service into a narrow-gauge one. In 1869 the broad gauge was abandoned north of Oxford. The change, however, carried with it no engineering difficulties, for the section had been from the first mixed gauge, and meanwhile the inner third rail had been extended from Oxford to London.

On October 1st 1861, the first narrow-gauge train ever started from Paddington left at 9.35am for Birmingham, being due there at 12.55pm. But the new narrow-gauge service included some faster connections than that. The 6.30pm down made Birmingham in 2 hours 50 minutes, the 53 mile run to Didcot being accomplished in the hour, inclusive of a stop at Slough; while on the up journey there was one 3 hour train, and one taking five minutes less. The rival North Western service gave two down trains and one up at 3 hours.

For many years after the triumph of the narrow gauge there appears to have been no change worth noticing in the time tables of either route. Early in the seventies, however, the Great Western Railway entered upon a long period of lackadaisical, unenterprising management, and their Birmingham service suffered accordingly. In 1878 the North Western service, for the first time since the competition had existed, was morally the best. Euston then gave one train each way in 2¾ hours, an up one in 2 hours 55 minutes, and several others at from 3 hours 5 minutes to 3 hours 15 minutes. On the down journey the Great Western had only three fast down trains, the best taking 3 hours 18 minutes, and an up in 2 hours 55 minutes. The time by the remainder was very poor, averaging about 3 hours 40 minutes.

In the winter of 1880/1 Paddington woke up and inaugurated an accelerated express service, which once again forced the pace. A down train left London at 4.46pm and made Birmingham in 2 hours 42 minutes (the fastest timing between the two cities hitherto scheduled), and an up one leaving Birmingham at 2.35pm reached Paddington in 2 hours 50 minutes. These two trains were nicknamed the "Afghans," since they made their appearance just when Lord Roberts' grand march to Kandahar was in every mouth. At the present day one often hears them alluded to as the "Zulus," but the "Zulus" are the afternoon West of England expresses, inaugurated in 1879 at the triumphal close of the Zulu War. To compete with the new Great Western trains, the North Western put on a new down train, leaving Euston at 4.10pm, and reaching Birmingham at 6.55pm.

Professor Foxwell's exhaustive train statistics made during the summer of 1888 revealed the fact that the London and North Western Railway then gave six down and five up express trains between London and Birmingham. All these trains, with the exception of one up, ran via Northampton, a distance of 115½ miles. The average time for the whole was 2 hours 49 minutes, giving an inclusive rate of speed of 40½ miles per hour. The Professor only noticed those trains which attained an inclusive journey speed of 40 miles per hour. It was not, therefore, such a complete contemporary record as that up-to-date one furnished on the next page which takes into account "fast" as well as express connections. By 1891 the best North Western time had been reduced to 2 hours 35 minutes on the down, and 2 hours 30 minutes on the up journey, while the best Great Western trains were still the two "Afghans" on their original timings. In July, 1893, the Great Western made their 1.30pm down train and 5.45pm up one into what are now well-known as corridor trains, these two trains being the first of the complete corridor type ever run in the country. In 1895, the North Western strengthened the Birmingham service, but without increasing the speed, and also deleted the Rugby stop by a few expresses.

On July 1st 1898, the Great Western ran, for the first time, a train from Paddington to Birmingham without stopping, performing the break of 129¼ miles in 2 hours 27 minutes, which was at the rate of speed of 52.7 miles per hour. This train, however – a summer tourist express for Wales –, was hardly intended for local traffic, but the acceleration paved the way to an important improvement that took place in the following summer, when the departure time of the 1.30pm ex-Paddington was altered to 2.10pm, the stops at Oxford and Leamington cut out, and Birmingham reached in 2 hours 27 minutes. The North Western immediately responded with a new train, leaving Euston at 2.35pm, making Birmingham in 2¼ hours. This train, which is running today, and forms the fastest connection between London and Birmingham, during the summer performed the 82½ miles from Euston to Rugby in 93 minutes, the speed being 53.2 miles an hour, this timing being the fastest ever given to any North Western express over that section of the line. This is the arrangement during the three summer months. During the remainder of the year the train leaves Willesden at 2.47pm, and runs thence to Birmingham, via Rugby, without a stop, performing the break of 108 miles in 123 minutes, speed 52.18. On July 1st 1899, the run of the 9.30am Great Western train to Birmingham was accelerated by 2 minutes to 53.4 miles per hour, and in July 1900, the same timing was given to the 2.10pm. This summer two more minutes have been knocked off the run of the 9.30am, so that the rate of speed now attains 54.2 miles per hour, which is the second fastest booked rate of speed on the whole Great Western system.

It is worthy of remark that in the September working time-tables, both the 9.30am and 2.10pm are scheduled to pass Oxford in 70 minutes from Paddington, which is identically the same timing as that given to the broad-gauge expresses of fifty years ago. But the latter stopped at Oxford, whereas the best stopping train today, the 4.55pm down, requires 73 minutes.

The rival services in September 1901, were as follows: - On the down journey the North Western gave six trains, via Northampton, averaging 2 hours 46 minutes, inclusive speed 41.7 miles per hour, and eight trains, via Blisworth, averaging 2 hours 46 minutes, inclusive speed 41.0, while the Great Western had eleven trains, averaging 3 hours 16 minutes, inclusive speed 39.6. On the up journey the North Western gave two trains, via Northampton, averaging 2 hours 30 minutes, inclusive speed 46.2, and eight, via Blisworth, averaging 2 hours 58 minutes, inclusive speed 38.2, while there were three trains running via Marton which took from 3 hours to 3 hours 50 minutes. The Great Western had nine up trains averaging 3 hours 4 minutes, inclusive speed 42.1. The Midland, whose route via Leicester and Wigston Junction is 138½ miles in length, do not seriously compete, but they have one train, or rather connection off the 5.30pm ex-St. Pancras, which accomplishes the journey in 3 hours 9 minutes, and furnishes an inclusive rate of speed of 43.9 miles per hour.

Chapter 22

The Opening of the Liverpool and Manchester Railway

by G.J. Stoker (LNWR retired)

It is but repeating a truism to say that the opening of the Liverpool and Manchester Railway marked the beginning of a new era in the history of this country, and of the world. As might be expected of such a notable event, some good descriptions of the proceedings were published at the time; from these we propose to gather the necessary particulars, and, so far as the limit of a short article will permit, give a more full account than is usually to be found in works on railways written at a later period.

Although the honour of providing the first public railway for the conveyance of passengers by means of a steam locomotive must be conceded to the Stockton and Darlington Company it was, without doubt, the success of the Liverpool and Manchester line that decided public feeling in favour of the new mode of travelling. The early working of the Stockton and Darlington was necessarily to a great extent experimental. It commenced with three modes of traction, horses, stationary engines, and locomotives. All its arrangements as to traction, rolling stock, signalling, permanent way, etc., were of the most elementary order, and had not emerged from the experimental stage when similar questions with regard to the projected Liverpool and Manchester line were under consideration. Something was to be learned from the earlier line, something could also be learned from other sources, but still more had to be initiated by the ingenuity and skill of the engineers and men of business. So little had really been decided by previous experience that almost up to the completion of the permanent way it was an open question whether locomotives or stationary engines were to be used. Even the employment of horse power was strongly urged; more than one writer entering into elaborate calculations to prove that by its use only could a dividend be earned.

No better illustration can be given of the comparatively little knowledge possessed by engineers of the construction of earthworks than the well-worn one of taking the line over Chat Moss – a simple matter according to modern ideas. The most eminent engineers professed to regard it as a stupendous task involving incalculable expense. We should be sorry to appear unjust to the memory of the able gentlemen who made so much of this difficulty when the Bills were before Parliament, but we are sometimes disposed to think that if they had been retained by the promotors instead of the opposition they would not have given themselves away quite so readily – the point of view makes such a difference. It could hardly have been pleasant for them to see the ease with which Stephenson surmounted the obstacle, nor to reflect that the greater they had endeavoured to make it appear the more credit accrued to the man by whom it was overcome. He did it in such a simple manner, too! – by merely carrying out on a larger scale a plan adopted by farmers and others for centuries for laying tracks across morasses and other marshy places. The achievement was not to be undervalued on this account; indeed, we have never heard that anyone was so ungenerous

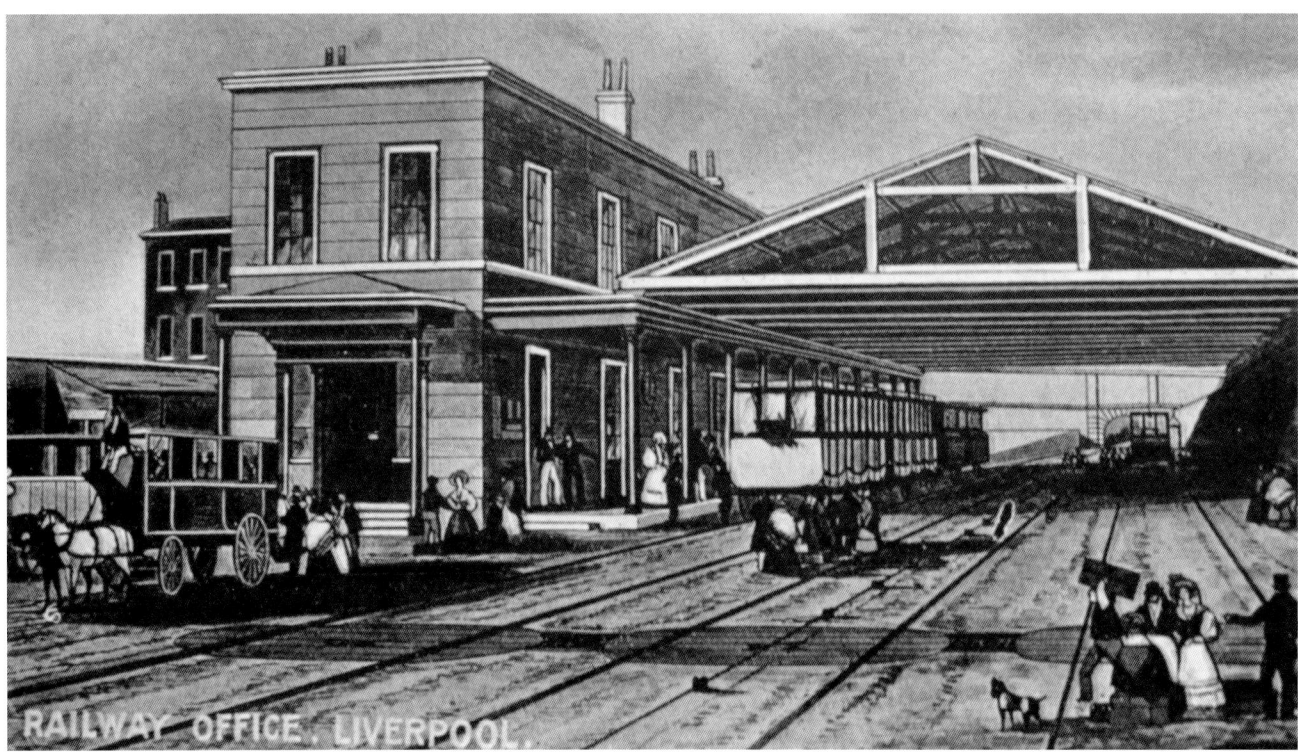

First Liverpool Station and Offices 1830s (from postcard).

as to attempt to do so. In its very simplicity there is an element of grandeur, and the patience with which Stephenson persevered in spite of all discouragement, proves the fine quality of the man.

As to the power to be adopted, suggestions came from all parts of the world and from all sorts and conditions of men. "Every scheme," writes Mr Charles Booth, the secretary of the company, "which the restless ingenuity or the prolific imagination of man could devise was liberally offered to the company." A sad waste of time and trouble. The vignette on the original share certificate, issued 1825, shows that the directors had pretty well decided in favour of the steam locomotive long before the trial at Rainhill. In it are represented two trains, each finished off with an engine at the head, a flight of imagination on the part of the designer which would hardly have been sanctioned if any doubt had existed on the subject.

The discussion as to the best form of rails, and the best mode of laying them down, which resulted in the adoption of forms and methods long since discarded, would be an unprofitable study. The controversy continued for many years, until, taught by experience and expenditure of much capital, engineers gradually settled down to the almost uniform system at present in use.

We need touch lightly on the causes that led up to the construction of the line; they have frequently been explained. The prime mover was *necessity*, the hard taskmaster who has been keeping the world at work from the very beginning, and to whom we owe all the progress made since Adam was turned out on the world to earn his own living. Neither would it be of much advantage, even if it were not foreign to our present purpose, to endeavour to trace to whom the invention of railways, or of this particular railway, is due. Like Topsy, they *grow'd*. In the first plank laid to diminish the friction of a wheel lay the germ of an idea. The old granite tracks of the Romans, the wooden way-leaves of Tyneside, with the later introduction of iron rails, form a succession of advances in the march of improvement, the first steps of which have left no imprint on the page of history.

The necessity of improved means of communication between Liverpool and Manchester was brought painfully home to all concerned in the trade of the two towns in many ways. There were two modes of transit – by road and by canal; if a merchant were asked which was the more exasperating, he would probably have replied – both! The first was excessively dear, but was frequently chosen in preference to the canals, because the saving by using these was more than counterbalanced by the delays – which were not infrequently extended to weeks – and the uncertainty of delivery. Of course, as trade grew these difficulties of transit increased, until they became a serious obstacle to the progress of the country.

As he looked out on the Mersey and saw the twin steam ferry-boat "Etna" (precursor of the "Castalia") puffing across, Mr Sanders, corn merchant and shipper, who had suffered many things of the carriers, may have often wished something of the same kind could be applied to land carriages.

Perhaps he was in one of these moods when, in 1821, Mr W. James, a London surveyor and land agent, armed with a letter from his friend, Mr Cowlishaw, of Manchester, called upon him and explained his views as to the benefits to be derived from a railway to Manchester. Mr James was enthusiastic about railways. He was the originator of several tram lines in the Midlands, and had just returned from the North, where he had inspected the working of the most recent locomotives, and seen what they could do when placed on rails. Mr Sanders was a willing listener, and in the end commissioned him to make a survey for a line such as he suggested, the expense of which he guaranteed. He took up the scheme heartily, wrote a pamphlet in its favour, induced the Mayor and other leading men to take it up, and formed a committee to carry it through.

Mr James made the survey and submitted plans, but he was not destined to construct the line. A series of unfortunate circumstances prevented him from being able to complete his survey in time, or to give the necessary attention to the Parliamentary business. The committee, therefore, very reluctantly took the work out of his hands, and sent for George Stephenson, who had been recommended to them by Mr James, and was becoming known beyond the Northern coal districts, to which his work had hitherto been confined. He speedily supplied plans. His estimate of £400,000 looked big compared with James' modest £100,000. Both were sufficiently wide of the mark to entitle their authors to take rank with other eminent engineers. The total cost was £1,089,818 17s.7d. It is only fair to say that a large portion of the discrepancy between the estimates and the actual cost was due to the enlargement of the ideas of the promoters as time went on and they realised more clearly the scope of the undertaking to which they were committed.

In 1825 application was made to Parliament, but the opposition of vested interests, and of a prejudiced and short sighted public, was too strong. The bill was thrown out, the motion for its rejection being seconded, very appropriately it was thought, by a member named *Coffin*.

Those who hoped it would then be decently interred were disappointed. The directors did not believe in the demise of their bantling. They had fresh plans made out, this time by Messrs. G. and J. Rennie, the leading engineers of the day. With these they again went to Parliament and got their Bill passed on April 6, 1826. Messrs. Rennie, having prepared the successful plans, were offered the option of carrying them out. But as they hampered their acceptance with terms to which the directors would not agree, the ever-ready Stephenson was again applied to, and he took charge of the work, and never relinquished it until he had made the line, and engines to run upon it.

Practical men were sent to Darlington, Killingworth, and other districts where useful information was likely to be obtained. Their reports, the chief value of which lay in the facts they contained, were rather in favour of stationary engines, but no very decisive opinion was expressed. Before finally deciding, the directors thought it would be well to have a few engines on approval. To induce makers to submit these, they offered a prize of £500 for the engine that best fulfilled certain conditions in a trial to be commenced at Rainhill on October 5, 1829. It is well known that George Stephenson's "Rocket" distanced all competitors, gained the prize, and obtained for his firm orders for the engines to form the first locomotive stock of the company. Sir George Findlay relates that Stephenson was so elated by his success that he presented his (Sir George's) father, who was a sub-contractor under him, with a silver watch, a valuable present at that time, to mark the occasion.

The "Rocket" is the most famous locomotive engine ever built. Amongst the general public its name stands as a synonym of Stephenson's success. Afterwards Stephenson constructed the "Planet", a locomotive built on lines including the main principles underlying engine construction at the present day, and in it were combined the blast pipe, the multitubular boiler, the horizontal cylinder, and the crank axle, and it had the firebox firmly attached to the boiler; beside the "Planet" all previous engines look antiquated. It soon showed its quality by conveying a train from Manchester to Liverpool, 33½ miles, in 60 minutes.

All this time money was being poured out at what seemed in those days an alarming rate – to speculators in our time it would appear a mere dribble – and subscribers were becoming impatient for some return. Great pressure was put on the engineer; on some parts of the line work went on night and day without cessation. On New Year's Day, 1830, a special train with directors and friends passed over Chat Moss – nine months

Stephenson's "Rocket" – a replica seen at the National Railway Museum in York with an 'open' and 'closed' carriage.

Close-up of the "Rocket" replica with side cut out to show inner working.

L&M No.9 "Planet" a 2-2-0 working replica seen at the Manchester Science Museum. "Planet" was the ninth loco built by Robert Stephenson for the railway and was the first to have inside cylinders (11in x 16in). It had 5ft driving wheels and weighed 8 tons. On 23 November 1830 it ran from Liverpool to Manchester (30 miles) in 62 minutes. A further 15 of the 'planet' class of locomotives were built 1831-33 later the iron bands, called by Gray, of Norwich, the "main springs of civilisation" stretched from the Mersey to the Irwell, and notice was given that the opening ceremony would take place on September 15, 1830. The locomotive engine, set on the rails by Trevithick a generation earlier, and for want of encouragement allowed to drop out of public notice, had been improved by various hands, chiefly by the "stern featured man with dark and deeply-marked countenance," as Miss Kemble describes Stephenson, and was on this day to take its place as the foremost force of the earth. King Steam had come to his throne, and the directors determined to give him a right royal welcome.

Invitations to be present were accepted by the Duke of Wellington, the Marquis and Marchioness of Salisbury, Sir Robert Peel, Prince Esterhazy, and many other distinguished persons, including eminent members of both Houses of Parliament, mayors of important towns, and business men, who watched with eagerness the result of an experiment they were prepared, if it appeared successful, to follow up in other districts. Strangers arriving from distant parts crowded the hotels and lodging houses; famous people like the Kemble family were glad to obtain a "tiny garret," secured for them as a special favour by a friend. The streets were blocked all night by vehicles for which there was not room in the inn yards. The country houses of the neighbouring nobility and gentry were filled with visitors.

It was arranged that all the trains should start from Crown Street Station, Liverpool, in the morning, run to Manchester and return to Liverpool in the afternoon; the invited guests to be at the station at 10 o'clock. Both lines of the railway were to be occupied; the trains running in the same direction on each, all crossings from one main line to the other were taken out, a precaution for the prevention of accidents, which led to much difficulty on the return journey.

After a stormy night, the morning opened bright and cheerful. The approaches to the station were filled with an immense concourse of people, and all along the route, and at Manchester, vast crowds assembled. The station at Liverpool was not in the central position it now occupies. Lime Street Station was not opened until 1835. The area in front was crowded with vehicles of every description, from the nobleman's carriage to the costermonger's cart, pressed into service by the favoured ones, who, dressed in their brightest array, were about to undertake the exciting expedition through gloomy defiles, amid Cimmerian darkness of abysmal tunnels, across giddy heights, and over Serbonian bogs of unknown depth. Such was the flowing language used in contemporary descriptions. Nothing less than the superlative would suffice.

The most ordinary things became wonders. One writer describes how an engine looked small when at a distance, and seemed gradually to enlarge as it approached – apparently surprised that the laws of perspective should affect such an uncanny beast. In the station yard all was life and animation. The gay dresses of the ladies, the varied colours of the flags, which were displayed in profusion, with the strange collection of vehicles, composed, as a rather cynical writer remarked, "Such a scene as might be made up by a combination of the Lord Mayor's Show and Epsom races." The Duke of Wellington, who entered the yard a few minutes before 10 o'clock, was much amused, and showed his enjoyment by bursting into a hearty fit of laughter.

On one line stood the carriages forming the train for directors and distinguished guests, including a "Moorish" car for the Duke of Wellington and his friends. This vehicle is described as resembling an Eastern pavilion rather than a carriage. The floor was 32 ft. long by 8 ft. wide; gilt pillars supported a crimson canopy 24 ft. long. A "Grecian" car of equally gorgeous appearance accommodated a band of musicians.

On the opposite line stood a long procession of trains, each drawn by one of the seven engines that with the "Northumbrian" (driven by George Stephenson himself), which was attached to the

First class carriage of Liverpool & Manchester Railway 1838.

Duke of Wellington's train, composed the entire locomotive stock of the company. Each train was decorated with silk flags of a particular colour, and every visitor (about 700 in all) to whom a seat was allotted had a card of similar colour, with a number on it corresponding to the number on the seat.

A grand musical display was provided for the amusement of the company. Throughout the trains trumpeters were stationed, each of whom as the Duke came in sight took up in succession the martial strain, "See the Conquering Hero Comes" until, by the time the band in the Grecian car was reached and struck in, bar, time and tune were inextricably mixed, producing a striking and unexpected effect. Other bands stationed in close proximity, if they did not improve the harmony, added to the gaiety of the crowd by joining in as occasion offered.

The signal to start was given by the firing of a cannon, and the trains got away in good style at 11.20 am. When nearing Parkside a wheel of one of the engines got off the rail and ran along the ballast for some distance. When the train came a stand it was heavily bumped into by the engine of the train immediately behind. Fortunately, no damage was done, the engine was re-railed, and the passengers, who were enjoying themselves too much to be disturbed by such trifles as the engine off the road and a collision, went on in high spirits. One occupant of the front train, moralising on the mishap, comes to the conclusion that it was rather of a satisfactory nature than otherwise, inasmuch as it proved that what would theoretically be considered perilous, might practically be of no consequence at all. A comforting doctrine worthy of being pondered over by others besides railway passengers.

At Parkside a stop was made for the engines to take water, and here occurs the sad accident to Mr Huskisson, Member of Parliament for Liverpool, which threw a gloom over the whole party and marred the pleasure of the day. The

Taking water at Parkside (Newton le Willows) 1830s Site of the fatal accident to William Huskisson MP on the opening day when he was run over by the "Rocket".

ducal train was brought to a stand in such a position that the other trains, on the opposite line, could, after taking water, make a display of their powers by passing it at a good speed. Many of the distinguished passengers alighted and walked about on the line or stood speaking to the Duke of Wellington. Amongst the latter was Mr Huskisson, between whom and the Duke it was said there was a coolness on account of the circumstances under which Huskisson ceased, a short time previously, to be Chancellor of the Exchequer in the Wellington Cabinet. It was noticed that the Duke and Huskisson shook hands very cordially as if to publicly indicate that any unpleasantness, if such ever existed, was at an end. Three of the trains had passed, and there were still several gentlemen standing outside the ducal car, the door of which was open, when an alarm was raised that the "Rocket" (in charge of Mr Joseph Locke) was approaching. Mr Huskisson endeavoured to pass round the edge of the door, but became confused, and was knocked down by the "Rocket." He fell across the off side of the road on which the "Rocket" was moving, his left leg and thigh being crooked in an angle so that two parts of the leg rested on the rail, one part about the middle of the thigh, and the other part about the calf of the leg. At this moment the wheel went over him. As originally laid, the space between the up and down lines, now called the "six foot", was much less than at present; it was only 4 ft. 8in., the same width as between the rails of the running lines. This would much increase the peril of Huskisson's position, and render it impossible for him to get safely round the door, as he attempted. Mr. Huskisson was placed on the musician's car and taken to Eccles, where he died at the Vicarage the same evening. At the inquest a verdict of "Accidental death" was returned. The jury also found that no deodand attached to the engine, thus doubly absolving all concerned from blame.

A very remarkable circumstance occurred in connection with the accident. Mrs Blackburne, the wife of the Vicar of Eccles, was staying with her husband at Hale Hall, near Liverpool, in order to take part in the fetes of the day. Suddenly a presentiment came into her mind that she was wanted at home. So strong did the feeling become that in spite of all remonstrances she, at much inconvenience, returned to Eccles, and was waiting at the side of the line with her children to see the procession pass when the engine rushed up with the injured man, to whom she rendered invaluable aid. Poor Huskisson himself when he heard it was proposed to take him to the Vicarage, exclaimed, "Pray take me there; there indeed I shall be taken care of." Mrs Huskisson witnessed the accident to her husband, and was with him when he died.

Mr Huskisson was not favourably disposed towards railways. Only the day before the accident he replied to a deputation who waited on him to solicit his influence in favour of another line, "Gentlemen, I supported the Liverpool and Manchester Railway as an experiment, but so long as I have the honour to hold a seat in Parliament, I will never consent to see England *gridironed by railways.*"

When the "Northumbrian" had gone a consultation was held as to whether the journey should be continued to Manchester. Several of the party, including the Duke of Wellington and Sir Robert Peel, were in favour of turning back. The Borough-reeve of Manchester advised them strongly to proceed, stating that if the procession did not reach there he should be fearful of the consequences to the town. The departure of the "Northumbrian" having left the ducal train with no engine on the same line, the "Phoenix" and "North Star" engines were attached to it by a strong rope, and in this inglorious fashion it was *towed* to Manchester. The passengers were so shocked by the accident that they no longer had any pleasure in the trip. The band ceased to play, and the trumpeters, who had exerted themselves almost to a deafening extent to enliven the journey, were ordered to remain silent. The spectators ranged alongside the line or seated in the huge stands erected at frequent intervals, not knowing what had occurred, cheered loudly as the procession passed, but there was no response from the trains. The passengers were too much impressed by the terrible scene just enacted to feel disposed to return the compliment as they did in the earlier part of the journey. Heavy rain came on and distant thunder was heard when the trains were passing over the dreary expanse of Chat Moss.

On approaching Manchester it was with the greatest difficulty a passage was made through the mass of people crowding the line, the majority of whom maintained a sullen silence and evinced feelings the reverse of friendly towards the Duke of Wellington, who was just then most unpopular amongst the working classes. The railway, too, was regarded with strong disfavour, as another advance of the dreaded machinery which had already thrown so many handloom weavers out of employment. To emphasise this point, a loom was erected on a high stage, at which a ragged scarecrow of a man worked with all his might, as if his life depended on his continued exertions, whilst the trains were passing. Some few of the crowd went so far as to wear tri-coloured ribbons on their coats. Loud hootings mingled with the cheering of the better-disposed; it was even said that the ducal car was pelted with mud and turf. All this was in strong contrast to the Liverpool end, where amongst the classes the utmost good humour and rejoicing prevailed.

At Manchester everything looked gloomy and miserable. Frequent showers, accompanied by rolling thunder, had drenched the spectators, who waited hour after hour past the appointed arrival of the trains. The depression was intensified by the news of the accident to Huskisson, brought by Lord Wilton, who ran up on the "Northumbrian" to fetch a doctor from Manchester. Strong fears were felt for the safety of the Duke, which were increased by the sight of a detachment of dragoons galloping towards Eccles, a false report having been received that rails had been torn up, and the Duke attacked by the mob. At length, to the intense relief of the waiting crowd, the trains arrived. The passengers gladly alighted to partake of much-needed refreshment, provided by the directors in one of the goods warehouses.

The Duke of Wellington remained in his carriage, making himself as agreeable as possible, shaking hands, with both hands, with the people who thronged around, climbing the carriages in their eagerness to engage his notice, ladies holding up their children to be blessed by him. In the meantime, the aspect of the crowd became so menacing that it was thought advisable to hurry the Duke's train away without waiting for the return of the engines of the other trains, which had gone to Eccles to take water. The Chief Constable was most urgent, telling the magistrates that so long as the Duke remained he could not be responsible for his safety or the peace of the town. At half-past four, the time at which it should have been at Liverpool, the train started. The Duke was very anxious about Mr Huskisson, and stopped at Eccles to enquire as to his condition; he wished to go and see him, but as Mr Blackburne, the Vicar, who was with him, relates, "The crowd was so immense, the police dared not let him get out." A curious predicament for the "hero of a hundred fights." The crowds must have been enormous. It was estimated that from four to five hundred thousand people altogether turned out to see the show. One writer records an odd reflection by the sight of so many faces, he began to speculate as to where sufficient earth could be found to bury such a multitude. Then he bethought him that they might all be comfortably accommodated in Chat Moss – a cheerful train of thought for a festive occasion!

On arrival at Eccles it was found that three of the engines of the other trains were on the same line, and there being no means of crossing them out of the way – all intermediate crossings having been taken out, as already mentioned, they had to go forward in front of the train towards Liverpool. At Prescot two of them were got on the opposite line and turned back. The third went on to Liverpool, whence it also returned. The Duke alighted at Roby, the train then proceeding to Liverpool, where it arrived about 7 pm.

In the meantime, the other unfortunate passengers were left in Manchester with small prospect of getting away. About 5 o'clock three engines which had not been captured by the ducal train turned up, the remaining six trains were tied together with ropes, the three engines attached, and a start made for Liverpool. When about half-way the other three engines were met returning to look for them, two were attached in front, and one sent on ahead. The monotony of the journey was varied by the trains occasionally breaking loose and having to be tied together again, an additional element of interest being imparted by the inability of the united efforts of the five engines to pull the trains up Sutton incline. The gentlemen, numbering about five hundred, got out and walked, much as they would from a coach to ease the horses. Whether they pushed behind is not on record. One who participated in the enjoyment says, "There was something more striking than agreeable" about this part of the day's work.

When the melancholy procession got to the top of the incline they again took their seats, rejoicing in the prospect of speedily seeing an end of their troubles, but their adventures were not yet over. Further delay was caused by the pilot engine running over a wheel-barrow, placed on the line by some malicious person. Alas! What a climax to the grand doings of the morning. At half-past ten, six hours after the appointed time, they arrived in Liverpool, where they found the people in much anxiety owing to a report that George Stephenson had been killed. A man named Stephenson had met with a fatal accident, which gave rise to the rumour. Thus ended in gloom and disaster the first great railway excursion.

On the following morning the "Northumbrian" took the first public train from Liverpool to Manchester, returning in the evening. Next day, Friday, September 17, 1830, a regular service

Original Liverpool & Manchester Railway "Lion" seen in Crewe Works following restoration. This 0-4-2 loco was one of the first built in this country by Todd, Kitson and Laird at Leeds in 1838. It had 5ft driving wheels, a maximum speed of 40mph and could haul a 200 ton load. It worked on the L&M until 1859 when it was sold to the Mersey Docks & Harbour Board. It was restored by Crewe works in 1929/30 for the centenary of the opening of the line.

of three trains per day commenced to run. On November 10th the mails, consisting of four bags daily, were first despatched by rail. Goods trains commenced to run on December 4, 1831.

Many of the arrangements were more primitive than we should have expected to find even at that period. Space will not permit of our enlarging on this. One little-known instance may be given, on the authority of Mr Abel Turton, one of the latest survivors of the original staff of the Liverpool and Manchester Railway, and of those who were present when the accident occurred to Mr Huskisson. Mr. Turton entered the service as a lad a few weeks after the line was opened. He relates that when he first started the lamps were tied on the carriages with tarred rope. Part of a porter's equipment consisted of a ball of this cord and a clasp knife, the one for tying on the lamps, and the other for taking them off when the knots proved recalcitrant.

Mr Turton, who died in 1894, was for forty years at Parkside Station, the greater part of the time as stationmaster. Before the line was extended to the North he saw a good deal of the nobility and gentry, who travelled by road as far as Preston, then had their private carriages placed on trucks on the railway and conveyed to Birmingham – the family retaining their seats in their own conveyance. At Birmingham, until the opening of the London and Birmingham Railway, post horses were again put into requisition for the reminder of the journey. Such great noblemen as the Dukes of Argyle, Buccleuch, and Montrose were amongst the first to adopt this plan. On occasion Mr. Turton was witness to a *canny* joke on the part of the Duke of Argyle. Hearing he was on the station, the passengers waiting for the train were very desirous of seeing him. One enterprising individual, in his anxiety to know which was the Duke, asked his Grace himself, who indicated a rather distinguished-looking gentleman who was promenading the platform. The inquirer spread the news, and the gentleman, much to his surprise and annoyance, found himself the object of considerable attention. Meanwhile, the Duke retreated to his own carriage chuckling at the success of his little stratagem.

At the same time that the Liverpool and Manchester Bill was before Parliament, other railway projects, of which the same promotors were the ruling spirits, were being pushed forward. Authority was obtained for branches to some of the larger towns in Lancashire; the great schemes for the Grand Junction and the London and Birmingham lines, to connect Liverpool and Manchester to London, were projected, and in due time carried out. As the various companies were formed and the lines completed, leases were made, agreements entered into for division of receipts,

Early trains on the Liverpool & Manchester Railway.

Local train on the L&M line just east of Patricroft c1870 with No.402 a Sharp Stewart 2-2-2 saddle tank built for the Manchester & Birmingham Railway in 1840 (later rebuilt at Longsight in 1856 and 1868). The first five carriages are believed to date from 1863. Posed with group of staff from the station. Slotted post Home signal.

and running powers granted over each other's lines, until the whole thing became a bewildering maze. At length matters were simplified by the union in 1846 of all the companies concerned into the great corporation known as the London and North Western Railway. Under this comprehensive title many important railways, the original names of which served as route marks through the country, have lost their identity and faded from the mind of the public. The name of the Liverpool and Manchester Railway, however, will never be forgotten. It will live as a monument to the genius and enterprise of the men by whom it was conceived and executed, from whose success and failures the world has learned lessons the value of which can never be fully estimated.

Chapter 23

LNWR Locomotive and Rolling Stock in the United States

by Brunel Redivivus

It is well known that the London and North Western Railway exhibited at the celebrated International Exhibition held at Chicago in 1893. The exhibits with which we are now more particularly concerned consisted of the compound locomotive "Queen Empress," a West Coast Joint Stock sleeping saloon and a West Coast Joint Stock composite carriage.

The engine "Queen Empress" was built at the Locomotive Works of the London and North Western Railway Company at Crewe, early in 1893, from the designs of Mr F.W. Webb, Chief Mechanical Engineer.

The engine is carried on four pairs of wheels, the leading pair being 4ft. 1½in. in diameter, and fitted with Mr Webb's arrangement of radial axle box with central controlling spring. The high and low-pressure driving wheels are 7ft. 1in. diameter, and are placed in front of the fire box; this arrangement giving a more even distribution of the weight on the wheels. The trailing wheels are 4ft. 1½in. diameter, the axle boxes in this case being allowed a side play of one-half an inch. A special feature of this engine is the design of the boiler, which is made with an extra-long barrel (18ft. 6in. in length) to allow of both the driving axles being placed in front of the firebox. An intermediate combustion chamber is placed in the length of the barrel which divides the tubes into two lengths, those extending from the firebox to

Webb 3-cylinder compound No. 2054 "Queen Empress" at Madeley in 1895.

the chamber being 5ft. 10in. long between tube plates, and those reaching from the chamber to the smoke box 10ft. 1in. long between tube plates, the diameter outside in each case being 2½in. The mean diameter of the barrel outside is 4ft. 3in.

The combustion chamber has an opening at the bottom large enough to allow a man to enter when necessary for repairs, and to this is attached a hopper fitted with a valve for the discharge of any ashes which may accumulate in the chamber. The valve is so weighted that in its normal position it is closed and air-tight, but is connected by a rod to the footplate, so that the driver may open it when required. This chamber is also fitted with a steam blast apparatus for cleaning the soot out of the tubes, which is arranged as follows; A steam valve is fixed within the boiler barrel, over the top of the combustion chamber, controlled by a handle outside the barrel. The valve is fitted with a T pipe, the long or vertical stem of the T being connected with the valve, and the cross part placed at right angles with the tube plate, with a "rose" at each end, through which the steam is directed against the tube plates. When the valve is opened the steam rushes with considerable force out of the "rose" in each end of the T, and passes through both sets of tubes, driving before it any soot or ashes deposited therein.

The two high pressure cylinders, which are 15in. diameter by 24ins. stroke, are firmly bolted on the outside of the main frames, one on each side, immediately behind the leading wheels and close up under the outside footplate, the steam chests being inside the frames.

The low-pressure cylinder, 30in. diameter by 24in. stroke, is fixed between the frames immediately under the smoke box, of which it forms the base. The high-pressure cylinders (balanced slide valves) are fitted with the ordinary curved link motion, the gear being arranged inside the frames. For the low pressure slide valve Mr Webb's single eccentric motion is used. Steam is first supplied to the high-pressure cylinders from the regulator placed in the dome, by a copper pipe 5½in. diameter, which is connected to a T shaped casting fixed on the outside of the smokebox tube plate. From this casting a copper pipe, 3¾in. diameter, is carried round each side of the smokebox and along the inside of the frames to the high-pressure cylinder steam chests. The exhaust steam from these cylinders is then returned through copper pipes, 5in. diameter, to the low-pressure steam chest, but the pipes before reaching there are carried almost to the top of the smokebox and back, so that by this means the exhaust steam before it reaches the low pressure cylinder gets superheated by the waste gases in the smokebox, and also, owing to the large capacity of the pipes obtained by this arrangement between the high and low pressure cylinders, no separate steam receiver is required.

All axle and other bearings are made as large as possible, and ample provision made for keeping them properly lubricated, so that although the engine runs long distances at high speeds everything is kept perfectly cool and free. The total wheel base of the engine is 23ft. 8in., and is divided as follows: from centre of leading to centre of low-pressure driving wheels, 8ft. 5in.; from centre of low pressure to centre of high-pressure driving wheels, 8ft. 3in.; and from centre of high-pressure wheels to centre of trailing wheels, 7ft. The total weight of the engine in working order is 52 tons 2 cwts., of which 15 tons 10 cwts., is carried by each pair of driving wheels, 12 tons 16 cwts. by the leading and 8 tons 6 cwt. by the trailing wheels.

The tender carrying the coal and water is fitted with the water "pick-up" apparatus, by means of which, whilst running, the tanks are re-filled with water from troughs laid between the rails of the permanent way at convenient points, so that long distances may be run without stopping for that purpose. The tank carries 2,000 gallons of water; and the total weight of the tender in working order is 26 tons 12 cwts.

The engine is fitted with an automatic steam brake, which is applied to both pairs of driving

No.2054 "Queen Empress" was specially painted a creamy white in honour of Queen Victoria's Diamond Jubilee in 1897. The royal coat of arms is on the rear splasher and on the cabside is the gold medal awarded at the 1893 Chicago Exhibition.

wheels, and also with an ejector and air pump for working the automatic vacuum brakes on the train, both these brakes being applied simultaneously by either the driver or guard.

The "Queen Empress," on her completion in the shops, was not tried in steam, as is the usual practice, but was sent direct to Chicago, and it was not until after the close of the Exposition that she was run with her own steam for the first time at Chicago.

The sleeping saloon, together with the standard composite carriage forming part of the London and North Western Railway exhibit at the World's Columbian Exposition, were at that date the latest achievement of the art of English carriage building, and both emanated from the carriage shops of the London and North Western Railway at Wolverton, having been constructed under the superintendence of Mr C.A. Park.

The sleeping saloon, 42ft. long, contains four sleeping compartments, each having a separate lavatory, the two end compartments contain four berths each, two upper and two lower, the middle compartments have two berths each only.

The corridor runs the length of the two centre compartments joining smoking and attendants' compartments, with entrance door at the ends.

The woodwork is carved black walnut, panels of sycamore, figured walnut or mahogany and satin-wood borders.

Pockets for valuables are placed above the pillow of each berth, and under the berth is found a commodious black walnut wardrobe, into which the occupant may place all of his clothing.

The upholstery is rich terra-cotta frieze, the beds are made in spring mattresses, and can be changed into parlour compartments for day travel.

There is also a smoking compartment for gentlemen, and an attendant's compartment.

The saloon is fitted with compressed oil gas, electric bells, and it is heated through pipes from a coke stove located in the attendant's compartment. The carriage is run on bogie trucks, and is fitted with vacuum and Westinghouse high pressure system brakes.

The composite carriage exhibited is also 42 ft. long; it is, however, divided into first, second and third class compartments, *coupé* and baggage compartment.

The woodwork, which is very rich, is made up in panels of sycamore, maple and walnut. In the *coupé* are two beautiful panel *placques,* with a representative of Truth and Justice burned on sycamore with a hot metal pencil.

The upholstering is figured saladin moquette; cork carpets surmounted by rich rugs cover the floor.

The compartments are entered by side doors, they are provided with lavatory accommodation, lighted by gas and fitted with vacuum and Westinghouse brakes.

The chief interest in this train, however, arises from the fact that at the close of the Chicago Exhibition it ran for hundreds of miles in America on the tracks of the Lake Shore and Michigan Southern Railway and the New York Central and Hudson River Railroad.

Before describing this run, it is necessary to emphatically deny the statement that there ever was any racing or semblance of racing – between the English "Queen Empress" and the American locomotive "999" of the New York Central and Hudson River Railroad. There is a small and otherwise unknown coterie who hold themselves out as authorities on railway matters and are always willing to belittle British railways and locomotives, especially in comparison with American roads and engines. Someone or another of these hare-brained individuals, after the passing of the London and North Western Railway train over the American railway, gave out that there had been a race between the English "Queen Empress" and the American "999", and that the former has been beaten by the later. We believe that Mr Webb, knowing full well the source from which this absurd canard emanated, at the time never deigned to deny the silly tale, considering both the originator of the statement and the story itself beneath notice. He has now, however, authorised the Railway Magazine to state emphatically that no elements of a race were ever contemplated or took place.

What really happened is that No "999", drawing the celebrated Wagner train, acted as "pilot" to "Queen Empress," and preceded her by a space of 10 minutes on the circuitous journey which the English train performed in travelling from Chicago to New York.

This lengthy trip over American railways was made for the purpose of giving to as many as possible of the American railroadmen and others interested in the English engine and coaches, an opportunity of inspecting them, and needless to say, advantage was taken at every place where the train stopped by crowds of people to inspect the engine and coaches.

A remarkable feature of the trip, and one that goes to show the high degree of the workmanship and finish of the "Queen Empress," is the fact that although she had never been in steam before, she performed the whole of the long trip without mishap or delay of any kind. The following is an account of the run:

On Monday, November 20th 1893, the locomotive "Queen Empress" and carriages left the Chicago Exposition grounds and proceeded over the Illinois Central and Baltimore and Ohio Railroad to the freight yards of the Lake Shore and Michigan Southern Railway, Chicago, where they were placed in a siding and the locomotive taken to the Round House. On Wednesday, November 22nd, at 7.30am, the engine made a short trial trip of about 5 miles, and at 9.20am the same day it was attached to what was known as the Special British Train, which was composed of and weighed as follows :-

	Tons	Cwts.	Qrs.
"Queen Empress" No. "3435" and tender	77	2	0
W.C.J.S. composite carriage	26	14	2
W.C.J.S. sleeping saloon	29	2	2
Wagner sleeping car	50	0	0
Wagner sleeping car	50	0	0
L.S. and M.S. dining car	50	0	0
Total	**282**	**19**	**0**

At a little before 10am the train left Chicago preceded by the Wagner train, which acted as pilot all the way to New York, an interval of 10 minutes being kept between the two trains. The British train was full of guests, comprising railroad officials, city officials, members of the Boards of Trade and Chambers of Commerce, merchants, shippers and newspapermen, etc. All stops at different places en route were made as per schedule previously arranged and at 2.40pm the train arrived at Elkart, where it was stationed for the night.

On the following day (Thursday), the train left Elkart at 6.30am and was due to arrive at Toledo at 2.30pm but owing to a severe snowstorm which prevailed during the whole day the train was somewhat late in arriving at its destination.

On arrival at Toledo the carriages were thrown open to the public and several hundred passed through them.

On Friday, November 24th, the train left Toledo at 7.30am for Cleveland. During the trip the speed attained at some points of the journey was 1 mile in 52 seconds. On Saturday the journey was resumed, leaving Cleveland by 9.10am, due at Buffalo at 4.30pm.

Sunday and Monday were spent in Buffalo. On the latter day at 9am the Wagner train and the British train were exhibited at one of the siding stations of the New York Central Railway. The exhibition continued until 12.30pm. After this a tour was made round the city of Buffalo on what is termed the "Belt" line. At 4pm the same day the trains started for Rochester, which place they reached at 6pm. On the following day (Tuesday, November 28th) the trains were thrown open for inspection from 10am until 2.30pm. At 3.20pm they left for Syracuse, which place they reached at 5.45pm.

Owing to the American national holiday, known as "Thanksgiving Day", occurring November 30th, it was decided to remain in Syracuse the whole of Wednesday and a portion of Thursday. During this time the trains were inspected by thousands of people. On Thursday the trains left Syracuse at 2pm for Watertown, arriving there at 6pm. On the following day (Friday, December 1st) the trains were thrown open for inspection soon after 9am. Watertown being located in the vicinity of the St. Lawrence, The Thousand Islands and ease of access with Canada, a large crowd of visitors came from the surrounding towns and from Canadian points to see the trains. At 3pm the same day the trains left Watertown for Utica. During the trip they were delayed some hours owing to a breakdown of a freight train, and when at length the journey was resumed, a severe snowstorm was encountered. Utica was reached at 3am on the Saturday. A stay was made here until 3pm, when the journey was resumed and Albany reached at 5.30pm the same day. It was arranged that the trains should remain at this place until the following Tuesday, and in the meantime were on exhibition outside the Central Station.

On Tuesday December 5th, the train left at 6am for Poughkeepsie, reaching there at 8.30am. At 2pm the train left for Yonkers, arriving at 4.20pm and stopped there 25 minutes, leaving at 4.45pm for New York, which it reached at 5.10pm. On the two following days the train was open for inspection by the public from 10am to 3pm, when thousands of the people availed themselves of the opportunity of inspecting the first British train that had run on American railways. After that the work of dismantling and packing the train was commenced and it was afterwards shipped on board the White Star SS "Runic," which left New York for Liverpool on December 19th 1893.

As proof of the superior construction of British locomotives, readers of the RAILWAY MAGAZINE will be interested to learn that whilst the "Queen Empress" is still as effective and useful to the London and North Western Railway as she was when constructed nine years ago, her United States compeer, the once famous "No. 999", the locomotive on the New York Central Railway which attracted so much attention at the World's Fair in 1893 in Chicago, and has done well known service hauling the "Empire State Express," has come down to hauling a train of eleven milk cars and a caboose on the "West Shire" between Albany and Oneida. Although "999" may be as good as she ever was, the fact remains that the addition of but one car to the "Empire State Express" made it necessary to assign the new "Central Atlantic" type engines to that service. They haul the train with ease, but "999" was worked too near her limit of power, which explains the change. The Empire State Express even now consists of only five cars – not a long train by many means according to British notions.

Chapter 24

Preston

Notable Railway Stations
by J.L. Lawrence M.A.

Visitors to the recent Merchant Guild – a very ancient festival which is held in Preston under an old charter every twenty years – found themselves confronted, wherever they turned, by the device 'P.P.'

This device, it was explained, stood for 'Proud Preston.' Why the Prestonians should be credited with the exclusive haughtiness which is to be inferred from this appellation it is hard to say. As far as the present is concerned, the town has no especial claims to greatness, either political or commercial. In coaching days, it occupied an important position as a centre of traffic, both passenger and postal, and now that the railway has superseded the road, that importance is still maintained. If Preston has nothing else of which to be proud, it is entitled to be proud of its railway station, for probably no similar structure in England can compete with it, either for comfort or convenience, or even as to its size.

Its position in the railway system of the country is analogous to that of York, in that it is a great distributing centre. But there is one important distinction. York Station affords hospitality to the rolling stock of no less than seven railway companies; whereas the conservatism of Preston extends even to its station, and whilst possibly foreign vehicles may have found their way into its precincts, the writer has never heard of any foreign locomotive venturing there.

It is 209 miles from London, 191 from Edinburgh, 31 from Manchester, 28¼ from Liverpool and 103 from Birmingham. It is thus a sort of halfway house between England and Scotland. Whilst the London and North Western Railway's main line runs through, due north and south, looking neither to the right hand nor the left, the lines of the Lancashire and Yorkshire Railway approach it and leave it in all directions.

As far as the former company is concerned, the objectives are London and Carlisle, a hand being held out to Liverpool and Manchester at Wigan, 15¼ miles to the south. But both of

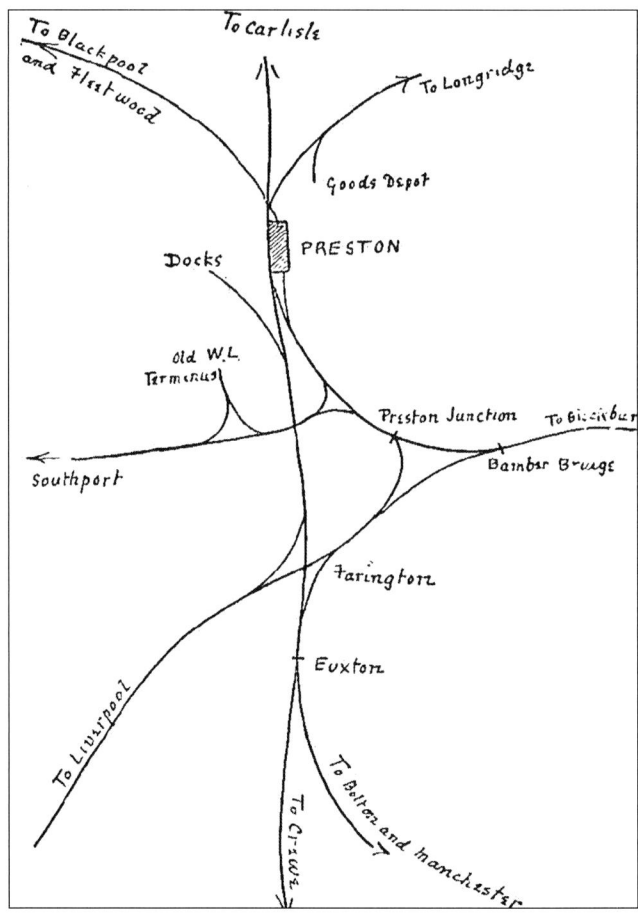

Preston area map.

these towns are more readily reached by the Lancashire and Yorkshire Railway, which goes to Liverpool via Ormskirk, and to Manchester via Bolton and via Atherton. The same company reaches Southport by two routes, the one being their original one by way of Burscough, and the other over the West Lancashire line, now the property of the Lancashire and Yorkshire Railway.

The line from Blackburn and Yorkshire completes the approaches from the south. On the north the Lancashire and Yorkshire Railway objectives are Blackpool and Fleetwood. To the former there are alternative routes, via Lytham and via Poulton and a third is promised, being a short cut via Kirkham.

The only branch line pure and simple from Preston is that to Longridge. The little line penetrates into the fells which abound in mid-Lancashire and it needs no great skill in prophecy to predict that in time to come it will be extended to Clitheroe, and thus be linked with the Midland system via Hellifield, affording an alternative route into Yorkshire.

It is no detraction from the town's commercial importance to suggest that the greater part of the railway traffic is of the 'through' description, and most of the trains using the station are long distance.

The main line to the south comprises four tracks as far as Euxton, 6¼ miles distant. As far as this, the line is used by both companies, but from that point the line to Bolton and Manchester branches off to the east.

The Lancashire and Yorkshire Railway's Liverpool trains in some cases use the same metals, leaving the main line at Farington, 2½ miles distant.

The line to Blackpool, known as the Preston and Wyre Railway, is used by both companies.

Preston Station is really two stations, although to the uninitiated public there seems to be but one. Platforms 1 to 6 constitute a joint territory, and the staff serves both Lancashire and Yorkshire Railway and London and North Western Railway traffic. Platforms 7, 8 and 9, together with several bays, form what is now and then called Butler Street Station, and it is exclusively Lancashire

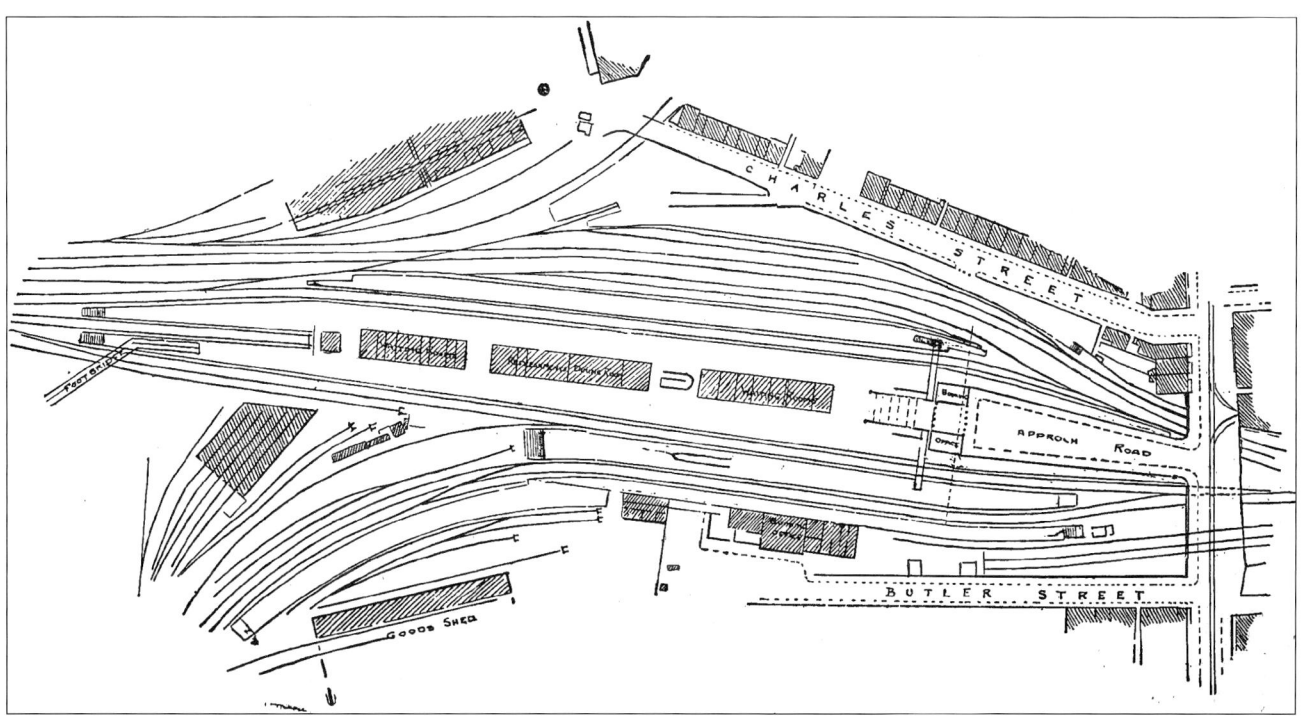

Preston Station Plan.

and Yorkshire Railway property and manned by a Lancashire and Yorkshire Railway staff. Mr Barlow is the chief of the former, and Mr Bridson of the latter. Platforms 1 and 2 are not yet open to the public, although they were used to contend with the exceptional traffic of the Guild week.

The present station was built about twenty-two years ago, and took the place of a much inferior structure.

The dimensions of Preston Station are imposing. The length of the chief platform is 1,225ft. and its width is 110ft. The space occupied by the station buildings reduces this width in places from 35ft. to 40ft. The platform area is 4½ acres and the covered area 6¾ acres. What this means can be best appreciated by comparing it with some other well-known stations. The platforms at Paddington are from 800ft. to 850ft. in length and 28ft. broad. At St. Pancras the corresponding dimensions are 770ft. and 25ft. At King's Cross, 990ft. and 25ft. The length of the longest platform at Liverpool Street is 900ft. and at Waterloo it is 850ft. with a maximum breadth of 30ft.

In fact, one of the officials at Preston suggested to the writer that the main platform would make an ideal track for cycle races.

Of the total length of 1,225ft. the refreshment rooms and other offices take up 575ft. and they are in three blocks. At the north end are the commodious waiting rooms and sundry offices, then come the refreshment rooms, over which is the post office, and at the south end are other waiting rooms and offices.

The booking hall at the entrance to the station is reached by the approach from Fishergate. On leaving this we pass through the gates at which tickets are collected and then a foot-bridge stretches right and left, traversing the whole station. A broad and easy slope leads on to the platform. Besides the foot-bridge there are two

Preston Station entrance c1880.

subways, one for passengers and the other for their luggage. In one respect the station fails to come up to modern requirements, in that it has to depend for its light on gas, and, moreover, with the old-fashioned burners. We cannot have everything, however, and in some respects the proud Prestonians stand by the old order. Are not some of the best residential streets paved with 'petrified potatoes'?

The main line platforms are nine in number, but to arrive at the full accommodation we must add that which is provided by the several docks or bays; and we have then no less than fifteen 'quays' in addition to a platform specially intended for dealing with horses and carriages.

The approach from the south – that is from Warrington – affords an excellent view of the town. The line is on a viaduct, which has been enlarged three times, and is 700ft. long, with five arches.

Preston is a seaport, and has its own docks. The sea is a long way off, certainly, but the docks are there all right, and the London and North Western Railway provides a special dock line, which leaves the main line on the south of the station and reaches its destination by means of a bank of 1 in 27 and curve of eight chains radius.

On July 13th 1896, a very serious accident occurred in the station yard. The 8pm from Euston – the train which occupied so large a place in the public imagination during the preceding summer – was timed to run from Wigan to Carlisle without stopping, the time allowed for the 105¼ miles being 112 minutes. On the occasion in question it comprised seven carriages, six heavy West Coast sleepers, and a composite, all of them running on four wheeled steel framed bogies. Two engines were drawing it, "Vulcan" (No. 275) being the train engine, and "Shark" (No.2159) the pilot. Both of these were six wheeled, and they ran through Preston at a speed which some witnesses at the enquiry estimated to be nearly 50 miles an hour. At all events, it was admitted that the speed considerably exceeded the ten-mile limit prescribed.

At the north end of the station was a very sharp curve, and in taking this the train was derailed, and one death was the result. Whilst the undue speed at this particular point undoubtedly contributed to the disaster, the technical Press had something to say on the absence of leading bogies, a peculiarity of construction in which Mr Webb has found very few imitators. One immediate result of the accident was the deceleration of the train, and a secondary result was the re-alignment of that portion of the permanent way on which the derailment occurred. This was accomplished by the purchase of a large amount of property on the North-West side of the station, including a whole street; and the land thus acquired served for the extension of the passenger station and for enlarging the curves to a radius of 15 chains.

The new accommodation comprises three new platforms, two for passenger service and one for dealing with horses and carriages. This extension will probably not be officially open till the spring of 1903, and it will then relieve the congestion caused by the pleasure traffic.

At times this threatens to become serious, for there are not only Blackpool and Morecambe to be considered, but the Lake District and passengers for these resorts converge at Preston from all parts of England and Wales. A surprising amount of Yorkshire traffic comes through Preston en route for Morecambe. It consists largely of trippers from Batley and Dewsbury and neighbouring towns, to whom the companies hold out special inducements in the way of through trains and cheap fares.

Morecambe is exploited not only for its own attractions, but because it is a favourite way to the Lake District, the shortest way to Grange lying across the bay.

The Blackpool traffic is a marvel. During the past summer the service to this notable watering place was provided for by no less than forty-seven trains every day, five of these being run by the London and North Western Railway; and even in the winter the trains number thirty-six. There are in addition the non-stopping expresses and the specials. On one given day nearly 180 special and ordinary trains arrived at Blackpool, and 150 of these would pass through Preston. As the great majority of these would return the way they came, it means that more than 300 Blackpool trains were dealt with. The Blackpool "trip," and the lordly London and North Western Railway "grouse special," represent probably the antipodes of railway travel and Preston gets them both. Ordinarily the total number of trains dealt with in the summer is 442, made up of 136 Lancashire and Yorkshire Railway departures and 150 arrivals and 79 London and North Western Railway departures and 77 arrivals. In the winter the departures are 193 and arrivals 191.

The glory of the refreshment rooms has to some extent departed. Before dining-car trains were the rule and principal up and down Scotch expresses were timed to arrive at Preston at about the same hour. The Edinburgh and Glasgow train leaving Euston at 10 arrived at 2.20, the Perth express leaving at 10.30 came in at 2.50 and the corresponding up trains were due at 2.5 and 2.20. One needs to have been there to properly appreciate the scene that used to be enacted between 2 and 3 o'clock every day in July and August.

The impetuous charge of hungry passengers endeavouring to get through half-a-crown's worth of food in 20 minutes and scalding their throats with hot soup in the process, was a sight in itself worth seeing, but most to be admired was the perfection of the arrangements made for dealing with such a high pressure. No one ever saw a Preston railway official flurried. The waitresses are the pink of courtesy and overflowing with attention and absolutely indifferent to tips; the porters brim-full of information and knowing

Preston station c1880 looking south along Down Main Platform (later Platform 5) This was before the island for platforms 3 and 4 was built on the right.

with exactitude whence and at what time, and whither bound every train started; luggage treated as tenderly and with as much solicitude as if every item were a first-class passenger – all these are recollections that make Preston a grateful memory to the passenger.

Now, alas! This is changed. We do not mean, of course, that the courtesy and the attention and the discipline have changed, but we fancy that many a sigh is heaved when some stately 'Scotchman,' made up of corridor coaches and dining-cars, and drawn by two engines, flits through, and not one of the two or three hundred passengers deigns to look at the station. Non-stopping trains are officially supposed to crawl through at the rate of 10 miles an hour, but we might remark in this connection that motor cars are also supposed to travel only 2 miles an hour faster. The train has this advantage over the motorcar, in that there is no official with a stop-watch stationed at the end of the platform and it is impossible to say, therefore, whether practice conforms to precept.

In our description of Preston as a railway centre, it will have been noticed that to most places alternative routes exist. This is, of course, a necessary result of the gradual growth of the railway system. The several routes do not, however, compete with one another aggressively.

Preston Junction is a sort of under-study to the chief station. At all events, it saves it from what might be, at certain hours of the day, a congestion of traffic. It serves as the exchange station for passengers between East and West Lancashire and thus not only saves congestion on the platform, but also on the metals, inasmuch as the train from Preston to Liverpool, say, need not wait for that from Burnley and Accrington, but get away some 5 or 10 minutes before the latter is due and thus leaves the dock free for the incoming train. It also serves as the exchange station for Southport, inasmuch as when the Lancashire and Yorkshire Railway bought up the West Lancashire Railway, they left the old terminus on the south side of the river, and running under the London and North Western Railway, joined the line from Blackburn by two curves, north into Preston Station and south into Preston Junction.

Preston has not much suburban traffic of the residential type, but the greater part of what there is has been developed on this particular line.

The accommodation even of Preston was taxed to the utmost during the interesting festival known as the Merchant Guild. For a whole week Preston was *en fête* and the town was one seething mass of humanity.

Whether the railway people sent for the Doncaster officials to give them some hints born of an annual St. Leger experience, the writer is not aware, but nothing could have been better done. The only way of dealing with the increased traffic was by insisting upon absolute punctuality and once this idea had taken root and germinated in the mind of every railway servant concerned, the rest was easy. Everything went like clockwork. Trains arrived and got away with absolute adherence to time-table promise, and no mishap of any kind occurred. Some exceptional arrangements were, of course, made. The Longridge trains had to make Deepdale, the first station out, their terminus for the time being. The old West Lancashire Station, now only used for goods, was once more opened for passenger trains, and the two new platforms in the joint station were temporarily requisitioned. It is noteworthy that there were no excursion fares into Preston, but that all visitors had to pay ordinary fares. This was the only feature of the arrangements that failed to command universal approval.

We must not omit to mention the postal department. As at Crewe, there is a branch of the G.P.O. located within the station. The chief office in the town is concerned with office and counter work, but all the sorting is done at the station in a very commodious suite of rooms situated above the refreshment rooms. At one end of the suite, the chief of the staff, Mr Edwards,

Preston view looking north from the south end of the station. Signal gantries in centre with rings on some arms. Covered footbridge on right.

has his little office, which reminds one somewhat of a pulpit, designed thus, doubtless, to allow him to command a bird's eye view of the whole establishment. Something like 1,200 letter bags and parcel post baskets pass through in the twenty-four hours, but this number conveys little idea of the work really got through.

A bag comes in, say, from Kendal, labelled Preston. It is emptied and is found to contain letters for some fifty different towns and villages, and these have to be sorted, and the similar contents of hundreds of other bags are added in their proper order, and then in due course what to the outsider seems to be irredeemable chaos, becomes order, and some 400 bags have been emptied and re-sorted and their contents sent off to their proper destinations.

High pressure in the postal department begins with the arrival of the up "limited," at 10.42, and things reach a crisis at 11.25, when the up postal special comes in. The latter conveys for the most part parcels. About an hour later the down trains begin to come in, and then the work recommences. Special departments of the office are set apart for dealing with letters and newspapers. Just as there are some people of perverted mind who enjoy a railway journey all the more if they have been able to accomplish it without the formality of purchasing a ticket, so there are so-called newspapers which necessitate the employment of a special detective staff in the Post Office.

The railway staff at Preston Station is numerous. On the Lancashire and Yorkshire Railway side there are 101 employees. In the joint station there are seventy-eight employed on the platforms, including collectors, porters, lampmen, etc; twenty-nine in the parcel office, including vanmen; ten in the booking office; and there are besides the signalmen, probably forty in number, who man eleven cabins and the telegraphists. The total will be about 270. Certainly, therefore, Preston is a 'Notable Railway Station.'

Chapter 25
New LNWR Royal Saloons

"King Edward of England received from the London and North Western Railway Company a remarkable Christmas gift, which was nothing less than a luxuriously furnished special train with a new especially designed engine. The train is perfectly equipped, and will be used only for transporting the King and members of the Royal Family. The cost of the railroad company's present is given as $300,000."

Although the London and North Western Railway has not been so generous as the above paragraph (extracted from an American railway paper) indicates, there have recently been turned out from the Wolverton Carriage Works two saloons for the use of their Majesties when travelling over the London and North Western Railway. With regard to the cost, however, it should be stated that $300,000 is quite a guess, as the London and North Western Railway has never given any information as to the cost of the two new saloons. From the illustrations we give of these vehicles the readers of the RAILWAY MAGAZINE will be able to judge in

New Royal Saloons for King Edward VII.

King Edward VII's Day Saloon.

how satisfactory a manner Mr C.A. Park, the Carriage Superintendent of the London and North Western Railway, has used his talent and experience to provide a down-to-date travelling palace for our King and Queen.

The twin coaches, which are connected by vestibule gangways, are carried on six-wheel bogies. Each saloon is 69ft. 6in. over the buffers. They have clerestory roofs and the exteriors are painted the standard London and North Western Railway colours. A special feature of the design is that the coaches can only be entered at the extreme ends, the double doors that are provided allowing an opening of about 4ft. 6in. The King's coach comprises an attendants' compartment, 7ft. 7½in. long, succeeded by a lavatory entered from the dressing-room, whilst a side corridor gives access to the dressing-room (8ft. long) from the attendants' saloon. Beyond is a bedroom, 14ft. in length, opening into the day saloon, 14ft. 7in. long, which in turn is succeeded by the smoking compartment, 10ft. in length, and at the extreme of the coach is an enclosed balcony, 6ft. long. The interiors of the saloons are fitted in a most luxurious style.

The King's smoking room is in mahogany, with fine inlays of rosewood and satinwood. The chairs are in green leather and the curtains, carpets, etc., are in similar tones of colour, while the gilding of the metal-work has been subdued in effect to keep the whole restful to the eye; yet at the same time a very pleasing and comfortable room has been produced.

The King's day compartment is decorated in the Colonial style and is in white enamel. The furniture is in satinwood inlaid with ivory. This room is also in green, though of the lighter tone of colour. The fine windows, which are of an unusually large size, keep the room very light, so that the whole makes a bright and cheerful compartment.

The special features in this and the other rooms are the methods of heating or cooling. Electric heaters have been introduced, and having very fine adjustments, each room can be heated up to any temperature desired. For the hot weather electric waving fans help to keep the temperature down, and if desired, the windows can be lowered and fine dust-proof ventilators inserted, so that without any discomfort from dust flying in, the saloon can be kept very cool and comfortable. His Majesty's bed and dressing rooms are also in white enamel, with finely silver-plated fittings, the upholstery generally being of a soft green shade. His Majesty's saloon is also fitted with electric cigar lighters.

The Queen's saloon is similar in general arrangement to H.M. the King's but accommodation is provided for H.R.H. Princess Victoria. From a balcony, 6ft. long, the day compartment, 17ft. 7in. in length, is entered. Beyond this is a dressing room, 7ft. long, then the sleeping compartment, 15ft. in length, succeeded by the dressing room, 7ft. long, opening out of which is a lavatory and side corridor leading to the attendants' compartment, 7ft. 7½in. long at the end.

All the rooms are in white enamel, and the predominating colour is blue, which is lightened in effect with light brocades and a very soft shade of pink to tone the electric lights.

Her Majesty's bedroom has been draped in soft pink and, with the silver-plated bed and the fittings in the room, has a very beautiful effect. Adjoining this is Her Majesty's dressing room in similar effect, but with finely-inlaid satinwood furniture.

The bedroom in the Queen's saloon is fitted up with two dressing rooms – one on either side of the bedroom.

At the end of each saloon is the attendants' compartment, which is fitted with a seat that can be turned into a bed for night journeys and is also fitted with electrical appliances for cooking.

There are balconies to each saloon which are so fitted with windows that they can be used as observation cars, and, being in richly carved and polished mahogany, make fine entrances

Queen Alexandra's Day Saloon in 1903.

The Royal Attendant's Compartment.

The Prince of Wales's Saloon.

to the saloons, which as a whole, create a distinct feature in the equipment of railway carriages, producing a note which is very rare and pleasing.

The attendants' ends in each saloon are fitted with electric plugs for connecting to heaters for providing tea, coffee, etc. Each compartment of the saloons is also provided with portable table lamps. The two saloons are gangwayed together, so as to enable anyone to pass from one end of the train to the other and the balcony ends of each vehicle are heated by steam.

The saloons are 12ft. 7½in. at centre from rail level to the top of the clerestory roof, the clear height inside from floor level being 8ft. 2in.

The width of saloons outside at waist is 9ft.

New LNWR Royal Saloons • 293

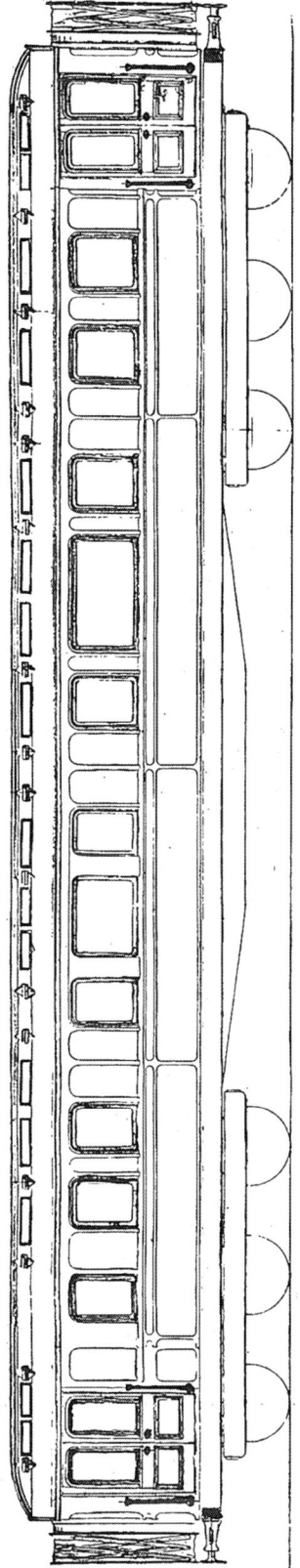

EXTERIOR OF NEW ROYAL SALOON, LONDON & NORTH-WESTERN RAILWAY.

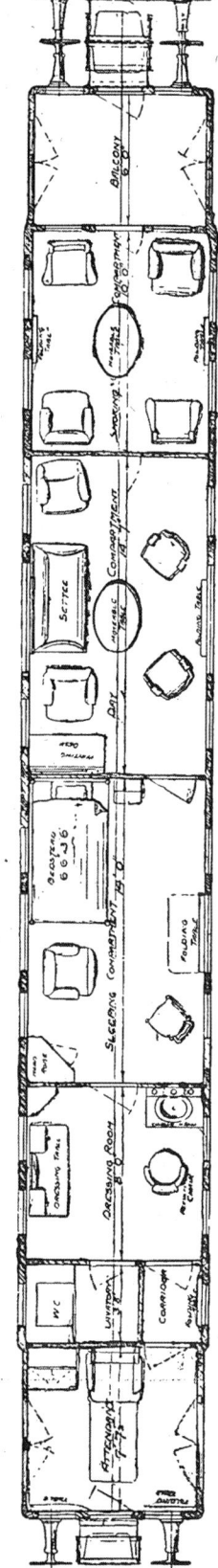

GROUND PLAN OF NEW SALOON, LONDON & NORTH-WESTERN RAILWAY, FOR HIS MAJESTY THE KING.

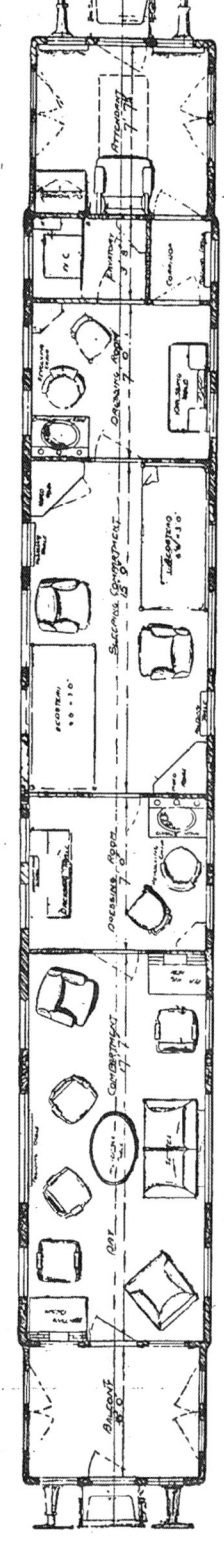

GROUND PLAN OF NEW SALOON, LONDON & NORTH-WESTERN RAILWAY, FOR HER MAJESTY THE QUEEN.

Plan of New Royal Saloons.

Chapter 26
New Goods Warehouse at Sheffield
by T. Booth

February 2nd of this year (1903) marked another red-letter day in the railway history of Sheffield. On this date the London and North Western Railway opened a new commodious goods warehouse at the bottom of Broad Street – a site in every way most suitable for handling the heavy classes of traffic for which Steelopolis is famous. In 1895 this company opened a goods, mineral and cattle depot in Bernard Road but, as was apparent from the first, the place did not meet the requirements of the city. This depot was situated on rising ground in the immediate neighbourhood of the Great Central Railway, over which company's line the London and North Western Railway people have running powers to their goods branch from Woodburn Junction.

The steep gradients which had to be overcome in hauling traffic from the city to the yard proved a source of considerable expense and some inconvenience and it became apparent to the powers that be that another and easier entry to the city would have to be accomplished. Fortunately, the London and North Western Railway was able to secure a site much nearer the centre of the town and at such a level as would permit of the heaviest kind of merchandise, up to 10 ton pieces, being handled with a minimum of trouble; heavier weights, up to 40 ton pieces, being handled at Bernard Road.

In February 1900, the new extension was begun. The piece of permanent way which has been constructed is barely three-quarters of a mile in length, but the engineering difficulties have been of such a character that an outlay of £250,000 has been necessary to complete the works. It says much for the enterprise of the London and North Western Railway in completing such a scheme, as it has no line of its own nearer Sheffield than Ardwick and Guide Bridge on the west and Market Harborough on the South; but all trains are worked by the London and North Western Railway Company's own engines and staff over the Great Central Railway into Sheffield. Heavy bridge work has been necessary nearly the whole length of the extension. Commencing at Bernard Road, the line runs under the private railway of the Nunnery Colliery Company, which is in tunnel. It was found necessary to carry the London and North Western rails for about a furlong in length in the tunnel beneath the colliery line and immense retaining walls have been built to support it and the property on the line side.

The bridging of the Midland Railway is the most notable feature in the whole work. The new railway had to cross this at Navigation Hill. To do this it was necessary to open out the road, remove several houses and take down part of the Midland tunnel. It was necessary to put in heavy girders 18ft. above the level of the Midland line, to carry forward the railway extension and over this, again, a long steel bridge to the road, which had to be reinstated on a gradient of 1 in 13½. These two bridges form a good example of various methods of steelwork erection. The main girders of the railway bridge were able, on account of the large angle of skew, to be launched over the Midland main lines by means of rollers and bogie trolleys, without interfering with the traffic below. Those over the branch lines were erected by means of derricks. In the case of the road bridges, however, neither of these former methods could be applied, and recourse was had to building a heavy timber

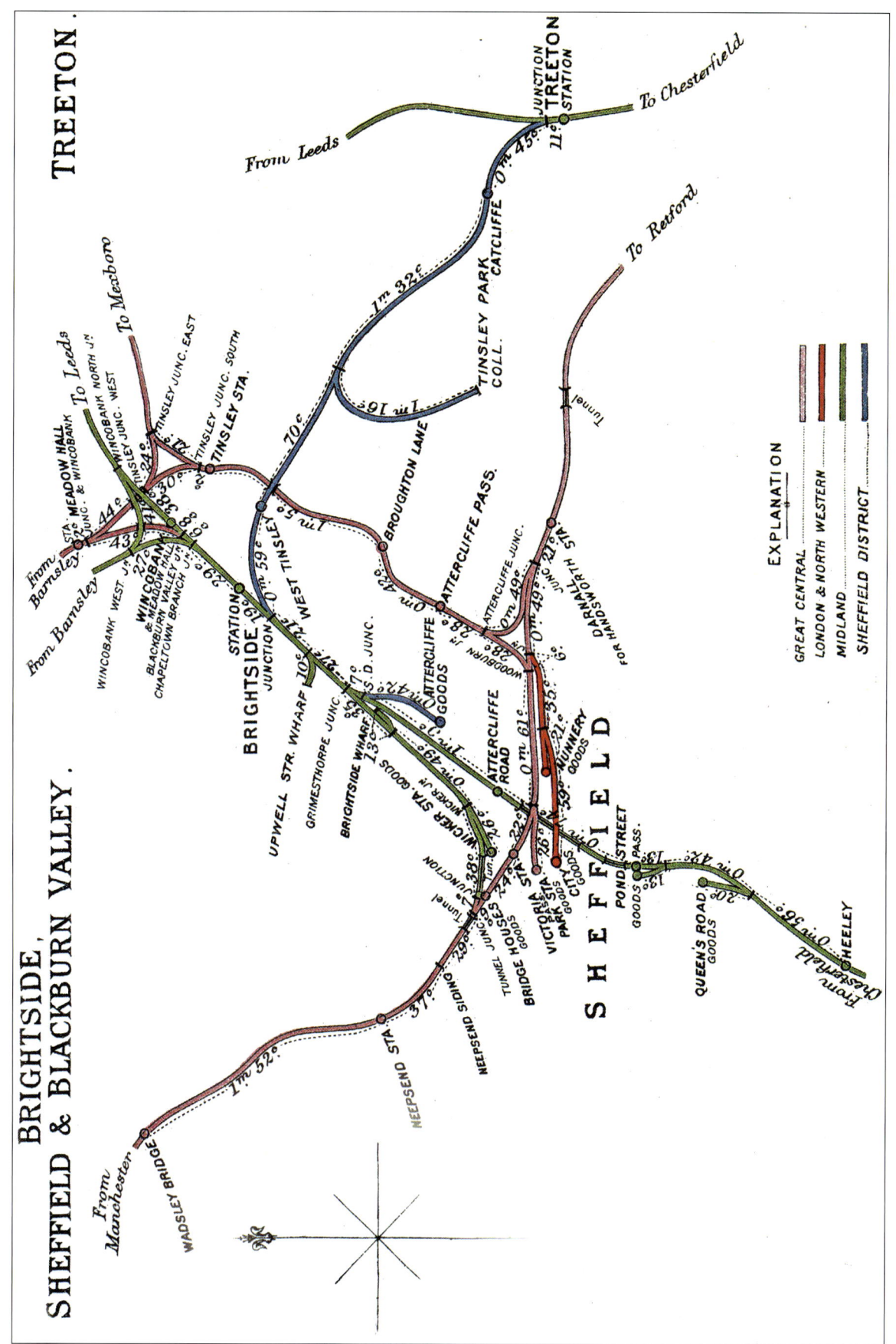

Sheffield area map 1912. LNWR lines are shown in red.

stage on the top of the new railway bridge. On this the main girders were built up, and then 'skidded' out to their respective positions. Steam cranes and derricks were employed for fixing the cross girders on both bridges.

From Navigation Hill the line runs on brick arches to the new depot, but the rails do not touch the ground level. To reach the basement two large hydraulic hoists have been provided and these are each capable of lifting a weight of 20 tons. The descent from the railway level, which runs alongside of the first floor of the warehouse, to the basement, is 29ft. 9in. Space does not permit of dealing at length with all the features of interest, but it should be recorded that the new warehouses are of a most extensive character. These are fronted with offices in every way suitable for dealing with outward and inward traffic. They have been divided into groups and all are abundantly provided with incandescent electric lights. Mr W.J. Shepherd, the agent, has his private office on the first floor and two large offices are set apart for the correspondence clerks on the same floor. Entering the yard from the offices a glance reveals the three stages which have been erected for dealing with the traffic. A double line runs parallel with each stage, and drays may be either loaded direct from the wagon or from the raised platform. The trucks are worked to and from the stages by hydraulic capstans. Three or four weighing machines are fixed at intervals on each stage and hydraulic cranes, with lifting capacity from 15 to 30 cwt., have been supplied by Messrs. Tennant, Walker and Co. Ltd., of Leeds. A 10-ton hydraulic crane has also been supplied by the same firm.

Above the basement is the mezzanine floor, 34,920 square feet; first floor, 26,040; and the second floor 33,300 – total 94,260 square feet. All traffic is loaded and unloaded under cover, and special accommodation has been provided for the storage and expeditious handling of bacon and hams, cheese, butter and lard and all kinds of provisions, fruit, vegetables and other market produce. Grain shoots have been constructed from the top storey to the basement and there are the usual outside grain hoists, which are caged in and connected with the floors beneath. The marshalling yard consists of twelve sets of rails, all of which are connected by means of turntables.

The total weight of steel work in the station is 1,770 tons and 3,500 tons constitute the total for the whole of the steel used for bridging, etc. The floors of the station are fireproof and sprinklers on the Grinnel system have been fixed throughout the building. Nearly two miles of these sprinklers have been fixed, and these are connected with a huge tank holding 13,500 gallons of water, which stands 104ft. high.

Access to the large cattle dock has been given from Navigation Hill. The yard is illuminated with the Davy enclosed arc light and the electric supply is drawn from the Corporation at about 200 volts.

The entrance to the station is in Broad Street and Wharf Street, immediately facing the Corn Exchange, and in close proximity to the Sheffield Canal. It will be known as the City Station and the old Bernard Road depot as the 'Nunnery.' Mr W.J. Shepherd, who is one of the youngest looking agents in the country, has had a wide experience of railway work. His unfailing courtesy and ready tact eminently fit him for the honourable position he now enjoys – a post he has filled with credit to himself and the interests of his company for some years. Sheffield is included in the sphere of the company's District Goods Manager, Mr Spencer Harley, who leaves Nottingham to take up his quarters at the Bernard Road Station. Mr F.D. Workman, the resident engineer, is to be complimented on the way in which the work has been carried out. This gentleman comes from the office of Mr Stevenson, late Chief Engineer of the London and North Western Railway at Euston. Messrs. Walter Scott and Middleton, of London, were the contractors for the line, and Messrs. Robert Neill and Sons, of Manchester, for the warehouse.

Chapter 27
A Depopulated Railway Town (Crewe During the Holiday Week)
by A Resident

"In consequence of the Works' Holidays, there will be no meeting during next week in connection with this place."

These words were uttered from the rostrum of the Nonconformist chapel during one Sunday evening's service and the words give a clue to the

Crewe Works General Offices with old Chester line in foreground.

social life of the town during the week's holiday of the workmen of the London and North Western Railway Company.

The time usually chosen by the management for the holiday is the first or second week in July.

About one-fourth of the population of Crewe are employed by the Railway Company. Those who are not in the employment of the company are the tradesmen who supply grocery, bread, meat and clothing; and the professional men, such as doctors, solicitors, Church and Nonconforming ministers.

But during the Works' holidays all the trades and professions, with few exceptions, are shut down until the return of the workmen and all activity ceases in the town.

The Work's Buzzer does not blow from half-past five on the Friday night preceding the holiday until ten minutes to nine on the morning of the Monday a week later. There are no means of setting your clock and your watch other than by going to the market clock or the church tower, or by a journey to the railway station to consult the clock there.

The works' buzzer is a most important institution in the town and its loss is appreciably felt by the few unfortunate beings who are left behind for this one week in Crewe.

The first buzzer usually blows at half-past five in the morning, the last at half-past five at night; but between these there are many others, and at least nine-tenths, if not ninety-nine hundredths, of the watches in the town are set to this wonderful and powerful hoot of the siren.

We have said that the first buzzer is at half past five in the morning, but this is not the starting signal for actual work by any means – far from it. The buzzer has to be blown three times yet again before work at six o'clock is to begin.

The first buzzer at half-past five is (it is said) intended to wake the men and rouse them to a sense that work is to be done. At ten minutes to six the buzzer is sounded again, and this, by some strange reasoning, is called the "first" buzzer. By this time all the men who live in Haslington or Coppenhall and the other outside districts, will be on their way to the dusty and grimy steel works or moulding shops; but the ten minutes to six serves the double purpose of acquainting these outsiders as to whether they are too near or too far away from the "time-clerks" gate, and it also serves the purpose, a very important one, of acquainting the dwellers just within the edge of the town that now they, too, must don the cap and overalls, and make their way to work. But the buzzer has not yet finished its work. At five minutes to six its hoot once more awakes the echoes, and this has the effect of producing acceleration in all those who hear it; it means that all who live just outside the gates must now lay down the morning pipe and waken the "missis" (for it is whispered that the wives of these workmen do not always rise before the second buzz); it quickens the step of the man and boy who twenty minutes before set off from the cottage in the country lane; and it accelerates the gait of the man who comes from just within the borough boundary; and in some cases – we hope not in many – it acts like the starter's pistol on the racers in the arena and youths who find themselves at the second buzzer in the locality where they should have been when the first buzzer "raised its tuneful note," now sprint for dear life down street and across square, the goal in view not being the white tape and the judge's desk, but a brass check and the time-clerk's box, the achievement being the placing of the check within the box, and this before the "pop" or third buzzer informs the town at large that work has now begun.

The Work's Buzzer, is, therefore, an institution in the town and without it one feels away from home – in the desert, far afield from civilisation.

It is a well-worn joke in Crewe that whilst it takes three buzzers to bring the men to work, yet it takes only one to send them home again, for one short blow at a quarter-past eight will undo all that it has taken half-an-hour's work with the siren previously to accomplish.

The same three hoots, at five-minute intervals, are given for the restart after breakfast and again after dinner, but as before, one short blow is alone necessary for the release of the hard-worked toiler of the Works.

But these are not alone the uses of the Crewe Buzzer (it quite deserves a capital B), for in the case of a fire in any part of the Works, three prolonged hoots will speedily bring the Works' fire brigade on the scene and will warn the town that something serious is going on within the walls of the great workshop. No clarion calls, no ringing bells, no shouts of alarm within the towns of centuries ago had more effect than the three successive hoots that denote that the dreadful thing "Fire! Fire!" has once more broken out; and in thousands of homes, when the man or boy returns, will the question be anxiously put, "Where was it? Is the danger over?"

The Railway Volunteers

Crewe is proud of being the headquarters, and the other quarters, of the 2nd Cheshire Volunteer Royal Engineers (Railway) and is more than proud of the fact that in proportion to the population of the town, more men were sent out to South Africa during the late war than in any other town or city in Great Britain.

Nearly three hundred men from Crewe have been at the front and did useful work whilst they were there. Many bridges and many lines of rails testify to the exceeding competency of the working man from Crewe.

The battalion was well-nigh one thousand strong and practically volunteered to go out to a man if the battalion could retain its unity and go out as the Crewe Regiment. These conditions were, however, not accepted by the authorities who ruled at the War Office, with the result that only a few actual volunteers went out with the reservists who were legally called upon to serve.

The railway engineer from Crewe is a most useful man to take out to a country situated like the late Transvaal and the now otherwise named the Orange Free State. He can rebuild bridges when the enemy have knocked them down and he can repair a locomotive when the enemy have blown it up. Not only this, but he can stoke, fire and drive that locomotive, and he can fix and rivet up the bridge again. He can both make and fight the armoured train, and he can relay the permanent way that the enemy have destroyed.

Many of the Crewe lads have not only been employed on this work, but were given positions of trust at the railway depots and junctions, and have proved themselves invaluable in any mechanical or clerical description of labour that had to be done.

But why introduce the 2nd Cheshire V.B.R.E. into this page? Why, simply because they, too, take a conspicuous part in the depopulation of the town of Crewe. They are off this year (1904) to Blackpool, and of course, they take the week of holiday when the Works are closed.

The writer has several times visited their orderly encampments at Rhyl, and at South Shore near Blackpool, but circumstances have altered since the camping-out was an affair of pleasure and of fun. A great and serious war has taught the country that there is a danger in too long a peace; that the Army was not properly prepared for the serious business it had to do; and the Crewe Volunteers have fully appreciated these things – this to some extent bitter awakening – and they are now prepared to give a week's hard work to their country, and this in a determined way, at a place where pleasure is not always the first and only thought; that is, they will undergo a thorough training in their work under the eye of responsible officers, and this infers by no means only beer and skittles.

A brilliant scene in the Market Square in Crewe is the muster of the citizen soldiers in their brilliant scarlet uniforms on the Saturday morning; a few bugle calls, a few sharp orders from the captains of the companies (who are also erstwhile managers in the railway works), a few words from the colonel and the adjutant (who are country gentlemen of fair Cheshire), a short march to the special train that is standing in a siding within the works, and a thousand men, husbands and brothers are gone, and will not be back before a week's hard work is done. The wives and children often follow their husbands, fathers and brothers to the camping place.

The school children are, of course, included in the exodus, and all the elementary schools are closed. There has been no School Board in the town, but the town is not without schools. There are Roman Catholic, Presbyterian, and several Wesleyan schools; but by far the greater number of scholars have been for the last few decades, and are yet, educated within schools built by the London and North Western Railway. Although this was not altogether a disinterested gift on the part of the Railway Company, yet the result is that education is cheap in the town.

The London and North Western Railway many years ago built a Mechanics Institution of considerable size, and not only fitted this up with class rooms, gymnasium, news and reading-rooms, but even went so far as to provide a library of several thousand volumes, a restaurant for workmen of the town and their visitors, a commodious fitting-shop with a set of lathes and other machinery, and a powerful gas engine to drive both the machinery and the dynamo which supplies the Institution with its own electric light.

A large room was built within the Institution and called the 'Town Hall' and it speaks well for the care exercised in the selection of teachers, and for the enterprise and perseverance of the pupils, that more Whitworth Scholarships and Royal Exhibitions have been gained in the Institution than in any other similar place of like population within the confines of Great Britain.

But all this by the way. What becomes of the children? Why, of course, most of the grown-ups who have left the town have taken their children with them, and peace, almost perfect peace, prevails at street corners, and in the North, South, and West Ward playgrounds, that a few short days ago resounded with the cries and shouts of budding railway engineers and their gentler sisters.

LNWR Mechanics Institute in Crewe Town Centre. It was well used for many public events in the town. The Euston Coffee Tavern was on the corner with the main entrance on the right. It provided a library, reading room and evening classes. There was also a social club and a ballroom. The LNWR company's laboratory was on the top floor – here water analysis was carried out.

The Sunday schools are nearly empty, those few teachers who have remained at the post of duty having little trouble to manage the two or three infants who have not gone away.

The sands of Blackpool, Morecambe and of Rhyl will be busy this week, and much "Blackpool rock" will soon be staining the fair lips of the children of Crewe.

But what about the food supply of those benighted beings who, not being in the swim of things, are left behind? The state of things at the Co-operative stores shall answer this.

The method of the management of the Crewe Friendly Society is peculiar. Cash is not paid when purchases are made, but all transactions are debited in a trading book, to be cleared at a later time. This system is safe, as each member must first invest in shares to twice the value of the allowed credit.

One drawback to the Co-operative system in Crewe is that in nearly all the shops there is much waiting for "turns." Whether this is due to the fault of the members themselves, or to those who serve them, is not to be argued here; but at certain hours in the evenings, and often on Saturday afternoons, there is such a scramble for "turns" that the management has to insist on the trading books being deposited as members enter the building, to be picked out in due order when attention can be given. This week, however, this has ceased. One may go through the shops and fill his trading book in his own time, at his own sweet will.

We ought to mention, however, that he will have to ask which days the stores are closed, for one of the days of this week the employees are going upon their annual picnic, and another day the shops are shut for yet another holiday, or perhaps are closed from sheer inanition.

There is really no food to be obtained; the bread is stale, the bacon is dry, the groceries are fusty, and everything is old. You cannot without difficulty buy even a small joint of meat, and you can only get that on one day this week, and even then, you will have to rouse up the butcher's boy from his doze upon the doorstep around the corner.

The Exodus

But we have yet to attempt to describe the outgoing of the people of Crewe.

We have said that the buzzer blows for the last time at half-past five on the Friday night, and within twenty-four hours of this the outgoing is accomplished.

Privilege fares at one-fourth the usual rates are allowed to all railway employees, and a special office for the issue of tickets at the reduced fares is open all day on Friday, and at certain times on preceding days as well.

Of course, the husbands and brothers cannot go during work hours to buy their tickets, but the wives and sisters can, and it is one of the sights of the time to see the long rows of waiting women, girls and children outside the booking office window.

A passage way formed of parallel rows of old sleepers, and of a length of several score of feet, is made to lead up to the ticket window, and this passage has the virtue of mercifully preventing much quarrelling and elbowing that would ensure were there no such lane for waiting ticket buyers.

There is little sleep in Crewe this Friday night. A large proportion have left the town when midnight arrives, but the exodus is still kept up in the early hours.

Relays of horses are arranged for and buses keep on running nearly all the night. If there should not be a train just to meet the bus, this makes no matter, the party and the luggage will wait. The top and the inside, the driver's seat and the conductor's stand, are all monopolised; hat boxes, brown paper parcels, hand baskets, large baskets, tin trunks, wooden trunks, portmanteaux and carpet bags – never was there so much of this sort of luggage on the station before! Mail carts and bassinets, some new, many old, roll down on to the station platforms in seething waves. Every man, woman and child carries his or her own box,

Crewe Station No.1 Down Platform 29.1.20.

bundle, or bag. The Porters in such a crowd are of no avail, and find it better policy to let passengers and things severely alone, and thank their stars when they are gone!

The Return

Most of the men, with their wives and families, return on the Saturday night of our holiday week. Every vehicle in the town that can carry a passenger and be pulled by a horse must now turn out – old and new, good and bad, great and small. Omnibuses are waiting for every train that arrives and cabs are kept constantly on the run all night long. At nine o'clock the climax is reached. The station platforms are full, the station entrance is packed – the special with the Volunteers has reached the railway town.

Of course, all are getting away as quickly as they can, but the pitiful forty who can crowd or hang on to one single 'bus are but a very few out of the hundreds who are here. Every passenger, young or old, has a parcel or box of some description in their hands and should the evening of this particular Saturday be wet, affairs are much intensified.

Wagonettes, with or without cover, are drawn up and despatched as quickly as they can be filled and driven away. The 'bus is simply packed as it approaches the station by boarders who run down the Nantwich Road to meet it.

People standing at the entrance of the station see that vehicles are snapped up and filled before they can draw up, and catching the idea, a husband leaves his family and his boxes and runs down the road to the first turning to hail the first returning cab he sees. Too late! Someone has been before him and jumped into the cab.

Wait a little longer! The next *Jehu* will probably take you in. Ah, here he comes! Hi! Stop! He pulls up, but before you can put your hand upon the handle of the door, two other men are on the step and are already half inside. Desperate, and thinking quick and hard, you start away to walk towards the town, and at a distance of perhaps half a mile you see a cab unloading fares down some side street. The driver does not leave his seat – he has no time for that – and you at once run up to the unloading cab, and before the driver has time to collect his fare for the last journey, and almost before the fares have landed on to the curb, you plump down on the warm seat, and bargain with the driver through the window.

Now you are alright. Cabby is off again to fetch your wife and child, and possession is nine points of the law just now more than it ever was before, you drive past all the other waving arms, sticks and umbrellas that are striving to arrest your cab; you fight off the crowd who greet you; you make a way through them with one hand whilst not leaving hold of the door handle for a single instant with the other; you manage to get into the cab, you drive away and the holiday and the struggle for you, as least, is now gone past once more.